IOM International Organization for Migration

WORLD MIGRATION 2008

MANAGING LABOUR MOBILITY
IN THE EVOLVING GLOBAL ECONOMY

VOLUME 4 - IOM World Migration Report Series

This volume is the fruit of a collaborative effort by a team of contributing authors and the editorial team under the direction of the Editors-in-Chief. The findings, interpretations and conclusions expressed herein do not necessarily reflect the views of IOM or its Member States. The designations employed and the presentation of material throughout the work do not imply the expression of any opinion whatsoever on the part of IOM concerning the legal status of any country, territory, city or area, or of its authorities, or concerning its frontiers or boundaries.

Unless otherwise stated, this volume does not refer to events occurring after August 2008.

IOM is committed to the principle that humane and orderly migration benefits migrants and society. As an intergovernmental organization, IOM acts with its partners in the international community to: assist in meeting the operational challenges of migration; advance understanding of migration issues; encourage social and economic development through migration; and uphold the human dignity and well-being of migrants.

Publisher: International Organization for Migration
17 route des Morillons
1211 Geneva 19
Switzerland
Tel: +41.22.717 91 11
Fax: +41.22.798 61 50
E-mail: hq@iom.int
Internet: http://www.iom.int

ISSN 1561-5502
ISBN 978-92-9068-405-3

Cover concept and design: Dominique Cherry, DEC Creatives, Bonnell's Bay, Australia

Printed in Switzerland by SRO-Kundig

IOM EDITORIAL TEAM

Editors-In-Chief and Concept	Gervais Appave, Ryszard Cholewinski
Editorial Board	Michele Klein Solomon, Frank Laczko, Sophie Nonnenmacher, Jobst Köhler, Nilim Baruah
Steering Committee	Juan Artola, William Barriga, Jean-Philippe Chauzy, Shahidul Haque, Jill Helke, Bernd Hemingway, Irena Omelaniuk, Robert Paiva, Richard Perruchoud, Jillyanne Redpath-Cross, Peter Schatzer, Irena Vojackova-Sollorano, Thomas Weiss
Editorial Assistance	Juan Artola, William Barriga, Shahidul Haque, Jill Helke, Michele Klein Solomon, Frank Laczko, Sophie Nonnenmacher, Irena Omelaniuk, Robert Paiva, Irena Vojackova-Sollorano, Elizabeth Warn
Publications Assistance and Layout	Clara Francia Anaya, Anna Lyn Constantino, Valerie Hagger, Caroline San Miguel, Alma Sy, Carmelo Torres
Executive Assistance	Dominique Jaud-Pellier, Antoinette Wills
Regional Overviews	Verónica Escudero, Claudia Natali
Cartography	Jana Hennig
English Language Editor	Ilse Pinto-Dobernig

ACKNOWLEDGEMENTS

The Editorial Team wishes to thank all contributing authors and is especially grateful to Brunson McKinley, former IOM Director General, for his vision and encouragement to produce this publication.

The Editorial Team wishes to thank the following persons, principally current and former IOM staff, for their kind assistance and support:

Christine Adam, Christine Aghazarm, Serhan Aktoprak, Carmen Andreu, Jorge Baca, Diego Beltrand, Andrew Billo, Philippe Boncour, Rosilyne Borland, Peter Bossink, Andrew Bruce, Cynthia Bryant, Anne-Marie Buschman-Petit, Audrey Carquillat, Laurentiu Ciobanica, Ricardo Casco, Sarah Craggs, Luca Dall'oglio, Richard Danziger, Anita Alero Davies, Priyanka Debnath, Alexandre Devillard, Flavio Di Giacomo, Françoise Droulez, Sylvia Lopez-Ekra, Disha Sonata Faruque, Berta Fernandez, Stephanie Fitzjames, Jorge Andrés Gallo, Nicoletta Giordano, Mary Haour-Knipe, Laurence Hart, Janet Hatcher Roberts, Dina Ionesco, Nayla Kawerk, David Knight, Sarah Költzow, Umbareen Kuddus, Lucy Laitinen, Kerstin Lau, Chris Lom, Marina Manke, Kristina Mejo, Ugo Melchionda, Susanne Melde, Françoise Moudouthe, Günter Müssig, Alina Narusova, Ndioro Ndiaye, Pierre Nicolas, José-Angel Oropeza, Paola Pace, Jemini Pandya, Niurka Pineiro, Carina Raisin, Felix Ross, Redouane Saadi, Ovais Sarmad, Scott Schirmer, Meera Sethi, Frances Solinap, Lucie Stejskalová, Alma Sy, Yorio Tanimura, Lalini Veerassamy, Galina Vitkovskaya, Shyla Vohra, Vassiliy Yuzhanin, Zhao Jian, Jennifer Zimmermann.

The input of the following external experts to the concept of *World Migration 2008* at a workshop in Geneva in January 2007 is also much appreciated:

Ibrahim Awad (International Labour Organization – ILO), Luca Barbone (The World Bank), Johannes Bernabe (International Centre for Trade and Sustainable Development – ICTSD), Scott Busby (Intergovernmental Consultations on Migration, Asylum and Refugees – IGC), Antonia Carzaniga (World Trade Organization – WTO), Verona Collantes (United Nations Conference on Trade and Development - UNCTAD), Jeff Dayton-Johnson (Organisation for Economic Co-operation and Development – OECD), Carla Edelenbos (Office of the United Nations High Commissioner for Human Rights – OHCHR), Lisa Eklund (United Nations Population Fund – UNFPA), Raquel Gonzalez (International Trade Union Confederation – ITUC), Geneviève Gencianos (Public Services International – PSI), Bela Hovy (Population Division of the United Nations Department of Economic and Social Affairs – UN DESA), Robyn Iredale (Australian Demographic and Social Research Institute, the Australian National University), Azfar Khan (ILO), Eleonore Kofman (Social Policy Research Centre, Middlesex University), Christiane Kuptsch (ILO), Virginia Leary (Emeritus Professor of International Law, State University of New York at Buffalo), Lindsay Lowell (Institute for the Study of International Migration, Georgetown University – ISIM), Frederick Muia (International Organization of Employers – IOE), Edmundo Murrugarra (The World Bank), Kathleen Newland (Migration Policy Institute – MPI), Pierella Paci (The World Bank), Dilip Ratha (The World Bank), Martin Ruhs (Centre on Migration Policy and Society, University of Oxford – COMPAS), Brigitte Suter (Malmö Institute for Studies of Migration), Siri Tellier (UNFPA), Sabrina Varma (United Nations Development Programme – UNDP), Stéphan Vincent-Lancrin (OECD), Martin Watson (Quaker United Nations Office – QUNO), Vincent Williams (Southern African Migration Project – SAMP).

Several organizations generously shared their data and other research materials:

Canadian Permanent Mission to the United Nations (Geneva), Centre for European Policy Studies (CEPS), COMPAS – University of Oxford, IGC, International Institute for Sustainable Development (IISD), International Migration Programme of the ILO, Internal Displacement Monitoring Centre (IDMC) – Global IDP Project, Norwegian Refugee Council, OHCHR, OECD, Pan American Health Organization (PAHO), Platform for International Cooperation on Undocumented Migrants (PICUM), Population Division of UN DESA, PSI, SAMP, Thai Ministry of Interior, Thai Ministry of Labour, United Nations High Commissioner for Refugees (UNHCR), UNFPA, The World Bank, WTO.

The Editorial Team is especially grateful to the following donors for their generous financial support towards the development and publication of *World Migration 2008*:

Governments of Australia, Denmark, Switzerland and the United States, The John D. and Catherine T. MacArthur Foundation, Agence intergouvernementale de la Francophonie (specific financial contribution towards the translation of the French version).

LDCs	Least Developed Countries	**OSCE**	Organization for Security and Co-operation in Europe
M&As	Mergers and acquisitions (cross-border)	**OWWA**	Overseas Workers Welfare Administration (the Philippines)
MDGs	Millennium Development Goals		
MENA	Middle East and North Africa	**OWWF**	Overseas Workers Welfare Fund (Sri Lanka)
MERCOSUR	Common Market of the South		
MFN	Most Favoured Nation	**PAHO**	Pan American Health Organization
MIDA	Migration for Development in Africa	**PEA**	Private employment agency
MIDSA	Migration Dialogue for Southern Africa	**PICUM**	Platform for International Cooperation on Undocumented Migrants
MIDWA	Migration Dialogue for West Africa		
MLDR	Migrant Labour Dependency Ratio	**PIELAMI**	Cooperation on preventing illegal employment of labour migrants with a view to promoting legal employment opportunities (IOM Helsinki ARGO project)
MLSA	Ministry of Labour and Social Affairs (Czech Republic)		
MOITAL	Ministry of Industry, Trade and Labour (Israel)	**POEA**	Philippine Overseas Employment Administration
MOU	Memorandum of Understanding		
MPG	Migration Policy Group (Brussels, Belgium)	**POLO**	Philippine Overseas Labour Officer
MPI	Migration Policy Institute (Washington, D.C.)	**PPP**	Purchasing power parity
MRU	Market Research Unit	**PRSP**	Poverty Reduction Strategy Paper
MSR	Market Situation Report	**PSI**	Public Services International
MWF	Migrant Welfare Fund		
		RCM	Regional Conference on Migration (Puebla Process)
NAFTA	North American Free Trade Agreement		
NAMA	Non-agricultural market access	**RCPs**	Regional Consultative Processes
NBER	National Bureau of Economic Research (U.S.)	**RTA**	Regional trade agreement
NESC	National Economic Social Council (Ireland)		
NGO	Non-Governmental Organization	**S&T**	Science and technology
NHS	National Health Service (U.K.)	**SAARC**	South Asian Association for Regional Cooperation
NRB	Non-resident Bangladeshi		
NRI	Non-resident Indian	**SADC**	Southern African Development Community
		SAMP	Southern African Migration Project
ODA	Official Development Assistance	**SAMReN**	South Asia Migration Resource Network
ODI	Overseas Development Institute (U.K.)	**SAWP**	Commonwealth Caribbean Seasonal Agriculture Workers Program (Canada)
OAS	Organization of American States		
ODIHR	Office for Democratic Institutions and Human Rights (OSCE)	**SAWS**	Seasonal Agricultural Workers Scheme (U.K.)
		SIEMMES	Statistical Information System on Migration in Mesoamerica
OECD	Organisation for Economic Co-operation and Development		
		SLBFE	Sri Lanka Bureau of Foreign Employment
OFW	Overseas Filipino Workers	**SMEs**	Small and medium enterprises
OHCHR	Office of the High Commissioner for Human Rights		
		TNCs	Transnational corporations
OPF	Overseas Pakistani Foundation	**TOEA**	Thailand Overseas Employment Administration
OPT	Occupied Palestinian Territories		

TOKTEN	Transfer of Knowledge Through Expatriate Nationals	**UNODC**	United Nations Office on Drugs and Crime
		UNRISD	United Nations Research Institute for Social Development
UN	United Nations		
UNCTAD	United Nations Conference on Trade and Development	**UNRWA**	United Nations Relief and Works Agency for Palestine Refugees in the Near East
UN DESA	United Nations Department of Economic and Social Affairs	**UNSD**	United Nations Statistics Division
		UN-WIDER	United Nations World Institute for Development Economics Research
UNDP	United Nations Development Programme	**UNWTO**	United Nations World Tourist Organization
UNECE	United Nations Economic Commission for Europe	**UP**	Unió de Pagesos
		U.S.-CAFTA-D.R.	United States-Central America-Dominican Republic Free Trade Agreement
UNEP	United Nations Environment Programme		
UNESCO	United Nations Educational, Scientific and Cultural Organization	**VoTs**	Victims of Trafficking
UNFPA	United Nations Population Fund		
UNGA	United Nations General Assembly	**WHO**	World Health Organization
UNHCR	United Nations High Commissioner for Refugees	**WMO**	World Meteorological Organization
		WTO	World Trade Organization
UNICEF	United Nations Children's Fund		
UNIFEM	United Nations Development Fund for Women		
UN-INSTRAW	United Nations International Research and Training Institute for the Advancement of Women		

migration to the country of origin is also much more frequent, as is the circular or pendular movement between two countries. It is also the case that many persons viewed administratively as students or visitors are in some instances indistinguishable from migrants. In the midst of all that diversity, traditional administrative distinctions continue to be maintained – for instance between those who have permanent or temporary visas, or between those who have authority to work and those who do not – but category-bridging or category-switching options are nonetheless often available.

Part A: The Worlds of Contemporary Mobility for Economic Purposes

Part A of the Report is an exploration of contemporary mobility, presented in the form of a mosaic of independent studies developed by specialist researchers invited to offer individual perspectives on different facets of economically-related mobility. While they are not identical in structure, in general terms they all deal with issues of definition, attempt to map out the magnitude and distribution of movements, address major issues that arise, discuss possible policy responses and identify priorities for further research.

All too often, the impact of globalization on labour mobility is studied and discussed from separate and isolated domestic and international perspectives, as though each of these two realms of work existed independently from the other. **Chapter 1** argues instead that workers, irrespective of their geographical location, are now living, by and large, in the same world of work, one offering a wide range of opportunities but, at the same time, characterized by increased competition and calls for greater flexibility in work practices. It looks at how the forces of globalization are changing the way enterprises do business, giving rise to more integrated labour markets and, consequently, creating demand for increased labour mobility. The chapter provides an overview of the forces that determine the nature

and patterns of employment worldwide, especially the globalization of financial flows, trade and production. It considers how these dynamics affect employment in terms of both jobs and wages and goes on to look more closely at how international labour migration features in the global economy, as a strategic response to the demand for increased efficiency in production on the one hand, and, on the other, as an increasingly important contributing factor to the development of the economies in the South. Finally, the chapter discusses what might be meant by the concept of a "global labour market" and calls for greater attention to be given to the labour factor in theoretical studies on globalization and trade, to provide a clearer and stronger basis for decisions by policymakers.

While migrant workers are to be found in a wide range of employment sectors and at all skill levels, it is possible to discern some distinct patterns. Clustering is obvious at the extremes of the skills spectrum, with a strong, and officially recognized, demand for highly skilled migrants at the one end and a noticeable, but often officially ignored, demand for low or semi-skilled migrants at the other. **Chapter 2** surveys the first of these patterns. Highly skilled migrants appear on the migration scene in various guises. Most of them are permanent residents, but a growing number is admitted under various temporary migration schemes, which, in due course, may provide an opening to permanent residence status. At the same time, the foreign student population is increasingly seen as an attractive source of talent. The chapter outlines the major trends in highly skilled migration across the regions of the world, identifies the main geographical poles of attraction and lays out the different sets of policy issues facing the two major global constituencies, which are, respectively, the countries of origin and of destination. For countries of destination, the challenge is to beat the competition through the formulation of policies that will attract the "best and brightest" (Kapur and McHale, 2005). For their part, countries of origin feel the need to protect themselves against the loss of their highly skilled citizens and/or to secure their return or at least the return of the resources, both financial and in terms of skills, know-how and networks, acquired by their expatriates. In that connection, key policy options are canvassed and attention is drawn to the importance of bilateral and multilateral efforts.

The focus of **Chapter 3** is on the re-emergence of low and semi-skilled migration programmes – a seemingly surprising development considering the economic and socio-political problems that brought large-scale temporary worker programmes in both western Europe and the U.S. to an abrupt halt more than 30 years ago, but one which reflects the recognized need for foreign labour as spelled out above. While this type of movement occurs predominantly between developing and developed countries, it also affects a wide range of middle-income countries. The chapter maps out broad global distribution patterns before addressing the triple challenge of ensuring positive outcomes for countries of origin, countries of destination and for the migrants themselves. It argues that for "win-win-win" solutions to be achieved, policymakers must resolve problems of distortion, or unevenness, in labour supply, dependence or undue reliance on migrant labour, and address the difficult question of possible trade-offs between human rights and numbers. Carefully designed economic incentives may be a promising means to encourage employers and migrants to maintain programme integrity.

A distinction has long been made between permanent migration and short-term admission policies. Though these two categories are not necessarily mutually exclusive, the migration policies of countries of destination almost always distinguish between those who arrive with the intention of staying and becoming part of the host community and those who come with the main intention to study or to work for a limited period of time before returning to their country of origin. Chapters 4 and 5 focus on the often overlooked migratory objectives and itineraries

of students and visitors and their increasingly felt impact on global employment trends.

Chapter 4 tracks patterns of student movements and policy developments since the 1990s, and highlights the shifts in both government motivations and the design of educational programmes during that period. Broad academic, political, cultural and development goals of an essentially humanitarian nature have not completely disappeared, but they are now overshadowed by sharper-edged economic objectives. Governments see their education programmes as a convenient and effective means for the subsequent recruitment of highly skilled migrants, while for foreign students they offer an entry to the international job market. The chapter outlines major trends in student mobility and discusses the underlying factors, while pointing to new forms of cross-border higher education offers where establishments or programmes move to meet the demands of student populations. The identification of four major strategies characterizing government policy stances that reflect the different motivations at work in this field (mutual understanding, skilled migration, income generation and capacity building) opens the way for an assessment of the increasingly close interplay between student mobility and migration policies and a discussion of the need for international cooperation and harmonization in this area of mobility.

In terms of sheer numbers, short-term travel, generally not exceeding 6 to 12 months, occurs on a much larger scale than for any other form of mobility, although this type of movement is not usually addressed in migration-related research and is, in fact, generally dealt with as an entirely separate policy category. **Chapter 5** sets out to investigate the complex, often overlooked bidirectional relationship between tourism and migration. It points out that many flows for leisure and business purposes are related to, or are inspired by, earlier migratory movements and that, in turn, tourist movements

Computer-based information systems have been instrumental in the development of flexible production methods (e.g. computer-integrated manufacturing)[19] and, more broadly, facilitated the management of companies with units located around the world. Reductions in the costs of transport and telecommunications and the lowering of trade and FDI barriers have also contributed to the emergence of global chains of production taking advantage of lower labour and material costs and more favourable policy environments.

According to this scheme, the production process of goods is divided and each segment located where it can be carried out most efficiently and at minimum cost. A considerable proportion of employment in manufacturing has thus been relocated to low-wage countries, including to Export Processing Zones (EPZs), creating job opportunities that often attract low-skilled workers, including women, from rural to urban areas.

The strategy of "outward processing for reverse importing" is, at least in part, responsible for the transformation of corporate structures and activities. Some companies send materials, components and supplies for processing or assembly abroad for which, when returned, duty will be charged only on the value added abroad. This approach has been widely adopted by developed countries, especially in the textile and electronic industries, and has helped secure an important share of import business in the U.S. and the European Union.

While the share of the industry sector (mainly composed of manufacturing processes) remains at about 21 per cent of total global employment,

reflecting a decrease in developed countries and an increase in developing countries, total global employment in industry rose by 83 million between 1995 and 2005, half of which occurred in East and Southeast Asia (ILO, 2006b).

(b) Global resourcing of services

Offshoring or outsourcing of services to lower-wage locations is a recent phenomenon that has been encouraged (as with manufacturing) by lower telecommunication costs, as well as by decreased risks in locating services in developing countries (e.g. by the introduction of intellectual property protection measures).

The McKinsey Global Institute (2005: 14) defines "global resourcing"[20] as the "process a company goes through to decide which of its activities could be performed anywhere in the world, where to locate them and who will do them". According to the McKinsey study (2005), offshoring of services to emerging markets was expected to grow at 30 per cent annually between 2003 and 2008. It argued further that, in 2008, 11 per cent of worldwide services employment (160 million jobs) could in theory be performed by people located anywhere in the world (undertaken, for instance, by engineers, finance professionals, accountants and analysts). However, it is estimated that, in practice, companies will offshore far fewer jobs, growing from 565,000 to 1.2 million for the eight sectors of the economy covered by the study.[21]

Global resourcing can have positive outcomes for developed and developing countries through reduced costs, repatriated profits and new markets for home country goods and services. Indeed, the McKinsey

---

[19] A computer-automated system in which individual engineering, production, marketing and support functions of a manufacturing enterprise are organized; functional areas such as design, analysis, planning, purchasing, cost accounting, inventory control and distribution are linked through the computer with factory floor functions such as materials handling and management, providing direct control and monitoring of all process operations.

[20] "Global resourcing", "offshoring", "international outsourcing" are terms often used interchangeably when referring to the transfer of services operations or production processes to a foreign country.

[21] Automotive services, health care, insurance, IT services, packaged software, pharmaceutical products, retail and retail banking.

Global Institute (2003) estimated that for one dollar spent on outsourcing, the U.S. economy gained USD 1.12 to 1.14, while the foreign host country received USD 0.33.

(c) The role of TNCs

The globalization of production is largely carried out by TNCs. According to UNCTAD's 2006 World Investment Report, *FDI from Developing and Transition Economies: Implications for Development*, the EU, Japan and the U.S. still host most of the world's dominant TNCs. However, more than 20,000 TNCs have their headquarters in developing countries and there is a growing and significant presence of FDI by firms from developing and transition economies. Significant differences exist nonetheless between the top TNCs from the developing and developed world, with the former in general having fewer foreign assets and a less extended global outreach and presence.

In 2005, TNCs generated USD 4.5 trillion in added value, employed some 62 million workers and exported goods and services valued at more than USD 4 trillion (UNCTAD, 2006). Three per cent of global trade is intra-firm. TNCs have not only played an important role in directing FDI flows, but also contribute to more labour market openness. Specifically, the internationalization of the activities of firms for the production of goods and services is accompanied by increased international mobility of their workers among branches in different countries to perform services or undertake business visits abroad.[22]

3. Impact of Globalization on Employment

Starting with some key global figures on employment in 2005 (see Textbox 1.2), this section examines the impact of globalization on wages and job security, the way the structure of economies are modified and the predominance of certain economic sectors, and the repercussions on the movement of jobs (offshoring) and workers (labour migration).

---

[22] For the link between business visits abroad and labour mobility, see Chapter 5.

Textbox 1.2

Some Key Figures on Employment in 2005

- **The global labour force**[1] **comprised over three billion workers**. Of these, 84 per cent lived in the developing countries of Asia and the Pacific region, Africa, Latin America and the Caribbean, as well as the transition countries of the Commonwealth of Independent States (CIS) and south-eastern Europe (ILO, 2006b).

- **Women represented around 40 per cent of the world's labour force (1.22 billion)**.

- **2.85 billion individuals aged 15 and above were employed**. However, about half did not earn enough to raise themselves above the poverty line of two U.S. dollars a day. These figures are the same as those of ten years ago. Agriculture had the highest employment share (40.1%)[2] as compared to industry (21%) and services (38.9%) (ILO, 2006a).

- **The global unemployment rate was 6.3 per cent** (ILO, 2006a), affecting some 191.8 million people,[3] with young persons accounting for approximately half of the unemployed, a relatively high proportion given that they represented only 25 per cent of the total working age population (ILO, 2006a).

- **86 million persons were identified as migrant workers** (ILO, 2006c).

- **TNCs** comprised 77,000 parent companies with over 770,000 foreign affiliates, the latter **employing some 62 million workers** (UNCTAD, 2006).

that are at best unfair, at worst equivalent to forced labour or slavery. There are also smuggling and trafficking networks, which are often in the hands of organized crime. These adverse effects show how inefficient administrative barriers can be at keeping people out, and lead to questions about how such flows should be managed to ensure, at a minimum, that national labour market policies reconcile the competitiveness sought by employers with the protection of workers' rights and interests.

At the individual level, as well, the decision to move is driven by both economic and non-economic considerations. Differences in wages and general economic prospects between countries of origin and destination are obviously important, but other matters such as political stability, freedom from conflict, levels of human rights protection, labour standards and access to social services, such as health and education, can also play a role. The existence of a diaspora providing support to new migrants and acting as an information network (see Chapter 12) enters into consideration in the selection by the migrant of the destination country, together with employment prospects and possible access to secure or permanent residence status. Geographical proximity also plays a role, especially for low-skilled workers, as it affects their travel costs unless these are taken care of by the employer. Finally, elements as disparate as the possibility of being accompanied or joined by a family member, the difficulty of severing connections with one's community and life style in the country of origin, the costs of living, exchange rate differentials, taxation, the climate, language and the rules relating to recognition of qualifications will, in the end, all be weighed in the individual worker's decision to opt for mobility or not.

5.4. Prospects for Enhanced International Cooperation in the Management of Labour Mobility

Given the complexity of the economic, social and political equations that have to be resolved before significant progress can be made, the slowness and cautiousness of inter-governmental negotiations in this field is hardly a surprise. With regard to mobility, the unequal balance powering the supply/demand equation between countries of origin and destination creates no strong incentive for the latter to enter into a multilateral framework encompassing the admission of migrant workers. Destination countries are still largely in a position to satisfy their labour market needs through unilateral policies, and adjust them according to changes in their labour markets. This is clear from the limited commitment made under GATS Mode 4 to date and the absence of a significant outcome in the current negotiations.[50]

The General Agreement on Tariffs and Trade (GATT) and its successor, the WTO, were created to ensure that the negative and positive impacts of free trade would be shared equally, and are supported by the economic reasoning that, through specialization in production, most countries, both developing and developed, could gain from the establishment of such a regime. The IMF and the World Bank have been given a role in managing international finance, and there is widespread support for the development of a framework which would ensure more stable exchange rates and strong currencies. On the other hand, the case for an international regime establishing freer movement of workers does not yet attract a critical mass of support because of the perceived asymmetries of supply and demand, the lack of reciprocity in potential gains and the social and political implications that remain to be addressed.

---

[50] Major developed and destination countries have made only limited offers under GATS Mode 4, principally for top managers, highly skilled professionals and intra-corporate transferees.

While prospects for a global regime opening the way to the freer mobility of workers remain guarded, there are concrete indications of progress in regional settings, where economic disparities are often more limited and consequently less likely to act as obstacles to liberalization (see Chapter 13). Even in such restricted settings, however, it is the more highly skilled who are most likely to benefit from movement facilitation arrangements.[51]

Countries are more interconnected through trade, capital flows and the global production system than ever before. Changes in the economic situation and regulations in countries that are the most important economically have repercussions for the rest of the world. Therefore, increased globalization requires the elaboration of new ways of approaching the world of work in its domestic and international dimension, with renewed emphasis on consultation and cooperation.

Coordination among the actors involved in the formulation of policies impacting on employment (i.e. labour market policy, but also labour migration, social security, education policies, etc.) is first required at the national level, while national actors also need to devote more attention to the international dimension of this phenomenon both at the regional and global levels. This could be facilitated by the creation of a roadmap on "globalization and labour mobility" to guide discussion in international fora and maximize the potential for collaboration between global agencies with mandates in this area (e.g. ILO, IMF, IOM, World Bank, WTO, among others).

An important objective of such a roadmap would be to recognize the interrelationships between globalization, the world of work and the international movement of workers. It could provide an analysis of the challenges arising from these interactions in terms of creating new work opportunities in the developed and developing worlds while protecting the most vulnerable individuals who are not in a position to tap into these opportunities. It could look at what can be done at the national level, but also how regional and global frameworks as well as institutions mandated to address trade, finance, employment and migration issues could help countries to better manage these challenges by creating more synergies in their endeavours in these different fields.

6. Conclusion

An examination of the place, present and future, of international labour mobility within ongoing processes of globalization leads to three main observations. First, workers in the developing world provide a pool of human resources that can respond to demand in the developed world now and well into the future, although much remains to be done to realize this in practice and to make it beneficial for both countries of origin and destination; for instance, through the elaboration of human resource development strategies and the creation of effective mechanisms to match demand with supply.

Second, the relationship between trade and migration needs to be better understood. There is a greater need to focus on labour in trade theory than in past globalization phases, because the current phase is characterized by an increase in trade in services and knowledge-based trade, both of which rely heavily on human resources. New trade theories (and supporting evidence) are needed to better inform policies that seek to address the need for increased international labour mobility.

Third, policy coherence needs to be improved on a number of levels. The transformation of the world of work has led to a change in the roles of traditional stakeholders (e.g. public authorities, employers and

---

[51] From a purely economic perspective, there is a paradox here as movement is liberalized in a setting (i.e. of the highly skilled and between countries that are at a similar economic level) where the gains from the liberalization are not the most significant.

trade unions) or at least in their ability to perform the role traditionally assigned to them. They face the task of having to formulate and implement policies and protect interests at the national level in the face of global economic forces.[52] The state also tends to have a more limited role in the regulation of the economy than before as new prominence is given to enterprises as regulators.[53] As roles and relationships change, there is a challenge in ensuring that the mobility of workers and the role of key players, including TNCs, are properly integrated within employment and migration policies and strategies at the national and international level.

At the broadest policy level if, as it is likely, the gathering forces of globalization – as evidenced and implemented through trade reforms that have already taken place with respect to liberalizing the movement of goods and capital – increase the pressure for greater labour mobility, but systems of migration management are not adjusted accordingly, a serious disconnect will be created between policies and realities. There are manifest social costs to be paid for this in terms of irregular migration and the related exploitation involved.

To date governments have chosen to manage migration essentially from a domestic perspective.[54] This is unlikely to change radically but, in so doing, governments are confronted with the challenge of maintaining their sovereign prerogative to manage movements across their borders, while having to cope with the inefficiencies of regulating a transnational phenomenon with national level policies. Regional processes may provide helpful consultative and experimental platforms for the exploration of approaches that may reconcile needs for security, mobility and worker protection. Attention is now focused on building interstate cooperation in the migration field from the bottom up rather than the top down and, in particular, with respect to labour mobility. In parallel to the pursuit of legally binding international instruments regulating the movement of persons and protecting the human rights of migrant workers at the global level,[55] bilateral cooperation, regional dialogue and consultation, and even non-binding global consultative mechanisms are exploring means to achieve greater cooperation in managing migration and labour mobility. A period of confidence building in the ability to manage labour mobility to mutual benefit is needed – at national, bilateral, regional and global levels – and may pave the way in the future for more comprehensive and coherent approaches to labour mobility that would be more supportive of freer movements.[56]

---

[52] As a result, some actors are modifying their strategies. For instance, some trade unions are developing more international strategies (setting up international branches, or creating international networks) or recognizing new realities with the inclusion of migrant issues in their agendas and/or opening their membership to migrant workers. See the Global Union Research Network (GURN) website at http://www.gurn.info/topic/migrant/index.html.

[53] Not only through the impacts of their economic weight but also, for example, through the adoption of corporate social responsibility norms.

[54] One evolving exception is the migration law and policy of the European Union.

[55] E.g. temporary movement of persons through GATS Mode 4; the 1990 International Convention on the Protection of the Rights of All Migrant Workers and Members of Their Families (see Textbox 13.1).

[56] See Chapter 13 for a fuller discussion of interstate cooperation.

REFERENCES

Castells, M.
1996   *The Rise of the Network Society: (The Information Age: Economy, Society and Culture, Volume 1)*, Blackwell Publishers, Oxford.

Chang, H.
2007   "The Economic Impact of International Labor Migration: Recent Estimates and Policy Implications", *Temple Political and Civil Rights Law Review*, 16.

Commission of the European Communities
2006   *Report on the Functioning of the Transitional Arrangements set out in the 2003 Accession Treaty (period 1 May 2004-30 April 2006)*, COM (2006) 48 final, 8 February.

Farrell, D., M.A. Laboissière and J. Rosenfeld
2005   "Sizing the emerging global labor market. Rational behavior from both companies and countries can help it work more efficiently", *The McKinsey Quarterly*, No. 3 (August), http://ce.mdic.gov.br/SOFTWARE/McKinsey%20-%20Labor.htm#foot4up.

Freeman, R.B.
2005   "What Really Ails Europe (and America): The Doubling of the Global Workforce", *The Globalist*, 3 June, http://www.theglobalist.com/DBWeb/printStoryId.aspx?StoryId=4542.

2006a   "People flows in globalization", National Bureau of Economic Research (NBER) Working Paper No. 12315, June, Cambridge, MA.

2006b   "Labor Market Imbalances: Shortages, or Surpluses, or Fish Stories?", Boston Federal Reserve Economic Conference on Global Imbalances – As Giants Evolve, 14-16 June, Chatham, MA, http://www.bos.frb.org/economic/conf/conf51/papers/freeman.pdf.

Gammage, S.
2007   "El Salvador: Despite End to Civil War, Emigration Continues", *Migration Information Source*, July, Migration Policy Institute (MPI), Washington, D.C., http://www.migrationinformation.org/Profiles/display.cfm?ID=636.

Ghosh, B.
2005   "Managing Migration: Whither the Missing Regime?", Draft Article of the UNESCO Migration without Borders Series, Doc. SHS/2005/MWB/4, 15 February, http://unesdoc.unesco.org/images/0013/001391/139149e.pdf.

Ghose, A.K.
2002   "Trade and international labour mobility", Employment Paper 2002/33, ILO, Geneva, http://www.ilo.org/public/english/employment/strat/download/ep33.pdf.

Global Commission on International Migration (GCIM)
2005   *Migration in an interconnected world: New directions for action*, Report of the GCIM, October, SRO-Kundig, Geneva, http://www.gcim.org/attachements/gcim-complete-report-2005.pdf.

International Monetary Fund (IMF)
2000   "Globalization: Threat or Opportunity?", IMF Issues Brief 00/01, 12 April (corrected January 2002), http://www.imf.org/external/np/exr/ib/2000/041200to.htm.

International Labour Organization (ILO)
2004a   *Towards a Fair Deal for Migrant Workers in the Global Economy*, Report VI, International Labour Conference, 92nd Session, June, Geneva, http://www.ilo.org/public/english/standards/relm/ilc/ilc92/pdf/rep-vi.pdf.

2004b   *Trade, Foreign Investment and Productive Employment in Developing Countries*, Governing Body, 291st Session, November, ILO, Geneva.

2004c   "Facts on Migrant Labour", June, International Labour Office, Geneva, http://www.ilo.org/public/english/region/asro/bangkok/child/trafficking/downloads/migrantsfactsheet.pdf.

2006a   "Global Employment Trends", Brief, January, International Labour Office, Geneva, http://www.ilo.org/public/english/employment/strat/download/getb06en.pdf.

2006b   *Changing Patterns in the World of Work*, Report of the Director General, Report I (C), International Labour Conference, 95th Session, June, Geneva, http://www.ilo.org/public/english/standards/relm/ilc/ilc95/pdf/rep-i-c.pdf.

the board would appear to be about right in terms of the numbers necessary to generate linkages to the global economy and to yield positive feedback effects from the diaspora. But many Latin American, African and Caribbean countries have a much larger share of their highly skilled nationals living abroad, which poses a serious challenge to their own socio-economic development.

This chapter first reviews some of the trends in highly skilled migration in major countries of destination. The distribution of highly skilled migrants in different countries is reviewed, as well as their share of migrants from different source regions. Next, data on permanent immigrants are presented together with a brief discussion of the limited data available on temporary skilled foreign workers and foreign students, a subject addressed in more detail in Chapter 4. This is followed by a discussion of the major elements in admission policies associated with the trends in highly skilled migration. The chapter then turns to the impact of highly skilled migration on countries of origin. A brief discussion of the literature dealing with such impacts then leads to a discussion of policies that could contribute to optimizing highly skilled mobility for the benefit and development of countries of origin. The chapter concludes with some observations on policy and research implications.

2. The Increasing Mobility of the Highly Skilled

In recent years, new data sets based on the collection of national census data have revealed the patterns of highly skilled migration. They demonstrate that skilled migration is indeed increasing and that there are many and complex relations between major countries of origin and destination. Student migration also shows a marked increase and is likely to significantly influence the future volume, composition and destination of highly skilled migration (see also Chapter 4).

Migratory movements tend to be influenced by regional affinities. While policymakers and researchers have focused their attention mainly on migration from developing to developed countries, there are other types of flows that deserve attention. According to Ocampo (2006), South-North, South-South, and North-North migration flows account for roughly one-third each of the global distribution of migrant stocks. Moreover, the growing share of tertiary educated migrants in migration movements is notable, accounting, for instance, for a 46 per cent increase in migrant flows in OECD countries between 1990 and 2000.

2.1 Defining Highly Skilled

It is not always clear just who the highly skilled are. The most obvious indicator is either the level of education or occupation. Depending on the objective to be achieved, one or the other is preferred. If relevance to policy is important, most governments typically use a combination of both education and occupation to select the highly skilled. Ultimately, data availability often constrains the definition used for the purpose of analysis.

The most basic definition of highly skilled migrants tends to be restricted to persons with tertiary education, typically adults who have completed a formal two-year college education or more. This is also the most readily available international statistic and, by default, the most widely studied measure of highly skilled mobility. When possible, additional information regarding an academic or professional degree would be desirable. The National Science Foundation of the United States, which has some of the most complete international data on the stock of scientists and engineers, tends to focus on data for holders of doctoral degrees.

The Manual on the Measurement of Human Resources of 1995, or the "Canberra Manual", is a response to the work of both the OECD and the European

Commission's efforts to prioritize standardized data on human resources devoted to science and technology (S&T). It draws on best international and national practice and classifications and provides definitions in terms of qualifications (levels and fields of study) and occupations (Auriol and Sexton, 2002). While it is, perhaps, one of the most detailed definitional guidelines for comparative international statistics, its focus on S&T occupations limits its general usefulness.

Most frequently, governments define highly skilled migrants not in terms of either/or, but in terms of both education and occupation. For example, the United States' well-known "specialty worker H-1B visa" is based on a list of specific occupations and a minimum academic requirement of a Bachelor's degree. The definition of "highly skilled" depends on both an educational component and a threshold defining minimum competence in a knowledge-based society.

Professional activity and experience are important as selection criteria as this allows to filter out workers with little education and to target desired skills. The S&T occupations defined in the Canberra Manual are an example in point as they focus on technical skills regarded as crucial for research and development (R&D) and the engineering requirements of knowledge-based economies.

However, to restrict the meaning of highly skilled to S&T occupations would be too narrow an approach as it would disregard other high-skill categories that are in significant demand, such as business persons, managers, teachers or healthcare providers. Of course, it is possible to go beyond narrowly defined immigration policy interests by extending it to include a "creative class" that includes S&T workers as well as writers and artists (Florida and Tinagli, 2004). Arguably, such an expanded definition goes beyond the domain of immigration policy, as creativity has, or should have, deeper endogenous

wellsprings, although it raises an interesting point about what might be considered as most important for national productivity — education, skills or creativity? Other than for the specific purpose of constructing international norms in statistics, occupation is important precisely because it points to what is being done; and what is being done is ultimately of critical importance. Highly skilled persons are mainly in high value-added and high productivity activities that are essential to the global knowledge society. S&T workers, physicians and business persons bring different competencies and their professional activities at various levels combine to advance economic and social development and national wealth.

2.2 Flows and Stocks of Highly Skilled Migrants

The existing data on the mobility of highly skilled individuals are limited to the assessment of persons with tertiary education and have only recently been compiled for the World Bank and the OECD using national censuses. Putting these estimates together is a substantial task requiring the collection of data from national censuses in destination countries, which often work with different definitions. More refined estimates, for instance regarding more detailed levels of education, or for the mobility of men versus women, or by occupation, have yet to be developed.

Using tertiary education, Figure 2.1 shows that the growth of highly skilled migration to EU countries already started in the early 1990s, preceding the "New Economy" and the boom in the information, communications and technology (ICT) sectors. Once underway, the percentage of highly skilled migrants increased until the end of the ICT-led cycle in 2001. From just under 15 per cent of all migrants in 1991, the share of the highly skilled grew to just over one-quarter of all migrants by 2001.[2]

---

[2]   For the EU, the new immigrants are those who arrived in the respective year. For the United States, new immigrants are those admitted during the past five years.

The application of these regulations may vary significantly among countries. However, there has been little national or comparative evaluation of the success of admission programmes. In fact, there is rather little international effort to evaluate programmes, other than all-too-often perfunctory administrative/legislative reviews, and very few countries have attempted to either collect the necessary data or carry out rigorous analyses.

Certainly, countries have different criteria for measuring success and particular countries may even have conducted experiments with different programmes intended to achieve different ends. However, it appears that there is very little interest in policy evaluation when it comes to the impact of admission policies on highly skilled migration. According to McLaughlan and Salt (2002), the five approaches most often used to determine success are qualitative assessments to see whether policy objectives have been met; measurement of work outputs; level of complaints lodged by stakeholders; surveys of public opinion; and research conducted internally or externally. The authors note that only Australia, Canada, Germany and the United States have carried out such systematic research. Comparative frameworks for programme evaluation are therefore still at the development stage.

In fact, most international policy studies to date do little more than specify criteria deemed important for comparative purposes. The most detailed comparative study so far, completed in 2000 (Christian, 2000), covers some 15 countries and compares them in terms of class of admission (type of migrant/business stream), the use of quotas, the type of employment authorization (employer or employee-based), and application procedures (employer or employee-based). Rollason (2002), whose main focus is on the United Kingdom, remarks on the comparative features of temporary or permanent programmes in 11 countries in terms of the categories of workers, general/specific admissions, tests for the availability of domestic workers, quotas, period of stay and possibilities for renewal, and the permissibility of family reunification. Having constructed major criteria for comparison, however, none of these studies goes on to draw firm conclusions about effective practices. Even the regular reporting on policy changes in the OECD's annual *Trends in International Migration*, rarely draws any strong conclusions.

One exception to this tendency to make systematic comparisons while drawing few conclusions is found in Papademetriou (2003), who identifies four major strategies to admit skilled immigrants: employment-based admissions where employers apply to hire a worker under conditions that safeguard domestic labour; labour market testing where government agencies identify sectors with labour shortages; talent accrual where points are awarded for characteristics like education or language ability; and "filtration systems" where permanent residence status is awarded to students or temporary workers who first demonstrate their value. He suggests that a combination of the best of these strategies might be a good approach and might be accomplished using a points system, similar to those used in Australia and Canada, awarding points for sub-elements of each of the four strategies. In this regard, he starts with an evaluation of the strengths and weaknesses of various strategies, not recommending one or the other, but rather a combination of the best elements of each.

In addition, there have been policy recommendations for the orderly management of migration on a worldwide basis that are in some ways supplementary to legally binding standards, such as those found in international trade agreements. They offer ideas for the cooperative management of highly skilled workers between developing and developed countries. Such projects include the Transatlantic Learning Connection (1999) or the International Regime for Orderly Movements of People (Ghosh, 2000). In partnership with the International Organization for Migration (IOM), the Swiss Government launched the Global Consultative Process for Inter-State Cooperation on Migration Management in 2001 (Berne Initiative), which contributed to the development of the International Agenda for Migration Management (IAMM) (2005) containing a set of common understandings and effective practices for a planned, balanced and comprehensive approach to the management of migration.

The Global Commission on International Migration was launched by the U.N. Secretary-General and a number of governments in December 2003. The Commission's final report in October 2005 makes recommendations on how to improve the national, regional and global management of international migration (GCIM, 2005). In the European Union, the recent enlargement to 27 members has renewed pressure to go beyond the harmonization of national policies to a common legal migration policy (Van Selm and Tsolakis, 2003), including a proposal for a EU Directive on the conditions of entry and residence of highly skilled workers from non-EU third countries (European Commission, 2005). In October 2007, the European Commission published a Communication introducing this draft directive. The proposal establishes a fast-track procedure for the admission of highly qualified workers from third countries, based on a common definition and criteria. Workers admitted would be provided with an "EU Blue Card", essentially a residence permit allowing them to work and also affording them a set of rights, including favourable family reunification conditions. The proposal envisages restrictions on access to the labour market for the first two years in the Member State of residence. Thereafter, such workers would enjoy equal treatment with nationals as regards access to highly qualified employment. Moreover, after two years of lawful residence in the first Member State, the proposal would enable the migrant to move for work to another Member State subject to certain conditions (European Commission,

2007). While there has been progress in the development of common policies on asylum seekers and refugees and on the treatment and movement of long-term third-country residents, the achievement of consensus on the establishment of common criteria for the admission and residence of highly skilled migrants in EU Member States will require a great deal more work.

4. Policies that Address Brain Drain[7]

It is fair to say that the greatest competition has been for highly skilled migrants from the developing world, the source of the largest and growing numbers of highly educated persons. Despite Europe's increasing intake, the United States remains the dominant destination country for highly skilled workers from developing countries. Already at the outset of the 1990s, the U.S. had just over half of the world's highly skilled migrants from the developing world (Carrington and Detragiache, 1999). In fact, Table 2.2 shows that the traditional North American destinations of the United States and Canada have been the place of residence of nearly two-thirds (65%) of the world's tertiary educated foreign-born adults in 1990 and 2000. The traditional countries of immigration, along with Sweden and Norway, are the most successful countries relative to the size of their own populations in attracting highly skilled migrants (Lowell, 2006).

These figures translate into substantial losses of highly skilled populations for the developing world. As of 2001, nearly one in every ten tertiary educated adults born in the developing world resided in North America, Australia or western Europe. About five per cent of the developing world's emigrants with secondary education live in industrialized countries and the figures for the upper echelons are even higher. It is estimated that 30 to 50 per cent of the developing world's population trained in science

---

[7] See also Chapter 12, which discusses some of these policies.

REFERENCES

Antecol, H., D. Cobb-Clark and S. Trejo
2004   "The History of Selective Immigration in Australia, Canada, and the United States", *Brussels Economic Review*, Special Issue on Skilled Migration, 47(1): 45-56.

Borjas, G.J.
1999   "The Economic Analysis of Immigration" in O.C. Ashenfelter and D. Card (Eds), *Handbook of Labor Economics*, Vol. 3A, Elsevier, Amsterdam, 1697-1760.

Carrington, W.J. and E. Detragiache
1999   "How Extensive is the Brain Drain?", *Finance and Development*, 36(2), http://www.imf.org/external/pubs/ft/fandd/1999/06/carringt.htm.

Chiswick, B.R.
2005   "High Skilled Immigration in the International Arena", IZA Discussion Paper No. 1782, September, Forschungsinstitut zur Zukunft der Arbeit (Institute for the Study of Labour), Bonn, http://ftp.iza.org/dp1782.pdf.

Christian, B.P.
2000   "Facilitating High-Skilled Migration to Advanced Industrial Countries: Comparative Policies", Working Paper, Institute for the Study of International Migration (ISIM), Georgetown University, Washington, D.C.

Docquier, F.
2006   "Brain Drain and Inequality Across Nations", IZA Discussion Paper No. 2440, November, Institute for the Study of Labour, Bonn, http://ftp.iza.org/dp2440.pdf.

Docquier, F. and A. Marfouk
2006   "International Migration by Educational Attainment (1990-2000)" in C. Özden and M.W. Schiff (Eds.), *International Migration, Remittances and the Brain Drain*, Palgrave-Macmillan, London, 151-200.

Ellerman, D.
2003   "Policy Research on Migration and Development", World Bank Policy Research Working Paper 3117.

European Commission
2003   *Employment in Europe 2003. Recent Trends and Prospects*, Directorate-General for Employment and Social Affairs, September, Office for Official Publications of the European Communities, Luxembourg, http://ec.europa.eu/employment_social/employment_analysis/employ_2003_en.htm.

2005   *Policy Plan on Legal Migration*, COM (2005) 669 of 21 December.

2007   *Proposal for a Council Directive on the conditions of entry and residence of third-country nationals for the purposes of highly qualified employment*, COM (2007) 637 of 23 October.

Faini, R.
2003   "Is the Brain Drain an Unmitigated Blessing?", United Nations University, World Institute for Development Economics Research (UN-WIDER) Discussion Paper No. 2003/64, http://www.wider.unu.edu/publications/working-papers/discussion-papers/2003/en_GB/dp2003-064/.

Findlay, C. and T. Warren
2000   "The GATS and developing economies in the ESCAP region", *Studies in Trade and Investment*, 37: 11-60.

Florida, R. and I. Tinagli
2004   *Europe in the Creative Age*, February, Carnegie Mellon Software Industry Center, co-published in Europe with DEMOS, http://www.demos.co.uk/files/EuropeintheCreativeAge2004.pdf.

Ghosh, B. (Ed.)
2000   *Managing Migration – Time for a New International Regime?*, Oxford University Press, Oxford.

Global Commission on International Migration (GCIM)
2005   *Migration in an interconnected world: New directions for action*, Report of the GCIM, October, SRO-Kundig, Geneva, http://www.gcim.org/attachements/gcim-complete-report-2005.pdf.

Hanson, G.H. and A. Spilimbergo
1996   "Illegal Immigration, Border Enforcement, and Relative Wages: Evidence from Apprehensions at the U.S.-Mexico Border", Inter-American Development Bank (IADB) Working Paper Series 328, Washington, D.C.

Hatton, T.J. and J.G. Williamson
2003 "What fundamentals drive world migration?", National Bureau of Economic Research (NBER) Working Paper No. 9159 (September), Cambridge, MA.

International Organization for Migration (IOM) and Swiss Federal Office for Migration
2005 *International Agenda for Migration Management*, IOM and Swiss Federal Migration Office, Geneva/ Berne.

Jones, H. and T. Pardthaisong
1997 "The commodification of international labour migration", Centre for Applied Population Research Paper 97/4, University of Dundee, Dundee, United Kingdom.

Koivusalo, M.
2003 "The Impact of WTO Agreements on Health and Development Policies", Globalism and Social Policy Programme, Policy Brief No. 3 (January), http://gaspp.stakes.fi/NR/rdonlyres/3000F54A-DDCF-48C4-AFFE-056867902724/0/policybrief3.pdf.

Kutznetsov, Y. (Ed.)
2006 *Diaspora Networks and the International Migration of Skills: How Countries Can Draw on Their Talent Abroad*, The World Bank, Washington, D.C.

Lowell, B.L.
2004 "Policies and Regulations for Managing Skilled International Migration for Work", United Nations, Department of Economic and Social Affairs (UN DESA), Population Division, New York, http://www.un.org/esa/population/meetings/ittmigdev2005/P03-LLowell.pdf.

2006 *An Evaluation of an Extended Index on Pro-Development Migration Policies*, Report to the Center for Global Development, Washington, D.C., http://www.cgdev.org/doc/cdi/2006/lowellMigration.pdf.

Lowell, B.L. and M. Bump
2006 "U.S. Competitiveness: Foreign Students in Science, Technology, Engineering and Math", ISIM, Georgetown University, Washington, D.C.

Lowell, B.L., A. Findlay and E. Stewart
2004 "Brain Strain: Optimising Highly Skilled Emigration from Developing Countries", Asylum and Migration Working Paper 3, Institute for Public Policy Research (IPPR), London, http://www.ippr.org.uk/ecomm/files/brainstrain.pdf.

Martin, P.L.
2003 "Highly Skilled Labor Migration: Sharing the Benefits", May, International Institute for Labour Studies, ILO, Geneva, http://www.ilo.org/public/english/bureau/inst/download/migration2.pdf.

Mayda, A.M.
2005 "International Migration: A Panel Data Analysis of Economic and Non-Economic Determinants", IZA Discussion Paper No. 1590, May, Institute for the Study of Labour, Bonn, ftp://repec.iza.org/RePEc/Discussionpaper/dp1590.pdf.

McLaughlan, G. and J. Salt
2002 *Migration Policies Towards Highly Skilled Foreign Workers*, Report to the Home Office, Migration Research Unit, University College London, http://www.geog.ucl.ac.uk/research/mobility-identity-and-security/migration-research-unit/pdfs/highly_skilled.pdf.

Meyer, J-B.
2001 "Network approach versus brain drain: Lessons from the diaspora", *International Migration*, 39(5): 91-110.

Massey, D.S., J. Arango, G. Hugo, A. Kouaouci, A. Pellegrino and J.E. Taylor
1994 "An Evaluation of International Migration Theory: The North American Case", *Population and Development Review*, 20(4): 699-751.

Ocampo, J.A.
2006 "International Migration and Development", presentation to the United Nations International Symposium on International Migration and Development, 28-30 June, Turin, http://www.un.org/esa/population/migration/turin/Turin_Statements/OCAMPO.pdf.

Organisation for Economic Co-operation and Development (OECD)
2004 *Trends in International Migration: Annual Report*, SOPEMI, OECD, Paris.

Textbox 2.3 - Social Costs of the Migration of Women Health Workers

Van Eyck, K. (Ed.)

2005   *Who Cares? Women Health Workers in the Global Labour Market*, Public Services International (PSI) and UNISON UK, Ferney-Voltaire, France, http://www.world-psi.org/Content/ContentGroups/English7/Publications1/Who_Cares.pdf.

LOW AND SEMI-SKILLED WORKERS ABROAD[*]

CHAPTER 3

1. Introduction

The world appears to be on the threshold of a new era in temporary labour migration programmes, characterized by more sources and destinations of migrant workers at all rungs of the job ladder (Martin, 2003b; Abella, 2006). Current temporary labour migration programmes aim to add workers temporarily to the labour force, but not settlers to the population. This may seem surprising, since programmes such as the Mexico-U.S. Bracero and the German *Gastarbeiter* (guest worker) programmes ended when destination country governments were persuaded that large numbers of temporary migrant workers adversely affected local workers and could result in migration getting "out of control".[1]

In a world of persisting demographic and economic inequalities and better communication and transportation links, young people in particular want to cross national borders for higher wages and better opportunities. There is general agreement that the world is about to enter a new stage in international labour migration, with more labour migration sources and destinations and migrants employed in a wider range of industries and occupations.

The improved management of labour migration in the 21st century is likely to require temporary migrant worker programmes that include economic incentives to encourage employers and migrants to abide by programme rules. For example, employer-paid taxes on migrant earnings that finance the restructuring of migrant jobs can allow the programmes to shrink over time, while the refunding of worker-paid taxes can encourage migrants to return home as programme rules require while providing funds to stimulate economic development and to reduce the incentive to emigrate in the future. Adding such economic mechanisms could help to better align temporary labour migration programme objectives and outcomes, and convince industrialized countries that such programmes will not turn into furtive "side door" or de facto permanent immigration, but lead to more border gates being opened for regular migrant workers.

---

[*] This chapter was written by Philip Martin, Professor, Department of Agricultural and Resource Economics, University of California, Davis, California, United States.

[1] It is generally agreed that the Bracero programme sowed the seeds for later irregular Mexico-U.S. migration (Martin, 2004: Ch. 2), and that Germany faces major integration challenges with settled Turkish guest workers and their families (Martin, 2004: Ch. 6).

There seems to be no widely accepted definition of temporary labour migration. Abella (2006: 4) suggested a definition based on a destination country's perspective and considers "temporary migrants" as "those whose legal status is temporary, regardless of the amount of time they may actually have stayed in a country". It goes without saying that this is a very wide definition and would apply to an

> extremely broad array of different movements, conditions and durations, [including] *au pairs*, seasonal workers,[4] trainees, intra-corporate transfers, contract workers, working holiday makers, exchange visitors, highly skilled professionals, cross-border service providers, installers, performing artists and sportspersons, etc. (OECD, 2007: 51).

3. Global and Regional Distribution of Temporary Migrants with Particular Reference to Low and Semi-skilled Workers: Flows and Stocks

3.1 Global Distribution

Today, the world community consists of some 200 countries with their respective annual per capita incomes in 2004 ranging from less than USD 250 to over USD 50,000 (World Bank, 2006b). Such economic differentials provide a significant incentive, especially for young people, to migrate in pursuit of higher wages and better opportunities.[5] In 2004, one billion people, or one-sixth of the world's population, lived in the 30 high-income

countries with a gross national income of USD 32 trillion, representing four-fifths of the global wealth of USD 40 trillion.[6] The resulting average per capita income of USD 32,000 in high-income countries was 21 times the average USD 1,500 in low and middle-income countries, and this 21:1 ratio has remained stable over the past quarter of a century (Martin et al., 2006).

Migration is an age-old response to variations in economic opportunity, security and other factors, but the crossing of international borders is a relatively recent phenomenon, as international borders have multiplied along with the sharp rise in the number of independent states making up the international community as it is known today.[7] The number of international migrants has also doubled during the past two decades to 191 million in 2005 (UN, 2006). As shown in Table 3.1, some 62 million migrants moved from South to North, i.e. from a developing to a developed country; 61 million moved from South to South; 53 million from North to North; and some 14 million migrants moved from North to South.[8]

Table 3.1:

Migrants in 2005 (millions)

Origin	Industrialized country	Developing country
Industrialized country	53	14
Developing country	62	61

Source: UN, 2006.

Given that about half of these migrants are absorbed into the labour force of the destination countries,

---

[4] Seasonal labour migration is also by definition temporary in nature, and many of the policy issues discussed below and in Chapter 11 in relation to temporary labour migration, apply to mobility for the purpose of seasonal employment, which, however, has certain distinguishing characteristics. Importantly, seasonal labour migration comprises particularly short-term movements (3-9 months), which are dependent on the natural rhythm of the seasons, such as sowing and harvesting time in agriculture, and demands for workers in the hospitality sector especially during peak periods in the year (e.g. ski resorts in the winter, coastal resorts in the summer months in Europe).

[5] Young people are most likely to cross borders as they have invested the least in jobs and careers at home and have the most time to recoup their "investment in migration" abroad.

[6] At purchasing power parity (PPP), which takes into account national differences in the cost of living, the world's gross national income was USD 56 trillion, including 55 per cent in high-income countries.

[7] From only a small number of recognized independent states at the beginning of the 20th century, the number of countries making up the international community as we know it today has risen to 193 by 2007, when the CIA World Factbook listed 193 "independent states", one "other" and six other entities (CIA, 2007).

[8] These are stock estimates in 2005, meaning that migrants may have arrived recently or decades ago.

the 60 million migrant workers in high-income countries account for an average of 12 per cent of the local labour force (ILO, 2004). The labour force distribution of the 31 million migrant workers moving South-North is quite distinct from that in destination countries: 40 per cent of the 3.2 billion workers worldwide are in agriculture, 20 per cent in industry and construction, and 40 per cent in services (World Bank, 2006b), and migrant workers from developing countries largely originate from societies characterized by this 40:20:40 distribution. In industrialized countries only about three per cent of the total workforce is in agriculture, 25 per cent in industry and 72 per cent in services (OECD, 2005). However, a look at the distribution of migrant workers in these countries shows 10 per cent to be in agriculture, 40 per cent in industry and construction, and 50 per cent in services (OECD, 2006) (Table 3.2).

Table 3.2:

Migrants and Local Workers by Sector, Percentage Distribution

	Agriculture	Industry	Services
Industrialized countries	3	25	72
Developing countries	40	20	40
Migrants in industrialized host countries	10	40	50

Note:
Industry includes construction.

Sources: OECD (2005), (2006), World Bank (2006b).

The difference in migrant worker distribution reflects the three types of employers and respective demands for migrant workers in: (a) sunset industries – e.g. agriculture, light manufacturing, garment industry; (b) industries that cannot be moved – e.g. construction; and (c) services at all levels of the skills ladder, from IT and health care to domestic work and janitorial services.

Migrant workers from developing countries who move to industrialized countries also have personal characteristics that differentiate them from native-born adults. The best single determinant of individual earnings in industrialized countries is years of education. In most developing countries, the distribution of adults by years of education has the shape of a pyramid, a few well educated persons at the top and most workers with less than a secondary-school certificate or high-school diploma grouped near the bottom.

A graph showing native-born adults in high-income countries by years of education has a diamond shape. About 25 per cent have a college degree, 60 per cent a secondary-school certificate and 15 per cent have less than a secondary certificate or high-school diploma. Migrants from developing countries in industrialized countries differ from both adults at home and abroad, as their distribution resembles an hourglass or barbell shape when arranged by years of education. About 35 per cent have a college degree, 30 per cent a secondary school certificate and 35 per cent less than a high-school diploma (Figure 3.1). International migration from developing to industrialized countries takes persons from the top and bottom of a pyramid distribution and adds them to the top and bottom of a diamond-shaped distribution.

Figure 3.1:

Native-born and Migrant Adults in Industrialized Countries by Education, 2005 (percentage)

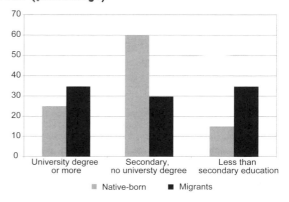

(a) East and Southeast Asia and the Middle East

The growth in the numbers of temporary migrant workers can be seen across East and Southeast Asia and the Middle East. In Japan, 146,000 temporary workers were admitted in 2004 compared with 114,300 in 2000, although in 2005 admissions dropped to 110,200 (OECD, 2007). However, the numbers of trainees admitted has risen steadily (54,000 in 2003; 75,400 in 2004; 83,300 in 2005) (OECD, 2007). Stocks of temporary foreign workers in East Asia have also risen, particularly in South Korea and Taiwan Province of China, where they rose by half, and then doubled respectively between 2000 and 2004 (Abella, 2006: Table 3.4). In Japan, however, the total number

of foreign workers, including various categories of temporary migrants, is relatively low and estimated at around 650,000 by the end of 2005, or less than one per cent of the labour force (OECD, 2007). Table 3.4 includes estimates of undocumented migrants who are prevalent in many low and semi-skilled employment sectors (e.g. construction) in Malaysia and Thailand.

In the GCC States the number of overseas contract workers rose by 2.5 per cent annually between 1985 and 2000, though this rate of increase is relatively small compared with the rates of expansion from the mid-1970s to the mid-1980s (Abella, 2006; Table 3.4).

Table 3.4:

Temporary Foreign Workers in Asian Destinations (stock estimates)

Country of Employment	1985	1997	2000	2004
East Asia[1]				
Brunei			80-90,000	
China		82,000	60,000	80,000
Hong Kong SAR		171,000	217,000	217,000
Malaysia		1,720,000	800,000	1,359,000
Republic of Korea		245,000	285,000	423,000
Singapore			612,000	580,000
Taiwan Province of China		246,000	327,000	600,000
Thailand		1,126,000	1,103,000	1,624,000
Viet Nam			30,000	
West Asia[1] [2]				
Bahrain	99,000		180,000	
Jordan			35,000	
Kuwait	574,000		976,000	
Lebanon			75,000	
Oman	91,000		55,700	
Saudi Arabia	2,722,000		3,060,000	
United Arab Emirates	784,000		1,300,000	

Notes:

[1] For East Asia, the figures include work permit holders and estimates of undocumented migrants. For "West Asia", only work permit holders are recorded.

[2] "West Asia" is the region referred to in the original Table – it denotes Arab Mashrek countries and GCC States covered in the Middle East Migration Overview (see the Asia Overview).

Source: Adapted from Abella (2006), citing sources from the Gulf Cooperation Council (GCC), OECD (2003) and Hugo (2005).

Israel is also a significant destination for temporary foreign workers, who, since the early 1990s, have been admitted to replace Palestinian workers. At the end of 2003, official estimates counted approximately 189,000 such migrants, with many employed in low-wage and low-status jobs. Over half of the migrant workers in Israel come from Southeast Asia: about 50,000 from the Philippines, employed mainly in home healthcare, 30,000 Thai migrants mostly working in agriculture, and 15,000 Chinese migrants in construction. There are also approximately 65,000 foreign workers from eastern Europe, with over half from Romania working by and large in construction. One-third of the migrants are women employed chiefly in the home healthcare sector (Kruger, 2006).

(b) Established countries of immigration: Australia, Canada, New Zealand and the United States

In the admission systems of established countries of immigration, which are primarily geared towards permanent migration for employment, temporary labour migration remains nonetheless an important feature with the objective of filling labour shortages in specific sectors (Table 3.5). In the periods 2004-2005 and 2005-2006, these countries received approximately 1.14 and 1.24 million temporary migrant workers (including dependants) respectively, and their numbers are rising steadily.

Table 3.5:

Temporary Migration for Employment to Australia, Canada, New Zealand and the United States, 2004-2006

	2004-2005	2005-2006
Australia[1]	100,758	118,181
Canada[2]	93,481	99,141
New Zealand[3]	118,460	142,536
United States[4]	831,715	883,706

Notes:

[1] Figures for fiscal years 2004-2005 and 2005-2006, respectively, relating to the issue of temporary resident visas (skilled visa, social and cultural, international relations and other), but excluding working holiday visas (see Chapter 5).

[2] Figures for 2004 and 2005, respectively.

[3] Figures for fiscal years 2004-2005 and 2005-2006, respectively, relating to work applications and including young persons employed under Working Holiday Schemes with specific countries, which are described in Chapter 5. These include principal applicants and secondary applicants. The applications also include individuals who apply for more than one visa or permit in a given year.

[4] Figures for fiscal years 2004 and 2005, respectively, including spouses and children, but excluding intra-company transferees (L-1 visas) and foreigners coming to the U.S. for work-and-learn experience (exchange visitors – J-1 visas).

Sources: *DIMA (2006), CIC Canada (2006), Immigration New Zealand (2007), U.S. Office of Immigration Statistics (2006).*

Although seasonal labour migration is not a common occurrence in the Asia-Pacific region, in April 2007 the New Zealand Government started a bilateral Seasonal Labour Scheme for Pacific Islanders, in partnership with the World Bank. It aims to enable up to 5,000 low-skilled and semi-skilled Pacific Islanders to take up specific agricultural jobs left unfilled by local workers (see Textbox 3.3).

Textbox 3.3

Expanding Job Opportunities for Pacific Islanders through Labour Mobility

In a world of rapid globalization, the economic competitiveness of a number of countries is coming under increasingly severe strain owing to their limited territory market size and remote location, while rapidly eroding trade preferences also no longer suffice to support competitiveness. Furthermore, international economic aid, which had enabled the development and construction of local infrastructure and the delivery of important services, may no longer be able to mitigate their growing cost disadvantages. Hence, for small and remote island economies to be viable, economic integration and export diversification – particularly in niche markets able to overcome the limitations of small size – are important. Facilitated labour mobility may be considered as responding to such a niche market.

were administration, business and management (37%), hospitality and catering (20%), agriculture (10%), manufacturing (7%), and food, fish and meat processing (5%). "Administration" in the above list may be slightly misleading, as the majority of workers in this sector work for recruitment agencies and can therefore be employed in a broad range of occupations (U.K. Home Office, 2007).

A principal feature of temporary low-skilled labour migration in Europe is seasonal employment (Table 3.3), particularly to the southern European countries, Austria, France, Germany, Norway and the U.K. Germany, for example, has a relatively large-scale scheme that, on the basis of bilateral arrangements, provides over 300,000 seasonal jobs annually for a period of up to four months in the agriculture, forestry and hospitality sectors to migrant workers from central and eastern Europe (German Federal Ministry of Interior, 2007; Table 3.3). A recent development, undoubtedly related to the considerable out-migration from the new EU Member States to the former EU-15, is the growing labour shortage in central and eastern European countries, particularly in the low and semi-skilled sectors. The shortages of agricultural workers in Poland have led to the introduction of a policy in 2006 allowing farmers to recruit seasonal workers from neighbouring countries (Belarus, Russian Federation and Ukraine) for a period of thee months within a six-month period without the need for a work permit (OECD, 2007).

In recent years, Italy has implemented labour migration schemes covering both temporary and seasonal workers. In the 2006 quota-setting decree, provision was made for the entry of 45,000 temporary migrant workers in the domestic and personal assistance sectors, and for an additional 50,000 seasonal workers in agriculture and tourism out of a total migration contingent of 170,000.[19]

---

[19] Decree by Prime Minister DPCM No. 7 of 15 February 2006, published in the *Gazzetta Ufficiale* (Official Journal) on 7 March 2007.

(d) Africa

In sub-Saharan Africa, most temporary labour migration is across borders and circular, involving also irregular movements (see Chapters 7 and 8). More reliable information is available concerning specific types of regular movements in the Southern African Development Community (SADC), such as contract labour migration to the principal mining centres in the region (Textbox 3.1). While labour recruitment figures for mines in South Africa for 1990-2000 show a decline in the number of migrants from all countries except Mozambique, there was an increase in foreign workers in the mining industry, from 40 per cent in the mid-1980s to almost 60 per cent in 2000. Lesotho, Mozambique and Swaziland are the three main countries of origin. In 2000, the numbers of migrants from these countries stood at 58,224, 57,034 and 9,360, respectively (Crush and Williams, 2005). According to more recent figures provided by officials from Swaziland, 13,000 of their nationals were working in South African mines in 2005 (MIDSA, 2007). In addition to mining, the principal sectors employing migrants in South Africa are construction, domestic services and factory work. Commercial agriculture is another important sector employing migrants both with and without authorization (Crush and Williams, 2005). Botswana and Namibia, both of which are experiencing rapid economic growth, are also important destination countries in the region, mainly for skilled migrants from other SADC countries (MIDSA, 2007).

The numbers for both regular and irregular Asian migrant workers in the Southern African region are increasing, such as for Chinese workers in Lesotho's textile industry and Chinese, Indian and Pakistani workers in Swaziland and Tanzania, who appear to be filling jobs left vacant by both skilled and less-skilled nationals who moved abroad for employment. Mauritius is a country of both origin and destination for migrant workers (MIDSA, 2007; see also Textbox

12.2).[20] Labour migration in West Africa is more complex, and movements have fluctuated in recent times because of economic downturns in what were until recently relatively prosperous countries and destinations for migrant workers (e.g. Côte d'Ivoire and Nigeria) and because of conflicts in others (e.g. Liberia and Sierra Leone) (Adepoju, 2005; see also Textbox 13.2).

Labour migration is also occurring within and to the Maghreb from sub-Saharan Africa, and it appears that most of these workers are either low or semi-skilled (see Textbox 3.4).

[20] In Mauritius, labour shortages exist in the manufacturing and hotel industries. In March 2007, 29,400 work permits had been issued in Mauritius, mostly to Chinese and Indian nationals. However, the country is also undertaking a major 10-year reform programme to restructure the economy, which, according to World Bank estimates, will result in the loss of 12,000 low-skilled jobs. Consequently, the Mauritian authorities are looking to offer employment abroad for some of their nationals through bilateral temporary (circular) labour migration programmes (MIDSA, 2007).

Textbox 3.4

Mobility of Skilled and Low-skilled Workers from, within and towards the Maghreb

In the immediate post-independence era, most Maghreb countries faced an unbalanced labour market due to a surplus of relatively low skilled and a shortage of qualified and highly skilled workers. Owing to geographical proximity and social and historical links, a number of Maghreb countries pursued an emigration policy with Italy, France and Spain, which went hand in hand with the recruitment of skilled foreign personnel to develop and manage services and enterprises. This arrangement was terminated in the context of Franco-Maghreb relations in 1973 against a backdrop of global recession. One year later, other European countries also ended the Maghreb labour migration programmes.

As concerns migration towards the Maghreb, 2006 United Nations data (Figure 3.2) show that out of a total Maghrebin population of 90 million, over one million were migrants. This represented 1.23 per cent of the population in 2005, with female migration accounting for 40.3 per cent. Since the 1970s, Libya has been the country with the largest number of foreigners on its territory. In 2005, they numbered just over 600,000, or five per cent of Libya's population. Libya is still the leading destination country for migrants from other Maghreb countries.

Figure 3.2:

Evolution of the Foreign Population in the Maghreb from 1960 to 2005 (thousands)

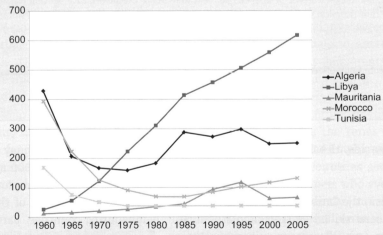

Source: *UN, Department of Economic and Social Affairs, Population Division 2006, Country Profile, World Migrant Stock: The 2005 Revision Population Database, http://esa.un.org/migration.*

Temporary migrant worker programmes in the mid-20th century were usually "macro" in the sense that there was one major programme per country, and the overall unemployment and job vacancy rate played a determining role in deciding the need for temporary migrant workers. Today's multiple programmes are "micro" in aiming to respond to specific labour market needs, such as filling job vacancies in nursing and IT. Overall unemployment and job vacancy rates play only a small role in determining admission to these specialized sectors. Government employment services, which have shrunk in size, have less credibility in determining whether foreign workers are "needed" to fill job vacancies.[24]

With admission procedures giving employers more say in deciding whether foreign workers are needed, employers have gained an important voice in admission policy. In many industrialized countries, if an employer decides that a college-educated foreigner is the best person to fill a vacancy, the hiring and admission procedure is relatively straightforward. For example, available H-1B visas in the U.S. are generally exhausted well before the end of the year, in part because the admission process is easy – most employers simply "attest" that they will be paying at least the prevailing wage to a college-educated foreigner who is filling a job normally requiring a college education. As a general rule, the admission procedures are more stringent for low-skilled workers. For instance, in Canada, employers wishing to hire low-skilled workers for employment in agriculture or under the new Low Skill Pilot Project discussed in Section 3.2(b) above, are still required to obtain a Labour Market Opinion from Human Resources and Social Development Canada (HRSDC). However, in some regions, where labour market information indicates that the demand for labour in particular occupations exceeds the available supply, the labour market test is relaxed considerably. For occupations found on Regional Lists of Occupations under Pressure, developed by HRSDC and Service Canada, employers do not need to conduct lengthy or comprehensive job search efforts before obtaining permission to hire foreign workers (HRSDC, 2007), with Labour Market Opinions issued for the number of workers required by a specific enterprise.

5. "Win-Win-Win" Migration: The Economic Argument for More Low and Semi-skilled Labour Migration

Moving low and semi-skilled workers from lower to higher-wage countries can be a "win-win-win" situation, with migrants benefiting from higher wages, destination countries from more employment and a higher GDP, and countries of origin from jobs for otherwise unemployed workers, remittances, and returns. The first two "wins" are well established, as migrants demonstrate a strong desire to go abroad by taking considerable risks to move to higher-wage countries. Most studies in destination countries conclude that the major beneficiaries of economically motivated migration are the migrants who receive higher earnings, and that the presence of migrants slightly expands economic output, albeit by depressing wages slightly (Smith and Edmonston, 1997).

The third "win", the effect of emigration on countries of origin, has been in the spotlight as migrant numbers and remittances are rising rapidly. The Global Commission on International Migration (GCIM, 2005), the World Trade Organization's GATS Mode 4 negotiations,[25] the UN High-Level Dialogue on Migration and Development[26] and the Global Forum on Migration and Development (GFMD)[27]

---

[24] In the U.S., there are two major ways of determining whether an employer "needs" migrants. Under certification, the U.S. Department of Labor (DOL) controls the border gate, not allowing migrants to enter until the employer conducts recruitment activities supervised by DOL. Under the alternative attestation process, the employer controls the border gate, opening it by attesting that she is paying the prevailing wage, and DOL responds to complaints of violations.

[25] See www.wto.org/english/tratop_e/serv_e/serv_e.htm.

[26] See http://www.unmigration.org.

[27] See Textbox Int. 2.

have recently lent support to the belief that more temporary labour migration from developing to industrialized countries can enhance "win-win-win" outcomes, citing remittances and the contributions of migrants who return and create new jobs at home, and the diaspora that maintains links to the country of origin (see Textbox 3.5).

Textbox 3.5

Promoting Temporary Labour Migration: Policy Response of the International Community

Global Forum on Migration and Development (GFMD)

"Temporary labour migration can work to everyone's advantage if it is legal, protective and linked to real labour needs. It is a flexible way of meeting labour surplus and shortage across countries. Assuring legal access to a varied labour market, protecting the basic rights of migrants, especially women, and assuring temporariness of the migration are key to maximizing the mutual benefits. In the absence of a functional multilateral system, bilateral arrangements have been found to operate effectively in certain countries. Individual countries can also adopt institutional and policy frameworks that contribute to realizing the objectives of temporary migration. Joint arrangements between origin and destination countries, particularly for lower-skilled migrants, can help enforce the laws to protect temporary migrants and enhance their contribution to their families and home communities."

GFMD (2008: 65).

UN Secretary General's Report on International Migration and Development

"84. Temporary migration programmes are becoming more numerous. They are a response to the rising demand for labour in receiving countries. Although the number of migrants admitted under the more recent programmes is modest, there is potential for these programmes to result in beneficial synergies for migrants, countries of origin and countries of destination. Under such programmes, migrants benefit from having a legal status and countries of origin gain from remittances and the eventual return of migrants, provided the experience they gain abroad can be put to productive use at home. Receiving countries secure the workers they need and may enhance the positive effects of migration by allowing migrants to stay long enough to accumulate savings."

UN (2006: 18).

World Bank

"Greater emigration of low-skilled emigrants from developing to industrial countries could make a significant contribution to poverty reduction. The most feasible means of increasing such emigration would be to promote managed migration programs between origin and destination countries that combine temporary migration of low-skilled workers with incentives for return."

World Bank (2006a: xi).

ILO Multilateral Framework on Labour Migration

"Chapter IX. Migration and development

...15. The contribution of labour migration to employment, economic growth, development and the alleviation of poverty should be recognized and maximized for the benefit of both origin and destination countries.

Guidelines

The following guidelines may prove valuable in giving practical effect to the above principles:

...

15.8. Adopting policies to encourage circular and return migration and reintegration into the country of origin, including by promoting temporary labour migration schemes and circulation-friendly visa policies."

ILO (2006).

Global Commission for International Migration

"States and the private sector should consider the option of introducing carefully designed temporary labour migration programmes as a means of addressing the economic needs of both countries of origin and destination."

GCIM (2005: 16).

International Agenda for Migration Management (IAMM)

Temporary migration

... "The effective management of temporary migration offers States the opportunity to channel migration to address a range of domestic needs and policy priorities, such as short-term labour market requirements or the acquisition or improvement of skills, knowledge and resources through training and work abroad. Different criteria and conditions may be developed for each temporary migration category. The key elements of a comprehensive and balanced temporary migration programme are that it is transparent, non-discriminatory, orderly, efficient, reliable and safe.

Effective practices in regard to temporary migration:

- Promotion of the use of certain forms of temporary migration, such as short-term and project-related migration, as a means of meeting labour market needs, improving the skills of nationals of countries of origin, especially developing countries and countries with economies in transition.
- Facilitation of regular consultations on a bilateral or multilateral basis to identify and meet temporary migration needs through orderly channels, including through conclusion of bilateral or multilateral agreements.
- Identification of employment sectors that would be designated as suitable for temporary migrant workers.
- Definition of categories for temporary migrants according to specific intended objectives, for example business, family visit or study.
- Implementation of measures to enable and facilitate temporary migration and multiple short stays, including through efficient registration systems and delivery of multi-entry visas based on available technology and information sharing for tourists, business visitors, family visits and other temporary purposes.
- Provision of clear, accessible and user-friendly information on temporary migration opportunities and procedural requirements, migrant rights and responsibilities, as well as means to access such information, including through such services as migrant information centres.
- Implementation of temporary migration programmes which provide temporary migrants with a secure legal status, with rights and responsibilities that reflect their temporary status.
- Promotion and implementation of measures to ensure that temporary migration remains temporary, such as conditioning subsequent re-entry on timely return.
- For those States utilising temporary migration programmes as a possible route to permanent migration, articulation of clear conditions under which those who qualify can gain permanent status.
- Promotion of data collection and analysis regarding temporary migration."

IOM/Swiss Federal Office for Migration (2005: 35-36).

UN Department of Economic and Social Affairs (World Economic and Social Survey 2004: *International Migration***)**

"It is widely recognized that a liberalization of the movement of people (workers and services providers) that is not for resettlement purposes would result in gains to the world economy and especially to developing countries. ... Improving the way temporary migrant flows are managed is a promising option. A step forward would be to implement such arrangements for the less skilled. (...) The movement of [less-skilled] workers from developing to developed countries promises to yield the greatest gains because this is where the difference between factor prices is largest and where there is considerable scope for movement."

UN DESA (2004: 139).

Economists estimate that more workers moving across borders could significantly increase global economic output as workers would be placed where their productivity is higher. One of the first studies was conducted by Hamilton and Whalley (1984), who estimated that global GDP could double if migration were to increase sufficiently to equalize the marginal productivity of labour (and wages) between seven world regions that included 179 countries.[28] Even if migration were insufficient to equalize wages, global GDP would still increase significantly if there were more migration, since the initial migrants face the largest gaps in marginal productivity or wages and thus gain the most by moving.

In its Global Economic Prospects Report 2006 on *Economic Implications of Remittances and Migration*, the World Bank (2006a) estimated that if an additional 14 million migrants were to migrate from developing to high-income countries that would generate a global income gain of over USD 350 billion, exceeding the anticipated USD 300 billion gain from completing the Doha round of trade negotiations.[29] The press release accompanying the report argued that more

> managed migration programs, including temporary work visas for low-skilled migrants in industrial countries (...) would contribute to significant reductions in poverty in migrant sending countries, among the migrants themselves, their families and, as remittances increase, in the broader community.[30]

If more labour migration produces "win-win-win" outcomes, how should it be organized? "Carefully" would seem to be the answer. The GCIM (2005: 79, para. 1.3) recommended "carefully designed temporary migration programs as a means of addressing the economic needs of both countries of origin and destination". The need for a careful design of temporary migrant worker programmes is especially urgent in countries such as the U.S. and Germany, where governments have not had a great record of keeping temporary worker programmes true to their design as past programmes did not function as expected. An understanding of why

---

[28] In Hamilton and Whalley's simulation, massive migration to equalize wages would have added USD 5 – 16 trillion to global GDP in 1977, when it was USD 8 trillion. Their simulation relied on a number of assumptions, including full employment of the world's workers, who produced a single output with a CES production function (i.e. constant elasticity of substitution between labour and capital). They estimated differences in 1977 in the marginal productivity of labour across seven multi-country regions and assumed that these differences were due to migration restrictions. Migration that equalized marginal productivity and wages (factor price convergence via migration) would result in workers in destination countries losing and capital owners in these countries gaining, and the opposite distributional effects in countries of origin. (The full employment assumption is necessary to justify equating wages and marginal productivity; they assume that the wage:profit ratio is one in both rich and poor countries before migration barriers are lifted and that capital does not move even as labour migrates.)

[29] Two-thirds of this USD 300 billion gain would come from liberalizing farm trade.

[30] World Bank, "Migration Can Deliver Welfare Gains, Reduce Poverty, Says Global Economic Prospects 2006", Press Release, 16 Nov. 2005, citing Uri Dadush, Director of the Bank's Development Prospects Group.

temporary labour migration programmes tend to get larger and to last longer than originally intended is a prerequisite to designing programmes that can come closer to fulfilling the goal of adding workers temporarily to the labour force, but not adding settlers to the population.

6. The Problems of Distortion and Dependence and Possible Solutions

Temporary migrant worker programmes tend to get larger and to last longer than intended because of distortion and dependence. Most employers in the majority of host countries do not hire temporary migrant workers. Distortion means that the minority who do have access to a supplementary labour supply – those hiring temporary migrants – face generally limited supplies of low-skilled workers at home and almost unlimited supplies abroad.

Employers hiring temporary migrant workers often do so assuming that migrants will continue to be available and make investment decisions reflecting this assumption. Thus, farmers who depend on migrants may plant fruit trees in areas with few people, assert that they will go out of business without migrants to pick their crops, and resist efforts to reduce the number of migrant workers because doing so would reduce the value of their investment. This is economic distortion in that some employers face more stringent labour supply constraints than others. Employers relying on migrant labour can either avoid raising wages when local workers are no longer available or willing to do the work, or they can expand production because they are able to recruit migrant workers.

Dependence reflects the fact that some migrants and their families as well as their regions and countries of origin may assume that foreign jobs, earnings and remittances will continue to be available. If the opportunity to work abroad legally is curbed, but the "3 Rs", i.e. recruitment, remittances and

returns, have not been set in motion to remove or reduce migratory push factors, migrants may continue to migrate to avoid a reduction in their income. Most researchers conclude that the U.S.-Mexico Bracero programmes sowed the seeds of subsequent unauthorized Mexico-U.S. migration, via distortion in rural America (the expansion of labour-intensive agriculture) and dependence in rural Mexico (population and labour force growth without economic development) (Martin, 2003b: Ch. 2).

The realities of distortion and dependence should encourage governments considering new temporary labour migration programmes to proceed cautiously, and to include economic mechanisms to minimize distortion and dependence. These mechanisms include taxes to encourage employers to look for alternatives to migrants and subsidies to encourage temporary migrant workers to return to their countries of origin as their contracts require.

Dealing with distortion requires recognition that employers always have choices when they make investments and fill jobs. By the time government is involved in a request for temporary migrant workers, the employer has usually found the migrants desired, so that a supervised period of recruitment usually fails to find local workers. Government employment services are ill suited to second-guess employers in such situations, which is one reason why labour certification processes (i.e. labour market/resident worker tests) can become very contentious, especially if unemployment rates in the areas where migrants will be employed are high.

Once the employers who turn to guest workers learn how to have their "need" for migrants certified, most assume they will be able to continue to hire foreign workers. As a result, investments in alternatives to migrants can dwindle, and distortions may increase as migrant-dependent sectors become isolated from national labour markets. For example, agriculture may not offer workers' health insurance to its employees because the young male migrants who dominate the seasonal workforce prefer cash wages to costly benefits, but this also makes farm work less attractive to local workers who are interested in benefits. Networks linking migrants and work places soon span borders as current migrants refer friends and relatives to fill vacant jobs. One result is that labour market information may flow far more freely from a migrant workplace to migrant countries of origin than to pockets of unemployment nearby.

International norms and local laws usually call for migrant workers to be treated equally, receiving the same wages and benefits as local workers. One way to minimize distortion is to realize that social security and health insurance payments increase the overall payroll expenditure of employers by 20 to 40 per cent. These amounts could be collected on migrant payrolls to level the playing field between migrant and local workers.

The employer share of migrant payroll taxes could be used to combat distortion through the restructuring of migrant jobs, such as promoting labour-saving mechanization. For example, in an industry such as agriculture, it is often hard for one farmer to finance or implement mechanization, since peach packers and processors want fruit that is either picked by hand or mechanically, but not both (Martin, 2003b: Ch. 8). Thus, a mechanization programme funded through payroll taxes could help to provide alternatives to migrants.[31]

Mechanization is not the only alternative to migrants. Sometimes local workers may be attracted to "migrant jobs" once they have been restructured, as has been the case with garbage collection in the U.S., whose labour force has been "renationalized" by switching to large containers lifted by a truck operator. In other cases, subsidized research could develop alternatives to

migrants, as when some elderly persons have in-home migrant caregivers and others use technology such as cameras linked to computers to live alone but under video monitoring that can summon help quickly. The universal truism is that wages held down by the presence of migrants will lead to more labour-intensive ways to get work done, and pressures to increase wages by the absence of migrants will encourage the development of alternatives to high-wage workers.

The other half of the equation involves giving migrants incentives to abide by the terms of their contracts, which usually require them to leave when jobs are no longer available or their work contract ends. To encourage returns, the worker's share of payroll taxes can be refunded when the migrant surrenders his/her work visa upon return in the country of origin. Given the increasing global interest in using remittances to hasten development, governments and development institutions could match payroll tax refunds to support projects that create jobs in the migrants' home country.

Minimizing distortion and dependence with taxes and subsidies will not have the desired effects on employers and migrants if unauthorized workers are readily available and labour laws are not enforced. Some employers hire unauthorized workers to save payroll taxes, and some migrants will resist departing when their work visas expire despite refund offers if they believe that they can continue to work abroad in an irregular status and have only few options to earn income at home. Thus, the enforcement of immigration and labour laws is a prerequisite to the development of temporary labour migration programmes that minimize distortion and dependence.

7. Numbers vs. Rights

The new approaches to the management of temporary labour migration give rise to a difficult discussion

---

[31] To recognize that each sector is different, boards representing employers, workers and governments could decide how to spend the accumulated funds to reduce dependence on temporary migrant workers over time.

In relative terms, i.e. as a percentage of the size of the higher education systems of various countries, the situation varies somewhat. Cyprus, Fiji, New Zealand, Switzerland and Macao SAR are among the countries and regions with the largest proportion of foreign students in their national higher education systems, while the United States drops from first place (Figure 4.1a) to rank thirty-second among host countries (Figure 4.1b). Against a country average of 5.7 per cent of foreign students worldwide, the average for OECD countries stood at 7.3 per cent of their total student body in 2004 (up from 4.5 per cent in 1998). In 2004, the overall student body in nine smaller, English-speaking countries included at least 15 per cent international students. Generally speaking, the fewer foreign students a country receives, the greater the tendency for those students to come from neighbouring countries or from within the same continent. Hence, 99 per cent of foreign students studying in sub-Saharan African countries are themselves from sub-Saharan Africa, and the percentages are about 80 per cent for the countries in Latin America, South Asia and the Pacific, and almost 70 per cent for the Arab and Central Asian countries - as against a mere 27 per cent for western Europe and North America taken together (UNESCO, 2006).

In the OECD area, Europe is the main destination with 1.2 million, or 52 per cent of foreign students on record there (see Table 4.1). It is the leading host region for students from Europe and Africa and is also attractive to students from the Americas and Asia. North America is host to 31 per cent of foreign students, and the Asia-Pacific region to the remaining 17 per cent.

The geographical distribution of foreign students varies across the major OECD regions (Table 4.2). While North America receives fewer foreign students (707,000 in the United States, Canada and Mexico in 2004), it is the most attractive region for Asian students (Table 4.1). Accordingly, over half (61%) of all foreign students in North America come from Asia, compared to Europe (14%), South America (12%), Africa (8%) and North America (5%). In the European OECD countries, students come first and foremost from Europe (44%), followed by Asia (29%), Africa (18%), and the Americas (8%), while Asian countries receive 85 per cent of students from within the Asian region.

Asia ranks first in terms of students going abroad to pursue higher studies. In 2004, almost half (48%) of the foreign students in the OECD area came from Asia, followed closely by Europe (27%), Africa (12%), South America (7%), North America (4%) and Oceania (1%).

International students choose their study destinations according to their region of origin. As Table 4.1 shows, student mobility in Europe occurs largely within Europe. Among European students registered abroad, 81 per cent are studying in another European country, while among Asian and North American students registered as studying abroad, 28 per cent and 44 per cent, respectively, remain within their continent. The preference of European students to remain in Europe can no doubt be attributed to the Bologna Process and to the new Erasmus Programme promoting this type of mobility (though the introduction of Erasmus Mundus has since expanded the new Erasmus Programme to cover the whole world). For their part, African students have a clear preference for Europe – France alone receives 55 per cent of all African students in Europe and 42 per cent of all international African students enrolled in the OECD area. In turn, students from the Americas most often choose to stay in the region, though almost 40 per cent also opt to study in Europe. Asian students aim mainly for North America (40%) and, though 28 per cent also go to study in the Asia-Pacific region, in particular in Australia, 32 per cent also choose to go to Europe. Here again, the averages conceal major variations, as the United Kingdom (43%) and Germany (29%) together host 72 per cent of Asian students studying in Europe.

Table 4.1:

Destinations of Foreign Students Studying in OECD Countries by Origin, 2004 (%)

Origin	Destination			
	North America	Europe	Asia-Pacific	OECD
Africa	20	77	3	100
North America	44	43	13	100
South America	56	41	2	100
Asia	40	32	28	100
Europe	16	81	3	100
Oceania	27	19	54	100
World	31	52	17	100

Source: OECD.

Table 4.2:

Composition of Foreign Student Bodies in the OECD Area, 2004 (%)

Origin	OECD area			Total OECD
	North America	Europe	Asia-Pacific	
Africa	8	18	2	12
North America	5	3	3	4
South America	12	5	1	7
Asia	61	29	85	48
Europe	14	44	5	29
Oceania	1	0	3	1
Total	100	100	100	100

Note:
The percentages do not always add up to 100 per cent because of rounding.
Source: OECD.

At the country level, China (including Hong Kong SAR) ranks first as the country with the largest share of its nationals studying abroad, i.e. 17 per cent of all foreign students in the OECD area, followed by India (5%), South Korea (4%), Germany, Japan, Morocco and France (3% each). Two-thirds (66%) of all Asian students abroad are concentrated in four English-speaking countries, namely Australia, Canada, the United Kingdom and the United States. Whereas Asians generally turn to cross-border education to follow full courses, bearing the real cost of their studies themselves, American and European students prefer short stays, mainly to attend courses

subsidized by European institutions (OECD, 2004a).

In relative terms, the situation again differs (Figure 4.2). The small countries are often those with the largest numbers of nationals studying abroad relative to the size of their higher education system. Frequently their offer, both quantitatively and in terms of the range of disciplines available is limited, and, consequently, their nationals most often study in neighbouring countries under more or less tacit agreements. A case in point is Luxembourg, which, in 2004, had twice as many students enrolled abroad than at home. For many larger African countries, the high degree of student mobility is no doubt attributable to limited capacity at home. In absolute terms, the number of students from the major source countries studying abroad is, in fact, relatively low considering the size of their system of higher education.

Figure 4.2:

Countries with over 20 per cent of all Tertiary-level Students Studying Abroad, 2004

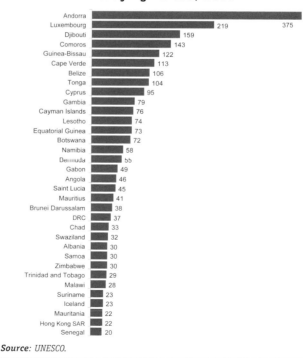

Source: UNESCO.

REFERENCES

Böhm, A., D. Davis, D. Meares and D. Pearce
2002   *Global student mobility 2025: Forecasts of the Global Demand for International Higher Education*, IDP Education, Sydney.

Bound, J., S. Turner and P. Walsh
2006   "Internationalization of U.S. Doctorate Education", National Bureau of Economic Research (NBER), mimeo.

Cervantes, M. and D. Guellec
2002   "Fuite des cerveaux: Mythes anciens, réalités nouvelles", *L'observateur OCDE*, March, Paris.

European Association for International Education (EAIE)
2005,   *I gotta use words when I talk to you: English and international education*, Edited by M. Woolf, EAIE Occasional Paper No. 17, Amsterdam.

Finn, M.G.
2003   "Stay Rates of Foreign Doctorate Recipients from U.S. Universities, 2001", November, Oak Ridge Institute for Science and Education, TN, http://orise.orau.gov/sep/files/stayrate03.pdf.

Huisman, J. and M.C. van der Wende (Eds.)
2004   *On Cooperation and Competition, National and European Policies for the Internationalisation of Higher Education*, Lemmens Verlag, Bonn.

IDP Australia
2007   The independent guide to Australian study opportunities, http://www.idp.com/.

Iguchi, Y.
2003   "The Movement of the Highly Skilled in Asia: Present Situation and Future Prospect" in *Migration and the Labour Market in Asia: Recent Trends and Policies*, OECD, Paris, 29-50.

Institute for International Education (IIE)
2005   *Open Doors 2005: Report on International Educational Exchange*, Sewickley, PA.

Knight, J.
2004   "Internationalization remodeled: Definition, Approaches, and Rationales", *Journal of Studies in International Education*, 8(1): 5-31.

Larsen, K. and S. Vincent-Lancrin
2002   "Le commerce des services d'éducation: est-il bon? est-il méchant?", *Politiques et gestion de l'enseignement supérieur*, OECD, Paris, 14(3): 9-45.

McBurnie, G. and C. Ziguras
2007   *Transnational Education: issues and trends in offshore education*, Routledge Falmer, London.

Middlehurst, R. and S. Woodfield
2004   "The Role of Transnational, Private and For-Profit Provision in Meeting Global Demand for Tertiary Education: Mapping, Regulation and Impact", Summary Report for UNESCO and the Commonwealth of Learning, Commonwealth of Learning, Vancouver, BC, http://www.col.org/colweb/site/pid/3108.

Organisation for Economic Co-operation and Development (OECD)
2004a   *Internationalisation and Trade in Higher Education: The Cross-border Challenge*, OECD, Paris.

2004b   *Quality and Recognition in Higher Education: The Cross-border Challenge*, OECD, Paris.

2005a   *E-learning in Tertiary Education. Where do we stand?*, OECD, Paris.

2005b   *Guidelines for Quality Provision in Cross-border Higher Education*, OECD, Paris, http://www.oecd.org/dataoecd/27/51/35779480.pdf.

2005c   *Trends in International Migration*, SOPEMI 2004, OECD, Paris.

2006a   *Education at a Glance 2006*, OECD, Paris.

2006b   "The internationalisation of higher education: towards an explicit policy", in OECD, *Education Policy Analysis 2005-2006*, OECD, Paris.

2006c   *International Migration Outlook*, SOPEMI 2006, OECD, Paris.

Salmi, J. and A. Saroyan
2007   "League tables as policy instruments: uses and misuses", *Higher Education Management and Policy*, 19:2, 31-68.

Suter B. and M. Jandl

2006   *Comparative Study on Policies towards Foreign Graduates. Study on Admission and Retention Policies towards Foreign Students in Industrialised Countries*, International Centre for Migration Policy Development (ICMPD), Vienna, http://www.icmpd.org/774.html?&F=2&tx_icmpd_pi2%5Bdocument%5D=548&cHash=10fde5b0ec.

Tremblay, K.

2005   "Academic Mobility and Immigration", *Journal of Studies in International Education*, 9(3): 1-34.

United Nations Educational, Scientific and Cultural Organization (UNESCO)

2006   *Recueil de données mondiales sur l'éducation 2006: Statistiques comparées sur l'éducation dans le monde*, L'Institut de statistique de l'UNESCO, Montréal, http://www.uis.unesco.org/TEMPLATE/pdf/ged/2006/GED2006_FR.pdf.

United States Department of State

2005   "We Don't Want to Lose Even One International Student", U.S. Department of State, http://travel.state.gov/news/info/press/press_1511.html.

Vincent-Lancrin, S.

2005   "Building capacity through cross-border higher education", *Observatory on Borderless Higher Education*, London.

Textbox 4.2 - National and Regional Retention Policies for Foreign Graduates in Industrialized Countries

Australian Education International

2006   International Student Data, Australian Education International, http://aei.dest.gov.au/AEI/MIP/Statistics/StudentEnrolmentAndVisaStatistics/Default.htm.

Birrell, B., L. Hawthorne and S. Richardson

2006   *Evaluation of the General Skilled Migration Categories Report*, Australian Government, Department of Immigration and Citizenship (DIAC), http://www.immi.gov.au/media/publications/research/gsm-report/index.htm.

Dolin, B. and M. Young

2004   "Canada's Immigration Program", Parliamentary Information and Research Service, Library of Parliament, Background Paper BP-190E, Ottawa, http://www.parl.gc.ca/information/library/PRBpubs/bp190-e.htm.

Lebrun, D. and S. Rebelo

2006   "The Role of Universities in the Economic Development of Atlantic Canada: A Focus on Immigration", January, Atlantic Canada Opportunities Agency (ACOA), Moncton, NB, http://www.acoa.ca/e/library/reports/univ_econ_dev.pdf.

Martin, P.

2004   "Universities as Immigration Gatekeepers", Mimeographed draft paper.

Organisation for Economic Co-operation and Development (OECD)

2007   Project on supporting the contribution of higher education institutions to regional development, OECD, Paris, http://www.oecd.org/document/48/0,3343,en_2649_35961291_39872432_1_1_1_1,00.html.

Suter, B. and M. Jandl

2006   *Comparative Study on Policies towards Foreign Graduates. Study on Admission and Retention Policies towards Foreign Students in Industrialised Countries*, ICMPD, Vienna, http://www.icmpd.org/774.html?&F=2&tx_icmpd_pi2%5Bdocument%5D=548&cHash=10fde5b0ec.

2008   "Train and Retain: National and Regional Policies to Promote the Settlement of Foreign Graduates in Knowledge Economies", *Journal of International Migration and Integration*, forthcoming.

Worldwide, international tourism receipts were estimated at USD 680 billion (EUR 547 billion) in 2005 (UNWTO, 2006), with all regions and subregions sharing in the increase from 2004. Europe gained an additional USD 20 billion, raising receipts to over USD 348 billion (51% of the world total); the Americas added USD 13 billion to USD 145 billion (21%) and Asia and the Pacific increased their total by USD 11 billion to USD 139 billion (20%). Estimates based on still limited available data point to an increase of USD 2 billion to USD 21 billion for Africa and of USD 2 billion to USD 28 billion for the Middle East, representing three per cent and four per cent of the world total, respectively.

The number of international tourist arrivals worldwide exceeded 800 million in 2005, an increase of 42 million (5.5%) over 2004, representing an all time high. The majority of international tourist arrivals concerned leisure, recreation and holidays (50% of the total, or 402 million), while business travel accounted for some 16 per cent or 125 million, and visiting friends and relatives (VFR), religious purposes/pilgrimages, health treatment and the like for 26 per cent or 212 million. For the remaining eight per cent of arrivals, the purpose of the visit was not specified (UNWTO, 2006).

Between 1950 and 1990, Europe and the Americas received the largest numbers of tourists, representing a joint market share of over 95 per cent in 1950 and 82 per cent forty years later. However, by 2000 their combined share had declined to 76 per cent. This points to a greater diversification of destinations, as also of origins of tourism. Between 2004 and 2005, Africa recorded the highest relative growth (+ 9%) in arrivals, followed by Asia and the Pacific (+ 8%), the Middle East (+ 8%), the Americas (+ 6%) and Europe (+ 4%).

For many destinations visitor expenditure on accommodation, food and drink, local transport, entertainment, shopping, etc. is an important pillar of their economy, creating much needed employment and opportunities for development. Some 70 countries earned more than USD 1 billion from international tourism in 2005. (...) Total receipts from international tourism, including international passenger transport, exceed USD 800 billion. (...) [F]or many destination countries, in particular developing countries and islands, tourism counts as the most important category of export earnings (UNWTO, 2006).

Table 5.1 lists the origins of international tourists from 1990 to 2005. It shows that international tourists still originate mainly from industrialized European countries (55.7%), the Americas (17%) and Asia and the Pacific (19.1%). However, over the last decades and with rising levels of disposable incomes, many emerging economies have shown rapid growth as sources of tourism, in particular in Northeast and Southeast Asia, central and eastern Europe, the Middle East and Southern Africa. By region, Africa recorded the largest increase in relative terms (+ 8.2%), followed by Asia and the Pacific (+ 6.9%) and the Middle East (+ 6.9%). The penultimate row in Table 5.1 shows that 78.6 per cent of international travel takes place within the same region.

Table 5.1:

International Tourist Arrivals, 1990-2005

	International Tourist Arrivals (millions)			Change (%)		Share (%)
	1990	2000	2005	2003/02	2005/04	2005
World	439.4	686.8	806.3	-1.8	5.5	100
Europe	252.6	396.7	449.0	1.0	4.1	55.7
Asia and the Pacific	59.1	115.5	154.3	-8.2	6.9	19.1
Americas	100.3	116.1	137.1	-4.8	5.3	17.0
Middle East	8.3	17.0	21.9	-2.1	6.9	2.7
Africa	10.0	17.7	20.3	1.1	8.2	2.5
Origin not specified*	9.2	13.3	23.6	-	-	2.9
Same region	350.8	540.9	634.1	-1.4	-	78.6
Other regions	79.4	133.0	148.6	-3.5	-	18.4

Note:
* Countries for which a specific region of origin could not be allocated.
Source: UNWTO, 2006.

Many countries now see tourism, especially international tourism, as a large potential source of revenue and are diversifying their production and marketing strategies to attract increasing numbers of tourists. There are clear economic and social benefits of tourism, but there are also social as well as environmental costs (see Textbox 5.1). The two countries experiencing the fastest growth in international tourist receipts between 2004 and 2005 were China and Turkey. In terms of numbers of arrivals, three out of the top ten countries are developing countries: China (ranking 4th), Mexico (7) and Turkey (9). Some countries experienced remarkable growth in 2005: Laos (65.1%), Cambodia (34.7%), Papua New Guinea (17%), Fiji (10%), Honduras (25.9%), Venezuela (45.2%), Swaziland (82.8%) and Senegal (15.3%). However, the figures are volatile and often start from a low base.

Textbox 5.1

Economic and Social Benefits and Costs of Tourism

Tourism can have both positive and negative impacts, but the main focus is on the gains to be made. Seen in this light, many countries are investing heavily in infrastructure projects and upgrading their human resources and facilities to become attractive destinations for more tourists. For example, the Greater Mekong Sub-region (GMS) attracted around 18.7 million international arrivals and more than 24 million border-pass tourists in 2004. This number is expected to rise to 30.6 million by 2010 and to 46.1 million by 2015 (International TravelDailyNews.com, 2006). Many initiatives are being launched to foster this development; however, the difficult part will be to manage such growth.

The potential benefits from tourism in terms of alleviating poverty, generating employment and stimulating various sectors of the economy are well known in many countries, and are being touted in others. In the GMS, for example, the impact of tourism on poverty alleviation is considered to potentially outweigh that of other productive sectors, since tourists are often attracted to poor areas. The tourism industry is also labour intensive and more easily accessible to local workers at the lower segments of this growing service sector and, if properly managed, can build and strengthen poor people's access to and control over their cultural and natural assets (Asian Development Bank, 2005).

On the other hand, tourism can also place enormous pressure on the fragile balance of natural environments at major tourist sites, especially World Heritage sites, and the development of tourism will have to be managed so as to ensure that natural resources are not depleted nor the absorption capacity exceeded (International TravelDailyNews.com, 2006).

The potential social impacts of tourism are also of major concern, including the proliferation of sex tourism and the trafficking of human beings, especially women and children.

within the EU, the "Schengen visa", which allows third-country nationals to enter countries included in the Schengen area[1] for up to three months within a six-month period, is required of most African country nationals as well as those from Bolivia and Ecuador (EU Council, 2001). However, in the absence of relatively accessible and enforceable regular migration channels, such additional controls are also viewed by some as ineffective to dissuade and mostly failing to curtail further irregular migration from the countries concerned and thus to reduce irregular entries. Clearly, a viable solution to and the proper management of this issue calls for closer cooperation and coordination by the parties concerned regarding the control of such movements, and of the respective employment and immigration policies in effect.

2.5 The Place of Working Holiday Schemes in Tourist Management Policies

Many countries and regions have introduced working holiday schemes over the last few decades.[2] Such programmes are usually reciprocal and enable young people to travel and work in countries parties to bilateral arrangements, subject to certain conditions. The schemes vary as to the degree to which they are explicitly aimed at filling sectoral or seasonal gaps in the labour market concerned. Although they are not usually targeted at particular sectors, experience reveals various employment patterns among young

persons participating in such schemes, making it possible to target groups known to accept work in particular hard-to-fill positions. A growing tendency to attract young and highly skilled people, who could potentially become permanent or long-term immigrants, can also be observed. The following three case studies illustrate the various schemes and trends.

(a) United Kingdom

In the U.K., the Working Holidaymaker Scheme entitles young citizens of any Commonwealth country, aged 17 to 30, to work for any employer in any type of work for up to two years. According to Salt (2005), annual numbers have risen from around 23,000 in 1990 to 45,800 in 1999, to fall again to 35,775 in 2001 before rising steeply to 62,400 in 2004. The dominant source countries are the "Old Commonwealth" — Australia, Canada, New Zealand and South Africa, which together accounted for the bulk of working holidaymakers (81.5%) in 2004. However, this was a drop from 88.3 per cent of the total in 2003, suggesting that the scheme is now attracting people from a wider constituency; for example, the number of participants from Ghana, India, Malaysia and Zimbabwe has risen substantially.

Though "little is known about the characteristics of working holidaymakers (including a breakdown of figures by sex) in the U.K., it may reasonably be assumed that they are generally well educated and adaptable" (Salt, 2005: 86). It is not possible to know how many of them will be working at any one time, nor what their total contribution to the labour market is. However, given the numbers it is likely to be substantial. "There is no regional breakdown in the statistics for working holidaymakers, nor is it known what jobs they take" (Salt, 2005: 86). Nevertheless, they provide a supply of young, mobile, largely English-speaking workers who may eventually become permanent residents. According

---

[1] The 1985 Schengen Agreement was originally an agreement among the Benelux countries, France and Germany providing for the abolition of systematic controls at their internal borders. The 1985 treaty was implemented by the 1990 Schengen Implementing Agreement and participation has since expanded to include most EU countries and three non-EU members Iceland, Norway and, in the near future, Switzerland. By way of the 1997 Treaty of Amsterdam, which amended the Treaty Establishing the European Community, most of the Schengen measures were incorporated into the body of EU law. While the Republic of Ireland and the United Kingdom are not parties to Schengen, they participate in the EU measures relating to police cooperation and the prevention of irregular migration, but not the common border control and visa provisions.

[2] Australia, Belgium, Canada, Cyprus, Denmark, Estonia, Finland, France, Germany, Hong Kong SAR, Ireland, Italy, Japan, the Republic of Korea (South Korea), Malta, the Netherlands, Norway, New Zealand, Sweden, Taiwan Province of China and the United Kingdom.

to the website of Y-AXIS, a large overseas career and immigration consultancy in India, the scheme now specifically targets students, young professionals, students who have returned home after having studied in the U.K., nurses and allied health professionals, doctors interested in locum work, teachers and IT professionals.

(b) Australia

The Australian Working Holiday and Work and Holiday Programmes "provide opportunities for people aged between 18 and 30 to holiday in Australia and to supplement their travel funds through incidental employment" (DIAC, 2007). Table 5.3 shows a significant increase in the number of one-year visas issued from 2001-02 to 2005-06. There are no numerical caps or quotas.

Table 5.3:

Australian Working Holiday and Work and Holiday Visa Approvals, 2001-2006

Visa Category	2001 - 2002	2002 - 2003	2003 - 2004	2004 - 2005	2005 - 2006
Working Holiday (subclass 417)	85,207	88,758	93,759	104,352	113,936
Work and Holiday (subclass 462)[1]	n.a.	0	85	254	751
Total Visa Approvals	85,207	88,758	93,845	104,606	114,582

Note:

[1] Visa subclass 462 was introduced in March 2003 and is only available to applicants from outside Australia. However, from 1 January 2004, Subclass 462 visa holders became eligible to apply for a further Subclass 462 visa while in Australia.

n.a. = not applicable

Source: DIAC, 2007.

For 2005-06, agreements were concluded with 20 countries, with the largest cohorts of Working Holidaymakers (WHMs) coming from the U.K. (28,821), followed by Republic of Korea (South Korea) (24,077), Ireland (12,554) and Germany (12,089). In recent years, there has been a notable diversification of source countries and regions with the addition of Belgium, Estonia and Taiwan Province of China. A 1997 survey conducted by Harding and Webster (2002), at a time when eight WHM agreements were in effect, found that 85 per cent of WHMs were in paid employment during their visit, averaging 2.9 jobs each during that period.

Around three-quarters of WHM jobs were low-skilled, covering basic or intermediate office duties, production and transport and general manual activities, relative to 46 per cent across the whole workforce. The main occupations were as waiters, harvesting fruits, providing basic services, secretarial work, labourer and similar manual and construction work. There were some differences among countries: Canadians were more likely to be employed as waiters, and a higher proportion of Dutch nationals were employed as fruit pickers, while Irish nationals were more likely to be active at both ends of the skills ladder as construction labourers and also in more professional occupations.

A positive effect of the Working Holiday and Work and Holiday Programmes was the creation of an additional 8,000 full-time jobs in Australia for every 80,000 WHMs through the employment generation effects of WHMs (Harding and Webster, 2002). Though WHMs were active in a range of low-skilled jobs, they were not shown to displace Australians who had not been interested in taking up these positions. The under-utilization of the skills offered by WHMs was

(a) Asia-Pacific Economic Cooperation (APEC)[3]

The APEC Business Travel Card (BTC) was introduced to lower trade transaction costs. This is a national visa waiver or three-year multiple entry visa valid for all participating economies for persons who satisfy the requisite visa conditions. Other provisions may eventually be attached to the APEC Business Travel Card, namely, an agreed 30-day service standard for intra-company transferees (executives, managers and specialists, the latter as defined by each economy), and an agreement to consider the streamlining of access to employment for spouses of intra-company transferees.

The aim is to move towards common agreed standards for the short and long-term entry of business people; to date, however, most countries, including a number of APEC participating economies, impose additional visa requirements on business people wishing to visit. Some of these are outlined below.

(b) Australia

Australia defines short-term business visits as covering (a) attendance at a conference or training session; (b) the conduct of business with an Australia-based company; (c) the conduct of business negotiations, or (d) an exploratory business visit. A choice of five business visitor visa options is available:

1. Short Stay Business Visitor (subclass 456): 3 months — for business people to make a short business visit to attend a conference, conduct negotiations or make an exploratory business visit.
2. Sponsored Business Visitor (subclass 459): 3 months — for business people who have an approved sponsor in Australia and may not be eligible to apply for an Electronic Travel Authority (ETA).
3. ETA (Short Validity) (subclass 977): 3 months — an electronically stored authority available to passport holders from a number of countries and regions. Applications must be made from outside Australia.
4. ETA (Long Validity) (subclass 956): 3 months, repeat visits — for business people to make regular short business visits, granted for the length of the validity of the passport.
5. APEC Business Travel Card (see above): 2 months, repeat trips — to streamline travel for business people from 16 participating economies in the APEC region. Nationals of all APEC members, besides New Zealand, must still apply for a subclass 456 or 977 visa (DIAC, 2007).

Table 5.4 shows the number of visas issued in four of these categories from 2001 to 2006. The short stay (subclass 456 and 977) visas are by far the most numerous. The persons in the sponsored 459 subclass are most probably intra-company transfers.

[3] Australia, Brunei Darussalam, Canada, Chile, China, Hong Kong SAR, Indonesia, Japan, Republic of Korea, Malaysia, Mexico, New Zealand, Papua New Guinea, Peru, the Philippines, Russia, Singapore, Taiwan Province of China, Thailand, United States, Viet Nam. For a description of APEC and its labour mobility-related activities, including a fuller discussion of the Business Travel Card, see Textbox 13.5.

Table 5.4:

Business Visitor Visas Granted Outside of Australia, 1 July 2001 to 30 June 2006

Visa Category	2001-02	2002-03	2003-04	2004-05	2005-06
Business Visitor Visas					
Short Stay Business Visitor (Subclass 456)	133,726	126,767	147,701	174,617	185,656
Sponsored Business Visitor (Subclass 459)	18	11	4	107	634
Electronic Travel Authority - Business Entrant - Long Validity (Subclass 956)	33,420	28,057	24,721	18,417	15,410
Electronic Travel Authority - Business Entrant - Short Validity (Subclass 977)	90,874	99,356	126,413	146,283	166,633
Total Business Visitor Visa Approvals	258,038	254,191	298,839	339,424	368,333

Source: DIAC, 2007.

It is interesting to note that a number of temporary entrants and visa categories, including the Class 457 Temporary Business (Long Stay) visa and the Working Holiday and Work and Holiday programmes, are linked to business migration. Class 457 entrants are actually sponsored employees. Their visas are valid for a stay of up to four years whereupon they may be converted to permanent resident status.

According to Khoo et al. (2005), the majority of 457 visa holders had applied for long-term temporary residence in Australia after a previous stay there under the Working Holiday and Work and Holiday programmes or as students. This was particularly true of Europeans, and their prior exposure to the country is considered to have facilitated their integration and adaptation to local living and working conditions. Conversely, 457 visa holders from India are least likely to have visited the country prior to their present stay.

Drawing on the findings of Coleman and Rowthorn (2004), Khoo et al. (2005) suggest that temporary skilled migration is the source of many economic benefits to Australia because it brings in young, well qualified and highly skilled people. Given that 457 visa holders are more likely to come from higher-income countries in North America and Europe, they note that the current temporary skilled migration policies link the Australian economy to other advanced economies.

(c) Canada

Canada receives a very large number of short-term visitors every year, with around 20 million annual crossings of the Canada/U.S. border alone. There is no statistical breakdown of the particular motives for a visitor's stay in Canada. A large majority of the many millions of business visitors entering Canada every year would not need visas as they are from visa-exempt countries, particularly the U.S. and Europe.

Around one million visas are issued annually to visitors who do require them and, although a global breakdown is not available, Table 5.5 demonstrates that regarding the Beijing issuing office, the business caseload accounts for a substantial proportion of the total number of visas issued to visitors.

Table 5.5:

Canada – Business Visitor Visas issued in Beijing

Business Visitor Applications	2005	2006	2007 (to 27 Nov.)
Total Number	36,835	43,701	37,721
% of all visitor visas issued in Beijing	60%	60.5%	54.9%
Official passport	25,281 (68.6%)	30,019 (68.7%)	24,316 (64.5%)
Private passport	11,554 (31.4%)	13,682 (31.3%)	13,405 (35.5%)

Source: Canadian Permanent Mission, Geneva.

In contrast to Australia and New Zealand (see below), however, Canada does not participate in the APEC BTC scheme (Citizenship and Immigration Canada, 2006).

(d) Japan and Republic of Korea

Both Japan and South Korea require short-term business visas for visits of up to three months for most business entrants. However, Japan and South Korea also waive visa requirements for nationals of certain APEC economies (APEC, 2007). South Korea offers multiple-entry visas for nationals from Australia, Canada, China, Japan and the U.S., in accordance with relevant bilateral agreements.

(e) New Zealand

The possibilities for short-term business visits to New Zealand are limited. The Long-term Business Visa (permit) requires the prior submission of a business plan. After nine months, the permit is subject to

3.4 Business Travel in the Developing World

(a) Developed to developing countries

Globalization and deregulation have opened up many developing countries where conditions are seen to be economically, socially and politically conducive to significant inflows of short-term business travellers or visiting nationals from more developed countries. In the 1960s and 1970s, the Asian "Tigers" were probably the best example of emerging economies that attracted much investment and technical input from more developed countries.

In recent years, temporary business visits from countries in Asia, Europe, North America and Oceania to many of the world's global cities and other major sites have become very prevalent. The expansion of multinationals and the establishment of offshore branches or client offices in mining, manufacturing and the services sector have given rise to countless and repeat visits by managers, technicians, engineers and supervisors.

Similarly, most non-resident Indians (NRIs) who have set up businesses in the IT sector in India (see Textbox 2.2) return home to attend to their business interests but do not go back permanently.

(b) Developing to developing countries

Disparities in economic development between neighbouring countries frequently give rise to short-term and often irregular movements for the purpose of trade.[5] For example, in 2003, over 300,000 individuals crossed the border from Mongolia into China, mostly for trading purposes. People come from Russia and eastern European countries, as well as from Mongolia, to buy cheap goods and to sell them elsewhere. The building of a free-trade zone and a new Trading Hall in Erlianhaut in Inner Mongolia led

to an increase in cross-border activities (Zheng and Ren, 2004).

The dismantling of the apartheid regime in South Africa led to a more liberal migration regime and, since the early 1990s, many people from other parts of Africa have been able to enter on a 30-day visitor's permit issued at the border. The declining contract labour migration to the mines has led to the growth of informal migration for work or to conduct business (Andersson, 2006). Economic growth has also acted as a magnet for petty traders from other parts of sub-Saharan Africa.

For years, cross-border shoppers from Southern Africa have flocked to Johannesburg, South Africa's financial centre, to buy cheap goods that can be taken home and sold at a profit. Officials have quickly become aware of the profitability of such trading practices, after a study showed that the influx of African "tourism traders" added R 20 billion annually to the local economy. The shoppers' spending bonanza includes cash-register sales and expenditure on overnight accommodation, meals and transportation. In 2004 – the latest year for which data are available – the major points of attraction for more than half a million African visitors were South Africa's array of shops, mainly wholesalers. "These are typically low to middle-income people who come because there is a wide variety of goods and good quality. And these stores may just be popping up in their own country", says urban consultant Neil Fraser of the newly formed Joburg Cross-Border Shopping Association. Most visitors are from Lesotho, Swaziland, Botswana, Zimbabwe, Mozambique, Namibia, Zambia and Malawi, where many people live on less than a dollar a day (Star and Reuters, 2006).

(c) Developing to developed countries

Many irregular migration flows from China and other parts of Asia (India, Pakistan, the Philippines), Latin

---

[5] Cross-border migration is discussed in more detail in Chapter 7.

America and Africa (Morocco, Senegal), as well as from eastern Europe (especially Albania and Romania) to the more developed countries in Europe have been associated with the establishment and operation of small businesses. In recent years, southern Europe has attracted many new irregular migrants (see also Chapter 8), including Chinese nationals, to take up job opportunities in the informal sector.

> [An] important reason is that these new destinations provide fresh business niches for the Chinese. Communities of Chinese in western Europe have usually been concentrated in the catering business. The catering business has become increasingly saturated since the 1990s, however, and there is not much evidence that the communities are entering new industries. By contrast, the Chinese in eastern and southern Europe are often engaged in the import/export trade between China and Europe, and even manufacturing (e.g. the leather and garment industries in Italy), partly encouraged by the economic structures particular to these countries (Laczko, 2003).

New types of flows have often emerged in response to tighter regulatory systems in developed countries. Peraldi (2004) documents the rise of Algerian suitcase traders throughout the Mediterranean region, replacing traditional labour migration to France. "Often serving tourist markets, their moves take place within family networks which allow them to seize trading opportunities in whichever city they are present" (Salt, 2006: 18). Such business movements are generally unrecorded or included in tourist figures.

3.5 Economic and Social Benefits of Short-term Business Movements, Especially in the Developing World

The circulation of people as part of international business activities, aid programmes and projects and for other reasons is significant, but difficult to quantify. However, both countries of origin and of destination stand to gain from short-term business migrants. Host countries can sell more goods and provide accommodation and other services for business clients, and are themselves introduced to new products, technologies and business and management practices. It is with these benefits in mind that the city of Johannesburg is seeking to develop a visitor-friendly approach, for instance by setting up a welcome booth for cross-border traders, and building a new passenger boarding area. The private sector is considering to contribute to the effort through the construction of basic lodgings with cheap overnight rates.

At an early stage of its industrial development, Taiwan Province of China realized the value of the contribution its citizens abroad, particularly in the U.S., could make to its economy and society. Beginning in the 1950s, it implemented a series of policies and programmes to encourage the return of highly educated expatriates. Such return was to be preferably permanent, but short-term exchange and business trips were also promoted. The major incentives included a travel subsidy for returnees and their family, helping them to find jobs, providing business investment assistance, facilitating visits of academics and experts, setting up recruitment programmes by offering competitive salaries and improving working conditions (Tsay and Lin, 2000).

The contribution of short trips to economic growth is evident, but the means to measure such contributions are mostly lacking. One exception is research by Tani (2006), who surveyed business travellers at Sydney Airport and found that most Australian business persons going abroad were male, aged 35 to 54, highly skilled, had a university degree (83%) and were born abroad (64%). His survey reported that 38 per cent of these business travellers go to attend a conference or trade fair or to look for international alliances (37%), that is, to seek out information or to share knowledge. Only 31 per cent travelled for developing countries (de Hart, 1999). Increased international mobility and subsequent marriage do not only result from citizens travelling abroad, but also from the increasing presence of transient and long-term migrants in a society, leading to rising percentages of mixed marriages. Increasing cross-border marriages in Asia and Europe often involve men of wealthier countries marrying women from economically less-developed countries, and intermediated marriages. The majority of the couples are introduced with the prior intention of marriage and have either no or only a comparatively short period of courtship (International Institute for Asian Studies, 2006). The internet is increasingly replacing face to face contact (hence the rather derogatory "mail-order bride" label) as a means of introducing potential spouses. In Asia, the demand for foreign brides has sharply increased to the point where half the total foreign population in Taiwan Province of China are brides. Since 1990, nearly 100,000 Vietnamese women have married Taiwanese men (Wong and Chang, 2002; UNFPA, 2006). Similarly, in the Republic of Korea (South Korea) and Japan, foreign women are marrying local men. An estimated 10,000-15,000 Russian women migrate as fiancées each year, of whom 80,000 have entered the U.S. in the past decade (UNFPA, 2006).

There is a third category of family migration where the **entire family** migrates. In the absence of official permanent immigration, as in settler societies, which encouraged this form of migration on the assumption that it would facilitate integration and contribute to population growth, this category is less common in Europe. Many countries do not allow temporary permit holders to be accompanied by family members (OECD, 2000), except the very highly skilled. The U.K. is the most liberal of the EU Member States, in allowing spouses of students, work permit holders and those undertaking training to enter with the right to work. With the increased demand for skilled labour (especially in the information technology (IT) and welfare sectors, such as education and health) and acceptance of long-term migration for this group

in countries such as Germany and the U.K., family migration is likely to become more prevalent. Some refugees, especially those entering on settlement schemes or quotas, also enter with their whole family.

A fourth category, largely restricted to settler societies, consists of **sponsored family members** who are not necessarily defined as being of the immediate family and, as discussed more fully below, constitute discretionary flows. In settler societies, a wider range of family members may be sponsored (Khoo, 2003), but stricter conditions and capping[1] of numbers are applied, as in the U.S., for categories such as unmarried children over 21 years, married children, and brothers and sisters.

Figure 6.1:

International Migration by Category of Entry in Selected OECD Countries as a Percentage of Total Inflows, Standardized data, 2005

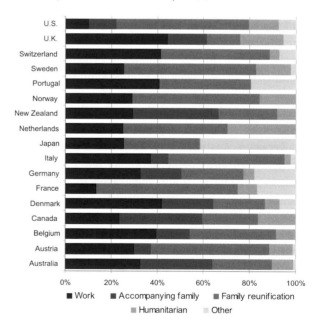

Source: OECD, 2007.

---

[1] This administrative procedure allows the government to set annual limits on the number of entries under a given migration category.

Table 6.1:

Proportion of Family Migrants among Long-term Migrants, 2005

Country	Family Migrants ('000)	Long-term Migrants ('000)	Family (%)
Australia	102.3	179.8	56.9
Austria	32.3	56.8	56.0
Canada	158.0	262.2	60.3
France	102.5	168.6	60.8
Germany	89.1	198.6	44.9
Italy	106.7	184.3	57.7
Japan	26.9	81.3	33.1
Netherlands	27.6	60.7	45.5
New Zealand	37.1	59.4	62.4
Norway	12.6	21.4	59.9
Portugal	5.3	13.3	39.6
Sweden	30.9	53.8	57.4
Switzerland	37.0	78.8	46.9
U.K.	113.8	362.4	31.4
U.S.	782.1	1,122.4	69.7

Note:
Family migrants in this table include family members of economic and work permit migrants, but not those entering either through humanitarian channels or through family streams.

Source: OECD, 2006.

Both Figure 6.1 and Table 6.1 show that in countries with low levels of permanent skilled migration, such as the U.S. or France, and with high levels of asylum seekers and refugees, such as Sweden, there are high levels of family migration, especially family reunification. In the U.S., the country with the largest proportion of family migration, family reunification has accounted for about two-thirds of lawful permanent migration since the mid-1980s, except for 1989-1994. If family members of other categories, such as migrants for employment and refugees, are also included, then family migration becomes even more significant, as indicated in Table 6.1. In some countries, such as Italy, the right to family reunification has been claimed by the growing number of foreign workers who have settled. In other countries, such as Australia, Canada and the U.K., the increasing emphasis on skilled migration has resulted in lower levels of family migration, though

in certain instances the decrease may partly stem from reclassifications. In Australia, for example, the category of concessional family migration covering the sponsorship of relatives with skills has been relocated to the skilled migration stream as skilled sponsored migration. Changing skilled migration policies may lead to increasing numbers of family members entering as dependants, as has been the case in the U.K., where the proportion of dependants among work permit holders rose from 25.5 per cent in 2001 to 33.4 per cent in 2006 (Home Office, 2007).

What constitutes the family for the purpose of migration differs among states, as these apply different rules to members of a family, as discussed above. The 1990 International Convention on the Protection of the Rights of All Migrant Workers and Members of their Families (see Textbox 13.1) defines the family in terms of those who can benefit from its provisions. These are the migrant worker's spouse, persons in a relationship with the migrant worker that, according to applicable law, produces effects equivalent to marriage, and dependent minors and unmarried children. It largely corresponds to the distinction between non-discretionary and discretionary family migration (OECD, 2006 and Table 6.2).

Discretionary family migration, which accounts for a high percentage of migrant entries in settler societies, includes those members of the family not recognized by human rights conventions or free movement provisions (e.g. EU) for family reunification, for example adult children, siblings and, in many countries, non-dependent parents. In Australia, though the number of visas issued to parents is capped, they do not have to prove economic dependence on their child(ren). In addition, there is a separate category for aged dependent relatives, remaining relatives or carers. These are the family members whose numbers may be subject to capping or restricted interpretations of dependence on the sponsor. This is very much at the heart of the

In contrast to migrants, French and EU citizens are not required to satisfy any resources conditions in order to bring in existing or future family members. Thus, renewed debates about immigration have led to further legislative changes marking a shift away from family migration to a selective policy to attract more skilled migrants. The immigration and integration law (No. 2006-911 of 24 July 2006) pursued four main objectives: recruiting skilled workers; facilitating entry and stay for foreign students; tightening the rules for family reunification; and limiting access to residence and citizenship (Murphy, 2006). It has tightened the conditions for the sponsor, for example by extending the period of residence from one year to 18 months, and requiring for non-EU migrants a probationary or conditional period of marriage of two to three years. The subsequent Bill No. 2007-1631 of 20 November 2007 aimed specifically at further reducing family migration, proved highly controversial in its introduction of DNA testing for children joining their mother in France. The test will be in place for an 18-month trial period, voluntary and paid by the French government (BBC News, 24 October 2007). In addition, the level of resources required to be eligible to bring in family members will depend on the size of the family. Parents will have to sign a parental contract vouching for the good behaviour of their children. The effects of these legislative changes in radically altering the migratory regime will depend not only on their capacity to reduce levels of family migration but also on an expansion of labour migration.

A number of countries, apart from France, have imposed mandatory integration conditions. In Austria, the Settlement and Residence Act foresees a mandatory integration agreement (Carrera, 2006). The Netherlands also foresees integration as a condition for family reunification to be legally sanctioned. Recent developments have meant that both newcomers and settled migrants will have to pass an integration test to demonstrate their actual integration into Dutch society. These rules are primarily aimed at non-EU

migrant family reunifications, where migrants have to complete a basic integration test in their home country before arriving in the Netherlands, to be followed by another test at a higher level five years after admission.[4] This was the first European country in recent times to require permanent immigrants to complete a pre-arrival integration course (Expatica, 2004). Other countries, such as France, Germany, Netherlands and the U.K., require family members to pass language tests as a precondition for obtaining a long-term residence permit (UKREN, 2007), as the inadequate knowledge of the language has been identified as a major barrier to integration.

Denmark has introduced restrictions on family migration, reducing numbers in this category since 2001. The 2001 elections saw the Danish People's Party introduce new provisions in force since 2003. The provisions foresee that Danish citizens cannot bring a foreign spouse into the country unless both are at least 24 years old and provide evidence that the sponsor is able to support the nominee (in most cases, this requirement will be met if the spouse/partner has not received public assistance for at least 12 months prior to the application being processed by the Immigration Service). More importantly, Danish citizens who are themselves first or second-generation migrants have to provide evidence that their ties with Denmark are stronger than with any other country (Denmark, Ministry of Refugee, Immigration and Integration Affairs, 2006). The effects of such changes can be seen in the drop of family reunification permits from 13,000 in 2001 to under 5,000 in 2003 (BBC News, 2005) and a substantial reduction in non-western immigrants (Hedetoft, 2006). In addition to the tightening of family reunification rules in recent years, since July 2005 applicants for family reunification and their

---

4 See, respectively, the Act on Preliminary Integration Abroad (*Wet inburgering in het buitenland*) of 22 December 2005, and the Act on Integration (*Wet inburgering*) of 7 December 2006. EU citizens, EEA nationals, Swiss citizens and non-EU nationals who are family members of EU citizens are exempt from these rules.

spouses have to sign a declaration of integration which obliges the applicant to actively participate with his/her children in Danish language courses and integration into Danish society.

Sham marriages have been in the spotlight in countries such as Denmark, France and the U.K. A sham marriage is characterized as a marriage that is contracted purely to procure the right of residence for one of the partners. In Denmark, prima facie or pro forma marriages, as they are also known, are assessed by the immigration services to determine, inter alia, whether the parties are able to communicate in the same language, whether there is a large age difference between them, and how well they knew each other before the marriage (Ministry of Refugee, Immigration and Integration Affairs, 2006). In the U.K., as of February 2005, any non-EU migrant with a short-term visa had to seek permission to marry from the Home Office. However, in April 2006, a High Court judgment found this to be in breach of human rights (Article 12 of the European Convention on Human Rights concerning the right to marry) and discriminatory on grounds of religion (i.e. those marrying in the Church of England were regarded more favourably) and nationality. The challenge was brought by a male Muslim Algerian irregular migrant and a female Polish Roman Catholic migrant, who had entered the U.K. following EU enlargement (Daily Telegraph, 2006) and who had been refused permission to marry in February 2005 under the U.K. regulations.

A further means of testing whether a marriage is bona fide or not is to impose what is known as a **probationary or conditional period**, during which the marriage must continue for the spouse to acquire a permanent right of residence. Recently, several EU Member States have extended the probationary period; for example, from two to three years in France as of 2007 and from one to two years in the U.K. in 2003. Many European countries have introduced exemptions for domestic violence. In the U.K., for instance, after continuous lobbying from women activists, a concession was introduced in 2002 to allow a woman indefinite leave to remain if she can prove that she left a relationship because of domestic violence (Southall Black Sisters, 2001; 2004). The U.S. also has a two-year conditional period, but differs from the U.K. in that it takes into account the duration of the marriage. In the U.S. the conditional residency provision applies only if the marriage is of less than two years' duration (workpermit.com 2006). In the U.K. all spouses are subject to the two-year conditional period.

In the EU, the sponsor generally has to meet minimum standards of income and accommodation when bringing in a third-country national spouse.[5] The Directive on family reunification, discussed in Section 4 above, enables Member States to impose similar conditions on sponsors who are third-country nationals lawfully resident in the country in question. In Denmark, which does not apply this Directive, further criteria have been introduced under which the person in Denmark is required to provide evidence that no financial assistance has been requested or received for one year prior to the application for the residence permit, and that there has been no conviction for a violent act against a former spouse or companion for a period of 10 years prior to the processing of the application (New to Denmark, 2006). Furthermore, it is often the case that during the initial years family migrants are not entitled to income-related public funds or welfare benefits. For example, in the U.K. there is no recourse to income-related public funds for two years for British citizens and settled residents.

The **arranged marriage** stands out as one of the forms of marriage migration that needs to be scrutinized, contained and managed (Gedalof, 2007).

---

[5] However, if the sponsor is an EU citizen who has taken up employment in another EU Member State, the more liberal EU rules on family reunion apply.

REFERENCES

Antecol, H., D. Cobb-Clark. and S. Trejo
2002   "Human Capital and Earnings of Female
            Immigrants to Australia, Canada, and the US",
            (IZA) Discussion Paper No. 575, September,
            Institute for the Study of Labour, Bonn, http://
            ftp.iza.org/dp575.pdf.

Arango, J. and M. Jachimowicz
2005   "Regularizing Immigrants in Spain: A New
            Approach", *Migration Information Source*,
            September, Migration Policy Institute (MPI),
            Washington D.C., www.migrationinformation.
            org/Feature/print.cfm?ID=331.

**Australia, Department of Immigration and Citizenship
(DIAC)**
2006   *Immigration Update Financial Year 2005-2006*,
            November, Research and Statistics Section,
            DIAC, Canberra, http://www.immi.gov.au/
            media/publications/pdf/Update_June06.pdf.

Bailey, A. and P. Boyle
2004   "Untying and retying family migration in the
            new Europe markets", *Journal of Ethnic and
            Migration Studies*, 30(2): 229-241.

Baldassar, L. and C. Baldock
2000   "Linking migration and family studies:
            transnational migrants and the care of aging
            parents" in B. Agozino (Ed.), *Theoretical and
            Methodological Issues in Migration Research*,
            Ashgate, Aldershot, U.K., 61–89.

Baringhorst, S.
2004   "Policies of Backlash: Recent Shifts in
            Australian Migration Policy", *Journal of
            Comparative Policy Analysis,* 6(2): 131-157.

BBC News
2005   "Denmark's immigration issue", BBC News, 19
            February, http://newsvote.bbc.co.uk/mpapps/
            pagetools/print/news.bbc.co.uk/1/hi/world/
            europe/4276963.stm.

2007   "French parliament adopts DNA bill", BBC
            News, 24 October, http://news.bbc.co.uk/2/hi/
            europe/7059186.stm.

Bouamama, S. and H. Sad Saoud
1996   *Familles maghrébines en France*, Desclée de
            Brouwer, Paris.

Borjas, G.
1995   "The economic benefits from immigration",
            Journal of Economic Perspectives, 9(2): 3-22.

Boyd, M.
1989   "Family and personal networks in international
            migration", *International Migration Review*,
            23(3): 638-670.

Boyd, M. and E. Grieco
2003   "Women and Migration: Incorporating Gender
            into International Migration Theory", *Migration
            Information Source*, March, MPI, Washington,
            D.C., www.migrationinformation.org/feature/
            print.cfm?ID=106.

Bryceson, D. and U. Vuorela
2002   "Transnational Families in the Twenty-first
            Century" in D. Bryceson and U. Vuorela (Eds.),
            *The Transnational Family. New European
            Frontiers and Global Networks*, Berg, Oxford,
            3-30.

Carrera, S.
2006   "Legal Migration Law and Policy Trends in a
            Selection of EU Member States", 4 December,
            Challenge: Liberty and Security, http://www.
            libertysecurity.org/article1190.html.

Citizenship and Immigration Canada (CIC)
2005   *Facts and Figures: Immigration Overview –
            Permanent and Temporary Residents*, CIC Canada,
            http://www.cic.gc.ca/ENGLISH/resources/
            statistics/menu-fact.asp.

Constable, N.
2005   "Introduction: Cross-Border Marriages" in
            N. Constable (Ed.), *Gender and Mobility in
            Transnational Asia*, University of Pennsylvania
            Press, Philadelphia, 1-16.

Cooke, T.J.
2005   "Migration of same-sex couples", *Population,
            Space and Place*, 11: 401-409.

Council of Europe
1981   *European Migration in the 1980s. Trends and
            Policies*, Council of Europe, Strasbourg.

Creese, G., I. Dyck and A. McLaren
1999   "Reconstituting the Family: Negotiating
            Immigration and Settlement", March, Research
            on Immigration and Integration in the
            Metropolis (RIIM), Paper 99-10, Vancouver
            Centre of Excellence, http://riim.metropolis.
            net/Virtual%20Library/1999/wp9910.pdf.

Daily Telegraph
2006   "High court overturns laws to combat sham marriages", *Daily Telegraph*, 11 April.

Denmark, Ministry of Refugee, Immigration and Integration Affairs
2006   New to Denmark 2006, Ministry of Refugee, Immigration and Integration Affairs, http://www.nyidanmark.dk/en-us/frontpage.htm.

Dumon, R.
1989   "Family and migration", *International Migration*, 27(2): 251–270.

European Migration Network (EMN)
2008   *Synthesis Report: Family Reunification,* January, EMN, http://ec.europa.eu/justice_home/doc_centre/immigration/studies/docs/emn_family_reunification_synthesis_report_jan08.pdf.

Expatica
2004   "Tracking the Dutch immigration policy", 19 May, Expatica, www.expatica.com/actual/article.asp?subchannel_id=10&story_id=7692.

Faist, T.
2000   "Transnationalism in international migration: implications for the study of citizenship and culture", *Ethnic and Racial Studies*, 23(2): 189–222.

Foner, N.
1997   "The immigrant family: cultural legacies and cultural changes", *International Migration Review*, 31(4): 961–974.

Fouron, G. and N. Glick Schiller
2001   "All in the family: gender, transnational migration and the nation-state", *Identities*, 7(4): 539–582.

Gedalof, I.
2007   "Unhomely homes: women, family and belonging in UK discourses of migration and asylum", *Journal of Ethnic and Migration Studies*, 33(1): 77-94.

Glick Schiller, N., L. Basch and C. Szanton Blanc
1995   "From immigrant to transmigrant: theorizing transnational migration", *Anthropological Quarterly*, 68(1): 48–63.

Guarnizo, L. and M.P. Smith (Eds.)
1998   *Transnationalism From Below*, Transaction Publications, New Brunswick.

Hedetoft, U.
2006   "Denmark: Integrating Migrants into a Homogenous Welfare State", *Migration Information Source*, November, MPI, Washington D.C., www.migrationinformation.org/Profiles/display.cfm?ID=485.

International Institute for Asian Studies/National Science Council
2006   Conference on Intermediated Cross-Border Marriage Migration in Asia and Europe, 18-20 September, Taipei.

Khoo, S-E.
2003   "Sponsorship of relatives for migration and immigrant settlement intention", *International Migration*, 41(5): 177-199.

Kofman, E.
2004   "Family-related migration: a critical review of European studies", *Journal of Ethnic and Migration Studies*, 30(2): 243-262.

Kofman, E. and A. Kraler
2006   "Civic stratification, gender and family migration policies in Europe", paper presented at the International Migration, Integration and Social Cohesion (IMISCOE) Cluster B3 Conference, 31 May - 1 June, Budapest.

Lahav, G.
1997   "International versus national constraints in family-reunification migration policy", *Global Governance*, 3: 349–372.

Lauth Bacas, J.
2002   *Cross-Border Marriages and the Formation of Transnational Families: A Case Study of Greek-German Couples in Athens*, Transnational Communities Programme WPTC-02-10, University of Oxford.

Le Play, F.
1871   *L'organisation de la famille selon le vrai modèle signalé par l'histoire de toutes les races et de tous les temps*, Paris.

Lethaeghe, R. and J. Surkyn
1995   "Heterogeneity in social change: Turkish and Moroccan women in Belgium", *European Journal of Population*, 11(1): 1-29.

Vatz Laaroussi, M.

2001   *Le Familial au Cœur de l'Immigration. Les Stratégies de Citoyenneté des Familles Immigrantes au Québec et en France*, L'Harmattan, Paris.

Vertovec, S.

1999   "Conceiving and studying transnationalism", *Ethnic and Racial Studies*, 22(2): 447-462.

2004   "Migrant transnationalism and modes of transformation", *International Migration Review*, 38(3): 970-1001.

Wang, H. and S. Chang

2002   "The Commodification of International Marriages: Cross-border Marriage Business in Taiwan and Viet Nam", *International Migration*, 40(6): 93-114.

Waters, J.

2001   "The Flexible Family? Recent Immigration and 'Astronaut' Households in Vancouver, British Columbia", January, RIIM Working Paper 01-02, Vancouver Centre of Excellence, http://www.riim.metropolis.net/Virtual%20Library/2001/wp0102.pdf.

workpermit.com

2006   http://www.workpermit.com (accessed 20 November 2006).

Yeoh, B., S. Huang and T. Lam

2005   "Transnationalizing the Asian family: imaginaries, intimacies and strategic intents", *Global Networks*, 5(4): 307-315.

Zlotnik, H.

1995   "Migration and the family: the female perspective", *Asia and Pacific Migration Journal*, 4(2-3): 253-271.

Textbox 6.1 - Social and Economic Costs of Migration on Family Members Left Behind - Bangladesh

Debnath, P. and N. Selim

2007   "Impact of Short Term Male Migration on Their Wives Left Behind: A Case Study of Bangladesh", September, Draft Study, IOM Dhaka.

UN-INSTRAW (United Nations International Research and Training Institute for the Advancement of Women) and International Organization for Migration (IOM)

2000   *Temporary Labour Migration of Women: Case Studies of Bangladesh and Sri Lanka*, IOM/UN-INSTRAW, Santo Domingo, Dominican Republic, http://www.un-instraw.org/en/docs/publications/tlmw.pdf.

UN-INSTRAW

2007   "Feminization of Migration 2007", Working Paper 1, Gender, Remittances and Development, UN-INSTRAW, Santo Domingo, Dominican Republic, http://www.un-instraw.org/en/downloads/gender-remittances-and-development/working-paper-1-feminization-of-migration/view.html.

INTERNAL MIGRATION*

CHAPTER 7

1. Introduction

Discussions on migration and globalization often tend to involve international migration; so much so, that the term **migration** has become synonymous with international migration. Yet, in many countries, **internal migration,** i.e. that which occurs inside the borders of a country, is actually far more important both in terms of the numbers of people involved and the resulting flow of remittances. This is especially true of countries with marked regional inequalities, but is not limited to the developing world.[1]

This chapter deals essentially with internal migration. In a slight departure from tradition, it also covers some types of cross-border migration, even though these are theoretically international movements. This is done to move away from simplistic typologies of migration that may lead to the impression that "internal" and "international" migrants are totally distinct. The borders in question are often highly porous, and the journeys undertaken are not very different from those within the country of origin. In the case of West Africa, as Adepoju (1998) notes, seasonal and short-term migrant workers regard their movements as simply an extension across national boundaries of internal movements and of rural-rural migration. In addition, in some cases it can be difficult to establish when, in fact, a traveller crosses international borders. Finally, borders often cut through the habitations of ethnic groups where their free movements across the region predates the drawing of colonial frontiers or the emergence of independent nation states and the creation of international borders and concomitant regulations governing immigration.

The chapter begins with a brief overview of the major patterns of internal migration. Rather than dwelling on what is already well known, the discussion focuses on five broad issues that have been highlighted recently in the international research and policy community and which have immediate implications for donor and government programming, namely:

- the growing incidence of temporary movements;
- internal remittance flows and their impact on development and poverty reduction;

---

* This chapter was written by Priya Deshingkar (Research Fellow, Rural Policy and Environment Group, Overseas Development Institute (ODI), London) and Claudia Natali (Associate Expert, Migration Policy, Research and Communications, IOM, Geneva).

[1] A new study by the Centre for the Study of Living Standards has found that even a developed country like Canada received a huge boost in 2006 due to high migration from low-productivity eastern provinces to high-productivity western provinces; the study provided evidence that migration to western Canada offers jobs to unemployed people from eastern Canada (Sharpe et al., 2007). While it is worth underlining that internal migration is also making a difference in richer countries, this chapter will analyse more closely the impact on the less-developed regions of the world.

eastern Nigeria by Okali and others (2001) found that nearly half the households in rural areas are headed by return migrants, who average about 50 years of age. In Ghana, about 35 per cent of migratory movements were urban-rural, 32 per cent rural-rural and almost one quarter (23%) urban-urban (Ghana Living Standards Survey, 2000).

2.4 Middle East and North Africa: Internal Movements are often more Significant than International Movements with Public Sector Downsizing an Important Cause

In the Middle East and North Africa (MENA), internal migration has increased with public sector downsizing (Al-Ali, 2004) and the resulting occupational diversification. Nonetheless, long-distance rural–urban migration to Cairo from Upper Egypt is a long-standing phenomenon that has existed for at least a hundred years. Greater Cairo, which includes Cairo, Giza, and Qualyoubyya governorates, attracted the bulk of internal migrants as shown by a number of studies mentioned in Zohry (2005). But successive censuses show only a slight increase in rural-urban migration. In contrast, return migration, i.e. urban-rural, has increased steadily and accounted for nearly a quarter (23%) of all movements in 1996. Urban-urban migration represented the bulk of movements (60.4% in 1996) between the large governorates of Cairo, Guiza, Qualyoubyya and Alexandria. Rural-rural migration was the least important type of movement, remaining at around four per cent at each census.

Internal migration in Morocco continues to be more important than international movements in numerical terms, notwithstanding the high number of international migrants originating from this country (De Haas, 2005). Interestingly, De Haas (2005) notes that patterns of rural-to-urban migration have changed lately, which is particularly the case in the provinces of the interior, as the policies of decentralization and improved road and electricity infrastructure favoured the growth of urban centres in rural areas. Therefore, urbanization and partial "de-agrarianization" are general processes that occur also within rural Morocco, as so-called rural populations increasingly earn additional income outside the traditional agricultural sector.

3. Cross-border Migration

The issue of cross-border migration needs to be viewed together with internal migration, especially for countries that are separated by porous borders and populated by people who are historically very similar in language and culture.

Ratha and Shaw (2007) assert, on the basis of datasets constructed by the University of Sussex,[9] that almost 80 per cent of South-South migration takes place across the land borders of adjacent countries and appears to occur between countries with relatively small differences in income. However, official statistics cannot capture the vast numbers of undocumented cross-border migrants.

An analysis of examples of cross-border migration in Africa and Southeast Asia will serve to illustrate the similarities with internal migration and the rationale for considering both types of movements within the same framework.

The NESMUWA surveys in Burkina Faso, Côte d'Ivoire, Guinea, Mali, Mauritania, Niger and Senegal recorded more than 6.4 million migratory movements between 1988 and 1992, of which 2.3 million were international, with flows between Côte d'Ivoire and Burkina Faso dominating. However, migration from Burkina Faso to Côte d'Ivoire has since dropped significantly due to the economic recession in the latter country. This has also been accompanied by return flows of migrants from urban areas of Côte

---

[9] The bilateral migration matrix was created for the Global Trade Analysis Project using national censuses, population registers, national statistical bureaux and a number of secondary sources (OECD, ILO, Migration Policy Institute (MPI), DFID, UNDP) to compile bilateral migrant stocks for 162 countries.

d'Ivoire. Most of the return migrants are active (93.8%) and are entrepreneurs.

The circular migration[10] by West Africans dates back to the pre-colonial period. This process has received a boost with the increasing liberalization of economies. New communication technologies are helping to consolidate historical social networks between peoples who are ethnically and linguistically similar, but artificially separated by political borders. This has led to unprecedented levels of flows of information, ideas, people, goods and money (Balbo and Marconi, 2005). The circularity of the movements allows migrants, a large proportion of whom are women, to maximize the returns from seasonal agricultural production.

The other major area of cross-border migration in Africa is to South Africa from countries in the sub-region, especially Lesotho, Mozambique and Zimbabwe. South Africa is home to an estimated three to eight million migrants, most of whom are employed in the mining industry (Stalker, 2000, cited in Sanders and Maimbo, 2003).

In Southeast Asia, Thailand has emerged as the major destination for migrants in the entire Greater Mekong Sub-region (GMS). As Thailand's own population has aged and the economy has grown, the demand for foreign labour has increased, especially for low-skilled labour. Thailand currently hosts an estimated 2.5 million migrants from Cambodia, Laos and Myanmar (Maltoni, 2006) with nearly 90 per cent in an irregular status (World Bank, 2005). Thousands of border crossers from Myanmar flow into the Thai border town of Mae Sot every year. Most of them

are looking for economic opportunities and are not eligible for refugee status. An estimated 50 per cent of Mae Sot's 80,000 migrant workers from Myanmar do not have proper work permits, which leaves them open to abuse from unscrupulous bosses, most of whom run garment factories (BBC News, 26 February 2007). Many others, especially women, commute on a daily basis from Cambodia to Thailand for petty trade, domestic work or agriculture, as the two countries share a very long and porous border. Men tend to migrate farther afield and for longer durations (Godfrey et al., 2001). Finally, in South Asia, India has a long history of migration from Bangladesh. Poorly demarcated borders between the two countries, cultural affinities (language and lifestyle) with certain Indian provinces such as West Bengal, physical proximity and the presence of earlier migrants contribute to the acceptance of these migrants as de facto members of local communities. These factors also explain why the largest numbers of migrants are believed to be concentrated in north-eastern India, close to the Bangladesh border, even though this region is not as economically robust as other areas in India that are now witnessing increased inflows from Bangladesh (Ramachandran, 2005).

4. Internal and International Labour Migration

The links between internal and international labour migration have recently begun to attract attention at the international policy level, especially in response to concerns by developed countries over migrant flows. Important questions are whether today's internal migrants are tomorrow's international migrants; whether international migration and internal migration are substitutes for each other; and whether internal and international migrants share the same profile. Needless to say, the answers depend very much on the local context and thus can only be arrived at through location-specific case studies. In very broad terms, the links between internal and international migration are of three types: step migration, where people move to one or more locations within their country before emigrating to

---

[10] Circular migration here refers to the livelihood strategy that has been traditional in West Africa for over 1,000 years as people followed livestock and crops on a seasonal basis; this concept therefore differs slightly from what is currently put forward in the European Union (EU) as a temporary labour migration policy (see Chapter 11): "Circular migration is a form of mobility that most closely ties migrants to their countries of origin, and allows them to build bridges between it and other (usually more developed) countries, thereby creating opportunity for the migrant's country of origin to make the most of its comparative advantages" (MPI, 2007: 3).

as much as those from the Kinh majority, are far less likely to have a work contract, or to receive help to find a job, and are far less likely to find work in a government organization (Deshingkar et al., 2006b). In Indonesia, too, minorities have faced difficulties in integrating into mainstream labour markets due to language differences. There are more than 200 distinctive ethno-linguistic groups in Indonesia, and although universal education has helped to some extent, difficulties in integrating in the mainstream remain.

6. The Internal and Cross-border Migration of Women and Children

6.1 Children

The independent migration of children (i.e. without their parents) appears to be very prevalent in certain regions such as West Africa and South Asia. Child migration has received much attention recently because of its similarities to trafficking, given the involvement of intermediaries, exploitation and infringements of rights. According to one estimate, approximately one to 1.2 million children are trafficked globally each year, and most of those in or from Africa originate from the West African region (Beyrer, 2004, quoted in Kiell and Sanogo, 2002). Burkina Faso has a high incidence of child migration. For example, a World Bank study by Kielland and Sanogo (2002) estimated that around 330,000, or 9.5 per cent of children aged between six and 17 years, lived away from their parents. Of these, 165,000 migrated for work, with poverty being the main reason for migrating. However, as case studies have shown, there are more sides to this phenomenon than blatant exploitation. For example, Hashim's (2005) study of the extremely poor Bawku East District of the Upper East Region in the very north-eastern corner of Ghana found that children viewed migration as a positive opportunity. Moreover, case studies on child migration in West Africa, published by the Development Research Centre on Migration, Globalisation and Poverty at the University of Sussex,

point to the negative, but also the positive aspects of this labour mobility. On the one hand, they confirm that young migrants are vulnerable – as shown by their efforts to obtain work, to remain in work, to receive their wages and to avoid being cheated or manipulated. On the other hand, these studies also give a strong sense that such children are not just passive victims of circumstances and that motivation for migrating often involves the child's own desire to earn an income (Anarfi et al., 2007).

Kiell and Sanogo (2002) also found that poor rural families see it as desirable, or even a good investment, to send a child to the city or abroad to work. This is probably why NGO and government initiatives to return trafficked children to their villages have sometimes been met with an unhappy response from children, incredulity from parents and teasing and humiliation from the children's peer group (Black et al., 2004). A much more differentiated and sensitive approach is needed, one that understands the aspirations of the poor and creates the conditions to enable them to better look after their children at home.

6.2 Women

There is no doubt that migration is becoming increasingly feminized, and this development has been driven by two main factors. On the one hand, the improved access of females to education and training opportunities has enhanced their employability in the organized labour market, locally and across national boundaries (Adepoju, 2006), but, on the other, women have also been obliged to seek additional income-generating activities to support the family due to the loss of male employment following structural adjustment policies. Adepoju (2006) notes, for example, that the traditional pattern of migration in sub-Saharan Africa – male-dominated, long-term and long-distance – is rapidly changing as more women migrate. Women in West Africa work mainly in the informal sector, which is less affected by economic recession compared to the wage sector, where most male migrants work. As the formal job market becomes tighter many families are relying on women to earn money. Bah et al. (2003) draw on research in six case studies in Mali, Nigeria and Tanzania and point out that the great increase in female migration in Africa in recent years is linked to employment opportunities as domestic workers in urban centres or in new international tourist resorts. They also highlight that women's migration is increasingly acceptable socially in as much as it contributes to their family's household income through remittances.

The INDEPTH surveys between 1996 and 2001 found that female migrants outnumbered male migrants in five sites and were equal at the other two. Female migrants are on average younger than male migrants. In particular, those aged between 15 and 35 years have the highest propensity to migrate. The 1999 Labour Force Survey in Ethiopia showed that roughly 55 per cent of migrants are women.

South African internal migration has also become more feminized as a recent study has shown (Posel, 2004). Overall, the migration of women has risen steadily between 1960 and 2000.

Bryceson et al. (2003) argue that the migration of women and children increased with the diversification of household livelihood strategies in response to the growing pressure on land and the deterioration of the international terms of trade for African small producers. Households increasingly abandoned the traditional pattern of growing food crops and relying on male migrant earnings in favour of one where everyone earns and non-farm activities are becoming central.

In Southeast Asia and Latin America the feminization of migration streams exceeds that of many other regions of the world. In Thailand, women are employed in five major export-oriented, labour-intensive industries, namely: the manufacture of small electrical appliances, electronics and computer parts; textiles and garments; chilled, frozen and canned food; precious stones and jewellery; and footwear. Work in the sex trade is also significant; however, while it provides more disposable income to women and their families at home, it also puts them at great personal risk. Cambodia experienced a sharp increase in female migration as more young girls and women migrated to urban areas to work in garment factories, as domestic helpers, beer girls and sex workers (Acharya, 2003). A similar trend can be observed in Viet Nam as female labour migration to Ha Noi and Ho Chi Minh City is increasing (Anh, 2005), reflecting a large demand for female workers in labour-intensive manufacturing (textiles, garments, footwear and food processing), commerce and service jobs (shopkeepers, housemaids, street vendors, café/restaurant workers, entertainers and trash collectors).

On the one hand, segmented labour markets reduce competition among migrants because different groups of migrants occupy different niches; but, on the other, there are also negative aspects that require urgent policy attention because the niches occupied by the most vulnerable and historically subjugated are often unregulated and authorities may turn a blind eye to exploitation.

7. Remittances, Poverty and Development

Remittances are an important additional or even principal economic resource for poor rural households worldwide, helping them to smooth income flows and to invest in assets and human capital. Yet, internal remittance flows are seriously under-reported, especially flows through informal channels.

Although generalizations are risky, there is some evidence to support the view that internal circular migrants often bring back more money than the remittances sent home by permanent migrants. For example, Van der Geest's study in Ghana (2003) found that seasonal migrant earnings amounted to about seven per cent of total household income and 14

Internazionale) and SID (Society for International Development) with the assistance of the Director General for Cooperation of the Italian Ministry of Foreign Affairs, were undertaken to forecast the pattern of migratory movements likely to emerge in Africa. Mazzali et al. (2006) assess the outcomes of a series of interviews with experts in the field of migration and development representing varying viewpoints and come to the conclusion that the largest migrations are likely to take place within continental boundaries. Similarly, the West Africa Long-Term Perspective Study (WALTPS), conducted by the Club du Sahel and the OECD (Cour and Snrech, 1998), warns that West Africa must come to terms with particularly high rates of intra-regional migration flows and rapid urbanization. Migration will continue from landlocked countries to the rest of Africa under the increasing constraints of climatic changes and environmental limits, as well as the demand for migrant labour in coastal countries. Such mobility is expected to reduce inequalities and foster growth.

Forecasts of labour mobility and migration trends in Asia, prepared by the Economist Intelligence Unit (2006), indicate that in all major Asian countries, especially the Philippines, Malaysia and India, but not Japan, working-age populations will increase. A positive outlook for economic growth of the region as a whole will drive demand for labour up to 2015. China will have one of the lowest growth rates because of its rapidly ageing population and as its working-age population is expected to peak by the early 2020s and decline thereafter.

In absolute terms, China and India will see the largest increases in working-age populations by 2015 (88 million and 148 million, respectively), followed by Indonesia and the Philippines. However, HIV/AIDS could impact on changes to the size of the working-age population.

9. Policy Developments

9.1 Policies Aimed at Labour Supply and Demand

Few countries have taken a progressive attitude towards rural-urban migration. In sub-Saharan Africa, for instance, current policies do not suggest that such is the case concerning either internal or cross-border migration. Adebusoye (2006) considers that in most African governments there is as yet insufficient awareness of the poverty reduction effects of internal migration. This view is supported by the UN (2002) review of policies affecting migration in sub-Saharan Africa, which shows that governments are averse or at best neutral to migration, especially rural-urban migration. This is based on the concern that movements from rural to urban areas burden urban services, and that housing, education, health and various welfare provisions will be strained because of a sudden influx of migrants, which is indeed the case as urban authorities are ill prepared to receive migrants. The focus of African governments has been on underdevelopment, poverty, socio-economic instability, population pressure on limited natural resources, and conflict as drivers of migration. Their main goal is to reduce migration and limit the formation of urban slums.

Similarly, internal migration was until very recently viewed negatively by many policymakers in Asia. Most governments have tried to control rural-urban movements through a combination of rural employment creation programmes, anti-slum drives and restricting entry to urban areas. However, this limited approach is changing for a variety of reasons, including: a) ineffectiveness of controls; b) the value of migration to poor households and growing industries becoming more visible; and c) the growing strength of the political voice of migrant workers. China is at the forefront of efforts to recognize the importance of internal migration, and the government is testing labour migration agreements between provinces of origin and destination.[15] The Ministry of Labour and Social Security has announced several measures aimed at improving conditions for millions of farmer-workers currently working in cities. The measures include approaching companies to abolish all limitations and unreasonable fees on workers seeking employment, and for charges for information and consultations provided by public agencies to migrants looking for work to be dropped. Local governments have been asked to establish professional training and education plans for workers. However, while controls on population movements have been relaxed, the right to settle still remains restricted under the household registration (*hukou*) system, which excludes rural migrant workers from claiming state benefits in urban areas as long as they remain registered in their place of origin.

A number of events in India have also signalled a change of attitude to internal migration in the country. There have been two high-level policy dialogues on internal migration and its potentially positive impact since 2005, and consultations at state level have been organized with the help of U.K. (DFID) funding by the Gramin Vikas Trust. Two state governments, Madhya Pradesh and Rajasthan, are actively engaged in developing policies to reduce the hardships faced by migrants. Rajasthan is piloting mobile ration cards[16] for 5,000 migrants, while Madhya Pradesh is introducing a comprehensive migrant support programme (see the next section on migrant support). At this point, it is difficult to say whether other states are likely to follow.

Viet Nam has an elaborate and complex KT registration system[17] for residents in urban and rural areas, which

restricts access to government services outside the authorized location of residence/work. The fact that the government conducted a special survey on internal migration, among other key issues, to understand the difficulties faced by migrants, is in itself an indication of their concern to make migration less costly and risky.

In the case of cross-border migration, bilateral and multilateral agreements in such areas as trade, migration, financial channels, labour standards and information have a particularly important role to play in regulating migration and maximizing the potential returns for both areas of origin and destination (see also Chapter 13). Adepoju (2006) welcomes the determination of the Economic Community of West African States (ECOWAS)[18] to abolish rigid residence permits and introduce modern border procedures, information sharing and staff exchange programmes. The adoption of an ECOWAS passport as a symbol of unity to progressively replace national passports over a period of ten years is intended to advance the concept of a borderless sub-region (Adepoju, 2002; see also Textbox 13.2). The Common Market for East and Southern Africa's (COMESA) Protocol on Free Movement of Persons has been established, but has not made much progress so far on the free movement of workers owing to the reservations of some of its member states,[19] notably South Africa, which is the

major recipient of migrant workers. Peberdy and Crush (1998) point out that within the Southern African Development Community (SADC)[20], agreements on free trade have been much more successful than

---

[15] Personal communication with Hans van de Glind, Manager/Chief Technical Advisor, ILO Programme on the Elimination of Child Labour (ILO-IPEC) project to prevent trafficking in girls and young women for labour exploitation in China (CP-TING project).

[16] Ration cards are issued to poor families in India to enable them to access subsidized foodgrains and other essentials. But entitlements through ordinary ration cards are based on proof of residence and cannot be transferred to another location.

[17] See n. 5 above.

[18] ECOWAS members are Benin, Burkina Faso, Cape Verde, Côte d'Ivoire, Gambia, Ghana, Guinea, Guinea Bissau, Liberia, Mali, Niger, Nigeria, Senegal, Sierra Leone and Togo.

[19] COMESA members are Angola, Burundi, Comoros, Democratic Republic of the Congo (DRC), Djibouti, Egypt, Eritrea, Ethiopia, Kenya, Libya, Madagascar, Malawi, Mauritius, Rwanda, Seychelles, Sudan, Swaziland, Uganda, Zambia and Zimbabwe. The Protocol on Free Movement of Persons has not yet entered into force. Members need to ratify the Protocol for it to come into force, and only four have done so to date.

[20] SADC Members are Angola, Botswana, DRC, Lesotho, Madagascar, Malawi, Mauritius, Mozambique, Namibia, South Africa, Swaziland, Tanzania, Zambia, and Zimbabwe.

those on free movement. In South Asia, the main focus of the South Asian Association for Regional Co-operation (SAARC) is on trade and transport rather than migration. The SAARC is working towards a South Asian Customs Union by 2015 and a South Asian Economic Union by 2020, which will have a bearing on the intra-regional mobility of the people of South Asia. However, progress has been slow so far.

Similarly, in Latin America a proposal within the Common Market of the South (MERCOSUR) for the gradual implementation of free movement of persons in the Southern Cone for Latin America was not followed up due to the subsequent redefinition of MERCOSUR,[21] and the current focus is mostly on the free movement of goods and capital (Maguid, 2007).

In Southeast Asia, efforts are being undertaken to match labour supply and demand across the borders of adjacent countries in a regular and orderly manner with a view to countering trafficking in human beings. For example, a Memorandum of Understanding has been drawn up between the Thai and Cambodian governments to create a bilateral administrative process for structured employment procedures regarding inter alia recruitment, a mechanism for the return of migrant workers at the end of their contract, labour protection guidelines and prevention and intervention mechanisms to combat irregular migration and human trafficking. However, the rules and procedures have been criticized for their complexity and lack of user-friendliness. In the meantime, people continue to move and face unnecessary hardship because they are often perceived as engaging in unauthorized activities (Maltoni, 2006).

Efforts are being made to reduce the costs and risks of migration in some countries, for instance in China, and by civil society organizations in others, such as in India and Viet Nam, often with donor support.

9.2 Migrant Support

(a) China

The Chinese Ministry of Labour and Social Security has rescinded the working card requirement for migrant farmer-workers in urban locations. Previously, farmers needed such permits to work outside their place of birth. The ministry has also asked local labour and social security departments to reform policies and cancel illegal charges targeting migrant workers. In addition, it is working on a draft law on household registration management to create conditions for free movement and settlement.

The All-China Federation of Trade Unions has submitted a proposal to the Legal Committee of the Chinese People's Political Consultative Conference, suggesting the ministry concerned issue a law concerning rural migrant employees to safeguard their legal rights, and advising the State Council to establish a special working committee on the protection of migrants.

The ILO CP-TING project in China, which aims to prevent the trafficking of young women and girls for labour, has succeeded in raising the level of understanding of migration and trafficking among policymakers. Hans van de Glind, project manager, believes that migration will continue and many will use irregular channels if regular channels are not made available.[22] This puts migrants at risk of trafficking and exploitation, as it is very difficult to protect the rights of migrant workers if their movement is not through safe channels. The project is trying to develop cheap, fast and transparent labour migration channels on a larger scale, geared especially towards those with low education and skills.

---

[21] MERCOSUR members are Argentina, Brazil, Paraguay and Uruguay

[22] See n. 15 above.

(b) India

In India, a large number of migrant support initiatives have emerged over the last two years, which can be broadly classified into five categories:

(i) The social protection model

This model provides a range of subsidized support services. Social protection aims to reduce poverty and vulnerability by promoting efficient labour markets, limiting risk exposure and enhancing the capacity of migrants to protect themselves against hazards and the interruption or loss of income. A well-known example is the DFID-funded Migrant Labour Support Programme implemented by the Gramin Vikas Trust. The project provides a range of services to migrants moving to the states of Gujarat and Rajasthan from poor tribal districts of Madhya Pradesh. These include identity cards issued through local government bodies, job information, creating awareness on rights, assistance with negotiating wages, communication facilities and help in accessing government programmes. The rationale of the social protection model is that poor migrants cannot fend for themselves in a job market that is dominated by labour market intermediaries and employers who are stronger, better informed and connected than they are. They are in need of support to reduce their vulnerability, but are unlikely to be in a position to pay for such services on a full-cost recovery basis immediately. The services provided will enable them to access better jobs and reduce the level of uncertainty and harassment that they face in the job market.

(ii) The market-based approach

This model works with existing labour market patterns and offers services on a cost recovery basis. An example of such an approach is the initiative launched by the NGO Samarthan and the District Poverty Initiatives Project (DPIP) in Madhya Pradesh, called Mazdoor.org, funded by the World Bank. This initiative will provide skills enhancement and certification programmes, advice and information on jobs, and help workers to link up with government schemes on insurance and workers' funds. The project implementers intend to work within the existing industry and labour market structures, i.e. recognizing that capital and labour are highly mobile and that capital/industry relocate where cheap labour is available. They also recognize that a majority of industrial workers are not listed on the employment registers of industries and are recruited by intermediaries who are not accountable to anyone under the existing law. Mazdoor.org will take on responsibility for the welfare of workers, even though by law it would be the responsibility of the industry and employers. For this, they plan to make industry pay service charges.

(iii) The labour union model

This is a rights-based approach for better implementation of labour laws and the regulation of labour flows. Some NGOs, such as Sudrak in Rajasthan and Disha in Gujarat, believe that unionizing migrant workers will go a long way towards realizing their rights, strengthening their bargaining power in the market and preventing exploitation. The Aajeevika Bureau, established by Sudrak, for example, has set up a union of migrant workers who work in cotton fields. One of its main objectives is to regulate the supply of labour as an oversupply of labour lowers the bargaining power of migrants. So far some 1,500 "mates" have enrolled, and the union has created a charter of demands and also set up around 16 manned check points at all the border crossings between Gujarat and Rajasthan. As a result, employers have offered partial wage rate increases and negotiations are continuing. A similar approach has been adopted by the Bandhkam Majoor Sangathan (BMS) established by Disha in Ahmedabad.

which the person is not a national or a permanent resident (Article 3(a)).

Trafficking is another process that feeds irregular migration flows, most frequently for work purposes, and is characterized by its exploitative nature and a disregard for the migrant's human rights. The Protocol to Prevent, Suppress and Punish Trafficking in Persons, Especially Women and Children, supplementing the United Nations Convention against Transnational Organized Crime (2000), defines trafficking as:

(t)he recruitment, transportation, transfer, harbouring or receipt of persons, by means of the threat or use of force or other forms of coercion, of abduction, of fraud, of deception, of the abuse of power or of a position of vulnerability or of the giving or receiving of payments or benefits to achieve the consent of a person having control over another person, for the purpose of exploitation. Exploitation shall include, at a minimum, the exploitation of the prostitution of others or other forms of sexual exploitation, forced labour or

services, slavery or practices similar to slavery, servitude or the removal of organs (Article 3(a)).

For the purpose of this definition, the consent of the victim is irrelevant if any of the identified means are used, and "the recruitment, transportation, transfer, harbouring or receipt of a child for the purpose of exploitation" is considered "trafficking in persons" even if such means are not used (Article 3(b), (c) and (d)). As this definition and indeed the very title of the Protocol indicate, many forms of trafficking affect mainly women and children, who are most frequently trafficked for sexual abuse or labour exploitation, although they may also be trafficked into forced marriages or delinquency. Victims of trafficking are exposed to physical and psychological abuse, denied human and labour rights and often found in a forced and unwanted dependency relationship with their traffickers, originating in the financial debt incurred for migration and placement services. A perspective on the extent of trafficking for forced labour of men, women and children, extrapolated from the data in the International Organization for Migration's Global Human Trafficking Database, is described in Textbox 8.2.

Textbox 8.2

Trafficking for Forced Labour

No discussion of the place of labour migration in an evolving global economy is complete without reflection upon the phenomenon of trafficking in persons.[1]

Traditionally, national and international counter-trafficking activity and policy have sought to combat the phenomenon by addressing the supply side, or what can be referred to as the root causes of trafficking in countries of origin, including economic inequality, gender discrimination, violence and corruption, and the lack of safe and regular migration opportunities. However, there has been increasing international recognition that serious attention must also be given to the root causes in countries of destination, and above all the demand for cheap and unprotected labour.

Irregular migration, and particularly the trafficking in persons for all forms of exploitation, cannot be separated from the process of globalization in general and the move towards a more global economy. New labour markets emerge, creating new employment opportunities across the globe for skilled and less-skilled workers, both men and women. But such economic growth has not been matched with the evolution of safe, humane and orderly migration channels to facilitate and satisfy this demand for labour. This tension between the growing need for labour and services on one side, and too few regular migration opportunities on the other, creates a niche for intermediaries to intervene and make profit. These intermediaries are the human traffickers, who exploit, abuse and victimize the migrant workers, especially those in an irregular, and hence more vulnerable, situation.

Only recently has the necessary attention been afforded to trafficking for non-sexual forms of exploitation as well as to men and boy victims. The exploitation of individuals by human traffickers exists in a number of employment sectors, often informal ones that are less subject to official labour inspections, including construction work, agriculture and food processing, the fisheries sector, domestic and care work, hospitality and entertainment. Women, men, boys and girls are also trafficked for the purposes of begging and low-level criminal activities.

While accurate figures on the number of persons trafficked each year are difficult to obtain given the clandestine nature of the phenomenon, one estimate states that, globally, there are at least 2.45 million people in forced labour as a result of internal or international trafficking in persons (Belser et al., 2005).[2] It is clear that significant numbers of male and female migrants are being exploited and their human rights abused by human traffickers. Child trafficking for sexual and labour exploitation also continues to exist to an alarming degree.

If human trafficking for all forms of labour exploitation is to be combated, it is necessary to tackle also the demand for cheap, unprotected and often irregular labour. Informal and unregulated work activities need to be brought within the protection of labour laws so that the rights of all workers are protected. And lastly, though by no means least, the demand for migrant workers needs to be matched with safe, humane and orderly migration channels, and with migration management policies between source and destination countries that fully stand to protect the rights of all migrants.

Information from the IOM Global Human Trafficking Database

The International Organization for Migration (IOM)'s Global Human Trafficking Database is a unique tool, which is used to collect information and monitor IOM's return and reintegration assistance to victims of (human) trafficking (VoTs). The database is the world's largest of primary data on registered VoTs, containing only primary data on registered victims of more than 80 different nationalities trafficked to more than 90 destination countries. At the end of December 2007, the database contained data on 12,681 registered cases of VoTs assisted by IOM, with a breakdown of 10,510 females (83%) and 2,169 males (17%) (Table 8.1).[3] Individuals assisted by IOM encompass all age groups, with just under half the caseload aged between 18 and 24 at the time of interview, and approximately one-fifth aged below the age of 18.

While the majority of individuals assisted by IOM are females trafficked for prostitution and other forms of sexual exploitation (8,326 cases to date), IOM's return and reintegration assistance programmes do not focus solely on trafficking for sexual exploitation; assistance is also provided to individuals who have been trafficked, both internally and internationally, for exploitation in such sectors as agriculture, construction work, food processing, domestic employment and childcare work, fisheries, and for the purposes of begging to name but a few.

Table 8.1:

Victims of Trafficking Assisted by IOM, by Gender and Type of Exploitation, 1999-2007

Type of Exploitation	Sex	1999	2000	2001	2002	2003	2004	2005	2006	2007*	Total
Labour exploitation	Female	0	17	50	78	172	161	392	367	303	1540
	Male	0	0	6	120	219	251	514	453	290	1853
Labour exploitation and low-level criminal activity	Female	0	0	0	0	1	0	1	0	1	3
	Male	0	0	0	0	1	1	0	0	1	3
Low-level criminal activity	Female	0	0	0	9	13	22	32	8	5	89
	Male	0	0	0	0	4	7	3	1	2	17
Other exploitation	Female	0	8	24	13	9	43	61	87	61	306
	Male	0	0	2	21	3	0	1	5	3	35
Sexual exploitation	Female	28	566	725	957	639	1,224	1,584	1,567	1,036	8,326
	Male	0	0	11	19	45	21	24	78	57	255
	Not known	0	0	0	0	1	0	0	0	1	2
Sexual exploitation and labour exploitation	Female	0	0	0	7	27	48	69	52	43	246
	Male	0	0	0	1	0	2	0	1	2	6
Total		28	591	818	1,225	1,134	1,780	2,681	2,619	1,805	12,681

Note:

* Based on cases registered in the database up to and inclusive of 31 December 2007.

Source: IOM Global Human Trafficking Database.

Although not readily citable as a trend per se, given that IOM counter-trafficking activities are project-specific,[4] it can be noted that IOM field missions are increasingly assisting individuals trafficked for labour exploitation (3,393 cases), and also an increasing number of male VoTs (2,169 cases). For example, IOM has provided return and reintegration assistance to Ukrainian males trafficked to Russia for labour exploitation. Within the IOM global human trafficking dataset, the most significant number of individuals trafficked for forced labour are indeed trafficked to the Russian Federation, with Ukrainian and Belarusian nationals appearing as the most represented nationalities of individuals trafficked for forced labour.

IOM has further assisted 2,046 VoTs under the age of 18 at the time of interview. The majority consisted of girls trafficked for sexual exploitation; however, it can be noted that IOM has a regional counter-trafficking project in Ghana, which, at the time of publication, had assisted more than 500 children (boys) internally trafficked for exploitation in the fishing industry.

Notes:

[1] See Section 2 above for the definition of trafficking under the Protocol to Prevent, Suppress and Punish Trafficking in Persons, Especially Women and Children, supplementing the United Nations Convention Against Transnational Organized Crime.

[2] The *Trafficking in Persons Report 2006* of the U.S. Department of State estimates that 600,000 to 800,000 persons are trafficked across international borders each year. Other organizations have stated similarly higher and lower figures.

[3] There are missing data for two cases.

[4] Further, as stated, policy and practice have predominantly focused on the trafficking of women and girls for sexual exploitation and thus there has arguably been a bias towards the number of VoTs identified as having been trafficked for sexual exploitation compared to the number of VoTs identified as having been trafficked for labour exploitation. Such a bias in turn impacts upon data collection.

3. Determinants of Irregular Migration

In very broad terms, the determinants of irregular migration are not different from those of regular migration. It can be argued that both movements are outcomes of the various and interconnected social and economic dynamics operating in our globalized world. However, while, by definition, regular migration proceeds along open and established channels, irregular migration seeks to circumvent them. In this regard, the Global Commission on International Migration (GCIM) draws attention to limitations of the meaning of a "global labour market":[7] highly skilled professionals such as information technology specialists or health professionals and world class athletes may be able to pursue their careers across the world, but "for the majority of people and in most regions of the world, national labour markets prevail and the opportunities for them to seek work in other countries remain limited" (GCIM, 2005: 15, para. 22). This mismatch between supply and demand is one of the factors underlying the so-called "nexus" between asylum and migration: the propensity of significant numbers of irregular migrants to make use of asylum procedures not because of a genuine need for protection, but to gain entry to new countries and access to their labour markets. This pattern is particularly evident when asylum systems are perceived as the primary or only official mechanism sanctioning the entry and stay of foreigners in the absence of an alternative means of access to the labour market.

Channels for regular migration, in particular labour migration, are defined by the policies of countries of destination, sometimes, but not always, in consultation with and the assistance of countries of origin (see also Chapter 13). They are, to a large extent, a response to the demand for foreign workers coming from domestic labour markets. When the supply through established channels does not match the demand, irregular migration dynamics come into their own. For instance, in Italy, 520,000 requests from employers for foreign workers contended with 170,000 available places offered in 2006 by government decree (see Section 5.1 below).

Another way of gauging the magnitude of opportunity, if not demand for irregular migration, is to examine the operation of informal economies,

[7] See Chapter 1 for a discussion of "global labour market".

their underlying social networks and, ultimately, the migrant-recruiting industry that services them. The informal economy is the natural point of insertion into the labour force for migrants who cannot find regular employment because of their lack of appropriate documentation. According to Schneider (2004), the informal economy as a percentage of official GDP accounted for 28.2 per cent in Greece, 25.7 per cent in Italy, 22.0 per cent in Spain and 21.9 per cent in Portugal in 2003 – all of them countries that have repeatedly implemented regularization programmes. However, the informal economy is not evenly developed throughout all sectors of the economy. According to conservative estimates by the Italian National Institute on Statistics (ISTAT, 2006), 11.5 per cent (2.7 million) of employed workers were in an irregular situation in Italy in 2004; the figures were much higher in the service (18.4%) and agricultural sectors (18.3%). It is important to note, however, that migrants accounted only for a very modest proportion (4.5%) of the informal labour market, with nationals actually making up the vast majority of those working in an irregular situation.

Social networks are constantly linked to irregular labour migration, as they provide the necessary information and contacts to migrants for both unauthorized entry into the country and subsequent insertion into the workforce. Some studies contend that the impact of social networks is limited compared to that of employers (Krissman, 2005), but there is much evidence that little irregular movement can occur without the information, advice, encouragement and support of family and friends, although it is by no means unknown for the latter to seek to exploit those who rely on them.

Beyond family and friends, there are more structured systems of recruitment, sufficiently developed to bear the collective name of a recruitment industry. The industry has a pervasive role in the phenomenon of irregular migration, from advertising and recruiting in the country of origin, to connections with migration officials and transportation employees,

to linkages with migration brokers, employers and social networks abroad. This, however, does not imply that there is one monolithic system overseeing irregular migration around the world. Rather there is a multiplicity of profit-making concerns that change their configurations at will, setting up and dismantling business fronts, initiating and reacting to market needs and opening or closing routes in response to enforcement patterns (Salt and Stein, 1997; Battistella and Asis, 2003).

4. Measurements of Irregular Migration

Virtually every research paper on irregular migration deplores the lack of reliable data on the subject since, by its very nature, it eludes established data collecting systems. Accurate statistics are rarely available and, at best, one generally has to make do with estimates, and at worst with wild guesswork. The data are often influenced by the methodology utilized and sometimes by the agenda of those reporting on the subject.

Jandl (2004) and Massey and Capoferro (2004) explore the limitations of both commonly exercised and less frequently utilized methods of measurement. Census data provide very sound and comprehensive information on immigrant populations as a whole since they identify the place of birth and citizenship of respondents, but they do not distinguish between regular and irregular migrants. Highly sophisticated residual techniques must then be applied to arrive at estimates of the irregular migrant contingent, but the results require careful interpretation (Costanzo et al., 2004).[8] Intercensal surveys are more focused and more frequently conducted than statutory censuses, but they are not based on sufficiently large samples for safe conclusions to be drawn about the size and composition of the irregular migrant

---

[8] According to these calculations, the estimated "residual" foreign-born population in the U.S. was 3.77 million in 1990 and 8.71 million in 2000. These figures include irregular migrants, arrivals residing lawfully, but not yet included in official figures, and arrivals awaiting finalization of their requests for regularization.

population. Some, but by no means all, countries have registration systems that require individuals to notify authorities of their arrival, departure or change in status, but irregular migrants are unlikely to bring themselves to notice, at least not until they can apply for regularization.[9] Matching arrival and departure records would appear to be a relatively simple and reliable way of determining the number of overstayers in a country. However, in addition to errors in reporting such information, there are many countries that do not require exit controls (for instance, the U.S. abolished them in 1957) and record matching can be costly in terms of both time and money.[10] Massey and Capoferro (2004) suggest the use of ethnosurveys, which combine quantitative and qualitative methods with ethnographic and survey techniques. The resulting databases are certainly rich in information, but the question remains whether they can really lead to a better approximation of the number of irregular migrants in a particular country.[11]

The European Union (EU) has established the Centre for Information, Discussion and Exchange on the Crossing of Frontiers and Immigration (CIREFI), which began its work in 1995. It gathers data on irregular migrants derived from different administrative operations, but the results are subject to numerous limitations, including the important issue of comparability of the figures among participating countries (Mitsilegas, 2004).[12] Officials are relying more on data from removals of non-nationals, although such data do not specify whether removal was forced or voluntary, nor whether the same person might have been involved and counted more than once.

Estimates of the number of irregular migrants based on those remaining after regularizations have been used in particular in southern Europe. One advantage of such data is that they concern the stock of irregular migrants present in the territory and that they contain a host of qualitative data. Obviously, this measurement does not capture those migrants ineligible for regularization or who decided for some reason not to take advantage of it. A similar data set results from mass registration exercises, which have often been conducted in Asia. In the case of registrations, however, as persons are invited to return to their country either immediately or after a short time, the danger of missing people who would prefer to remain in an irregular status is higher, and the possibility that the same person might be counted in a subsequent registration very real.

Given this rather bleak picture, it is hardly surprising that specialists in this field are reluctant to provide anything more specific than orders of magnitude or scales of possibility. On the basis of a national survey of employers, Piguet and Losa (2001) concluded, for instance, that there were between 70,000 and 180,000 foreign-born persons employed without authorization in Switzerland. Similarly, the estimated number of unauthorized migrants in France in the late 1990s was between 140,000 and 500,000 (Delaunay and Tapinos, 1998).

---

[9] An exception might be Spain, where even irregular migrants are registered at local municipalities.

[10] In the "Schengen zone", applicable for the time being to 25 of the 27 EU Member States as well as Iceland and Norway, the passports of all third-country nationals have to be stamped on entry and exit, which should make it easier to detect overstayers as well as the extent of the problem. See Regulation 562/2006/EC of the European Parliament and of the Council of 15 March 2006 establishing a Community Code governing the movement of persons across borders (Schengen Borders Code), OJ 2006 L 105/1.

[11] See also Chapter 9 for a discussion of the various sources of data on irregular migration.

[12] However, on 11 July 2007, the EU Council of Ministers and the European Parliament adopted Regulation (EC) No. 862/2007 on Community statistics on migration and international protection (OJ 2007 L 199/23), which establishes common rules for the collection and compilation of EU statistics on inter alia immigration to and emigration from the territories of Member States, including on third-country nationals refused entry, those found to be present without authorization and the number of undocumented third-country nationals who are obliged to leave (or who have in fact left) the territory of the Member State concerned (Articles 1, 5 and 7).

At the global level, ILO estimates refer to irregular migrants as representing 10 to 15 per cent of total migrant stocks and flows (ILO, 2004),[13] although this average obviously masks large regional or national variations.

5. Irregular Migration Flows and Trends

Any ambition to identify clear routes and patterns involved in irregular migration flows is quickly dispelled when one is confronted with the diversity of possibilities offered in an increasingly mobile world. Maps that try to depict such routes often appear as intricate webs of arrows and dots, with limited explanatory power. However, it is true, particularly for irregular migrants, that the migration process depends on information and that mediators play a crucial role. If clear routes might not always be identifiable, some cities and border-crossings have emerged as hubs, offering a high density of information sources on how to proceed with the journey. At these staging posts, smugglers set up their operations to offer travel packages, often proposing the guarantee of one or several repeat attempts should the first one fail.

Considering the difficulties and limitations of reporting on irregular migration flows by routes and hubs - and bearing in mind that a large proportion of regular migrants lapse into this status after entry through a legal point of entry - this section attempts to provide a broad overview of patterns of movement discernible across geographical areas that do not correspond to strictly defined migratory systems, but represent zones of more or less intense activity.

5.1 Southern Europe – Irregular Access by Sea

Countries in southern Europe were the source of large migratory outflows for almost two centuries during the industrial development phase in Europe and North America. Then, when the economies of these countries progressed to the post-industrial stage at the beginning of the 1970s, they became the main destination of new migrations, first from Africa, then from eastern Europe and Latin America. In the years following the fall of the Berlin Wall, Germany was the major net destination of migrants in Europe (almost 70% of the total) as it experienced the arrival of *Aussiedler*[14] as well as asylum seekers. Since 1998, Spain has become the leading net immigration country in the EU, accounting for 35 per cent in 2003, followed by Italy with 28 per cent, while Germany ranks fourth, after the United Kingdom (European Commission, 2005). Portugal's conversion to being a net destination of migrants occurred as recently as 1998.

As irregular migration is a component of migration flows, it is hardly surprising that Europe has also become a major destination of irregular migration. The major entry points are in the south and southeast of the continent. North Africa, for a long time an important region of origin, is now also a main region of transit. The short distance to the mainland or to islands that are constituent parts of European countries and the increasingly organized smuggling industry override the potential dangers of a journey at sea. Based on apprehension data, the UN Office on Drugs and Crime (2006) estimates that at least 200,000 irregular migrants enter Europe from Africa annually. However, although most prominent in terms of media exposure and numbers of tragedies, irregular migration from Africa is not the most important source of irregular migrants, as many irregular migrants enter over eastern land borders with a valid visa and subsequently, owing to intervening circumstances, such as overstaying and working without authorization, shift into irregular status (see Section 5.6 below).

---

[13] "Information obtained from regularization programmes and other sources suggests that 10 to 15 per cent of migrants are irregular" (ILO, 2004: 11, para. 37, citing Hatton and Williamson (2002)).

[14] Persons of German ancestry mainly from central and eastern Europe and the former Soviet Union.

The two main destinations for irregular migration in southern Europe are Spain and Italy, where the phenomenon has been resistant to both regularization programmes and reinforced interdiction efforts at sea.[15]

On the basis of the difference between the number of foreigners registered on the census lists and the number of residence permits issued, it was estimated that there were over one million unauthorized migrants in Spain in 2003 (SOPEMI, 2004). Two years later, nearly 700,000 applied under a major regularization programme. The overwhelming majority of irregular migrants in Spain come from Latin America (at 20%, Ecuadorians were the largest group, followed by Colombians (8%) and Bolivians (7%)). Eastern Europeans, especially Romanians (17%), were also present in significant numbers, as were Moroccans (12%). Information derived from the 2005 regularization exercise reveals that 59 per cent of migrants were male and 41 per cent female. Most of the applicants held low-skilled jobs: 32 per cent were domestic workers (83% women), 21 per cent construction workers (95% men), 15 per cent working in agriculture, 10 per cent in catering and 5 per cent in commerce (Karaboytcheva, 2006).

According to the Italian Ministry of Interior, the number of unauthorized arrivals by sea has increased by almost 50 per cent since 2003, reaching a total of 22,016 people in 2006 (Caritas/Migrantes, 2007). The corresponding figures for 2005 show that 96 per cent of the arrivals were male, while a disconcerting 7 per cent were minors (Caritas/Migrantes, 2006). To have a more realistic picture of the dimension of irregular migration in Italy, one can turn to the 2006 amendment to the decree establishing the number of residence permits to be granted to third-country nationals with a work contract in Italy. The

number was limited to 170,000, but 517,000 who were already present and working in Italy, filed an application. The approval of an additional 350,000 residence permits[16] puts the size of the irregular migration contingent living in Italy at that point in time at around 500,000. About 90 per cent of arrivals consist of 10 nationalities, among which migrants from North Africa and the Middle East are the most numerous, underlining that geographic proximity is still one of the main factors influencing the decision to migrate irregularly; Egyptians account for the largest group (45%), followed by Moroccans (15%), Eritreans and Tunisians.

Portugal and Greece rank after Spain and Italy as the two major recipients of irregular migrants in southern Europe. According to government estimates, Portugal would have had 500,000 irregular migrants at the end of 2004, with about 30,000 from Brazil. Results of the regularization process in Greece indicate that the total number of irregular migrants in April 2006 could have reached about 550,000, although fewer than 200,000 applied for regularization around that time, possibly because of the high application fees (EUR 1,176 per person) and the complexity of the application process.

Crossing the Mediterranean has always been, and still is, the main route for migrants to irregularly access southern Europe from Africa. This pattern seems to persist notwithstanding the recently increased controls. However, in response to this reinforcement of surveillance and interdiction activities, alternative routes have been developed. While the traffic was once concentrated in the Gibraltar Strait, through the two enclave cities of Ceuta and Melilla, the route via the Canary Islands has now become the preferred staging post into Spain from various departure points along the West African coastline. However, in the first seven months of 2007, the number of migrants intercepted on or off the Canary Islands dropped by

---

[15] It has been reported that EU patrols have substantially reduced arrivals since the beginning of 2007, although the European Commission has also called for improvements in EU cooperation (EU business.com, 2007a, 2007b).

[16] *Gazzetta Ufficiale della Repubblica Italiana* [*Official Journal of the Republic of Italy*], Anno 147, No. 285, 7 December 2006, p. 13.

55 per cent to 5,700 from 13,700 during the same period in 2006. This drop has been attributed inter alia to greater vigilance on the part of countries of departure and surveillance missions conducted by Spain alone or within the framework of the EU border agency FRONTEX (*Migration News Sheet*, September 2007).

Substantial patrolling operations have also been undertaken along the short route which connects the Libyan and Tunisian coasts to the island of Lampedusa, the main entry point for irregular migrants heading to Italy from Africa. While traffic along this route decreased by 4.5 per cent in 2006 (*Corriere della Sera*, 5 January 2007), it is very likely that migrants have opted to enter Europe through the alternative Canary route. In addition, patrolling operations have not been really effective in limiting the presence and power of organized gangs, who still handle the whole operation and charge between EUR 1,000 to 2,000 per person for the sea crossing from Libya to Italy (Moscarelli, 2008).

In both routes towards Spain and Italy, countless migrants perish along the way. If the numbers of irregular migrants can only be estimated, the number of migrants dying en route to their destination is even more uncertain. According to the NGO Andalusian Association for Human Rights [*Asociacion Pro Derechos Humanos de Andalucia*], 289 irregular migrants were confirmed dead or lost at sea in 2004, but some estimates suggest that the real number of deaths might have been closer to 500. Yet, approximately 1,200 to 1,700 migrants who left Mauritania in February and March 2006 never reached Spain and might have died. Finally, the then EU Commissioner Franco Frattini's conjecture was that during the summer of 2006 perhaps 3,000 people died while crossing the Mediterranean to reach Europe (Palidda and Cuttitta, 2007).

5.2 Western Europe – In and Out of Irregularity

Compared to the southern borders of Europe, western European countries appear less exposed to the large-scale entry of irregular migrants, particularly those entering without documents in a clandestine manner. In the past, intermediate central European countries operated as a buffer zone. Since the EU enlargement, to 15 and now to 27 countries, the former buffer role played by central European countries has become rather more complex. They are now the frontline states on the external EU border and are major suppliers of migrant workers to western Europe.

All western European countries are host to a number of irregular migrants, many of whom entered with a regular visa but then overstayed and worked without authorization. Figures on irregular migration are not published regularly, but at the political level there are frequent acknowledgements of both the magnitude and persistence of the problem. In France, the then Minister of Interior, Nicolas Sarkozy, estimated in June 2006 that there were between 200,000 and 400,000 irregular migrants (PICUM, 2006). In April 2005, a report on *"sans-papiers"* in Switzerland revealed that there were some 90,000 persons living in the country without authorization (Swiss Federal Office for Migration, 2005). In the United Kingdom, a report for the Home Office estimated the number of irregular migrants in 2001 at 430,000, suggesting that the actual number could be as low as 310,000 and as high as 570,000 (Woodbridge, 2005).

The participation of irregular migrants in the economy, especially the informal one, is a subject of much conjecture, but it is generally acknowledged that it is high, especially in agriculture and in the construction and service industries.

5.3 North America – The Focus on the U.S.- Mexican Border

Irregular migration is an issue affecting, in particular, the United States, where the number of irregular migrants has continued to increase, irrespective of countervailing legislative measures, beginning with the Immigration Reform and Control Act (IRCA) in 1986 and all control measures thereafter. The consistent demand for labour in the U.S. economy, the still hefty, though now reduced to a 1:6 ratio income differential between the U.S. and Mexico, the long border between the two countries, the increasing trade and industrial relations, the large Mexican community residing in the U.S. (about 12 million, approximately 10% of the Mexican population, perhaps half in an irregular status[17]) with large social networks, are among the determinants of a social phenomenon which remains a major concern of policymakers and public opinion.

Estimates of the number of irregular migrants in the U.S. are for the most part convergent. A report of the U.S. Department of Homeland Security estimated the number of irregular migrants at 11 million as of January 2006, an increase of 500,000 compared to January the previous year, while a report by the Pew Hispanic Center (Passel, 2006) put the estimate at between 11.5 and 12 million as of March 2006, two-thirds of whom would have been in the country for ten years or less. A breakdown by nationality indicates that six million are from Mexico, 470,000 from El Salvador, 370,000 from Guatemala, 280,000 from India, 230,000 from China, 210,000 from South Korea, 210,000 from the Philippines, 180,000 from Honduras, 170,000 from Brazil and 160,000 from Viet Nam. In terms of occupations, 7.2 million, almost five per cent of all workers in the U.S., were employed, with a significant presence in some occupations, such as farm work (24%), cleaning (17%), construction (14%) and food preparation (12%).

As to the mode of entry, the Pew Hispanic Center estimated that up to half of irregular migrants might have entered the country legally and overstayed their visa, while the rest entered by evading border inspection in many ways (hiding in vehicles, trekking through the desert, wading across the Rio Grande). Perhaps between 250,000 and 350,000 annually overstay their visa, a tiny fraction of the 179 million non-immigrant admissions, but a significant contribution to the stock of irregular migrants. A specific group of overstayers consists of holders of a Border Crossing Card (Mexicans and Canadians), who are authorized to stay for a maximum of 30 days within 25 miles of the border (75 miles at the border with Arizona) but fail to observe these conditions.

Mexico is not only the major country of origin of irregular migration to the U.S. (over 450,000 a year), but also a transit country for irregular migration from Central and South America. This flow has become more pronounced since the 1990s. At the same time, under pressure from the U.S., Mexico has increased the number of apprehensions and deportations of irregular migrants. In 2004, 215,695 Central Americans, half of them arrested in the border region of Chiapas, were deported. According to the Mexican Government's National Migration Institute (*Instituto Nacional de Migración*), deportations increased to 240,269 in 2005, to decrease again to 167,437 in the first 10 months of 2006. The decline could be a sign of a more general decline in migration from Central to North America, but some experts point instead to the development of alternative routes and the use of more effective methods to evade detection. The Central American region and the Caribbean are not only points of origin of irregular migration, but also transit areas, even for people coming from other continents, for example, the Chinese.

The 5,500 mile border between the U.S. and Canada (a third of which is with Alaska) is subject to increasing levels of border security. The U.S. is adding Border Patrol agents, and Canada plans to provide its agents with arms. The number of irregular migrants in Canada was estimated at approximately 200,000

---

[17] When not indicated otherwise, figures concerning irregular migration to North America are taken from the Internet quarterly *Migration News*: http://migration.ucdavis.edu/mn/index.php.

in 2006, employed particularly in construction and other blue-collar jobs. The government is not considering granting them amnesty as demanded by some employers. However, employer demands for more workers are being met to a certain degree through the recent expansion of Canada's temporary migrant worker programme (see Chapters 3 and 11).

5.4 Central America and the Caribbean – Mainly Labour Movements

Significant irregular migration flows also occur within the Central American sub-region.[18] Approximately half of the 500,000 migrant workers in Costa Rica have irregular status. Many of these irregular migrants come from neighbouring countries, particularly Nicaragua (somewhere between 65,000 to 100,000)[19] and are concentrated mainly in agriculture[20] but also in other forms of lower-skilled employment, such as construction, tourism and domestic work.

In the case of Haitian migration, the enhanced U.S. policies to protect its coastal areas and territorial waters from incursions over the past decade have reduced the number of attempts by irregular migrants to reach the State of Florida, with the result that the migration route has switched towards other Caribbean islands, especially the Bahamas and the Dominican Republic. Estimates of the number of Haitian migrants in the Dominican Republic vary from 500,000 to 1.5 million. However, reliable sources suggest there are between 500,000 and 700,000 Haitians living in the Dominican Republic, the majority of whom do not have valid visas or work permits (Achieng, 2006).[21] An estimated 40,000 to 50,000 Haitians or Haitian descendants reside in the Bahamas, most of whom work in low-paid, lower-skilled jobs in agriculture/landscaping, construction, domestic service and informal trading (Fernández-Alfaro and Pascua, 2006). Smuggling rings take advantage of the demand for labour by bringing in irregular migrants from Haiti.

5.5 South America – Fluctuating Policies and Fluctuating Flows

Migration in South America has traditionally been organized around two sub-systems: one involving the countries of the Andean region with Venezuela as the major destination; the other concerning the countries of the south, with Argentina as the main destination.

Migration in these two regions, as on the continent as a whole, has changed considerably in recent times. Both the Andean region and the countries of the south have become characterized by intensive out-migration, particularly from Ecuador and Peru, but also from traditional countries of destination like Argentina and Brazil. Increasingly, these migrants head towards North America and Europe as intra-regional movements have declined, especially in the years of economic crisis in Argentina. During the crisis, perhaps as many as 300,000 migrants left Argentina, by far the largest immigration country in South America with 1.5 million immigrants in 2001. This movement has already subsided, and Argentina once again attracts low-skilled foreign workers, particularly from Paraguay and Bolivia, who arrive to find seasonal employment and feed the informal economy.

Regularization mechanisms have certainly been one of the major policy strategies pursued by South American countries in an effort to tackle the phenomenon of irregular migration. Overall, changes in migration trends and policies have resulted in a drop in the numbers of irregular migrants in the southern part of South America. Chile, Bolivia and Peru regularized about 700,000 migrants in 2004 (O'Neil et al., 2005) within the Common Market of the South (MERCOSUR) cooperation

---

[18] Some of these movements are also described in Chapter 3 on low and semi-skilled workers.

[19] Most of this migration responds nevertheless to the demand for seasonal jobs (IOM, 2001).

[20] According to the Costa Rican Ministry of Labour and Social Security, in 2002-03 there were 50,400 seasonal migrants working in agriculture, of whom 40,900 (or 81%) were undocumented.

[21] Only some five per cent of these Haitian migrants are said to have identification (Achieng, 2006).

irregular migrants puts them under severe stress, as Morocco is under pressure from European countries to act to control irregular migration from its shores. The same can be said of Libya, where migrants break their journey to collect money for the crossing, and where they also end up if their attempts to proceed fail. In Libya, an economy for transit migration has flourished, both in Kufra, where people of many nationalities have settled to provide information to arriving new migrants, and the coastal cities where they prepare for departure (Hamood, 2006).

(b) Sub-Saharan Africa – diversity of movements

Sub-Saharan irregular migration is characterized by significant cross-border movements (see also Chapter 7) as well as flows to Europe and South Africa.

As opposed to migrants from North Africa, sub-Saharan communities are much less numerous in Europe and tend to gather by nationality. Irregular migrants from Senegal are found mostly in France and Italy, Nigerians are more numerous in the U.K. and Ireland. In the U.K., there are also irregular migrants from Zimbabwe and South Africa, while irregular migrants from Cape Verde, Angola and Guinea are found mainly in Portugal.

South Africa is the most prominent, although certainly not the only African destination of irregular sub-Saharan migrants (see also Chapter 3). Categories of irregular migrants include, among others, retrenched miners who remain in the country, tourists and students who work without permits, overstayers and migrants who entered evading border controls. A study estimated their numbers at anywhere between 390,000 and 470,000 (Crush and Williams, 2005).

5.7 East Asia – The Lure of Strong Economies

A region with diversified migration policies, East Asia experiences irregular migration mostly in the form of overstayers or persons engaging in work without proper documentation. In the Republic of Korea (South Korea), the phenomenon was connected in a very specific way to the presence of foreign trainees, employed in the textile, rubber and plastic industries (Ja-young, 2006), who turned into irregular workers in response to the ample employment opportunities provided by medium and small-sized companies but also to move away from stringent working conditions in their designated workplaces (UN Human Rights Council, 2007). The adoption of the Employment Permit System (EPS) in 2004, which was subsequently expanded to replace the industrial trainee system in January 2007, offered the opportunity to many irregular migrants to obtain regular status.[22] However, irregular migration – mainly in the form of overstaying – continues to be significant, but the number seems to be stabilizing: by mid-2006, about 190,000 individuals – half of all the migrant workers – lived and worked irregularly in South Korea (OECD, 2007). Similarly, in Japan, irregular migrants are mostly overstayers, and the Ministry of Justice estimated that at the beginning of 2005 they numbered approximately 207,000, while another estimated 30,000 persons were smuggled in by boat. Taiwan Province of China, is reported to be experiencing some irregular migration in the form of regular migrant workers who become clandestine residents because of problems with employers or as a result of lay-offs.

A new trend in East Asian irregular migration is the decrease of some intra-regional flows, while other less traditional destinations are becoming more attractive. On the one hand, "irregular migration" from mainland China to Hong Kong SAR and Taiwan Province of China has decreased, particularly because of the rapid development of the inland provinces (Hong Kong SAR is planning to attract skilled

---

[22] In 2003, the number of irregular migrant workers registered by the Ministry of Labour exceeded 227,000, and 80 per cent of them were afforded regular status under the Employment Permit System (UN Human Rights Council, 2007).

workers from mainland China under its Quality Migrant Admission Scheme). On the other hand, it is estimated that up to 200,000 irregular migrants from China are taking advantage of work opportunities created by the declining population in the Russian Far East (Akaha, 2004).

5.8 Southeast Asia – Cross-border Irregular Migration

Southeast Asia is a region of origin, transit and destination of migrants, where the most prevalent mode of entry is over land borders (see Chapter 7). Irregular migration in this region, however, takes many forms as illustrated in Portrait 8.1.

Portrait 8.1

Sailing to Nowhere – A Cambodian Migrant's Tale

Nang, aged 25, is a Cambodian fisherman from Banteay Meanchey province. He has very little formal education and, following the advice of some friends, decided to leave Cambodia in early 2004 to work in neighbouring Thailand to support his family.

He was recruited by a Cambodian broker (*mekhal*) who came to his village and promised him a job in the construction industry in Thailand paying up to THB 4,500 (USD 128) per month. The broker's fee, payable in advance, was THB 3,000 (USD 85).

Nang borrowed the money for the broker's fee from relatives, and he was then taken to the Malay district in Banteay Meanchey, where the broker helped him cross the border into Thailand unlawfully for an additional fee of THB 200 (USD 6).

Once in Thailand, he was taken to Patnam in Samut Prakan province, where he was kept in a guesthouse for several days before being told that there was no job in construction and that he would have to work on a fishing boat.

When he complained that he had been promised a job in construction, the broker threatened him that he could easily find himself in the custody of the Thai police as an irregular migrant. In fact, Nang believes that the broker sold him to the captain of the fishing boat for THB 5,000 (USD 150).

According to Nang, the conditions onboard his boat, which sailed towards Indonesian waters and remained there for six months, were extremely harsh. The crew had to work day and night for three days before having a day to rest, and was continually harassed and threatened by the captain.

Nang was never allowed to leave the boat, and even if the captain had allowed him ashore, he would have not gone for fear of being arrested by local police as an irregular migrant.

Eventually the boat docked in Ranong on the Thai-Myanmar border, where the Cambodian crew was replaced by a crew from Myanmar prior to moving on into that country's waters. Nang was paid a total of THB 2,000 (USD 57) for six months of work.

With no travel documents and unable to afford transport back to Cambodia, let alone the sum of THB 6,000 (USD 171) demanded by a broker to help him return home, Nang realized that it was only a matter of time before he would be picked up by the Thai police as an irregular migrant.

On the advice of other Cambodian fishermen stranded in Ranong, he signed up with another Thai fishing boat and was given forged papers identifying him as Thai.

In August 2004, while fishing illegally in Indian waters, the boat was intercepted by the Indian navy and escorted to Port Blair in the Andaman and Nicobar islands.

Before they arrived, Nang and the other Cambodian crew members were threatened by the crew that unless they stuck by their story that they were Thai, they would never be allowed to return home.

Textbox 8.4

Out-of-reach and Out-of-danger: Keeping Girls Safe from Traffickers in Nepal

Every year an estimated 12,000 Nepalese women and girls are trafficked into India. The Asian Development Bank estimates that 100,000 to 200,000 Nepalese women and girls are held against their will in Indian brothels, with roughly 25 per cent under the age of 18 years. Traffickers typically lure impoverished girls with promises of jobs in urban areas or abroad. Some families knowingly send their daughters to brothels because they consider them a burden. Many of the women and girls are illiterate and are not even aware that they have been taken across the border. The Government of Nepal has identified 26 districts from which women and girls have disappeared.

In response, the Reproductive Health Initiative for Youth in Asia (RHIYA), a partnership of the European Union and the United Nations Population Fund (UNFPA) working in collaboration with NGOs, is focusing on 19 "high-risk" impoverished districts. The programme educates parents, community leaders, district health officials and young people about the dangers of trafficking. It also provides girls and young women with training and empowerment opportunities. Trafficking survivors are reintegrated into their communities through efforts designed to reduce stigmatization and are referred to social and legal services for additional assistance.

The initiative is proving effective. In the district of Prasauni VDC, a RHIYA peer educator was able to rescue three adolescent girls the very same day they were scheduled to depart. She had learned that the young men who had promised the girls work were, in fact, traffickers. After the peer educator raised the alarm, villagers caught the traffickers and handed them over to the police. They soon admitted their guilt. In Rupandehi District, a young woman was asked by her brother-in-law to accompany him on a one-day shopping trip to Gorakhpur, just across the border. But when she arrived at the crossing, her brother-in-law introduced her to two other girls and asked her to accompany them into India, claiming that he would join them later after taking care of some personal business. She became alarmed, recalling the RHIYA educational sessions on trafficking, and realized that her brother-in-law must be a trafficker. She immediately sought help from the border NGO Maaiti Nepal, and all the girls were returned safely to their homes.

Source: UNFPA (2006: 50).

5.10 Middle East

Irregular movement for work is also an issue in the labour markets of Gulf Cooperation Council (GCC) States. As restrictions on work permits are progressively tightened, more migrant workers are prepared to enter without authorization or to stay beyond the expiration of their permits. In Kuwait, for instance, the Department of Immigration in the Ministry of Internal Affairs estimates the number of irregular migrants at up to 60,000 (UN DESA 2006, citing Shah, 2005). Two mechanisms working in favour of irregular migration are to be found in the employment sponsorship system, on the one hand, and the annual pilgrimage to Mecca (the *Hajj*), on

the other.[25] Another striking characteristic of the region, which to a certain extent nurtures irregular flows, is the high dependence on foreign workers (remittances sent home from the Gulf States in 2005 represent nearly 9% of GDP). According to United Nations figures, 12.8 million foreigners lived and worked in the GCC States in 2005. The proportion of non-nationals within the local population is as high as 62.1 per cent for Kuwait and 71.4 per cent for the United Arab Emirates (UAE) (UN DESA, 2006). The Gulf States are committed to reducing the number of irregular contract workers: for instance, in Saudi Arabia and the UAE by making the sponsorship system more flexible and allowing workers to change employer before the traditional one-year period,

---

[25] Approximately 700,000 persons are deported from Saudi Arabia annually. Many come for the *Hajj* and then stay and work in the country (Shah, 2005).

and in Saudi Arabia by discouraging nationals from harbouring overstayers by imposing a maximum fee of SAR 5,000 (i.e. USD 1,335) and imprisonment of up to two years. However, the effectiveness of these measures has yet to be determined. Other important patterns of irregular movements in the region include arrivals from Somalia, Ethiopia and other African countries in Yemen, and irregular Afghan workers (perhaps 800,000) in Iran, where the authorities have announced their intention to proceed with repatriations.

5.11 Summary Points

Following this broad, though cursory, overview of irregular migration in various regions some summary points may be offered:

- Irregular migration is present in all major regions; therefore, it is of general interest to the international community.
- The magnitude of irregular migrant populations differs significantly across the various regions. Irregular migration seems to be a function of the overall volume of migration in a given region, the proximity of places of origin and destination, the permeability of borders and the strength of migration networks.
- The existence of work opportunities for lower-wage, low-skilled migrant workers is an important incentive for irregular migrants.
- Although irregular migration is a complex phenomenon and resistant to analysis, it is a global industry with connections to both legitimate migration agencies and to criminal networks.
- The choice of regular or irregular migration channels depends on a variety of factors: availability of regular channels; time necessary for the migration process to be completed; bureaucratic difficulties in the process; excessive conditions and requirements; preference for immediate profit over long-term benefits; and lack of or difficult access to available alternatives.

- Although irregular crossings attract the highest attention, most irregular migration occurs through the lawful entry of persons who then drift into irregularity by violating the terms of their admission through overstaying and/or working without authorization to do so. It may, therefore, be argued that the possibility of finding work is the ultimate determinant of irregular migration.

6. Policies

Policies to address irregular migration have coalesced around a number of well-established policy objectives: the fight against organized smuggling in migrants; control of external borders to reduce irregular entries; inspection of labour sites to reduce irregular employment; and cooperation towards development to ease migration pressure from countries of origin; and repatriation and return programmes, and agreements between countries of destination, origin and transit. Another policy option, the regularization of migrants to lower the number of irregular migrants present in the country, does not attract general consensus. While some countries have implemented it repeatedly, others have remained sceptical.

6.1 Efforts against Organized Smuggling

There is international consensus on the need to combat the organized crime of smuggling in migrants and this is one of the few areas where a multilateral approach to migration management is pursued. The 1990 International Convention on the Protection of the Rights of All Migrant Workers and Members of their Families specifically calls for such cooperation (Article 68). The 2000 Protocol against the Smuggling of Migrants by Land, Sea and Air has attracted 114 ratifications. There are numerous declarations and statements of governments committing or re-committing themselves to action (among the most recent ones are the 11 July 2006 Rabat Plan of Action, adopted by the Euro-African Ministerial

Conference on Migration and Development,[26] and the 13 January 2007 Association of Southeast Asian Nations (ASEAN) Declaration on the Protection and Promotion of the Rights of Migrant Workers).[27] Many Regional Consultative Processes have the topic as a standing item on their agenda.[28] However, the constant reiteration of the need for common efforts against organized smuggling is in itself an indication of how difficult it is to translate intentions into practice.

6.2 Control of Borders

In recent years, and particularly after September 11, 2001, much attention was given to the link between migration and security and the control of borders. At times, this has resulted in the reinforcement of border controls as best exemplified perhaps by the U.S. decision to build a 700-mile long fence along the U.S.-Mexican border, under the terms of the 2006 Secure Fence Act. The construction of a wall at the border between Thailand and Malaysia, the fence between Bangladesh and India, and the fences around Ceuta and Melilla reflect the pressures governments are facing from people wishing to move irregularly in search of better life opportunities.

Increasing use is also being made of high technology, including movement and heat sensor devices, sophisticated radar systems and automated identification systems incorporating biometric components (Redpath, 2007).

6.3 Internal Controls and Labour Inspections

All countries of destination are faced with the problem of establishing the identity of irregular migrants. A major challenge is the prevalence of forged documents; hence the ongoing attempts to introduce tamper-proof travel documents through the inclusion of high-technology security features. Another is the fact that irregular migrants are routinely advised by smugglers to conceal or destroy their travel documents to delay identification and make repatriation more difficult.

As employment opportunities play a key role in encouraging irregular migration despite the administrative obstacles, inspections of labour sites constitute an important deterrent, and indeed there are indications that many governments are moving in that direction. In 2006, for instance, the U.K. Border Agency (2008a) carried out over 5,200 operations to detect unauthorized employment and removed more than 22,000 people from the country. At the end of February 2008, new rules have been brought into effect, whereby employers could be fined up to £10,000 for every unauthorized worker they negligently hire or, if they knowingly hire such a worker, an unlimited fine and/or a maximum two years prison sentence (U.K. Border Agency, 2008b). However, there are challenges in conducting such operations in a planned and systematic way over time rather than relying on highly publicized one-off interventions. Human resource limitations and differences in enforcement priorities among the relevant agencies are hurdles that have to be overcome. In addition, such inspections are very difficult in areas of employment where migrants are scattered, for instance in the agricultural sector, or where controls can be carried out only indirectly, as in domestic employment.

6.4 Prevention through Development

The idea that prevention should begin with the stemming of migration pressures at source has been much debated over the years without leading to the development of concrete and sustainable intervention strategies. Put simply, the argument is that prevention of irregular migration should begin

---

[26] The text of the Action Plan is available from the website of the Government of Morocco's Ministry of Foreign Affairs and Cooperation at http://www.maec.gov.ma/migration/Doc/PA%20final%20EN.pdf.

[27] See the ASEAN website at http://www.aseansec.org/19264.htm.

[28] E.g. the Regional Ministerial Process on People Smuggling, Trafficking in Persons and Related Transnational Crime, known simply as the Bali Process, is devoted largely to this issue. See http://www.baliprocess.net/.

with socio-economic development in countries of origin, although a reduction in flows in the short term is not to be expected, as theorists of the "migration hump" have articulated (Martin and Taylor, 1996). In more recent times, the linkage between migration and development has taken on renewed significance, but from a different perspective, as demonstrated at the UN General Assembly's High-Level Dialogue on International Migration and Development in September 2006, and the Global Forum on Migration and Development in July 2007.[29] The switch in international thinking is that migration, while not a panacea for economic distress, can itself be a development factor, contributing in the shorter term to the reduction of poverty levels in the longer term, to sustainable growth. The spectacular increase in the recorded levels of remittances transferred to developing countries has played a large part in ensuring broad acceptance of that shift of perception in the international community. Research and international consultations have yielded a wide range of recommended actions, some of which are being implemented, although a comprehensive global effort has yet to be attempted.[30]

6.5 Repatriation and Return Programmes and Agreements

Enforcement measures against irregular migration are often intended to lead to the repatriation of those identified as irregular migrants. Large-scale repatriations have been conducted in specific circumstances, for instance between Thailand and Myanmar or Malaysia and Indonesia. They appear to work best when coupled with offers of legitimate re-entry for the purpose of employment. In industrialized countries of destination, the acceptance rate is generally modest, even when return assistance is provided (see Portrait 8.2). Deportations are also practised, but are expensive to conduct on a large scale. It has been estimated, for instance, that the expulsion of one person from Spain to Romania costs USD 2,300, to Senegal USD 2,500, to Ecuador USD 4,900 and to China USD 8,600 (Caritas/Migrantes, 2005). Consequently, EU interior ministers decided in April 2004 to cooperate on organizing joint flights for the expulsion of third-country nationals to reduce costs.[31]

---

[29] For the GFMD, see also Textbox Int. 2.

[30] Chapter 12 offers a fuller discussion of the labour migration and development relationship.

---

[31] Council Decision of 29 April 2004 on the organization of joint flights for removals from the territory of two or more Member States of third-country nationals who are subjects of individual removal orders, OJ 2004 L 261/28.

Portrait 8.2

From Kayes to Tripoli and back

Diakite was born in Kayes, Mali, on 1 January 1943. The name Kayes comes from the Soninke word *karre*, meaning a low, humid place prone to floods in the rainy season. Kayes is also referred to as the "pressure cooker of Africa" because of its extreme heat, to which the iron ore found in the surrounding mountains is said to contribute.

Diakite has always been a farmer, working the five hectares of land he inherited from his father. A drought in 2004 made it difficult to eke out enough from the arid soil to live on, and his son decided to search for a better life by heading towards North Africa and later, perhaps, Europe. Then, one year later, Diakite also left to search for his son, who had disappeared. At the time of their last phone call, he had been working as an employee in Ghatt, south-western Libya.

Diakite travelled across his large country by any means he could find; he entered Algeria with the "assistance" of a smuggler, and then Libya. "Unfortunately, I did all this just to find my son's name written on a gravestone in a Ghatt cemetery. I never did find out how and why my son died", Diakite said. When he found himself a stranger and irregular migrant in a new country, without a job or money, he decided to go to Tripoli to find work that would allow him to earn the money needed to get back home. "Like many others from sub-Saharan Africa, I was sitting on the sidewalk of a street near a big market in Tripoli, with a brush and a tin of paint in front of me to indicate to passers-by the service I could offer for a few dinars. Sometimes I was lucky, and I found work for a few days or weeks decorating Libyan houses. At other times, I would wait in vain sitting under the sun the whole day", relates Diakite. For one year, he managed to survive by doing occasional jobs, but was unable to save enough money to return home. At the beginning of 2007, the Malian Embassy in Tripoli referred him to IOM as a possible candidate to benefit under an Assisted Voluntary Return and Reintegration (AVRR) programme. Diakite was able to return to Kayes, where he will buy a water pump to make his land prosper again. "This water pump will be beneficial to my family and the whole community, and I am glad to be back and able to tell the young people in my town how the dreams of emigrating can turn into nightmares."

Source: IOM Tripoli.

Another crucial aspect of repatriation is the willingness of countries of origin to accept expelled migrants. In December 2005, in response to a Parliamentary question, the Spanish Government announced that between 1 January 2001 and 31 May 2005 a total of 122,238 expulsion orders were not carried out (*Migration News Sheet*, December 2005). Most consulates of sub-Saharan countries refused to recognize the migrants to be returned as their citizens. Consequently, countries of destination have been eager to sign readmission agreements with countries of origin. Italy has signed more than 20 such agreements (IGC, 2002), but not all of them are yet operative. Spain has succeeded in signing agreements with some sub-Saharan countries (Cape Verde, Gambia, Guinea Conakry, Guinea Bissau, Mauritania, Nigeria, Ghana) (Embassy of Spain (London, U.K.), 2007), but others are resisting entering into readmission agreements. However, there are no indications of a close correlation between numbers of agreements signed and numbers of irregular migrants sent home.

Some lessons learnt from return programmes are described in Textbox 8.5 below.

Textbox 8.5

Return Programmes – Lessons Learnt

- Return programmes are best implemented as one important element within a comprehensive approach to migration management.

- To be successful, return interventions must not be a policy afterthought. Return interventions begin at the point of entry through the provision of timely and accurate information about options and consequences, not when weeks or months later a decision on return is eventually taken.

- Counselling by authoritative and credible interlocutors can create an appropriate context for return decisions.

- Protection of the dignity and integrity of the individual is essential.

- Both mandatory and voluntary programmes have their place in a properly designed approach to return, although there is a real challenge in ensuring that they are complementary and mutually supportive.

- Return programmes are best developed in partnership between countries of origin and destination. A prerequisite to this is the establishment of effective communication lines between the two parties, and the creation of mutual confidence.

- Carefully designed reintegration programmes that take account, where appropriate, of the needs of local residents as well as of returnees can contribute significantly to the sustainability of return.

- The range of available options is practically unlimited, ranging from preparation for return to return visits, on-the-job training, setting up of small businesses and community development activities.

Among the most successful return programmes are those that operate on a small scale and are tailored to the particular circumstances of particular returnees and countries of origin.

Source: Nicoletta Giordano, Former Head, Return Migration Management, IOM.

6.6 Regularizations

Beginning in the 1980s, regularizations have become a frequent means of addressing the presence of a large number of irregular migrants, especially those with a stable record of employment and other claims to local integration, for whom any other outcome would be politically or socially unacceptable or too difficult to implement. There are wide differences in both terminology and actual administrative measures: amnesties, regularizations, and registration have all been decreed from time to time (Levinson, 2005). In southern Europe, since the early 1990s, regularization campaigns have been conducted more often than anywhere else in the world (three in Greece, three in Portugal, four in Italy, five in Spain, involving more than three million migrants in total), to the point of being a major instrument of migration management. The last regularizations by Spain and Italy were directed only at migrants in employment with applications submitted on their behalf by their respective employers. While regularizations may represent a highly favourable outcome for irregular migrants (particularly if they do not fall back into irregular status) who can thus accede to legitimate employment and services, they are also criticized for creating the perception that irregular entry and stay is a calculated risk, and one worth taking as it pays off eventually. This reasoning explains the policy stance of countries, such as Germany, which have remained steadily opposed to the idea of regularization programmes.[32]

---

[32] But see the decision of the German Länder in November 2006 to legalize the situation of migrants with the precarious temporary *Duldung* status (referred to in Chapter 11), which may represent a turning point in the traditional line taken on regularization in Germany.

In the Gulf Cooperation Council (GCC) States and Southeast and East Asia, irregular migrants are not regularized as permanent residents. Rather, they are invited to register for the right to reside and work on a temporary basis (see Sections 5.7 and 5.8 above and Map 7b). The frequency of registrations is even higher than that of regularizations, indicating that this policy is not necessarily more effective in discouraging irregular migration.

In the U.S. there has been a vigorous ongoing debate about the policies that should be introduced to address the problem of the estimated 11 to 12 million irregular migrants present in the country. Since 2004, the government has tried repeatedly to put into place a plan to address the issue of undocumented workers within the context of a comprehensive temporary worker programme that would be accessible to both irregular migrants within the U.S. and applicants from abroad. The issue remains unresolved (Levinson, 2005).

7. Conclusion

Irregular migration is undoubtedly one of the most complex, sensitive and intractable migration management problems confronting the international community. Most of the responses to the problem have been and continue to be implemented essentially at the national level, but there is a clearly discernible evolution towards the development of cooperative approaches on either a bilateral or multilateral basis (for example, see Textbox 8.6).

One form of cooperation has focused increasingly on measures of control between countries of destination and transit. Such cooperation typically covers joint interdiction operations and capacity building – including the training of personnel and procurement of equipment. One unintended consequence of this approach is that irregular migrants become more inclined to seek to gain access to informal economies and settle in the country of transit (Collyer, 2006), thus giving rise in the medium to longer term to problems of social exclusion and petty criminality.

Another avenue of cooperation leads to migration and development initiatives, to lower the costs of remittance transfers, create savings schemes for migrants, apply the remittances to sustainable development enterprises and to mobilize the resources of diasporas.

In parallel with this, there is good reason to be optimistic about the part that managed labour migration programmes can play. While there is no evidence that labour migration programmes spell the end of irregular flows, they do offer an important, more manageable and more predictable alternative. And crucially, they provide better protection for the rights and dignity of migrants, which is what all policies should aim to do.

Textbox 8.6

Cooperation on Preventing Unauthorized Employment of Migrant Workers with a view to Promoting Regular Employment

In 2006, IOM Helsinki carried out a project called "Cooperation on preventing illegal employment of labour migrants with a view to promoting legal employment opportunities" (PIELAMI), involving partners from Finland, Latvia and North-West Russia. The project was funded under the European Commission's ARGO programme,[1] with co-funding from the Finnish Ministry of Labour, and largely focused on the service and construction sectors.

The impetus for the project came from IOM Helsinki's interest in exploring the interplay between unauthorized employment of migrant workers and labour market demand.

The project involved three main activities:

1. The drafting of working papers on the scope of unauthorized employment as well as regular employment opportunities for third-country nationals in Finland, Latvia and North-West Russia.[2]

2. A seminar in Helsinki in November 2006 attended by representatives from the Baltic Sea states.

3. A project report including the material and findings of the project (available from http://iom.fi/content/view/159/8/).

The working papers concluded that it was not possible to either generalize or simplify the causes or, indeed, the outcomes of unauthorized employment of migrant workers, as they reflected the very different migration contexts and labour market conditions of each country. Furthermore, different countries use different methods to combat unauthorized employment, often with little coordination between relevant authorities such as the police, tax authorities and migration officials. Officials who participated in the PIELAMI seminar pointed to the need for intensified administrative cooperation and exchange of information not only on methods to prevent unauthorized employment of migrant workers, but also to promote lawful employment opportunities.

Based on the papers and seminar discussions as a source of inspiration, IOM formulated a number of recommendations on the subject, which focused on the questions at issue from various angles. Some of the key recommendations are listed below:

• The encouragement of cooperative action among all stakeholders, including employers' associations and unions.

• Wide dissemination of information about employment opportunities and working conditions abroad.

- The creation of regular channels to enable workers to obtain access to the labour market in countries of destination.

- The protection of the rights of migrant workers, including through the signing and ratifying of relevant international conventions, the setting of minimum wages and the provision of access to justice and health care systems.

- The adoption of measures to combat intolerance, discrimination and xenophobia to facilitate the integration of migrant workers in host societies.

Notes:

[1] Action programme for administrative cooperation in the fields of external borders, visas, asylum and immigration (2002-2006).

[2] For North-West Russia, the term "foreign national" was used because in Finland and Latvia "third-country national" refers to a citizen from outside the European Economic Area (EEA).

Source: IOM Helsinki.

PART B

MANAGING LABOUR MOBILITY IN THE EVOLVING GLOBAL ECONOMY

ENHANCING THE
KNOWLEDGE BASE*

CHAPTER 9

1. Introduction

Migration management is a sensitive public policy domain where every policy proposal is the subject of close scrutiny by political parties, the media, interest groups and the community at large. Migration is increasingly recognized by countries of origin and destination as having the potential to provide appropriate solutions to problems of labour supply and demand, but public opinion is sharply divided over this issue. Some may see migration as the answer to demographic problems, such as low birth rates, population ageing and contracting labour forces. Others view migrants as competing for scarce resources. Policymakers therefore confront various challenges as they seek to develop balanced and effective migration policies. They are conscious of the risks they incur in generating unintended dynamics that can be detrimental to the labour market in particular, and economic growth in general (Boswell et al., 2004).

Governments considering the introduction of labour migration programmes as a means of addressing

labour market concerns need to base their decisions on reliable information and migration data.

This chapter discusses the ways in which governments can and do enhance their knowledge base and their capacity to devise timely and effective labour migration policies. As discussed in greater detail in Chapter 11, the governments of destination countries often rely on the available knowledge base in the labour market provided by, for example, employers and trade unions, to formulate, implement and evaluate their labour migration policies. Governments may, however, also develop their own knowledge base by collecting and analysing appropriate data and sponsoring/conducting their own research on migration, including labour migration. This chapter deals primarily with the knowledge base at the disposal of governments and the means to enhance it. Since labour migration is an integral part of international migration, some of the initiatives discussed in this chapter are of relevance to the management of international migration in general, but the main focus is on labour migration. Three areas of activities are emphasized.

The first addresses the nature and quality of existing data collection mechanisms. Official government statistics may suffer from a lack of reliability and

---

* This chapter was written by Jobst Köhler, Research Officer (Statistics and Survey Analyst), IOM, Geneva. The author would like to thank Christine Aghazarm for her research assistance and Marina Peunova for her comments.

comparability, in part owing to different definitions used, concepts of measurement and data collecting methods. Governments and international bodies are therefore looking for ways and means to improve the reliability and comparability of their official data.

Second, governments sometimes need to adjust their statistical systems in order to respond to new labour migration challenges for which only limited or no data are available. The chapter discusses different strategies and initiatives to collect data on emerging or rapidly evolving policy issues such as transnational communities or diasporas, circular migration, remittances, highly skilled migration, irregular migration and the impacts or outcomes of various migration programmes.

Lastly, a range of measures exists to improve the availability and policy relevance of data and information on migration. Though many and diverse sources are engaged in the collection and generation of migration data, such sources are not necessarily always known to policymakers, or may not be perceived to be of relevance to their decision-making processes or, indeed, such data as exist may not always reach or be available to them. The chapter discusses different approaches and mechanisms to make data more widely accessible and policy-relevant.

2. Enhancing the Knowledge Base on Labour Migration: A Comprehensive Approach to Data Collection

The collection of pertinent data is fundamental to appropriate and timely policymaking. As in other policy areas, data collection systems in the field of migration, especially concerning labour migration, face the challenge of having to serve and reconcile different, and at times conflicting, information needs at various levels of government.

Thus, to formulate and enact legal and policy frameworks, the legislative and executive branches of governments require reliable aggregate and analytical information from which to draw the necessary insights and understandings concerning the different trends and impacts of migration in various areas of interest to the public domain.

In the middle, there are those officials who run the agency offices that deal directly with migrants, in either service or law enforcement roles; they are largely involved in the effective day-to-day management of services offered and activities performed. At this level, the need is also for aggregated information, but of a somewhat different nature. Generally limited in detail or characteristics, the data consist of summaries – of the number of clients processed at a particular time or similar measures used to measure productivity and outcomes of a particular programme.

Finally, the various categories of staff involved in frequent and individual contact with migrants, such as case workers, require detailed and individual information and access to records of migrants to be in a position to align and conduct their programmes and activities in accordance with the particular characteristics, experiences and needs of individual or groups of individual migrants on a predominantly personal and individual basis (Pember and Djerma, 2005).

Although policymakers, programme managers and case workers have different interests in the data collected, they typically have to rely on the same data collection system. In fact, much of the data used for policy or programme management purposes and/or on which expert reports may be based, are initially generated by the programme staff who often have little stake in, or understanding of, how the aggregate records of their individual transactions are used by agency heads and policymakers. In order to generate accurate and timely data on labour migration for policy purposes, a data collection system needs to recognize the different information needs at the various levels of government and find ways to balance them.

3. Improving the Reliability of Existing Data Sources

The compilation of statistics on international migration, including labour migration will also depend on how "international migration" is defined. There are no universally agreed definitions. Although there are international recommendations on "international migration statistics", differing national definitions still persist, especially regarding subsets of international migration such as labour migration (UN DESA, 1998). Indeed, varying definitions and the methods used to assess labour migration can lead to very different results. The broadest definition includes all international migrants who are currently in the labour force (both employed and unemployed, regular and irregular) as migrant workers. A more restrictive definition counts as migrant workers only those who entered a country for the explicit purpose of employment.

Compared to data on demographic variables, such as fertility and mortality, international migration data are inherently difficult to obtain. For instance, while birth and death occur only once in an individual's life cycle, migration may occur repeatedly, and it is at times hard to determine with precision when it begins and when it ends. Furthermore, many official sources for migration data are frequently intended to achieve particular administrative objectives rather than to yield reliable measurements of migrant stocks and flows. For that reason, statistics compiled from such sources may often be unsatisfactory in terms of coverage and accuracy.

3.1 Main Data Sources and Their Limitations

To obtain quantitative information about migration, including labour migration, multiple sources are typically used to measure flows and stocks.

(a) Administrative records

Official international migration statistics are often a by-product of administrative processes and record-keeping related to the activities of institutions and agencies dealing with various aspects of migration or migration-related areas, such as, for instance, population management. Each country has its own data collection methods and traditions. This is one of the main reasons why the sources from which official statistics on international migration are compiled tend to differ from country to country.

A number of European countries (e.g. Austria, Estonia, Lithuania, the Netherlands) have comprehensive **population registers** and/or **registers of foreigners**, which are accounts of persons residing lawfully in a country. These registers can be used to measure the total stocks of international migrants in a country, as well as inflows when new migrants are recorded (usually after one year in the case of population registers) and outflows when people de-register and leave the country (Hoffmann, 1995; IOM/OSCE/ILO, 2006, 2007).[1]

Countries that do not have a population register often use **residence and work permits** to measure migration flows. These administrative sources generated from operations designed to regulate international migration are particularly suitable to produce information about specific subsets of international migrants. Records covering the grant of residence and work permits, for example, are popular sources for the measurement of labour migration statistics (IOM/OSCE/ILO, 2006, 2007).

Data on visa issuance are another administrative source that allows greater disaggregation of migration flows into specific subsets of international migrants. Such data are typically collected at the point of issue (usually an embassy or consulate) and allow

---

[1]   A problem with emigration statistics from registries, however, may occur when people leave the country and fail to de-register.

the foreign-born population for each OECD country by educational attainment. The World Bank has developed a similar database with greater coverage of countries and drawing on a wider range of data sources. The World Bank has also conducted a series of econometric studies on the impact of highly skilled migration on the economy of the country of origin (World Bank, 2006; Özden and Schiff, 2005).

These databases rely on statistics collected by host countries of highly skilled migrants. Few attempts have been made to assess the actual or potential level of highly skilled emigration from countries of origin. Although they are often the most affected in social or economic terms by the emigration of their highly skilled nationals, developing countries lack the resources to set up appropriate data collection mechanisms. Most initiatives in this field remain based on specialized surveys conducted by academic research institutions, such as the Potential Skills Base Survey of the Southern African Migration Project (SAMP), to assess the propensity to emigrate of final-year students at training institutions across the region. It is nonetheless encouraging to note that many developing countries are now calling for more importance to be accorded to the collection of reliable data on highly skilled emigration, as illustrated by the recent decision of the National Statistics Offices in India and Sri Lanka to identify the development of improved tools for the measurement of highly skilled migration as a priority for future work (Castro, 2006; Gunasekera, 2006).

4.4 Remittances

In recent years, remittances have received increased attention because of their visible and positive impacts on the economies of countries of origin. Relevant data for measuring remittances are collated by the International Monetary Fund (IMF) from national data compiled and reported by appropriate statistical authorities in IMF member countries, and reported as part of the IMF's Global Balance of Payments (BOP) statistics (Bilsborrow, 1997).

Useful as they are, however, official remittance data derived from BOP suffer from certain limitations. These include the inability of banks to distinguish between short and long-term migrants; lack of information about "informal" (e.g. hand-carried) or "in kind" remittances; the exclusion of transactions made at money transfer centres (which comprise a large percentage of remittances); the inability to identify flows (i.e. the origin and destination of remittances); and different recording and reporting practices of BOP across and even within countries over time (UN DESA, 2005; Schachter, 2006).

Detailed data on remittances are usually obtained from surveys. When they are conducted, nationally representative household surveys of income usually include questions on remittances, although they are not always identified separately. Specialized surveys on remittances and migration are also conducted on an ad hoc basis, for example to study remittance "corridors" and sending and receiving practices. There are also a number of surveys sponsored by the World Bank that include questions on migrant remittances, such as Living Standard Measurement Surveys (LSMS). The LSMS multi-topic questionnaires are designed to study multiple aspects of household welfare and behaviour, including remittances, and have been used for remittance corridor studies. IOM has also developed specialized surveys to explore the relationship between migration patterns and remittances (IOM, 2005, 2006; Petree and Baruah, 2007). Rather than conducting specialized surveys, ILO has developed a project that uses standard labour force surveys to measure remittances on the assumption that adding a migration module to pre-existing surveys reduces costs while ensuring a large sample size (Schachter, 2006).

4.5 Irregular Migration

As measures to prevent or reduce irregular employment and migration gain increasing prominence, reliable information on the size, structure and dynamics of irregular migration becomes more important. By its very definition, irregular migration is difficult to capture statistically as it concerns (mainly) undocumented and covert events. There are no official statistics on irregular migration. Statements about the magnitude of this phenomenon tend to draw on statistics of observed events that are usually collected for law enforcement purposes (e.g. by the police and border guards). Given the sensitivity surrounding this type of information, such data are rarely shared and generally not released for public use.

An exception is the data flowing from the Centre for Information, Discussion and Exchange on the Crossing of Frontiers and Immigration (CIREFI) developed by the European Commission and Eurostat. CIREFI is the only available Europe-wide source of data on law enforcement measures taken in the field of irregular migration. Three types of published data from the CIREFI database are linked to irregular migration: refusal of entry, apprehension of non-citizens present without authorization and foreigners removed.

Different assessments of the data show that all three types are inadequate to capture the various levels and trends in irregular migration. For example, the data on apprehensions submitted to CIREFI's database by EU Member States may not distinguish between stocks and flows, while data on refusal of entry often do not distinguish between the reasons for such refusals. Similarly, the data on removals do not specify the type and category of removals in question. The EU Regulation to govern national statistics, referred to earlier in Section 3.2(b)(i), may present an opportunity to improve the quality of the CIREFI data (Poulain and Singleton, 2006).

Another rich source of data on irregular migration is the annual survey and analysis of border management and border apprehensions carried out by the International Centre for Migration Policy Development (ICMPD) in central and eastern Europe. Besides data on border apprehensions, removal of non-citizens and refusal of entry, the survey yields data on the demographic breakdown of irregular migrants and information on their particular routes. ICMPD, the European Police Office (EUROPOL) and FRONTEX, the European agency for coordination of cooperation between EU Member States in the field of border management, have also sought to improve the data exchange and information on irregular migration from the Mediterranean basin and Africa to Europe by developing a map on African and Mediterranean Irregular Migration Routes[5] in the framework of the ongoing Dialogue on Mediterranean Transit Migration (MTM).

A more reliable official source of data on irregular migration can be derived from regularization exercises, if and when they occur (see Chapters 8 and 11). Regularization data can provide an estimate of the stock of irregular migrants, although not all irregular migrants may decide to seek or be eligible for regularization. Explanatory notes on the specific conditions of regularization programmes are, therefore, important to interpret the estimate of irregular migrants derived from regularization figures (Jandl and Kraler, 2006).

There are also databases that contain data on special categories of irregular migrants, such as trafficked persons. One such database, the Global Human Trafficking Database (see Textbox 8.2), has been developed by IOM to gather data from the counter-trafficking programmes it conducts. A unique feature of this database is that the information is collected directly from the victims of trafficking and therefore

---

5   For this map, see the FRONTEX web site at http://www.frontex.eu.int/gfx/frontex/files/mtmmapen.pdf.

6. Conclusion

As labour migration becomes more prevalent at the global level, the demand for reliable and comparable statistics on migration for employment becomes more insistent. The changing nature of current labour mobility makes the task of harmonizing statistics on international migration more complex. As new categories of labour migration flows are emerging, their origins and destinations also diversify. How these particular challenges are addressed will depend partly on the development of new concepts of measurement and data collection techniques, but also on improved quality of the administrative data collected for different labour migration programmes.

It is commonly recognized that governments require an appropriate knowledge base to effectively manage migration. It is also acknowledged that this is particularly so in the area of labour migration. Three types of initiatives to enhance the national knowledge base were discussed in this chapter, concerning: (i) the improvement of the reliability and comparability of existing data sources; (ii) the gathering of new data on emerging issues, especially regarding labour migration; and (iii) the dissemination and utilization of data and research on labour migration.

The chapter has also emphasized the importance of recognizing and catering to different data needs at the policy, programme and case management level. Success in this endeavour will depend on the development of a comprehensive approach to the collection, analysis and dissemination of data through the mobilization and coordination of all national bodies and instrumentalities involved, both generally in international migration management and specifically in the management of labour flows.

However, to be fully productive and meaningful, these national efforts need to be complemented by broader regional and global endeavours with the support of appropriate international bodies to promote the adoption of a new culture of measurement, record keeping and exchange of information in this field.

REFERENCES

Aalandslid, V.

2006   "Using Register Data to Monitor the Immigration and Emigration of Immigrants", presentation prepared for the UN Expert Group Meeting on Measuring international migration: Concepts and methods, 4-7 December, UN, New York, http://unstats.un.org/unsd/demographic/meetings/egm/migrationegm06/DOC%207%20Norway.ppt.

Asia Pacific Migration Research Network (APMRN)

2002   "Migration Research and Policy Landscape: Case studies of Australia, the Philippines and Thailand", APMRN Working Paper No. 9, Migration and Multicultural Program, Centre for Asia Pacific Social Transformation Studies, University of Wollongong, Australia, http://www.unesco.org/most/apmrpap9.htm.

Australian Bureau of Statistics (ABS)

2006   "Country Paper: International Migration Statistics in Australia", paper prepared for the Expert Group Meeting on the United Nations Economic and Social Commission for Asia and the Pacific (UN ESCAP) Regional Census Programme, 27-28 November, Bangkok, http://www.unescap.org/stat/meet/egm2006/ses.4_Australia_1.pdf.

Bilsborrow, R.E., G. Hugo, A.S. Oberai and H. Zlotnik

1997   *International Migration Statistics: Guidelines for Improving Data Collection Systems*, International Labour Office, Geneva.

Boswell, C., S. Stiller and T. Straubhaar

2004   "Forecasting Labour and Skills Shortages: How can Projections Better Inform Labour Migration Policies?", Migration Research Group, Hamburg Institute of International Economics, July, paper prepared for the European Commission, DG Employment and Social Affairs, http://ec.europa.eu/employment_social/employment_analysis/docs/forecast_short3.pdf.

Castro, L.V.

2006   "Measuring international migration in the Philippines", paper prepared for the UN Expert Group Meeting on Measuring international migration: Concepts and methods (Doc. ESA/STAT/AC.119/18), 4-7 December, UN, New York, http://unstats.un.org/UNSD/demographic/meetings/egm/migrationegm06/DOC%2018%20Philippines.pdf.

Corr, P., A. Hakim and J. Farrow

2005   "Measuring International Migration with Traveller-completed Passenger Cards: The Conceptual, Administrative and Statistical Challenges Experienced by Australia", paper prepared for the XXV International Union for the Scientific Study of Population (IUSSP) International Population Conference, 18-23 July, Tours, France.

Costello, A. and Z. Alimuddin

2000   "Moving to research partnerships in developing countries", *British Medical Journal*, 321, 30 September: 827-829.

Diallo, K.

2004   "Data on the migration of health-care workers: sources, uses and challenges", *Bulletin of the World Health Organization*, 82(8) (August): 601-607, http://www.scielosp.org/pdf/bwho/v82n8/v82n8a10.pdf.

Diallo, K., P. Zurn, N. Gupta and M. Dal Poz

2003   "Monitoring and evaluation of human resources for health: an international perspective", *Human Resources for Health*, 1(3), http://www.human-resources-health.com/content/1/1/3.

Dumont, J.-C. and G. Lemaître

2004   "Counting Immigrants and Expatriates in OECD Countries: A New Perspective", Directorate for Employment Labour and Social Affairs, OECD, Paris, http://www.oecd.org/dataoecd/27/5/33868740.pdf.

EUROPA

2007   "The European Union improves the framework for the collection of migration and asylum statistics", Press Release IP/07/804, 12 June, Brussels, http://europa.eu/rapid/pressReleasesAction.do?reference=IP/07/804

Folden, C., M. Manke and T. Mortensen

2007   *Sharing Data - Where to Start: An Emerging Approach to Migration Data Management*, Technical Cooperation Centre, IOM, Vienna, http://www.iom.int/jahia/Jahia/cache/offonce/pid/1674?entryId=15669

Textbox 10.1

HRD Planning and Maximizing Economic Gains from Labour Migration

What may be the objective of HRD planning for the whole education labour market (ELM) market, including foreign employment, albeit of selective skills? In theory, the government would wish to maximize the social returns to investment in human capital of the population as a whole. There are private (both economic and non-economic) and social returns to the investment. Most visible are the private returns that consist of monetary and non-monetary gains from the investment. There is enjoyment to be gained from the possession of knowledge, and there are benefits to be derived from the ability it offers for making life choices and to further develop the knowledge acquired. The calculations below focus on the more tangible monetary gains, i.e. the incremental income gain minus the cost of investing in a category of human capital formation, for instance nursing education. Theoretically, it is possible to think of maximizing private returns to individuals pursuing the best investment options/skills. The returns to a skill i relative to skill j are estimated as follows.

Returns to a skill i is estimated as:

$$R_{i,t} = \sum_{t=D}^{T} D_t W_{i,t} - C_i - \left(\sum D_t W_j - C_j \right)$$

Where: R = returns to investment in skill formation
   W = nominal wage rate
   C = cost of investment
   D = discount rate $1/(1+r)^t$
   r = interest rate (cost)
   i, j = skill categories
   t = time period in years

Note the returns to investment in skill i takes account of its opportunity cost, or returns to investment in alternative skill j. Skill i is preferred to skill j if its (net) return R is positive. Another way of assessing skills is to array the skills according to their own returns:

$$\left(\sum_{t=0}^{T} D_{t_r} W_t - C_t \right)$$

It is assumed that the skills with the higher returns will attract more workers or labour units. In the short term, labour supply would originate from the current stock of available workers with the required skill. In the long term, the increased supply would come from the existing stock of workers with the skill and from new entrants, i.e. the students who would pursue the skill and those workers who might switch from other skills by retraining. In the equation, the reservation wage is the total cost of investing in skill i, comprising the cost of investment in that skill and the opportunity cost in forgoing skill j, or

$$\left(C_i + \sum_{t=0}^{T} D_t W_j - C_j \right)$$

When there is migration, the return takes account of the foreign wage and the probability of finding a job abroad. Return to a skill is estimated as follows:

$$R_i = \left\{ P_d \sum_{t=0}^{T} D_t W_{i,d,t} + P_f \sum_{t=0}^{T} D_t W_{i,d,t} \right\} - C_i - \left\{ P_d \sum_{t=0}^{T} D_t W_{j,d,t} + P_f \sum_{t=0}^{T} D_t W_{j,d,t} - C_j \right\}$$

The gross returns are averages of expected domestic and foreign wages. Gross returns to a skill rise as the probability of obtaining a foreign job, P_f, rises, given that foreign wage rates are significantly higher than the domestic wage rate.

It is possible to view an efficient ELM as one where information about demand for various skill categories and their specific job qualifications exists and where persons can acquire skills without significant financial constraints. Foreign job openings are taken for skill i. These jobs pay much more than the domestic wage. Consequently, the youth and some workers already in the labour force will be drawn to invest in skill i. The supply in other skills will fall and raise their wage rate. Skill i will continue to attract people until its return equalizes the returns to the other skills. This adjustment leads to maximum private returns on the investment. An efficient market needs no government intervention. However, if the ELM is inefficient because information about demand, the required job qualifications and where to obtain the skill is unavailable, or if the youth are prevented by poverty from acquiring the skill, there will be supply rigidity.

Market imperfections are known to be serious in the ELM. There are millions of youth preparing for entry into the labour market and millions of employers in the domestic and foreign labour markets. Information is generally poor and unevenly distributed; it is usually concentrated among the more educated in the cities. Financial resources for education are notoriously lacking for the great majority of families who may wish to invest in their children's education/training. Additionally, there are some highly skilled professionals, such as research scientists, innovative business executives, historians or creative artists, whose outputs are in the nature of public goods or have large positive social impacts or externalities. Governments would be well advised to invest in their education/training in order to increase the number of persons pursuing them. Producing and disseminating information on employment opportunities, required job qualifications and where to acquire the necessary skills is essential so that members of the labour force, and young people especially, can make optimal choices. HRD planners should also identify where financial constraints on education or training choices arise. Which are the employment categories with significant positive externalities or that are public goods by nature and hence require government subsidies? What subsidy strategy ought to be developed to address critical financial constraints? The task is so daunting in scale and complexity that, in many cases, governments tend to be very selective when choosing areas of

intervention. The U.S. Government, for instance, poured resources in science education and research in response to the Soviet launch of Sputnik in the 1950s. The Kennedy administration established the Equal Opportunity Program to mitigate inequality of access to higher education. In a similar way, scholarship programmes have been instituted by many governments to address the inequality problem and/or to increase enrolment numbers and research in science and technology (S&T) so as to promote technological progress.

2.2 Defining Requirements (Quantity and Quality)

To define requirements at the national level, both a profile of current human resources and a forecast of future requirements are necessary, as well as reliable and up-to-date information about employment opportunities and skill requirements in relation to both the domestic and foreign labour markets. Although international demand for major skills categories, such as engineering, computer science, natural science, management and finance, education and medicine is high, detailed information, for instance, on the specific skills and levels of competence required is lacking. Such information is necessary to allow for realistic and timely national HRD policy planning and implementation, as well as to guide and support individuals in their choices regarding education, work and migration.

2.3 Quality Standards and Indicators

Quality standards used by foreign employers evolve through different means. Through observed performance of their workforce, foreign employers arrive at standards by which to gauge the competence of applicants from countries of origin and use these yardsticks to identify reliable sources of qualified professionals. As a result, universities and colleges acquire a reputation based on employers' experience with their graduates, consultations with other employers and academic ratings based on periodic assessments through independent evaluators of higher education. ICT companies in the U.S. and Europe, for instance, compete for graduates from the highly acclaimed Indian Institutes of Technology. Similarly, hospitals in other countries recognize the licensure examinations administered by the Philippine Professional Regulatory Commission. The Japan-Philippines Economic Partnership Agreement[3] provides for the employment of Filipino nurses on condition that they undergo two to three years' language and practical training in Japan before being recognized as professional nurses. The adoption in 1984 of the International Standard for Training, Certification and Watchkeeping of Seafarers has contributed greatly to the establishment of high quality standards of education/training for Filipino seafarers and to their recognition by international shipping companies.

For blue-collar occupations, the quality of experience is critical. The recently completed survey of placement agencies in the Philippines for the IOM by one of the authors (Tan, 2007) demonstrates that experience in operating modern equipment is essential for tool and die makers, welders, pipe setters, heavy equipment operators and other construction workers. However, the country's industrial base has only a limited capacity to produce experienced workers with these

skills, as the pool of heavy equipment and machinery operators is too small and only a few workers are able to become proficient at operating them. Less stringent qualifications may be required of other blue-collar workers, especially when employers are willing to provide the necessary training, as in the case of household workers. The Government of the Philippines has undertaken skill certification – accepted in most countries of destination – based on occupational tests for low-skill categories such as household employment, popular entertainment, hotel and restaurant services, and general welding. However, this initiative does not yet amount to a fully developed strategy for the training of skilled blue-collar workers.

As yet, no information system has been developed in countries of origin concerning the prospective demand for specific skill categories and the qualifications they call for and there is no known programme for collecting this information on a systematic and continuous basis and relaying it to the public and to education/training institutions in order to adjust their course offerings to coincide with world market requirements. It is difficult for potential migrants to obtain information about specific job opportunities and required levels of proficiency. Any available information on the qualifications required by foreign employers is generally disseminated by recruitment agencies to job applicants, and by job applicants to their friends and relatives. The reach of such informal channels is necessarily limited. Most, if not all, overseas employment initiatives of countries of origin have been concerned mainly with the protection of workers in their workplace and the fight against fraudulent recruitment agencies. They have not yet taken on the responsibility of guiding would-be migrants to acquire the skills and competencies that would maximize the returns on their investment in training and migration. The next section considers whether the education/training system can be relied upon to produce these skills.

---

[3]   The text of this agreement is available from the website of the Ministry of Foreign Affairs of Japan at http://www.mofa.go.jp/region/asia-paci/philippine/epa0609/.

2.4 The Education/Training System

The quality of formal education, especially at university/college level, is a serious issue in most developing countries. For example, only a small proportion of the numerous universities and institutions in South and Southeast Asia are of world standard. Asian countries have established large numbers of higher educational institutions. India has 10,403; China 4,102; Bangladesh 2,711; Indonesia 1,891; the Philippines 1,314; Pakistan 1,108; and Thailand 750 (Tan, 2006). Sri Lanka is the only country to have strictly limited the number of its universities or institutes, currently at 13. Each country also maintains a small number of prestigious universities and colleges. Graduates from the good universities account for only a small fraction of individuals with tertiary education. Many of the professionals who qualify for highly skilled jobs in destination countries are likely to have graduated from the elite institutions. The Indian ICT specialists in the U.S. are most likely to have graduated from the Indian Institutes of Technology and other well-known Indian schools (Murali, 2003). In the Philippines, placement agencies actively recruit nurses for American hospitals from reputable nursing schools, such as the Medical College of the University of the Philippines (Tan, 2006).

Two sources of data serve to indicate the scarcity of high-quality higher educational institutions: the McKinsey study, *The Emerging Global Labor Market* (2005), and the *Asiaweek* Rating of the best universities and Science and Technology Institutes in the Asia-Pacific region in 2000. The McKinsey study looked into demand and supply of high-level human resources by conducting a survey of transnational corporations (TNCs) from Australia, Canada, Ireland, Republic of Korea (South Korea), the U.K. and the U.S., to "quantify the supply of talent in 28 low-wage countries (including China, India, Malaysia and the Philippines) and eight mid and high-wage ones". The study points to the very large number of young university-educated persons in low-wage countries, but states that the surveyed TNCs found that only a fraction qualified for employment in professional jobs in their firms. Of Philippine graduates, only 20 per cent qualified in engineering, 30 per cent in finance/accounting and 25 per cent in general occupations. The corresponding figures for Indian graduates are 25 per cent, 15 and ten per cent. The respective shares for Chinese graduates are even lower – ten, 15 per cent and three per cent. Ratings for Malaysia are similar to those of the Philippines. The Asian sample countries have higher proportions of qualified graduates than the other low-wage sample countries. The differences in ratings between India and the Philippines in engineering and finance/accounting reflect the relative strength of India's science and technology institutes and the accounting schools in the Philippines.

When *Asiaweek* magazine undertook to assess the "best" multi-disciplinary universities and Science and Technology (S&T) centres in the Asia-Pacific region in 1999 and 2000, it focused on a small but representative sample of the region's more than 20,000 institutions. The institutions were rated according to several criteria: academic reputation, student selectivity, faculty reputation, research, financial resources, student/academic staff ratio, citations in international journals and internet bandwidth per student. The schools were ranked from the highest to the lowest according to the scores obtained overall. Among the 77 participating universities, five were in Thailand, four in China, four in the Philippines, four in Indonesia and two in India; all ranked below the median. Pakistan did not rate in the multi-disciplinary group of universities, but three of its science and technology institutes ranked, respectively, 20th, 23rd and 32nd. Three institutions in China participated in the science and technology rating and eight in India, all above the median ranking. According to the *Asiaweek* survey, the institutions with the highest ranking in the Asia-Pacific region were all located in the advanced economies – Australia, Hong Kong SAR, Japan, New Zealand, Singapore and Taiwan Province of China.

2.5 Experience as an Important Source of Training

On-the-job training is the most common form of training for most skilled workers in either the highly skilled or blue-collar category. While medical doctors and nurses have to complete their respective degree programmes and pass their respective licensure examinations, the quality of their experience matters as a gauge of their competence. The capacity to produce high-quality experience depends to a large extent on the size of the economic sector and the technology it uses. The more advanced and industrialized an economy, the larger the workforce with experience in high-tech skills. Consequently, a well-developed sector is required in this field to be able to produce a large number of high-tech experienced workers. Nurses and doctors need to be familiar with state of the art medical interventions. Engineers must work in industries that use modern machinery and equipment, as too must electricians, welders, pipe-setters and metal workers. The less developed countries of origin of the Asia-Pacific region face the challenge of a high demand for such workers while having only a small industrial base to train workers in modern and high-tech skills. There is said to be a large demand for a variety of aviation skills, but countries with a relatively small airline industry will not have the capacity to produce large numbers of specialists in this field. Similarly, most countries in the region have no petrochemical industry and their universities and technical institutes do not produce engineers and technicians in this field; neither do they produce design engineers when their firms are generally of small size. Faced with these industrial realities, what HRD strategy can the region adopt? Formal education and training could provide workers with technical knowledge that would pave the way for on-the-job training. But such formal courses need to be carefully identified and

developed. Another option is for foreign recruitment companies to establish training institutions in countries of origin to meet their employment needs. Several such institutions now operate in countries like the Philippines. Placement agencies for U.S. nurses provide instruction to nurses applying for U.S. visas to improve their chances of passing the U.S. nursing examinations (National Council for Graduates of Foreign Schools and the National Council for Licensure Examination). It is informally reported in the Philippines that U.S. hospitals face such a shortage of nurses that they are willing to pay recruitment agents USD 10,000 to USD 12,000 per nurse placed.[4]

2.6 Role of the Private Sector

Wherever there is the opportunity, the private sector will respond to demand for education, as indeed demonstrated in several Asian countries. Private colleges and universities have assumed a relatively large responsibility in higher education in Indonesia, Japan, the Philippines and South Korea. Thailand has begun to authorize private institutions to offer tertiary education. The participation of private schools naturally increases access to education. However, the challenge is to ensure quality. Moreover, as discussed in Chapter 4, the Asia-Pacific region is also a popular testing ground for the adoption by foreign universities of contractual arrangements with private or public institutions in the form of franchises or twinning programmes with the objective of offering their academic courses to local students.

2.7 Emigration of Skilled Human Resources

Skilled migration is a controversial issue (see also Chapter 2). From one perspective, the movement of highly skilled workers may be seen as equally benefiting developed and developing countries by reducing the supply-demand mismatch in the former

---

[4] Information obtained from interviews with recruitment agencies in the preparation of Tan (2007).

and reallocating unused human resources from the latter. Seen from a different perspective, however, this movement is seen as detrimental to both by creating an unhelpful reliance on the "import" of talent from abroad (as opposed to the development of home-grown skills) in developed countries, and by depriving developing countries of their scarce professional and technical resources. There is also an ethical dimension to be considered, as the poorer countries of origin bear the cost of educating their nationals and potential migrants (including through private funding of students), while the countries of destination reap the benefits.

Clearly, when there is a skills shortage or when skills are difficult to replace, the cost is high for the country of origin. This is the case in much of Africa as well as in the Caribbean. Two-thirds of Jamaica's nurses emigrated over the period 1980-2000 and only few return (Lowell and Findlay, 2001). According to Docquier and Bhargava (2006), Grenada and Dominica have lost more than 90 per cent of their physicians, while the small island nations of Saint Lucia and Cape Verde have lost more than 50 per cent (Ratha and Xu, 2008). The problem has not been as acute in other parts of the world, but it exists nonetheless. The shortage of high-quality professionals and high-tech experienced blue-collar workers can be symptomatic of brain or skill drain. The number of nurses leaving the Philippines has exceeded the number of those who pass the licensure examination over the past five years. Foreign employers usually select nurses who already have experience, leaving hospitals and clinics with new graduates or those who may not have passed the licensure examination (Tan, 2007).

The following steps can be taken to mitigate the adverse impact of brain drain, although they should not prevent migrants from exercising the right to leave their country:

- promotion of ethical recruitment to prevent indiscriminate international recruitment in sensitive sectors such as health, particularly in

small and fragile economies, through managed recruitment under bilateral labour agreements (see also Chapter 13);

- creation of a system to recoup some of the loss of investment in countries of origin by requiring the inclusion of practical training as part of some higher education programmes; investment by destination countries in training and education, proportional to the loss in investment suffered by the country of origin; and retention of skilled workers through voluntary means; and

- better targeting of subsidies in higher education by, for example, concentrating such subsidies in priority programmes of instruction and research.

2.8 Achieving Policy Coherence

Given the complexities of developing education and training policies to meet the prospective demand for skilled human resources, countries of origin cannot rely on one-dimensional modes of intervention, however important they may be. The concept of HRD planning needs to be mainstreamed to give purpose and coherence to efforts aimed at matching labour demand with supply while at the same time providing the necessary means to mitigate the loss of skilled workers.

3. Foreign Employment Policies[5]

Countries of origin have different profiles. Some have long-established labour migration programmes, while others are experiencing a migration transition characterized by both labour inflows and outflows, and finally there are those that are relative newcomers to organized labour migration. Nevertheless, as countries of origin, they all face some common challenges, such as:

- Protecting migrant workers from exploitative recruitment and employment practices, and providing appropriate assistance to migrant

---

[5] This section has been updated and distilled from the OSCE/IOM/ILO Handbook on Labour Migration (2006, 2007).

Unlike registration, requirements to obtain a license are more rigorous to fulfil.

The Philippines and Pakistan are two countries with an active private recruitment sector. In 2003, there were 1,327 licensed recruitment agencies in the Philippines. Table 10.1 illustrates licensing requirements in Pakistan and the Philippines.

Table 10.1:

Licensing Requirements in Pakistan and the Philippines

Requirements	Pakistan	Philippines
National	Yes	Yes
Application fee	USD 16	USD 200
Registration	Company	Company (with paid up capital of USD 40,000)
Character Certificate	Certificate of good conduct	Clean criminal record
Refundable Deposit	USD 5,000	USD 20,000
Other	Licence fee – USD 500	Licence fee – USD 1,000 Surety bond – USD 2,000 Minimum capital – USD 40,000
Validity of Licence	3 years	4 years

Note:
Original sums were in national currencies and converted to U.S. dollars by the authors.

Source: Mughal and Padilla, 2005.

(ii) Fees

ILO Convention No. 181 on Private Employment Agencies (1997), ratified by 20 countries and in force since 10 May 2000, stipulates that recruitment fees and costs should not be charged to workers other than in exceptional circumstances. While it is clearly preferable for all the costs to be borne by the employers, in practice this is often not the case, and many governments do allow fees and costs to be charged to migrant workers. Supply and demand factors underpinning migration also require attention

when regulating fees. In India, fees vary according to the worker's level of qualification (Table 10.2).

Table 10.2:

Fees Charged to Migrant Workers by PEAs in India

Type of worker	Fee (in USD)
Low-skilled	45
Semi-skilled	65
Skilled	110
Highly skilled	220

Source: Adapted from India, Office of the Protector General of Emigrants (2004).

In the Philippines, the recruitment fee must not exceed one month's salary, although charging fees is not permissible when the prevailing system in the destination country where the worker is to be deployed, either by law, policy or practice, does not allow the charging or collection of placement and recruitment fees.[7] Responding to problems of overcharging by recruitment intermediaries and exorbitant migration costs, some countries of destination have placed legal limits to such fees. In Israel, for example, the maximum fee the migrant worker can be charged is approximately USD 950, which includes the sums paid to recruitment agents abroad as well as the sum paid to the Israeli agency but which excludes the airfare (MOITAL, 2008).

(iii) Involvement of public employment agencies

While in most countries of origin the role of public recruitment agencies has been taken over by the private sector, there are arguments in favour of the deployment through state-run agencies of categories of workers that are especially vulnerable to malpractice and abuse, such as women domestic workers.

---

[7] See 2002 Revised POEA Rules and Regulations Governing the Recruitment and Employment of Land-based Overseas Workers (http://www.poea.gov.ph/rules/POEA%20Rules.pdf), Rule 5, Section 3.

International organizations like IOM with wide-ranging experience in migrant application processing and services can also be called upon to facilitate recruitment and are indeed taking up this role within the framework of bilateral arrangements (e.g. IOM, 2008) concerning labour migration to Canada, Italy and Spain. A particularly interesting example is the Seasonal Agricultural Workers Project: Guatemala-Canada (see Textbox 10.2 and Portrait 10.1).

Textbox 10.2

Seasonal Agricultural Workers Project - Guatemala-Canada

The Guatemala-Canada Seasonal Agricultural Workers Project is the result of joint efforts by the Ministry of Foreign Affairs and the Ministry of Labour and Social Welfare, and IOM cooperation.

The project was established in 2003 through an agreement with La Fondation des entreprises en recrutement de la main d'oeuvre agricole étrangère (FERME) of the Province of Québec under the supervision of the Department of Human Resources and Skills Development Canada (HRSDC).

The Government of Guatemala and FERME agreed to promote the migration of seasonal agricultural workers with the objective of benefiting the country of origin and the host country, while reducing irregular migration and the associated risks. The Government of Guatemala requested technical cooperation and implementation of the agreement by IOM as follows:

- Assistance in the selection of candidates to meet the Canadian needs for seasonal agricultural workers.

- Coordination with the Ministry of Labour to assure that the rights of Guatemalan seasonal workers are protected and compliance with other requirements of the Ministry in addition to immigration requirements.

- Travel arrangements for seasonal migrant workers.

IOM signed a Memorandum of Understanding with FERME regarding the project.

Guatemalan workers are also protected under Canadian labour laws and have access to life and medical insurance. The project is monitored by Guatemalan consular staff in Canada who supervise the farms where Guatemalans work, with the aim of supporting Guatemalan workers as well as Canadian employers.

Main Procedures

Demand: Associated farms in Canada submit requests for seasonal workers to FERME, which are then processed and assessed for approval. Once approved, they are sent by FERME to IOM Guatemala with copies to the Guatemalan Embassy in Canada. Each request includes the number of workers, expected date of arrival in Canada, duration of the work contract and type of farm crop.

Recruitment: Recruitment is carried out in different communities and municipalities in various departments in Guatemala. During that process, candidates are interviewed and assessed to ascertain that they meet the requirements under the project, and fill in a form with general information for their possible selection. Some Canadian entrepreneurs also participate in the recruitment process. Workers then visit the IOM office and submit the documents required for inclusion in the project. Once these documents have been received, a visa application is made and the respective file created.

Visa Application: The visa application and all the appropriate documents are forwarded to the Canadian Embassy for the relevant Medical Examination Forms to be issued. Depending on the test results workers are deemed to be fit to undertake seasonal agricultural work in Canada.

(i) Information dissemination

Pre-employment

As millions of people move across borders each year, the need for information has become fundamental to all migration decisions. Distorted perceptions and insufficient knowledge about the realities in the countries they are intending to go to only serve to increase the importance of ensuring that migrants have access to information. Most migrants are unaware of the practical, legal, social and economic consequences of moving to another country. This lack of awareness heightens the risk migrants may be exposed to, while also undermining orderly migration. The dissemination of relevant information reduces such risk and provides migrants with a sound basis on which to make informed decisions.

In recent years, countries of origin have recognized the need to provide their citizens intending to go abroad for purposes of employment with sufficient information to make informed choices about regular travel options, means of recruitment and travel and employment arrangements. Such information can be conveyed in two ways: through preparatory pre-employment sessions for particular contingents of workers or through broader mass information campaigns. The latter can be especially useful in drawing attention to the risks and dangers of irregular labour migration. Information resource centres for actual and intending migrant workers have also been established in some countries with the assistance of international organizations (see Textbox 10.3 and Portrait 10.2).

A variety of communication activities using various media can be used. Mass media ensure that information reaches large audiences quickly, while direct grassroots contacts provide the informal setting required for more in-depth and frank discussions.

Textbox 10.3

Information Resource Centre for Migrant Workers in Tajikistan

An Information Resource Centre for Migrant Workers was established in Dushanbe, Tajikistan, in 2004 by IOM and the Government of Tajikistan with the support of the Organization for Security and Co-operation in Europe (OSCE) to provide intending and actual migrant workers with reliable information on living and working abroad. Tajikistan's limited employment opportunities and mountainous terrain make it difficult for its inhabitants to make a living. As a result, to escape poverty, almost every Tajik family has at least one member who is a migrant worker. Tajiks seasonally migrate to neighbouring Kazakhstan, Kyrgyzstan and Uzbekistan, though most go to the Russian Federation. An IOM study on labour migration in the region revealed that some 600,000 Tajiks are migrants (Olimova and Bosc, 2003). Unfortunately, however, Tajik migrants are not well informed about the realities of life abroad.

Most Tajiks work in informal and low-skilled sectors in Russia and, even when they have regular status, labour exploitation is common. Many migrants do not know where to go to seek advice and information on travel and work abroad and are an easy prey for unofficial recruiters and traffickers.

The Government of Tajikistan, IOM and OSCE agreed to create a public resource centre with qualified counsellors to provide information relevant to the needs of migrants. The Resource Centre informs potential migrants about employment conditions, travel and documentation requirements, registration, the rights of migrants, press reports, maps and contacts, the risks of trafficking and smuggling in human beings, health risks and other useful tips. Through this project, information is also provided on community organizations and resources, social services and longer-term integration facilities.

Particular attention is paid to collecting, preparing and disseminating up-to-date information in the field of labour migration to intending migrant workers.

1. Travel and documentation:

- documents required for travel (passport and other documents);
- entry and exit (rights and responsibilities of border guards and citizens);
- customs (customs procedures, rights and responsibilities on both sides of the border);
- police (how to prevent abuse);
- transport means and ticketing (air and road transport);
- visa information and embassy addresses;
- information on the dangers of trafficking.

2. Admission and post-admission:

- regularization in destination country (registration);
- regularization of employment (work permit);
- health (first aid, HIV/AIDS prevention);
- education (admission);
- overseas representations of the Republic of Tajikistan and other contact addresses;
- relationship with employer (employment contract and possible risks);
- housing (rental and leases, and risks);
- employment in foreign countries (realities and possible risks for Tajik citizens).

The information is disseminated via booklets, posters, counselling services, tours, mass media, meetings, workshops and seminars.

Source: *IOM Dushanbe.*

Portrait 10.2

The Importance of Pre-departure Consultation

In June 2006, Oleg saw an advertisement in a local newspaper offering a well-paid job in the United States. Until then, he had only been able to find some temporary jobs and the money he earned was quite insufficient to pay for his family's daily needs and the education of his children. Working in the U.S. for a monthly wage of USD 2,500, as stated in the advertisement, seemed to offer a solution to his problems. Oleg called the agency and, when he got through, was told to prepay USD 1,200 for the agency to prepare the necessary documents and obtain a work visa from the U.S. Embassy. As this was much more than Oleg could afford, he borrowed USD 1,000.

Oleg went to Kiev, located the agency and met the manager. The staff seemed friendly and accommodating. Oleg spoke of his financial problems and the manager reassured him that the prospective job would not be difficult, and provide high wages, accommodation and meals. Oleg signed the contract without even reading it, trusting what he had heard, and deposited his passport and the requested sum of money with the agency, and returned home expecting to be contacted one week before his departure for the U.S. as agreed.

However, nothing happened, and when he again called the agency, there was no reply. Becoming suspicious, Oleg continued to call and eventually left again for Kiev to see what was happening. However, there was nobody at the address, only empty offices. The cleaner informed him that the agency had rented the room only for a few days before leaving again, but she did not know where to.

Oleg needed some time before he realized what had happened. Only now did it occur to him as strange that the office was so small, that there was no official sign or name, that only a laptop had been placed on the table, and that the "manager" had been far too friendly. He did not know what to do now.

Textbox 10.4

Philippine Overseas Labour Officers: Serving Overseas Filipino Workers Abroad

The Philippine Administrative Code and Labour Code provide the legal basis for a service delivery programme in countries of destination through the Philippine Overseas Labour Officers or POLOs. The Department of Labour and Employment (DOLE) is responsible for the development of policy and programme guidelines, while the International Labour Affairs Service (ILAS) of the DOLE provides ongoing administrative support. The Philippine Overseas Employment Administration (POEA) and the Overseas Workers Welfare Administration (OWWA) are the POLOs' key institutional partners within the DOLE for the implementation of their programmes and day-to-day operations. From a personnel management perspective, the POLOs are attached to the Philippine diplomatic missions abroad and subject to the relevant regulations of the Department of Foreign Affairs for service attachés. The POLOs' activities are therefore supervised by their respective heads of mission at the posting station.

To ensure organized legal entry of Filipino workers to the place of work, POLOs verify whether foreign employers, foreign recruiters, worksites, project sites, job vacancies and terms and conditions of employment meet the standards set by bilateral agreements or Philippine Government policy. They also negotiate with host governments and employers to secure improvements of the terms and conditions of employment and to facilitate worker recruitment and documentation.

Post-arrival orientation activities, worksite inspections, the social mobilization of workers and consultative dialogues are undertaken to address adjustment needs by promoting a sense of belonging in their temporary work setting, the fostering of cultural unity among Filipino workers and the maintenance of communication with the Philippine Mission. When problems and crises arise, Filipino migrant workers are given access to counselling, mediation, conciliation, medical services, legal assistance and court representation, as required. Visits to workers in detention can also be arranged, temporary shelter offered and evacuation or repatriation effected in case of civil conflict or unrest, or for health reasons. Where permissible under host country policy, referrals for employment transfer may be organized. In addition, POLOs help update and implement crisis response programmes with the Consular Division of the Philippine Mission, whenever necessary. In preparation for their post-employment options in the Philippines, Filipino workers are provided access to skills training, reintegration counselling and service referral.

POLOs are counted upon to establish cooperative linkages with a wide range of partners and stakeholders, including host governments, employers' associations, worker organizations, Filipino communities, NGOs, faith-based organizations and the media. They have the responsibility to provide regular situational analyses, identify new market opportunities or make a recommendation when they are of the view that a ban on the deployment of workers to a company or country is warranted. They can also make recommendations towards the imposition of administrative penalties against or blacklisting of abusive foreign employers and recruiters.

POLOs have been deployed in 34 countries around the world and are led by 42 labour attachés. In most posts, the complete staff establishment of a POLO team includes a welfare officer, an administrative assistant, an interpreter and a driver. The POLO team works in partnership with Philippine consular officers and, depending on specific issues of concern, with other members of the diplomatic service. For example, the POLO works closely with trade attachés whenever bilateral discussions on economic cooperation agreements involve labour and employment issues. While police matters relating to nationals, including those concerning irregular work, are handled by consular officials, the POLOs maintain an open system of informal cooperation to assist in such cases. At other times, the POLOs work hand-in-hand with social workers and medical attachés deployed by the Department of Social Welfare and Development and the Department of Health.

The Migrant Workers and Overseas Filipinos Act of 1995 reinforced the role of the POLOs and provided impetus for further experimentation in team management and mainstreaming of services within the Philippine diplomatic service to provide overseas Filipino workers with the services they need wherever they may be.

Source: Ricardo Casco, National Programme Officer, Labour Migration Services, IOM Manila.

3.2 Optimizing the Benefits of Organized Labour Migration

For countries seeking to promote foreign employment, labour migration policy must also address the broader question of the promotion and facilitation of managed external labour flows. Countries of origin have an interest in discouraging irregular migration (while advocating an increase in regular channels for labour migration, including through circular migration initiatives). The benefits of organized labour migration can be optimized through the promotion of foreign employment by way of marketing strategies, cooperation with the private sector, human resource development (see Section 2 above) and leveraging the funds migrant workers send home (remittances). The importance of marketing is considered below, while circular migration and the question of enhancing the development impact of remittances are discussed in Chapter 12.

3.3. Importance of Marketing

Since labour migration is primarily determined by demand, countries wishing to deploy their workers abroad must be able to seek out prospective employers and compete with other countries of origin. Thus, it can be argued, a "marketing strategy" is the lifeblood of any overseas employment programme.

Marketing is a necessary first step in the effort to "promote" a country's labour. It also points to a country's deliberate purpose in using labour mobility as a means to attain certain specific economic goals, such as easing unemployment or the generation of flows of remittances to augment its foreign exchange earnings. Countries intending to deploy their nationals abroad need to identify opportunities beyond their national boundaries in a highly competitive international market. In this case, market research becomes essential.

In the Philippines, the market research group maintains a "desk officer" system that allocates work responsibilities according to regions of interest (e.g.

the Gulf Cooperation Council (GCC) states, Europe, Asia, Oceania/Australia) or to occupational sectors (e.g. seafarers, nurses/health workers, domestic workers).[9] A monthly Market Situation Report (MSR) is provided to private sector associations, which in turn distribute it to their members. The MSR is a consolidated report on current international labour market developments and relevant economic trends and events that have a bearing on the Philippine overseas employment programme. In addition, comprehensive destination country reports are prepared, covering the labour, political and socio-economic conditions as well as prospects and problems in each country of interest. Information on immigration policies and labour laws of different countries are continuously gathered, analyzed and disseminated. This type of research is essentially based on analytical reading of secondary sources such as trade journals, regional economic magazines and national development plans of countries of destination. This is complemented by feedback derived from consultations and close liaison work with the marketing staff of private sector groups. Inputs are also derived from reports of labour attachés and whatever information can be culled from Philippine embassy reports.

In addition to disseminating market research information to the private sector, marketing missions are undertaken by the Philippine Government to negotiate bilateral agreements or arrangements for the deployment of Filipino workers.[10]

As part of an inter-regional project for legal and managed labour migration,[11] financed by the European Commission, IOM is helping to create or strengthen existing marketing activities in ten Asian countries of origin. Market research units, or MRUs, are to be located in the ministries of overseas employment/

---

[9] Information provided by Ricardo Casco, National Programme Officer, Labour Migration Services, IOM Manila and former POEA official.

[10] Information provided by Ricardo Casco, National Programme Officer, Labour Migration Services, IOM Manila.

[11] AENEAS: Regional Dialogue and Programme on Facilitating Legal Migration between Asia and the European Union. A brochure describing the programme can be downloaded from the Colombo Process website (see Textbox 10.5) at http://www.colomboprocess.org/.

labour to collect labour market information on selected European Union Member States and disseminate it to recruitment agencies.

3.4 Administration of Labour Migration - Sample Policy and Procedural Interventions

Ultimately, labour migration programmes are most effective when they are supported by comprehensive sets of policies and procedures. An analysis of those already in place in four Asian countries is shown in Table 10.3 below. While there are undoubtedly similarities in these countries' policies, there are also significant differences in their content and application.

Table 10.3:

Government Functions and Services Provided by Overseas Employment Programmes, Selected Countries of Origin

	Bangladesh	India	Sri Lanka	Philippines
Supervision of Recruitment				
Registration and licensing of private recruiters	*****	*****	*****	*****
Ban/restriction of direct hiring	*****	*****	*****	*****
Periodic inspection of recruitment agencies	*****	*****	*****	*****
Limit to recruitment fee charged to worker	*****	*****	*****	*****
Cash/security bond requirement	*****	*****	*****	*****
Regulation of job advertising	*****	*****	*****	*****
Joint liability			*****	*****
Complaints mechanism and adjudication	*****	*****	*****	*****
Performance-based incentives				*****
State recruitment agency	*****	*****	*****	*****
Departure Procedures for Migrant Workers (MWs)				
Minimum standards for employment contracts	*****	*****	*****	*****
Emigration clearance	*****	*****	*****	*****
Trade test		*****	*****	*****
Support Services to Migrant Workers				
State subsidized skills training	*****	*****	*****	*****
Pre-departure orientation	*****	*****	*****	*****
Migrant welfare fund	*****		*****	*****
Labour attaché assistance	*****	*****	*****	*****
Overseas Workers Welfare Centres			*****	*****
Insurance	*****	*****	*****	*****
Conciliation on-site	*****	*****	*****	*****
Legal aid on-site	*****	*****	*****	*****
Return assistance			*****	*****
Reintegration assistance			*****	*****
Marketing Support to Recruitment Agencies				
Client referral system				*****
Market research units			*****	*****
Labour attaché reports				*****
Interstate Cooperation				
Social security arrangements		*****	*****	*****
MoUs/agreements on deployment/protection of MWs	*****	*****	*****	*****

Notes:
A migrant welfare fund is currently being established in India.
Policies by governments have also been formulated in the area of remittances.
***** In operation.

Source: *Achacoso, 2002; updated in 2007 by IOM and author.*

4. International Cooperation

There are clear limits to what a country of origin can do to protect its migrant workers without the active cooperation of destination countries. Interstate cooperation and, more broadly, international cooperation, can play an essential part, not only in the protection and welfare of migrant workers, but also in the expansion of organized labour migration and the curbing of irregular movements. Cooperation may take many forms. For instance, it may be conducted at the bilateral level, or regionally, between a number of like-minded countries, or even at the global level.[12] Nor should such cooperation be restricted to government actors; the participation of other stakeholders, such as employers' or workers' organizations, is of crucial importance.

Formal mechanisms of interstate cooperation are essentially binding treaty commitments relating to cooperation on labour migration, which have been concluded either on a global level as in multilateral agreements and conventions protecting the rights of migrant workers under the auspices of the ILO and the UN, on a regional level as in the treaties establishing regional integration mechanisms, or on a bilateral level as in the case of bilateral labour agreements (see Chapter 13). The various forms of formal cooperation, such as mandated in bilateral agreements, regional integration and international conventions, often operate simultaneously.

Where it is not desirable or feasible to work on the basis of formal commitments, other forms of cooperation are available. These include non-binding consultative mechanisms, such as regional consultative processes (RCPs), joint commissions on labour, working groups and non-binding multilateral frameworks, such as the Berne Initiative which culminated in the elaboration of the International Agenda for Migration Management (IAMM) (Swiss Federal Office for Migration and IOM, 2005) (see also Chapters 11 and 13).

One of the most active RCPs in operation is provided by the Ministerial Consultations on Overseas Employment and Contractual Labour for Countries of Origin in Asia, commonly referred to as the "Colombo Process" (see Textbox 10.5).

---

[12] See Chapter 13 for a more detailed discussion of formal and less formal mechanisms of interstate cooperation on migration, including bilateral labour migration agreements, international agreements protecting the rights of migrant workers and their families and regional consultative processes (RCPs), as well as global means of cooperation. In the latter regard, see also Textbox Int. 2 on the Global Forum on Migration and Development (GFMD). Given its importance and cross-cutting nature, interstate and international cooperation is also discussed in other chapters in Part B of the Report (viz. on the exchange of migration data in Chapter 9; from the perspective of destination countries in Chapter 11; and between countries of origin and destination as well as with and among other pertinent stakeholders, with a view to harnessing the development potential of migration in Chapter 12).

Textbox 10.5

Ministerial Consultations on Overseas Employment and Contractual Labour for Countries of Origin in Asia: The Colombo Process

In response to a request from several Asian countries of origin, IOM organized Ministerial Consultations in 2003, 2004 and 2005. The ten original participating States (Bangladesh, China, India, Indonesia, Nepal, Pakistan, the Philippines, Sri Lanka, Thailand and Viet Nam) made recommendations for the effective management of overseas employment programmes and agreed to the implementation of a range of follow-up activities.

The aim of the Ministerial Consultations is to provide a forum for Asian countries of origin to:

- share experiences, lessons learned and best practices on overseas employment policies and practices;
- consult on issues faced by overseas workers, countries of origin and destination;
- propose practical solutions for the well-being of vulnerable overseas workers;

- optimize development benefits and
- enhance dialogue with countries of destination.

Achievements so far include:

- identification at ministerial and senior official level of policy challenges and needs, and exploration of the range of possible responses and exchange of experiences in programme development;
- development of training curricula for labour attachés and administrators and implementing joint training courses;
- establishment of Market Research Units (MRUs) and creation of more channels for regular labour migration; and
- implementation of specific recommendations at the national level.

The third Ministerial Consultations in Bali, Indonesia, were greatly enriched by the participation of countries of destination, with delegations from Bahrain, Italy, Kuwait, Malaysia, Qatar, Saudi Arabia, South Korea and the United Arab Emirates. Afghanistan was welcomed as a new member to the group after participating as an Observer in 2004. International and regional organizations participating in the Consultations included the Asian Development Bank, the Association of Southeast Asian Nations (ASEAN), the European Community, the Gulf Cooperation Council (GCC) countries, the U.K. Department for International Development (DFID), ILO, UNIFEM and the World Bank.

On 21 and 22 January 2008, Colombo Process countries met in Abu Dhabi with GCC countries and Malaysia, Singapore and Yemen. The Abu Dhabi Dialogue resulted in the adoption of the Abu Dhabi Declaration which provides a basis for cooperative action to be undertaken with the support of IOM. Four specific areas of partnership were identified:

- **Partnership 1**: Enhancing knowledge in the areas of: labour market trends, skills profiles, temporary contractual workers and remittance policies and flows, and their interplay with development in the region.
- **Partnership 2**: Building capacity for the effective matching of labour demand and supply.
- **Partnership 3**: Preventing illegal recruitment practices and promoting welfare and protection measures for contractual workers that are supportive of their well-being and preventing their exploitation at origin and destination.
- **Partnership 4**: Developing a framework for a comprehensive approach to managing the entire cycle of temporary contractual mobility to the mutual benefit of countries of origin and destination.

Sources: IOM and http://www.colomboprocess.org/.

At the global level, the constituents of the ILO have developed a non-binding Multilateral Framework on Labour Migration (see Textbox 10.6). The Framework aims to provide a rights-based approach to labour migration that takes into account labour market needs, proposing guidelines and principles based on best practices and international standards. The Framework also underlines the importance of international cooperation in dealing with labour migration. It is composed of 15 broad principles, each with corresponding guidelines and a follow-up mechanism.

Textbox 10.6

The ILO Multilateral Framework on Labour Migration

The *ILO Multilateral Framework on Labour Migration: Non-binding principles and guidelines for a rights-based approach to labour migration* forms the centrepiece of the ILO Plan of Action for Migrant Workers, adopted by the tripartite constituents (governments, and employers' and workers' organizations) at the 92nd Session of the International Labour Conference in June 2004. The Framework was the negotiated outcome of an ILO tripartite meeting of experts (31 October-2 November 2006), subsequently endorsed by the ILO Governing Body in March 2006.

The objective of the Framework is to provide practical guidance to its tripartite constituents and other stakeholders (civil society, international and regional agencies) on the development, improvement or strengthening, implementation and evaluation of national and international labour migration policies. The Framework supplements existing ILO and UN migrant worker instruments, and takes into account new global challenges and developments such as the growth of temporary labour migration programmes; the feminization of migration; the greater role of the private sector in arranging migration across borders; high incidence of irregular migration, including trafficking and smuggling of human beings; and the growing interest of the international community in migration and development linkages.

The ILO Multilateral Framework on Labour Migration is the most comprehensive international collection of principles, guidelines and best practices on labour migration policy. It is "rights-based" in the sense of bringing together the principles and rights that apply to labour migration and treatment of migrant workers already contained in various international instruments. The Framework consists of 15 principles and corresponding guidelines organized under nine broad themes, and a collection of 132 best practices worldwide. The five major themes that underlie the Framework are: decent work for all; international cooperation; governance and management of migration; promotion and protection of migrant rights; and migration and development. The Framework recognizes the important role to be played by social partners, social dialogue and tripartism in migration policy. It advocates gender-sensitive migration policies that address the special problems faced by women migrant workers. It is important to highlight that most of these principles and guidelines are already present in varying degrees in many parts of the world, as shown by the extensive compilation of examples of best practices.

At the same time, the Framework acknowledges the sovereign right of all nations to determine their own migration policies. Since it is a non-binding Framework, constituents can draw upon its extensive compilation of principles, guidelines and practices – in full or in part – in formulating, improving, implementing and evaluating their own legislative and regulatory frameworks on labour migration. Global trade union federations, such as the International Trade Union Confederation (ITUC) and international and regional NGOs (e.g. Migrant Forum in Asia), have incorporated the ILO Multilateral Framework on Labour Migration into their policy agendas.

The ILO will continue to promote and support implementation of the Framework principles and guidelines by Member States through its regular advisory services, advocacy work and technical cooperation programmes in active collaboration with its tripartite partners, the Global Migration Group (GMG), and other concerned international, regional and national organizations.

Source: *International Migration Programme, ILO, Geneva.*

International cooperation is vital to an orderly and managed labour migration system. In the absence of a widely accepted international migration system for labour migration – for instance, the expansion of the General Agreement on Trade in Services (GATS) to encompass broader categories of service providers thus increasing the mobility of temporary workers (see Textbox Int. 1) and considerably more ratifications of the International Convention on the Protection of the Rights of All Migrant Workers and Members of their Families, and of relevant ILO instruments (see Chapter 13) – there is a need to expand and develop concurrently bilateral, regional and international cooperation through formal and informal mechanisms on the basis of existing effective practices. Cooperation has to take into account the interests of countries of origin and of destination, of governments at all levels (central, regional and local), migrant workers and their representatives, social partners (employers and trade unions) and civil society.

5. Conclusion

An increasing number of developing countries and countries with economies in transition seek to adopt policies, legislation and administrative structures that promote foreign employment for their workforce and generate remittances, while providing safeguards to protect migrants. While job creation at home is their preferred option, these countries see overseas employment as part of a

Pritchett, L.

2006   *Let their People Come: Breaking the Gridlock on Global Labor Mobility,* Center for Global Development, Washington, D.C., http://www.cgdev.org/content/publications/detail/10174.

Ratha, D. and Z. Xu

2008   "Migration and Remittances: Top 10" in *Migration and Remittances Factbook 2008,* Migration and Remittances Team, Development Prospects Group, The World Bank, Washington, D.C., http://siteresources.worldbank.org/INTPROSPECTS/Resources/334934-1199807908806/Top10.pdf.

Swiss Federal Office for Migration and IOM

2005   *International Agenda for Migration Management,* 16-17 December, IOM/Swiss Federal Office for Migration, Geneva/Berne, http://www.iom.int/jahia/Jahia/cache/bypass/pid/1674?entryId=8005.

Tan, E.A.

2005   "Welfare Funds for Migrant Workers – A Comparative Study of Pakistan, the Philippines and Sri Lanka" in IOM, *Labour Migration in Asia: Protection of Migrant Workers, Support Services and Enhancing Development Benefits,* IOM, Geneva, 153-218, http://www.iom.int/jahia/Jahia/cache/offonce/pid/1674?entryId=7993.

2006   "Capacity of the Developing East Asian Region to Supply Skilled Manpower to Foreign Labour Markets", working paper submitted to ILO.

2007   "Supply Response to Foreign Demand for Skilled Manpower, the Philippine Case", draft paper prepared for IOM.

United Nations Development Fund for Women (UNIFEM)

2004   *The UNIFEM Asia-Pacific Arab States Regional Program on Empowering Women Migrant Workers in Asia,* Phase I: 2001-2004 (Report), UNIFEM, Bangkok.

Textbox 10.3 - Information Resource Centre for Migrant Workers in Tajikistan

Olimova, S. and I. Bosc

2003   *Labour Migration from Tajikistan*, IOM in cooperation with the Sharq Scientific Research Center, Dushanbe, http://www.iom.tj/publications/labour_migration_2003.pdf.

Textbox 10.6 - The ILO Multilateral Framework on Labour Migration

International Labour Organization (ILO)

2006   *ILO Multilateral Framework on Labour Migration: Non-binding principles and guidelines for a rights-based approach to labour migration*, International Labour Office, Geneva, http://www.ilo.org/public/english/protection/migrant/download/multilat_fwk_en.pdf.

FORMULATION AND MANAGEMENT OF FOREIGN EMPLOYMENT POLICIES IN COUNTRIES OF DESTINATION*

CHAPTER 11

1. Introduction

Foreign workers are employed in many countries at all skill levels, even though some of them may originally have arrived as students, tourists or family members (see Chapters 4, 5 and 6, respectively), and then remained in the country to work. There are significant numbers of foreign workers in the European Union (EU); established countries of immigration such as Australia, Canada, New Zealand and the United States; the Gulf Cooperation Council (GCC) states; new immigration countries such as the Russian Federation; as well as a number of middle-income countries in the developing world, viz. Malaysia, South Africa and Thailand. As described earlier in Chapters 7 and 8, cross-border labour mobility between neighbouring developing countries is common, while considerable irregular labour migration also occurs not only from developing to developed industrialized countries, but also among developing countries themselves.

The preparation of nationals in countries of origin for their temporary employment abroad, discussed

in Chapter 10, cannot be wholly successful without the development of partnerships between these countries and countries of destination, either on a bilateral basis or in the context of regional economic integration or trade agreements (see Chapter 13), and the adoption of transparent, flexible and complementary regulations and policies in countries of destination. But, a "one-size-fits-all approach" to policymaking in this field is not feasible because countries of destination have to address their own sovereign concerns regarding the employment of foreign workers.[1]

This chapter presents the principal policy options to be considered by countries of destination in their admission policies for both permanent and temporary migrant workers. It begins by underlining the increasing importance of labour mobility in the context of migration management and the need for an explicit official statement to guide public policy in this field and the appropriate administrative

---

* This chapter was written by Ryszard Cholewinski, Labour Migration Specialist, Migration Policy, Research and Communications, IOM, Geneva. The author is particularly grateful to Elizabeth Warn (Labour Migration Specialist, Labour and Facilitated Migration Division, IOM, Geneva), who provided material and assisted in drafting Sections 4 and 7.

[1] A country-specific approach to policymaking is inevitable because, as Ruhs (2005: 203) observes, "the design and implementation of immigration policy remain principally the domain of **domestic** policymaking of sovereign and self-determining states" (original emphasis) and because of significant contextual differences between countries (e.g. levels of economic development, regulation of labour markets, degree of democratic institutions).

structure to put such policies into effect. Regarding the design of temporary labour migration programmes, in particular, the chapter builds on the policy discussions presented in Chapter 3 and appraises some of the challenges involved in the effective implementation of such schemes. The chapter goes on to assess the main elements of a comprehensive post-admission policy, taking account of the concerns of destination countries regarding the protection of their labour markets, the economic and social integration of newcomers and maintenance of social cohesion. It also considers the principal tools at the disposal of policymakers in destination countries to comprehensively address irregular labour migration and the related issue of an informal labour market. Finally, the chapter provides an overview of the types of cooperation and partnerships destination countries might enter into with countries of origin and transit as well as other pertinent stakeholders, to formulate and manage their foreign employment policies more effectively and equitably.

While state sovereignty is the prevailing order in international relations, it is not absolute. Global economic interdependence, exemplified in the globalization process (Chapter 1), has a strong bearing on national policymaking in this field. States have also entered into agreements that foresee a certain balance of interest among the parties regarding their respective regulation of international labour mobility or the treatment of migrant workers. Such concerns have become an important subject of international negotiations and are reflected in bilateral or regional trade and/or economic integration agreements (Chapter 13), and regional and international human rights and labour standards.

2. Labour Mobility at the Core of Migration Management

An important line of argument in this Report is that labour mobility lies at the heart of migration management today against a background of economic globalization and labour shortages at all skills levels in such key sectors as health care, construction and agriculture; significant demographic decline in industrialized countries, and a decrease in asylum applications in these countries (see Textbox 11.1). Consequently, more attention to, and resources for, migration management in these and more recent countries of destination (e.g. the Russian Federation) (see Textbox Reg. 2 in the Europe Migration Overview) might be devoted to the development of a greater choice of regular labour migration channels, facilitated by explicit policy statements in support of appropriate policies and regulations involving the whole government structure and administration. Appropriate instruments to monitor and evaluate the efficacy of foreign employment policies are also integral to taking labour migration more seriously (Ardittis and Laczko, 2008). However, to do so requires the existence of appropriate mechanisms to allow the collection of accurate and reliable data (see Chapter 9).

Textbox 11.1

The Evolution of Asylum Applications in IGC Participating States, 1983-2007*

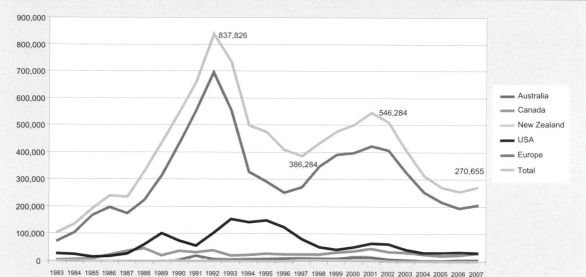

Note:

* The Intergovernmental Consultations on Migration, Asylum and Refugees (IGC) is an informal, non-decision making forum for inter-governmental information exchange and policy debate on the management of international migratory flows. The IGC brings together 16 Participating States, UNHCR, IOM and the European Commission. The IGC maintains databases on, among others, the number of asylum applications received in present and former IGC Participating States.

Present IGC Participating States are Australia, Belgium, Canada, Denmark, Finland, Germany, Greece, Ireland, the Netherlands, New Zealand, Norway, Spain, Sweden, Switzerland, the United Kingdom, and the United States. Former IGC Participating States from where IGC continues to collect data on asylum applications are Austria, France and Italy.

During the period 1983-2007, over 10 million asylum applications were filed in countries participating in the Intergovernmental Consultations (IGC; see above for a list of countries).

In 1985, some 100,000 asylum applications were received by IGC participating states. By 1989, annual applications had increased fourfold to 435,000. From 1983 to 1992, the major countries of origin were Sri Lanka, Iran, Turkey, Poland, the Czech Republic and former Zaire (today the Democratic Republic of the Congo).

In 1992, asylum applications reached a new peak of 840,000, with 85,000 applications received in July 1992, with most of the increase attributable to the rise in claims filed by persons from the former Federal Republic of Yugoslavia.

From 1993 onwards, numbers again dropped to a low of 390,000 applications in 1997; this was followed by a slight increase between 1998 and 2001, again owing to a rise in claims by persons from the former Federal Republic of Yugoslavia.

Since 2001, applications have continued to fall to stand at 240,000 in 2006, which corresponds to the number of annual applications in 1987.

In 2007, numbers increased for the first time since 2001 due to an increase in asylum applications by persons from Iraq.

Destination Countries

Throughout the period under review, Germany received the largest number of claims among all IGC participating states, with a peak of 440,000 in 1992, or 52 per cent of total claims filed in the IGC states for that year.

Distribution of Asylum Claims Among all IGC States, 1983-2007[1]

Germany	27%		Belgium	4%
United States	16%		Norway	2%
United Kingdom	10%		Spain	2%
France	9%		Denmark	1%
Canada	7%		Australia	1%
Sweden	6%		Italy[2]	1%
Netherlands	5%		Ireland	1%
Switzerland	5%		Finland	<1%
Austria	4%		New Zealand	<1%

Notes:

[1] Greece is not included in this chart because data is only available for 2006 and 2007

[2] Data for Italy are included only up to 2001.

France, the United States, the United Kingdom and Sweden receive most asylum applications, with Sweden, Austria, Switzerland and Norway receiving the largest number of claims in relation to their populations.

Source: The Intergovernmental Consultations (IGC) Secretariat, Geneva.

2.1 The Case for an Explicit Policy Statement to Guide and Inform the Elaboration of Transparent Regulations and Policies

Ideally, the immigration and labour migration policies and objectives[2] in destination countries should be clearly stated, and based on broad political and popular support, not only to enjoy wide legitimacy, but also to obviate the risk of subsequent policy inconsistencies espoused and pursued by different political formations, which often become apparent in the period leading up to general elections. For example, the importance of immigration to Canada's economic growth generally, and of labour migration in particular, to countervail the prevailing demographic profile and labour shortages together with the importance of integrating newcomers, is clearly articulated in the Citizenship and Immigration

Canada (CIC) Minister's *Annual Report to Parliament on Immigration*:

Immigration will play an increasingly important role in supporting Canada's economic prosperity and competitiveness. In a few short years, given our aging population, Canadians who leave school for the workplace will only offset the number of retirements. Immigration will therefore be a key source of labour force growth in the future. Moreover, the country is currently facing significant labour market shortages in some sectors and regions. Immigration can contribute to addressing both short- and long-term labour market needs by attracting people with the right mix of skills and talents to support economic growth today and in the future. With other industrialized countries confronting similar challenges with respect to sustaining population and economic growth, Canada will be operating in an increasingly competitive worldwide market for higher skilled workers.

...

Bringing immigrants to Canada is only part of the challenge. Just as important is ensuring that they

---

[2] For a list of the different types of impacts that policymakers should give regard to in defining policy objectives, see Ruhs (2005). High-level policy objectives (which may however also be conflicting) include: realization of labour market objectives, protecting national security, minimizing public expenditure, promoting social cohesion, compliance with human rights obligations, and promoting international development and cooperation (Spencer, 2003).

settle successfully upon arrival and integrate fully over the longer term. The challenges newcomers face are many: acquisition of English and/or French; recognition of their credentials, skills and work experience acquired abroad; and familiarity with the norms of the Canadian workplace and society, to name just a few. It will be important to look at ways in which the current range of settlement programs and services – including those provided by provincial and community partners – can be improved to better help immigrants in the early settlement period. (CIC, 2007a: 6).

The importance of migration for the economy of the United Kingdom and the contribution being made to the cultural and social fabric of the country are underlined in the proposal made by the government in 2006 concerning the introduction of a points-based system for migration management:

All the main political parties, employers' organisations, trade unions and educational institutions agree that migration is vital for our economy. Migration makes a substantial contribution to economic growth, helps fill gaps in the labour market, including key public services such as health and education, and increases investment, innovation and entrepreneurship in the U.K. Culturally we are enriched by people with diverse backgrounds from other countries (U.K. Home Office, 2006: 1).

Clear policy statements serve to guide and inform the elaboration and the adoption of comprehensible and coherent regulations and policies on foreign employment;[3] and this for two reasons. First, they

are an important part of the knowledge base on labour mobility, discussed in Chapter 9. Clear and coherent rules concerning migration and admission for employment, together with information about labour migration opportunities, would encourage regular labour migration and access to destination countries, with migrants either travelling individually and by their own means, or with the assistance of legitimate public or private employment agencies. Second, transparent rules also send a signal to host populations that the government has its labour migration policy "under control", provided that the rules themselves reflect a realistic policy response to the prevailing labour migration situation in the destination country concerned. For example, an otherwise clearly defined admissions policy that however fails to devote sufficient attention to an obvious demand for domestic[4] or agricultural workers (many of whom are often found in an irregular situation) will not be conducive to the development of a coherent and realistic response to the actual labour market situation in the country concerned.

2.2 Identifying an Appropriate Administrative Structure and the Need for a Coherent "Whole of Government" Approach

In many countries of destination, migration management falls within the responsibility of the ministry of the interior[5] or a government department set up specifically for this purpose.[6] Often, these ministries are also primarily responsible for the design and implementation of managed labour migration policies, which may result in the collision of two philosophies: an enforcement approach on the one hand, focusing on the control of borders and the prevention of irregular migration, particularly the eradication of its worst forms, i.e. human trafficking and smuggling, including trafficking for

---

[3] In the South African context, for example, it has been argued that "[p]erhaps, as the current Minister has pointed out on more than one occasion, the biggest problem with the [2004 Immigration] Act is that its provisions are not informed by any substantively agreed on set of policy outcomes, given that the process of developing policy (in the form of a White Paper) was not completed before the process to draft legislation was put in place. As a consequence, amendments to immigration legislation since 2002 have been ad hoc and by default rather than by design" (Williams, 2007).

[4] Also referred to as "household service providers".

[5] E.g. the newly established Border Agency of the U.K. Home Office.

[6] E.g. CIC Canada, the Department of Immigration and Citizenship in Australia, or the Singapore Immigration and Checkpoints Authority.

In addition to these general considerations, a number of specific policy elements can be identified that, in broad terms, are relevant to destination countries seeking to manage foreign employment: (i) assessment of the demand for foreign workers in the light of current and projected shortages on the national labour market, and demographic considerations; (ii) design of a foreign labour admission policy; (iii) the protection of migrant workers in the workplace and the host country generally, with particular attention to be paid to ensuring social cohesion (through integration and fighting discrimination and xenophobia); (iv) prevention or reduction of irregular labour migration; and (v) consultation and cooperation with countries of origin at the bilateral, regional and international level, as well as development of partnerships with other key stakeholders with an interest in labour mobility, i.e. the private sector, trade unions and civil society at large (NGOs, diaspora and migrant associations). These specific policy elements are discussed in the remainder of this chapter.

4. Assessing the Need for Foreign Labour

Regardless of the type of labour migration system in place in any particular country, one of its objectives is to address labour shortages. However, the mere existence of a labour shortage does not necessarily also express a need for foreign workers. For this to be the case, the causes of actual and potential labour and skills shortages and their potential scale have to be analyzed and the effectiveness of various possible policy responses to address them, including migration policy, evaluated (Boswell et al., 2004). Even where labour shortages are generally recognized to exist, political factors and the need to manage conflicting and competing migration policy concerns will determine whether, and to what degree, shortages call for the admission of foreign workers.

4.1 Detecting and Projecting Labour Shortages

There is no clear consensus as to what constitutes a labour shortage,[10] and much depends on how and where such a shortage is perceived. Shortages may occur not because there is an overall lack of workers to fill the jobs in question, but because of mismatches in the labour market:

> In most cases, such shortages are not caused by an aggregate shortage of labour, but can be attributable to problems of mismatch between labour demand and supply. Jobs remain unfilled despite high unemployment rates, because workers lack the relevant qualifications or skills, are reluctant to take up work in particular occupations or geographical areas, or have insufficient information about job opportunities. Alternatively (or in addition), employers are unwilling or unable to offer sufficiently attractive salaries or conditions to encourage occupational or geographical mobility (Boswell et al., 2004: 3).

In Ireland, the Expert Group on Future Skills Need in a report in 2005 also drew a distinction between skill shortages and labour shortages. The Expert Group found that foreign workers with specific skills would probably be needed in certain sectors in Ireland with skills shortages (e.g. foreign chefs received most of the work permits in the first half of 2005) for a period during which national workers are acquiring the necessary skills; while labour shortages (i.e. insufficient workers at prevailing wages and conditions) were identified generally in low-skilled employment (i.e. agriculture, food processing and jobs in services such as the security industry and catering) (NESC/IOM, 2006).

Further, labour shortages are difficult to predict as there may be limits to the accuracy of the available

---

[10] Boswell et al. (2004: 5) provide a working definition: "[I]n the most basic sense, labour shortages occur where the demand for workers in a particular occupation exceeds the supply of workers who are qualified, available and willing to do that job". They then proceed to make the further distinction between aggregate labour shortages and shortages resulting from mismatches in the labour market.

information sources (Chapter 9), while the types of labour shortage (e.g. long or short-term, absolute or relative) may vary considerably among destination countries. A key feature of labour shortages is that they may be prevalent in only some employment sectors and at certain skill levels; for example, in the EU labour shortages have been identified in the ICT, engineering, health and education sectors, as well as among low and semi-skilled workers generally (e.g. agriculture, construction, food production and hospitality). The causes of labour shortages are various and influenced by a number of trends in labour demand and supply (Boswell et al., 2004) that are also linked to national and global economic patterns and demographic factors (discussed in Section 4.2 below).

One trend affecting labour supply is emigration: "outflows of nationals (...) can have an important impact on skills composition where high-skilled workers leave because of more attractive business or research conditions in third countries" (Boswell et al., 2004: 14). For example, emigration from the U.K. has become quite significant in the last few decades, with the country experiencing a total net loss of approximately 2.7 million nationals between 1966 and 2005. More than 198,000 nationals left the country in 2005, while only 91,000 returned. Moreover, two-thirds of those who left the country did so to take up or seek employment opportunities abroad (Sriskandarajah and Drew, 2006). A similar net exodus, though to a lesser extent, was experienced in Germany (Landler, 2007).[11] However, not all countries quantify the emigration of their nationals and this question is rarely discussed in the context of designing foreign labour admission policies.

Conventional estimates of current labour shortages include, in particular, surveys and employers' reports on labour requirements in specific sectors.[12] However, such sources should be interpreted with some caution as they concern recruitment difficulties rather than labour shortages per se, and because employers may have unrealistic or overly ambitious expectations concerning growth in their sector. Governments can also conduct research into labour sectors and occupations. While such research may yield a more precise evaluation of the prevailing situation, it is less effective in predicting economic contraction or expansion and related changes in labour demand. More sophisticated econometric models are used to project future labour shortages, and these are considered essential for mid and long-term policy planning, especially for countries characterized by population ageing and decline, although theoretical and methodological shortcomings affecting their ability to produce accurate projections have also been identified.[13] Indeed, there is always the risk of error as when governments subsidize the training of teachers, nurses or engineers to meet projected labour shortages only to find that ultimately students graduate in a period of unemployment (NESC/IOM, 2006). Regardless of the difficulties, government interventions play a critical role in developing labour migration policies, particularly as concerns the different approaches needed depending on whether the problem to be addressed is one of labour shortage or rather tightness in a particular sector, and to provide the wider macroeconomic overview. As noted by one commentator:

> [I]t is necessary to recognize that, regardless of economic conditions and the number of vacancies advertised in a given economy, there is always the need for host countries to **manage the demand for migrant labour** [original emphasis]. This is

---

[11] In 2005, 144,800 Germans emigrated and only 128,100 returned – the first time in nearly four decades that more Germans left the country than returned (Landler, 2007, citing figures from the German Federal Statistics Office).

[12] E.g. the U.K. annual Employer Skills Survey (ESS) of approximately 4,000 employers, which inquires into the nature, extent, causes and implications of skills deficits, and the monthly Job Openings and Labor Turnover Survey (JOLTS) undertaken by the U.S. Bureau of Labor Statistics measuring labour market tightness and efficiency (matching) (Boswell et al., 2004; Abella, 2006).

[13] For an overview of such models in Australia, Canada, Germany, the Netherlands, the U.K. and the U.S., see Boswell et al. (2004).

shortages, such as health professionals, engineers, teachers and ICT specialists, and either do not apply the test or relax the rules. This more flexible and less bureaucratic approach has considerable economic advantages, since it enables a speedier and more efficient admission of migrant workers to fill shortages in important employment sectors.

(c) Occupational shortage lists

Occupational shortage lists can be an efficient way to channel foreign workers into sectors of the economy suffering from a lack of workers with specific skills. In the U.K., the National Shortage Occupations List, modified in July 2008, indicates shortages for certain categories such as engineers, doctors, social workers, veterinary surgeons and teachers for compulsory schooling posts in England and Scotland.[18] No labour market test is required to fill these posts under the ordinary U.K. work permit scheme.

In Australia, a Migration Occupations in Demand List (MODL) has been drawn up containing, as at 17 May 2008, 53 professional occupations/specializations and 49 trades persons' categories in which shortages have been identified nationally. The list is reviewed twice a year. Points are assigned to each category which can then be used by migrants applying for skilled migration visas (Australia, 2007; Abella, 2006) (see also Section 5.1(a) below).[19]

(d) Employer fees

Levying fees on employers for every foreign worker hired may be used to ensure that migrant workers are in fact brought in to fill genuine gaps in the labour market rather than just as convenient – and perhaps cheaper – substitutes for local workers. In Singapore, such fees are charged to employers wishing to employ medium-level skilled, semi-skilled or low-skilled workers in certain sectors, such as manufacturing, construction and services, and which are increased if the worker is less skilled.[20] The official website refers to the foreign worker levy as "a pricing control mechanism to regulate the demand of foreign workers in Singapore" (Singapore Ministry of Manpower, 2008). Such policies serve to minimize distortions in certain sectors of the economy, for instance agriculture, that often depend on a foreign workforce, and make funds available to restructure these sectors to make them less dependent on migrants (Martin et al., 2006).[21] However, the effective implementation of such policies depends on the extent to which governments of destination countries are prepared to recognize the merits of setting fees when weighed against the additional costs generated through increased government intervention and the introduction of adequate enforcement mechanisms to ensure that fees are not deducted from the wages of migrant workers (Ruhs, 2006; Ruhs, 2005).

5. Designing Foreign Labour Admission Policies: Permanent or Temporary Labour Migration?

Once there is a policy consensus on the need to admit foreign workers, policymakers need to decide whether to opt for employment-based immigration

---

[18] However, there is currently no longer a need for nurses generally in the U.K., with the exception of certain categories of registered nurses. The National Shortage Occupation List is available at http://www.ukba.homeoffice.gov.uk/sitecontent/applicationforms/workpermits/businessandcommercial/occupationshortagelist.pdf.

[19] The MODL is available at http://www.migration.gov.au/skilled/general-skilled-migration/skilled-occupations/occupations-in-demand.htm. The May 2008 list also included two occupations in an Associate Professionals category (Chef and Dental Technician) and two occupations under the general heading Managers and Administrators.

[20] Moreover, the levy for these categories of foreign workers in Singapore is combined with a Dependency Ceiling, which means the employer will have to pay higher fees in sectors such as manufacturing or services if the percentage of foreigners to nationals in the workplace is higher (Singapore Ministry of Manpower, 2008). A foreign workers' levy is also applied in Malaysia and Taiwan Province of China (Abella, 2006).

[21] Ruhs (2005) adds that such fees can also be used for a variety of other purposes: to generate funds for enforcement activities and integration assistance; to reduce the opposition of local workers to temporary labour migration programmes by compensating any losses suffered by such workers in terms of wages and/or working conditions; or to mitigate any adverse impact on local workers by funding their retraining and skills development.

or temporary labour migration, or a combination of both. As a general rule, employment-based immigration channels have usually been available to more skilled migrants, while temporary labour migration programmes are normally aimed at low-skilled workers (Chapter 3), largely because of a profound reluctance of local or resident workers to take up these jobs even in times of high unemployment.[22]

In principle, there is nothing to stop destination countries from opening up employment-based immigration to low-skilled workers, and a few examples of such opportunities exist, particularly in Canada and the United States (see Section 5.1(a) below). Skilled workers continue to be preferred for permanent settlement because they are considered more likely to be able to adapt their skills in the event of an economic downturn. However, low-skilled temporary migration programmes are seen increasingly as affording a number of advantages to all stakeholders in the labour migration process (see Chapter 3), and some of these are also discussed below.

The issue of circular migration, relevant to both employment-based immigration and temporary labour migration as well as to the question of return to the country of origin, is discussed in a separate section from the standpoint of policy formulation in destination countries.

5.1 Employment-based Immigration

(a) Established countries of immigration

Today's established countries of immigration (e.g. Australia, Canada, New Zealand and the United States) have long implemented immigration programmes to admit foreigners for the purpose of employment on a permanent basis from the moment of their entry with a view to promoting economic growth and ensuring a stable population and labour force. In the period 2005-2007, over 400,000 immigrants in total in this category were admitted annually for permanent residence in the four countries concerned (Table 11.1). Both Australia and Canada registered an increase in this type of migration. Indeed, the Australian Government enlarged the Skilled Stream visa category by 20,000 in 2005-2006 (DIAC, 2006).

The figures for skilled immigration to the four countries are somewhat misleading because the number of persons admitted for employment is actually much higher when taking into account dependants in both the economic and family classes (see also Chapter 6), as well as refugees admitted for permanent residence who are all permitted to take up work. In Canada, in 2006, a total of 251,649 persons were admitted for permanent residence, and Canada's Immigration Plan for 2008 is to admit between 240,000 and 265,000 permanent residents (CIC Canada, 2007a). The United States foresees a fixed annual employment-based immigration quota of 140,000, defined in the Immigration Act 1990, although this can be adjusted by means of a complex formula. Moreover, the majority of persons (59%) granted permanent residence in 2007 were already living in the United States, with women accounting for 55 per cent of all new permanent residents (U.S. Office of Immigration Statistics, DHS, 2008).

---

[22] "One of the most significant factors generating labour market mismatches is the unwillingness of resident workers to do certain low-skilled, low-status and low-paid work. ... Many professions have now become associated with immigrant or ethnic minority workers, often implying a social stigma for native, or non-minority workers. Occupational preferences may generate serious mismatches in situations of high unemployment, especially where social benefit systems provide limited incentives to take up low-paid or seasonal work" (Boswell et al., 2004: 15).

scheme was abandoned in the new compromise legislation that came into force on 1 January 2005.

5.2 Temporary Labour Migration

Given the prevalence of more "flexible labour market" practices in today's globalizing world, temporary migrant worker programmes have been increased in many industrialized destination countries to fill the (mainly low and semi-skilled) jobs available and that cannot be filled by drawing on the domestic labour force (Martin, 2003; Chapter 3). In the European context, the view that temporary migration of low-skilled migrants should be avoided because it inevitably leads to settlement and unpredictable social impacts has given way to a more positive attitude as not all low-skilled activities can be delocalized to developing countries, and owing to the concern over demographic imbalances and ageing populations and the decline in the working age population (Castles, 2006).

This section focuses in more detail on the policy challenges in making temporary labour migration programmes work, and builds on the more general policy issues outlined in Chapter 3, which also provides an overview of the global and regional trends relating to temporary labour migration with particular reference to low and semi-skilled workers.

(a) The potentially positive impact of temporary labour migration

The potentially positive impact of temporary labour migration for all actors involved in, or affected by, that process (i.e. countries of destination and origin, and migrant workers, especially low-skilled workers, and their families) has been widely recognized by the international community in recent years (GFMD, 2008; UN, 2006; World Bank, 2006; GCIM, 2005; IOM, 2005; ILO, 2005; UN DESA, 2004) (see also Textbox 3.5), and there is a convergence of interests by countries of destination and origin regarding temporary labour

migration (Ruhs, 2005). For countries of origin, such programmes provide authorized access to the labour markets of richer destination countries, particularly for their low-skilled workers, and the positive development impact on their economies (i.e. transfer of remittances and know-how and creation of business and trade networks) is arguably optimized if their citizens' stay abroad is temporary and they retain strong links with their home country. For destination countries,

> [t]emporary migration ... is viewed as contributing to greater flexibility in the labour market. For many countries this is of considerable importance given their ageing workforces, the demands of industry for new skills, and the tendency of people to become less mobile as societies become more prosperous. Secondly, compared to permanent immigration, liberalizing temporary admissions is politically easier to sell to electorates that have come to feel threatened by more immigration. And, thirdly, some societies have experienced increasing difficulties with integrating long-settled immigrant communities, hence they opt for solutions that would not compound their problems (Abella, 2006: 1).[26]

For migrant workers, such programmes provide access to authorized, albeit temporary, work abroad and the opportunity to earn higher wages (Ruhs, 2005).[27]

---

[26] With regard to the first reason, it has been observed that such persons will be less inclined to migrate for lower skilled employment abroad because they are more likely to be attracted by better opportunities at home. See also Nonnenmacher (2007a): "temporary labour migration is seen as a means to meet sectoral, seasonal and peak demands for labour **in a flexible manner**. Its temporary character ensures that **public opinion** is less negative towards it than towards permanent migration. It alleviates concerns relating to the social integration of migrants and their reliance on public services and welfare payments" (Original emphasis).

[27] But also at the risk of restricting some of their rights, a "trade-off" which temporary migrant workers might be willing to accept to improve their economic situation (Ruhs, 2005). For arguments relating to the trade-off between migrant numbers and rights, see the discussion below and Chapter 3.

(b) Policy challenges

Despite the opportunities offered by temporary labour migration, there are a number of difficult policy challenges for destination countries relating to the design of specific programmes (Martin, 2003; Ruhs, 2005). The principal challenge is to ensure the feasibility, equity and efficiency of such programmes on a reasonably large scale, given past policy failures,[28] which can be summarized as follows: (1) segmentation and distortions of national labour markets causing certain sectors, such as agriculture, food production, hospitality and low-skill domestic services to depend on foreign labour; (2) the failure of temporary migrants to return to their countries of origin on completion of their employment, which is also identified as a particular disincentive for destination countries to develop new programmes; and (3) the exploitation temporary migrants, especially the low-skilled among them, are prone to during the recruitment process and in the workplace, and the risk of social exclusion and discrimination and xenophobia in destination countries.

The policy challenges created by labour market distortions in certain sectors and the dependence on foreign workers this may generate have been discussed in Chapter 3. Levying realistic (monthly) fees on employers for the hiring of foreign workers in the sectors concerned, as discussed in Section 4.3(d) above, to ensure that they seek out local workers or consider other alternatives such as mechanization of production processes or outsourcing (Ruhs, 2005), has been advanced as one possible solution to addressing the segmentation of the labour market. However, the problem here runs deeper and also relates to systemic issues such as low pay or lack of decent work (exacerbated by intense global competition) in these sectors.

Second, a number of policy interventions are applied (or have been advanced) with the objective of encouraging the return of migrant workers admitted under temporary labour migration programmes, such as:

- issuing temporary but longer-term work permits to enable workers in low-skilled occupations to repay the expenses incurred in connection with their migration and to save enough money with which to return home;
- requesting migrants to announce their return at the embassy or consulate of their former destination country, which also serves to facilitate their subsequent return to that country for a further period of employment;
- enabling migrants with valid work permits to travel relatively freely between their countries of origin and destination for family and business visits;
- enabling the transfer of social security payments (for pension and health benefits) to the country of origin (see also Section 6.5 below);
- designing a sponsor system for employers whose record on return counts towards their future prospects to sponsor and hire foreign workers;
- the formulation and implementation of relevant procedures to ensure the return of migrant workers who overstay, and enforcement measures such as workplace inspections and employer sanctions;
- requiring workers to invest a portion of their wages in special high-interest bearing savings accounts, the funds from which may be accessed on their return to their home country; and
- subjecting employers to financial security bonds which may be retained by the authorities if the worker does not leave after his or her permit has expired (Agunias and Newland, 2007; Ruhs, 2006; Ruhs, 2005; U.K. Home Office, 2005).

Some of these measures, especially the last two, raise labour and human rights concerns on account of

---

[28] Two past temporary programmes frequently described in terms of failures are the Bracero programme involving Mexican migrant workers to the United States (1942-1964) and the *Gastarbeiter* ("guest worker") programme in Germany (1955-1973). See also Chapter 3 and Ruhs (2006).

"As undocumented migrant workers we do have rights, the trade unions and everyone else tell us that we do, but the problem is exercising them. It's like having a Porsche without knowing how to drive", said Henry Cardona of the Collectif des travailleurs et des travailleuses sans statut légal – Genève (CTSSL).

Nonetheless, the law protects undocumented migrant workers in many countries, and undocumented migrant workers in Europe and in the United States have won many cases.

9. Working with Government Agencies to Promote Undocumented Migrant Workers' Rights

Undocumented migrants tend to be reluctant to approach government agencies. Nevertheless, many government agencies and labour inspectors do not let the legal status of workers impede their main task of upholding fair working conditions and sanctioning employers who fail to observe labour requirements.

Liaising with these agencies can therefore be helpful, since they often can and will intervene to protect undocumented migrant workers.

10. Advocating for Legal Status of Undocumented Migrant Workers

A final means of preventing abuse and exploitation is regularizing the status of undocumented migrant workers.

There are many arguments for regularizing undocumented migrant workers: it leads to the increased visibility of this particular social group and thus to increased protection. It is strongly arguable that it is not only the workers who benefit, but society at a large. Regularizing undocumented migrant workers is a means to combat the informal economy and to stop the deterioration of general working conditions, which in the end affect all workers.

Source: Michele LeVoy, PICUM – Platform for International Cooperation on Undocumented Migrants.

Although there is no demonstrable evidence to sustain that the creation of **more opportunities for regular migration** will necessarily result in less irregular labour migration, the opening up of more channels for regular migration, that are equitable and sufficiently attractive in both scale and benefits to deter individuals from taking up irregular employment, has a place in any comprehensive approach.

Limited regular labour migration channels and the failure of some traditional preventive measures have drawn greater attention to **regularization policies** as a means of reducing irregular labour migration. While immigration rules in some destination countries contain limited regularization provisions applicable to individuals as apart of their overall immigration policy (e.g. U.K.) (Apap et al., 2000), the implementation of more visible and large-scale collective regularization exercises poses a dilemma. On the one hand, it has been argued that regularization rewards irregular migrants for entering without authorization or overstaying their entry entitlement and, indeed, encourages further irregular entries. On the other hand, it clearly provides a solution for individuals who, for legal, political, humanitarian or practical reasons, are unable to return to their country of origin. Proponents of regularization point out that there are also distinct economic and social advantages for destination countries in promoting regularization, including integration into the labour market of those irregular migrant workers who are unlikely to be paying taxes and social security contributions. For example, in November 2006, the Head of the Russian Federal Migration Service was reported as stating that the presence of approximately 10 million irregular migrant workers in the territory cost the economy more than USD 9.3 billion in unpaid taxes, which was equivalent to the Russian Federation's total budget on education and healthcare (Russian News and Information Agency, 2007). Moreover, regularization prevents the creation of a marginalized group of persons living and working in the midst of the host society. Consequently, policymakers have chosen to undertake both sporadic and periodic regularizations: the most recent examples being the collective decision of the German Länder in November 2006 to allow the regularization of persons holding the temporary and precarious "tolerated status" (*Duldung*) (Geyer, 2007); a pilot regularization of migrant workers in an unauthorized situation conducted in the Russian Federation in the last quarter of 2005 (OSCE/IOM/ILO, 2006, 2007); and the large-scale regularization of irregular migrant workers in Spain in 2005, which resulted in nearly 700,000 applications (Arango and Jachimowicz, 2005: see also Map 7a). Regularization and/or registration programmes have also been implemented recently in a number of Latin American and Southeast Asian countries (see Textbox 8.3 and Maps 7a and 7b). However, the downside is that regularizations may have limited application and thus not necessarily be of lasting effect as the individual in question may for a variety of reasons slip back into irregularity.[63] Some EU Member States, particularly in northern Europe, are negatively inclined towards large-scale regularizations as these may have adverse impacts on other Member States in view of the abolition of internal EU border controls.[64] ILO has argued in favour of an individual right to "earned adjustment" for irregular migrants who cannot be removed and have demonstrated good prospects of settling in the host country (ILO, 2004).

Return is often regarded as the counter measure to further regularization measures, and is sometimes seen as a means of guaranteeing the integrity of regulations concerning regular migration for employment. Return mechanisms are most effective when they include and promote an option for voluntary return (see Textbox 8.5). Readmission agreements, referred to in Chapter 8, are considered as a necessary deterrent by countries of destination,

but are often viewed with reluctance and scepticism by countries of origin, in particular concerning commitments to take back irregular migrants without papers but who are deemed to be their citizens, or non-citizens who transited their territory on the way to the destination country. Within the context of international cooperation (see also Section 8 below and Chapter 13), return measures, such as readmission, have been increasingly connected to the opening up of further regular migration channels, such as labour market quotas for some foreign nationals (e.g. Italy) (OSCE/IOM/ILO, 2006, 2007). Similarly, at EU level, readmission agreements have been negotiated with the Russian Federation, Ukraine and a number of Western Balkan countries,[65] in conjunction with visa facilitation agreements, and the European Commission (2007) has proposed the development of mobility partnerships between interested groups of EU Member States and third countries.[66]

7.2 Addressing the Informal Labour Market

It is increasingly acknowledged that irregular migration is essentially a labour market and not only a legal or security issue; the fact that many irregular migrants are able to find work in the informal economy indicates that there is a clear link between irregular migration and the labour market (Awad, 2006). In EU Member States, the informal economy accounts for between seven and 16 per cent of GDP (Mormont, 2002), although the majority of workers who comprise it are nationals.

The use of irregular migrant labour in certain employment sectors in countries of destination, especially in low-skilled sectors (viz. agriculture, construction, hospitality and catering, cleaning and domestic services), creates a dependence relationship

---

[63] E.g. if continued regular status is tied to employment and the migrant loses his or her job.

[64] Indeed, this approach resulted in the adoption of the EU Council of Ministers Decision referred to in n. 70 below.

[65] Albania, Bosnia and Herzegovina, Former Yugoslav Republic of Macedonia (FYROM), Montenegro and Serbia.

[66] The EU and a number of its Member States recently signed mobility partnerships with Cape Verde and Moldova (see Chapter 13).

able to exploit their knowledge of markets in both countries and thus may become good trade and investment intermediaries.

As remittances continue to flow into the local economy, they will fuel consumption and investment at home. Human capital accumulation is spurred in part by remittance flows and by the stronger incentives for personal advancement provided by the possibility of emigration. All of these phenomena boost productivity in countries of origin. Although growth may be accompanied by a reduction in absolute poverty, changes in the distribution of income and wealth depend in large measure on who migrates and how remittances are used. Growth alone does not guarantee that inequality will decline.

In most cases, by the time of the **return** stage, emigration will have contributed to skill formation for the migrant and to home country development and economic growth. As a result, the home country may begin to experience certain labour shortages, especially in some low-skill labour market segments, which may then be filled by internal migration or labour migration from neighbouring countries. The return of former emigrants may also coincide with such low-skilled labour migration and thus contribute to the local labour supply. As the number of returnees increases, the level of remittance transfers may decline. Irrespective of their original place of residence, returnees often choose to settle in cities on return, which increases pressure on urban labour markets, while new arrivals from neighbouring countries are more flexible and usually settle where there are labour shortages, finding employment as agricultural workers in rural areas or as household employees.

Whether growth is boosted or dampened at this stage depends upon the degree to which migrants either complement or "crowd out" native workers, upon the kind of skills introduced by return migrants and on labour market flexibility. Where regional markets are more integrated, flows of seasonal or contract migrant workers facilitate the creation of economic and social networks leading to positive externalities in trade and investment with neighbouring countries.

The impacts of the migration cycle on economies and societies in both home and host countries will differ depending on the characteristics and particular local socio-economic condition, and vary among countries. Some stages might be skipped or never reached in a given migration experience, and the duration of certain phases may differ significantly within the migration cycles themselves, as well as among countries. The critical lesson is that the net balance from migration for a country's development depends upon the particular stage in its migration history. Overall, the effect on growth can become more positive over time.

3. Managing the Labour Migration and Development Equation: The Role of Destination Countries

The joint consideration of migration and development cooperation policies, in a properly structured institutional setting, can form the basis of genuine migration and development partnerships between countries of origin and destination, as well as of transit countries, where applicable. Such partnerships should exploit the full range of benefits of cooperation – and the costs of non-cooperation – to pursue more effective management of labour mobility. This does not imply that migration policies do not need to take into consideration other major domestic policy concerns, including employment, social protection, security or social cohesion; nor does it imply that domestic policy priorities need to yield to development objectives of partner countries. Rather, the joint consideration of migration and development issues, including development assistance, could facilitate policy formulation and make difficult trade-offs (e.g. between development assistance for capacity building and recruitment of skilled workers) easier to handle.

Development assistance can help to resolve some of the challenges posed by international labour migration, particularly by enhancing the capacity of countries of origin to successfully adjust to emigration, for instance through support for infrastructure development, improvement of education and health systems, co-development projects, or support for appropriately designed fellowships and training schemes. However, it should also be pointed out what aid should **not** be expected to do: some observers suggest, for example, that aid be used by the OECD Development Assistance Committee (DAC) donors to stop or control immigration. This recommendation is misplaced for a number of reasons. First, the links from aid to growth are weak and, even if aid spurs growth, that does not mean that migration will necessarily diminish as a result.[6] In fact, the opposite might be true: as income rises in a developing country, households initially unable to afford the cost of migration now choose to move, a phenomenon referred to as the "migration hump".[7]

Second, using development assistance as a bargaining device to secure cooperation in controlling irregular migration, as is sometimes suggested, would be fraught with difficulties — not least because low and middle-income countries with limited resources, would be at least as hard pressed to enforce emigration border controls as destination countries are to enforce immigration border controls. Finally, the principal objective of development assistance is and should remain poverty eradication. Official development assistance (ODA) should not be intended to serve the double aim of poverty reduction and

migration control. Given that very little of the low-skilled migration to the European Union (EU), for example, originates from the least developed countries, redirecting development assistance towards the high-migration middle–income countries in order to influence migration patterns there, would run counter to the objective of eradicating the most severe poverty.[8]

3.1 Looking at Migration Policies Through a Development Lens

To improve migration management and to maximize the positive impact of migration, destination countries need to address the development impacts of their recruitment and admission policies, as well as development cooperation policies and the degree of mobilization and the channelling of remittances towards productive uses.

(a) Tackling the brain drain

Many developed countries have programmes to facilitate the entry of **highly skilled migrants**. Indeed, the global competition to attract the best and the brightest is intensifying (see Chapter 2). The disruption from the loss of key personnel, such as healthcare workers and educators, and the public costs incurred to train potential emigrants can be very real.[9] Of course, a highly educated diaspora could, in principle, provide benefits to the home economy – but the evidence for this remains weak and pertains more to upper middle-income countries, which are better placed to take advantage of technologies transferred from abroad and any fresh skills of returning diaspora members. Meanwhile, the poorer the country, the more it is likely to feel the loss of highly educated persons migrating to industrialized countries. How can these trends be

---

[6] The modern, largely pessimistic, empirical analysis of the effects of aid begins with the World Bank's report *Assessing Aid* (1998), which found that aid promotes growth, but only in good policy environments. Even this modest conclusion was called into question by subsequent research that suggested that it was not econometrically robust. The principal authors of the World Bank's research reviewed the criticism and responded in Burnside and Dollar (2004).

[7] On the "migration hump", see Faini and Venturini (1993), Hatton and Williamson (1998, 2002), Stark and Taylor, (1991) and Vogler and Rotte, (2000), among others. The cover of the 2006-2007 *Human Development Report* for Mexico (UNDP, 2007) suggests a variation on the migration hump, plotting an index of migration intensity against the human development index for many hundreds of Mexican municipalities.

[8] Cogneau and Gubert (2005) demonstrate that emigration rates are much higher for middle-income developing countries than they are for low-income countries. See also Dayton-Johnson and Katseli (2006b).

[9] For a discussion on the evidence of losses and potential gains from skilled migration, see Katseli, Lucas and Xenogiani (2006a and 2006b).

weather and price shocks, facing the prospect of overpopulation, multi-ethnic and with wide income inequalities, it had, in addition, experienced political conflict. And yet, within a decade, the country was able to turn such dire predictions around by diversifying its economy and promoting external investment. Within Africa, this small island in the southwest Indian Ocean became the "Mauritian miracle".

As during the 1970s, when Mauritius turned its fate around, it again appears that it will once more be able to turn some of its current disadvantages into distinct advantages in the international labour market. Mauritius has a vibrant and multicultural population; speaking both French and English, and local Creole; a mix of religions including Hinduism, Christianity, Islam and Buddhism - all factors which can potentially facilitate integration into host communities. Mauritians also pride themselves on their adaptability, which is evident from the 200,000 members of the Mauritian diaspora.

Apart from such natural advantages, the Government of Mauritius is also keen to implement its own policy direction and has set up an "Empowerment Programme", which aims to rapidly reduce unemployment by identifying and supporting new employment possibilities, retraining and investment. The Empowerment Programme has been allocated five billion Rupees (approximately USD 180 million) for the first five years to initiate the various components of the programme.

Through an IOM 1035 facility project,[1] the Government of Mauritius has been assisted in the development of an overseas employment strategy, the outcome of which was the establishment of a subcommittee on circular migration within the Empowerment Programme. Since May 2007, with a view to primarily addressing the unemployment problem, this subcommittee has met to formulate the conditions necessary for short-term placement of Mauritian workers to take up temporary employment abroad and to acquire skills and save money before coming back to start a small business or invest in other economic activities. The pilot placement of the first migrant workers abroad began in 2008. Perhaps this is the start of a new "migration miracle"?

Note:

[1] IOM's 1035 facility provides special support to IOM developing Member States and Member States with economies in transition for the formulation and implementation of joint government-IOM projects addressing particular areas of migration management.

Source: Elizabeth Warn, Labour Migration Specialist, Labour and Facilitated Migration, IOM Geneva.

Regional schemes among developing countries also deserve attention. Policies to facilitate cross-border regional market integration through improved infrastructure and appropriate visa policies, including perhaps also the introduction of regional passports, should be considered. This is supported by the evidence that a large part of the migration of less-skilled workers (and even more so of refugees) is intra-regional, and that migration by the less-skilled has the greatest potential to alleviate poverty.

(c) Mobilizing and channelling remittances for development

Remittances sent by migrants to families and friends in home countries constitute an important driver of development, particularly as a country's migration cycle moves into the consolidation phase,[13] although assessing the economic impacts of migration and remittances gives rise to a number of challenges (see Textbox 12.3). The actual amounts remitted by migrants will depend on economic and financial conditions in both countries of origin and destination, on the composition of migration flows as well as the conditions on which the migrants are admitted into the host country, and are therefore in part determined by admission policies in developed countries. The pro-poor effects associated with remittances are much stronger in the case of low-skilled as opposed to highly skilled migration, especially if highly skilled migrants settle permanently abroad with their families. Low-skilled migrants tend to remit a larger proportion of their income and direct their savings to their low-income families, who often remain in the home country.

---

[13] See Katseli, Lucas and Xenogiani (2006a) for a review of the evidence on the development impact of remittances and multiplier effects.

Textbox 12.3

Challenges in Assessing the Economic Impacts of Migration and Remittances

The rapid growth in the transfer of remittances has increased the interest in the economic impacts of migration and remittances on recipient developing countries.

It is frequently assumed that receiving households tend to spend all or a large part of the remittances they receive on consumption and that, in the absence of increased spending to improve human capital, i.e. on education and training, or to launch entrepreneurial activities, this might generate or perpetuate a cycle of dependency rather than lead to self-reliance and economic growth.

However, to gain a more realistic and detailed picture of the impact of remittances on receiving communities, a number of factors need to be considered:

- *The fungibility of money*: Remittances are an additional source of income for most households and, though they may be spent on consumption or traditional festivals and other celebrations, they nevertheless augment available household resources and enable the diversification of household expenditures, including on better nutrition which, in turn, improves health and well-being. Therefore, to concentrate only on "spending on consumption" falls short of the full picture and fails to measure the actual economic impact of remittances.

- *Self-selection concerning the decision to migrate*: To simply contrast the respective outcomes for households with and without migrants, or with and without remittances, is misleading, since those who in fact migrate are not a random sample of the population, rather they "self-select" for both observable and unobservable reasons. Many reasons underlying a desire to work abroad are closely tied to the actual outcomes used to measure the impact of labour mobility. For example, poor parents who value education very highly might send a migrant abroad to earn money to pay for schooling and also encourage their children to stay in school. Then, if it is observed that children in households receiving remittances are more likely to stay in school, this could reflect differences among households in how much they value education, rather than just the effect of receiving remittances.

- *Reverse causality*: Both migration and remittances may be driven by specific interests rather than be the cause of observed outcomes. For example, if remittances are sent in response to a household member's ill health, it may be observed in due course that households which receive remittances have poorer health than households which do not receive remittances. This does not in any way mean that receiving remittances is bad for one's health.

The consequence of these challenges is that estimation of the economic effect of migration requires comparing the situation of a household with a migrant to the unobserved situation in which the household would have been had a member not migrated. There are a variety of econometric methods available for approximating the latter. In a unique study, McKenzie, Gibson and Stillman (2006) are able to assess how well these different methods perform by taking advantage of a migration lottery used to select among Tongans applying to work in New Zealand. Comparing winners in this lottery (who migrate) to losers (who stay in Tonga) reveals an income gain from migration of NZ$274 per week, which is only half of what the difference in GDP per capita would suggest. Figure 12.1 below compares the performance of a number of non-experimental estimators against this mode of calculation. Using a good instrumental variable gives results close to the experimental estimates, whereas the other non-experimental methods overestimate the gains to migration by 20 per cent or more. This suggests that migrants in their study have higher unobserved ability than non-migrants.

With careful use of an instrumental variable, it is possible therefore to obtain reasonably accurate measures of the overall impact of migration on outcomes such as schooling, child health, poverty and inequality, and business ownership. However, most of these effects cannot be interpreted as being simply due to remittances. The main difference between remittances and other sources of household income is that the receipt of remittances is typically accompanied by the absence of a household member, which in turn will affect development outcomes. The absence of one or both parents may have a number of different direct impacts, on children, the single spouse left behind or grandparents (see also Textbox 6.1). Also, absent household members may transfer ideas and knowledge, as well as money; the migration of one family member may increase

3.2 Coherence of Policies for More Effective Management

Many of the factors that affect the labour migration and development equation span two or more policy domains, including policies related to migration and development, but also agriculture, trade, environment and security. The potential for international migration to contribute to economic development is greater if migration, trade, investment and development assistance considerations are jointly addressed at the national, regional and global level (Dayton-Johnson and Katseli, 2006a; Katseli, Lucas and Xenogiani, 2006b).

The trade policies pursued by developed countries should be crafted with due regard to their impact upon labour mobility. Being able to export products that make intensive use of low-skilled labour is a critical strategy for accelerated growth in countries of origin and a principal rationale for opening to trade. Expansion of such export industries might even have the effect of easing migration pressure as some workers may choose to work in export industries rather than emigrate. However, such a growth strategy is complicated by the trade policies of developed countries. For instance, the use of agricultural subsidies by many of the industrialized countries that depress world prices for agricultural products[14] hurt living conditions in countries that are exporters of cash crops, possibly exacerbating migration pressures. While the effects of such policies on potential migrants vary within and across developing countries, this example illustrates that the impacts of trade, migration and development policies of developed countries on specific low and middle-income developing countries need to be considered alongside migration policymaking.

Meanwhile, a new agenda on security and development would provide an opportunity to explore the many interlinkages between development, migration and security – links that have been sidelined in the wake of the September 11, 2001 terrorist attacks on the United States (Katseli, 2006). Such a new agenda calls for a broad conception of security. "Security" certainly includes the security from terrorist attack, but also the security from a broader class of negative shocks that make poor people vulnerable. Policies and programmes could explicitly aim to address the various sources of insecurity[15] that often cause people to emigrate and also hamper development. Strategies for risk prevention, risk mitigation and coping with risk should be incorporated ex ante into the design of policies in countries of origin; and, here too, development assistance can help. Improving access to land and water, supporting agricultural extension programmes and irrigation infrastructure, and promoting institutional capacity building, as well as appropriate land titling and regulatory modernization, are only a few examples of policy priorities that could significantly enhance security in countries of origin and stem the desire for relocation.

Linking migration and development cooperation policies at the national, regional or international level will require substantial rethinking of existing institutional parameters to address the current segmentation of policy competencies across ministries and various agencies and organizations.[16]

At the national level, inter-ministerial initiatives can promote coordination of development and migration policies. Sweden's 2003 Government Bill, committing

---

[14] See Verdier and Suwa-Eisenmann (2006) and Xenogiani (2006) for more discussion of these issues.

[15] Four proximate sources of insecurity include inability to access strategic assets, access to food or other inputs, large market volatility or failed institutional set-ups (Katseli, 2006).

[16] The momentum towards more coherent development policy is gaining in the European Union. In December 2004, the EU Council called for the further strengthening of policy coherence for development: "making wider and more systematic use of existing mechanisms for consultation and impact assessment and procedures to screen all relevant policies for their impact on developing countries" (European Commission, 2005: 18). Particularly noteworthy is the EU's December 2005 "European Consensus on Development", which explicitly calls upon the Commission and the Member States to observe coherence among their policies that affect development (European Commission, 2006).

various ministries to greater policy coherence in relation to measures that affect development through annual reporting to Parliament, is probably the institutionally most ambitious initiative (Sweden, 2003).

4. Managing the Labour Migration and Development Equation: The Role of Countries of Origin

The development impact of international labour mobility depends not only on the policies pursued by host countries or the choices migrants make, but also on the capacity of home countries to adjust successfully to emigration. This capacity will, in turn, depend on the active engagement of migrants themselves – consultation, cooperation, coordination with migrants and their various organizations – as well as on the institutions and policies in their home countries, and can furthermore be strengthened with the support of countries of destination.

In countries where emigration is a prominent feature, national development strategies (in particular "Poverty Reduction Strategy Papers" (PRSPs)[17]) need to pay adequate attention to the migration dimension in their policy development processes, and include it in their macroeconomic policies, human resource management, education policies, infrastructure investments and regional (including "South-South") initiatives.

4.1 Macroeconomic Policies

The budgetary implications of large-scale emigration and remittances can be profound and therefore warrant

explicit recognition in national poverty-reduction strategies. First, when migrants – particularly the highly skilled among them – leave, potential tax revenues decline. Consequently, alternative mechanisms of raising tax revenues so as to avoid a budget deficit need to be adequately addressed. Similarly, when remittances start flowing in, real exchange rate appreciation needs to be avoided through careful management of the exchange rate. Emigration may also shift expenditure priorities. Resources might need to be shifted towards public and social service delivery systems weakened by the loss of qualified staff (e.g. healthcare, education) or towards services for dependent children, spouses or elderly parents not effectively supported by absent migrant family members. However, any such scheme may have the undesired side-effect of weakening the personal responsibility and readiness of remittance-sending migrants to continue to offer support for their family back home, or to reduce such support over time. Thus, the design of transfer programmes (i.e. social assistance expenditures to support poor households) should be sensitive to the possibility that remittance receipts might level off where there are publicly funded alternatives. Some governments offer matching grants to encourage remittances.[18] However, such matching grants tend to go to communities already relatively well endowed through remittance receipts and may divert spending from other needier communities that do not benefit from migrant remittances.

4.2 Human Resource Management

Human resource management (see also Chapter 10), including employment policies, should also take into consideration current and projected effects of migration on domestic labour markets. The design of sufficient incentives for public sector posts (or for private sector companies hired to work for the public sector) is critical. Such incentives include not

---

[17] The PRSP, according to the World Bank's web site, is "a country-led, country-written document that provides the basis for assistance from the World Bank and the International Monetary Fund, as well as debt relief under the Heavily Indebted Poor Country initiative. A Poverty Reduction Strategy Paper describes a country's macroeconomic, structural, and social policies and programs to promote growth. It summarizes the country's objectives, policies, and measures for poverty reduction. A Poverty Reduction Strategy Paper should be country-driven, comprehensive in scope, partnership-oriented, and participatory."

[18] The *Tres por uno* [Three for one] programme in Zacatecas state, Mexico, is among the most celebrated examples; see Iskander (2005).

5. Effective Partnerships for Better Migration Management

Countries of origin and destination can use bilateral agreements and arrangements as a vehicle for maximizing the gains from international labour mobility by effectively linking recruitment with capacity building and development in countries of origin. Under such arrangements, developed destination countries offer to rethink their labour migration policies, including, notably, measures to promote circular mobility, accompanied by development assistance to increase adaptive capacity in countries of origin. In turn, developing countries could undertake to mainstream migration and remittances into their national development strategies.

For example, such a partnership approach could link migration policies in developed destination countries and human resource development policies in countries of origin. In the presence of emigration, countries of origin need to be encouraged to develop human resource development policies that take account of current and projected effects of migration on domestic labour markets as well as the potential loss of public resources invested in highly skilled emigrants (see also Chapter 10). This implies the provision of sufficient incentives for public sector posts, effective deployment of available personnel and possible restructuring of methods of financing higher education. The retention of highly skilled professionals in developing countries, especially in the health and education sectors, can be substantially improved through investments in public service delivery systems, continuous training of personnel and better working conditions. Development assistance can play an important role in such partnership arrangements by providing resources to the economies of countries of origin to strengthen their capacity to adjust. This capacity could include better transport and communication infrastructure to link up labour markets in different regions of the country of origin, and promotion of financial sector

development to encourage greater use of formal channels to transfer remittances.

6. Engaging Diaspora Networks

Migration management partnerships can be made more effective still if they engage diaspora networks: such groups include migrants (whether they have retained their original citizenship or adopted that of their new country) and they can include second, third and subsequent generations as well.[20] As a country's migration experience moves into the networking phase, the activities of diaspora groups, which can range from informal social relationships to formally constituted associations, become more visible and significant.

In general, the contribution diaspora networks can offer stems from the information advantages and social mechanisms at their disposal. The first information advantage has to do with the flow of information among various parties. Network members know about business opportunities in their host countries that might interest counterparts in their home countries, and vice versa.

Diaspora networks are familiar with labour market conditions in the host country or how to access social services. that can be of help to newcomers to the network (that is, newly arrived migrants). For example, 60 per cent of Moldovan migrants claim to have had a job lined up before they emigrated, based on existing networks (Borodak, 2006). These information flows are not limited to transmitting labour market information. In the field of public health, researchers in the U.K. show that immigrants have low take-up rates of preventative measures such as screening and immunization, and that uncertain immigration status is one of the main reasons why migrants do not access primary health care (Spencer

---

[20] This broad definition of "diasporas" is also that used by the European Commission in recent policy statements on immigration (European Commission, 2005). For a discussion of diaspora definitions, see Ionescu (2006).

and Cooper, 2006). Often migrants' command of English is insufficient to navigate among service providers, while the foreign-language competency of medical workers is too weak to meet them halfway. For their part, medical practitioners are equally unclear as to who is entitled to which service, while those outside metropolitan areas may lack the cultural competency to provide appropriate care (Spencer and Cooper, 2006). Could intermediaries in diaspora networks help to better match up care providers and migrants in need of care? More generally, diaspora intermediaries can help provide better targeting of social services, including, but not limited to, health care.

The second sense in which diaspora networks provide informational value has to do with what economists call an "asymmetric informational advantage" over other actors. Network members know more about their members than outsiders, and this information would be genuinely valuable in a credit or insurance market. Thus, diaspora networks can judge who among them is in need of material assistance, even if their members do not have easy access to formal insurance contracts (or publicly provided social assistance). Similarly, networks can assess whether a given immigrant is a good credit risk, though he or she may have no collateral of any value to a formal bank in the host economy. Indeed, a frequently cited benefit of ethnic (social) networks is the access to the financial capital they provide. Rotating credit associations, for example, often perceived as divided along ethnic or national lines, allow members access to capital for businesses through informal channels; members pool the sums so that each can raise money for small business operations (Rindoks et al., 2006).

A third asset of diaspora networks is that they have access to means of contract enforcement that are presumably unavailable to those outside the network. These may range from social norms of cooperative behaviour within the network (i.e. a network member feels shame if he or she breaches a contract with another network member, but not if

he or she does so in relation to an outsider) to social sanctions, namely, costly actions taken by network members to punish rule-breakers in their midst (the most draconian of which is expulsion). While these social norms are powerful, in diaspora groups, as in many social organizations, they might not be very democratic or fair; the negative aspects of such informal community powers must be acknowledged. Too often, for example, women's participation and voice in such organizations can be weak or non-existent.

These characteristics of diaspora networks allow them, in principle, to provide services more easily to their members that other members of society access directly from the public sector (e.g. information about the healthcare system) or from markets (e.g. a business loan). The promise of diasporas as a policy lever is that they can bridge gaps not filled by the public sector or markets; it remains an open question whether a more efficient solution would be to address market failures directly.

The role of diaspora networks may not be as productive or as positive as it appears at first glance. Experts voice some scepticism that the observed behaviour attributed to networks – loans, information-sharing, investment, cross-border trading, etc. – might often be more accurately ascribed to family contacts. Research on ethnic business networks shows that much of the putatively network-based financing available to ethnic entrepreneurs is, in fact, intra-family lending; moreover, family-based businesses of this type are at a competitive disadvantage when family objectives compete with profit maximization or other economic motives. Other observers point out that there are risks that while such organizations can effectively build social cohesion among migrants, they can also create barriers to broader participation, "filtering them out of mainstream politics into marginal spheres of political activity" (Spencer and Cooper, 2006). Indeed, this concern mirrors the distinction made between "bridging social capital" – institutions that create links between communities –

and "bonding social capital" – institutions that affirm fellow-feeling within communities. Some migrants' associations might be far more effective at providing the latter than the former. Additionally, the very fact that many migrant communities are marginalized reduces their capacity to be effective political or social intermediaries (Rindoks et al., 2006).

Keeping in mind these potential limitations, migrant networks can nevertheless help migrants find jobs and to integrate economically. Migrant organizations can often play a leadership role within social networks by providing guidance and services to migrants. While some organizations provide assistance in filing documentation for family reunification or citizenship, others offer second-language programmes (such as English as a Second Language in the U.K.) and vocational training to upgrade job skills. By partnering with local schools, community colleges, hospitals and vocational training centres, migrant organizations are able to provide meaningful services to their clients.

As the networking stage progresses and information flows through diaspora networks, migration increasingly promotes trade. Migrants may serve as trade intermediaries and facilitators because of their knowledge of opportunities and potential markets, their access to distribution channels, contacts and language. Membership in such networks (which may not be primarily economic in nature, as in the case of religious brotherhoods in North and West Africa, or village-based groups) may play a significant part in contract enforcement given the importance of reputation. Furthermore, access to information and knowledge not available outside the diaspora about market and trade opportunities among their members offer immigrants an advantage for setting up their own businesses (see Textbox 12.4). Thus migrants often create trading networks that increase trade flows between their host countries and their countries of origin (Xenogiani, 2006). This information channel implies that, for all these reasons, migration may actually have an impact both on exports and imports.

Textbox 12.4

Diaspora Linkage in Development: A Bangladesh Case

International migration from Bangladesh goes back to the 18th century and early colonization (de Bruyn and Kuddus, 2004), when sailors from the south-eastern part of Bangladesh, namely Chittagong and Noakhali, travelled from the port of Kolkata to different parts of the world in the British Merchant Navy (Siddiqui, 2005). In the 1940s and 1950s, Bangladeshi crews, especially Sylhetis, of British merchant ships used to land in British ports and settle in the U.K. to cater to the shortage of labour in low-skilled industries (de Bruyn and Kuddus, 2005). Over time, these migrants brought their wives and children and permanently settled there, creating Sylheti communities in different parts of the U.K. In the 1960s, mass migration occurred to the United States; however, it was mostly students and professionals who migrated (de Bruyn and Kuddus, 2005). During this period Bangladeshis also migrated to Australia, Canada, Greece and Japan (Siddiqui, 2004). In the late 1970s, educated Bangladeshis obtained political asylum in Germany and Switzerland and then students began travelling to different European countries in large numbers (Knights, 1996). These movements throughout Europe created small Bangladeshi communities in many European countries and such networks have facilitated chain migration of family and friends, for example in Italy and Spain (Zeitlyn, 2006). Although the long-term emigrant community of Bangladesh is spread throughout various countries, an overwhelming majority still resides in the U.K and the U.S. (Siddiqui, 2004).

Over the years, the diaspora linkages have evolved through the maintenance of social capital, family ties and assistance during natural disasters. However, the significant role of diasporas in the overall development of a country in areas such as business, trade links, investments, remittances, skill circulation and exchange of experiences (Ionescu, 2006) has been studied only in recent times. One such topic of study is the Nandan Group of Companies in Bangladesh.

The Nandan Group of Companies is a progressive initiative of a group of non-resident Bangladeshis (NRBs) living in the U.K. and the U.S. In 1999, Mr. Masrur Choudhury, now Chairman and Chief Executive Officer of the Nandan Group, encouraged 23 NRBs from the U.K. to pool resources and invest in a project in Bangladesh named "Nandan". This initiative led to the establishment of the Nandan Group of Companies, which has now expanded to over 800 employees and a customer base of over half a million (British-Bangladeshi Youth.net, 2007).

The initiative can be considered a success for two main reasons. Firstly, it delivered commercially viable and profitable projects from the funding of NRBs and, secondly, the initiative was an "eye opener" for all NRBs about the possibilities and benefits of investing profitably in their country of origin. The various projects undertaken by Nandan include the development of a theme park constructed in a 60-*bigha* (approximately 20 acres) property on the outskirts of Dhaka in collaboration with Nicco Park and Resorts, India (Amin, 2004). In addition, a major purpose-built supermarket chain, selling different items ranging from groceries to electronics to clothes to fresh fruits, was constructed in different parts of Dhaka.

Over the years, the Nandan Group has expanded further to include the Nandan Water Park – the largest water park in the country – and Nandan Tea and Fatehbagh Tea, which grows organic tea in Sylhet for export to the U.K. and the U.S. (British-Bangladeshi Youth.net, 2007).

The Nandan Group is now in its eighth year, and though the number of investors over the years has remained stable, as Mr. Choudhury observes, the amount invested by the diaspora group has increased substantially.

Future plans of the Nandan Group include the development of a resort behind the existing Nandan Park. In addition, as part of an attempt to establish a bridge between NRBs in the U.K. and Bangladesh, the Nandan Group has plans to take Bangladeshi investment to the U.K. through the creation of an amusement park in the U.K. built around an Eastern theme. Furthermore, the Nandan Group is considering opening a supermarket in the U.K. to sell Bangladeshi products, including foodstuffs and spices, predominantly for Indian and Bangladeshi restaurants based in the U.K.

The Nandan experience has been a revelation for many NRBs about the possibilities of having profitable links with their home countries. Such opportunities are excellent examples of how beneficial partnerships can be developed between the country of origin and its diaspora.

Source: *IOM Dhaka.*

Immigrants have a natural preference for home products, either because of habit or homesickness. If the products they used to consume at home are not available in the host country, then imports from the home country may increase to meet this demand. Several studies have demonstrated a strong link between trade and migration, in part based on such factors.[21] For migrants to act as trade intermediaries, the intention to return home is critical: their knowledge of trade and investment opportunities at home, ability to enforce contracts through personal contacts at home and specific knowledge about conditions at home deteriorate the longer they are away.

Finally, migrant and diaspora networks can be important partners in development cooperation. Traditionally, governments in developed countries and international organizations have engaged diaspora networks to facilitate the return of migrants by means of diaspora-focused return or circulation programmes,[22] and to assist them in their reintegration in home countries. Examples include the International Organization for Migration's Return of Qualified Nationals programme, which provided much of the inspiration for its Migration for Development in Africa (MIDA) capacity-building programme, or the Transfer of Knowledge Through Expatriate Nationals (TOKTEN) programme of the

---

[21] See the review of the literature in Xenogiani (2006).

[22] In general, however, voluntary return programmes have induced very few migrants to go home.

United Nations Development Programme (de Haas, 2006).

Recent initiatives have started engaging migrants' networks as development partners in more imaginative ways. That is, the diaspora is viewed as a reservoir not only of financial capital, but of human and social capital as well. In place of encouraging voluntary return (which has had mixed success), diaspora networks are being increasingly mobilized to foster a kind of "virtual return". The IOM's MIDA programme is a case in point. Initiatives of this kind focus on repatriation of skills and resources, but not necessarily of the migrants themselves (see Portrait 12.1). Remittances are among the most important of these resources. In addition to endorsing the idea of government matching funds (like the example of the *Tres por uno* programme in Zacatecas state, Mexico (Iskander, 2005), in which migrant remittances for community investment projects are matched by local, state and federal governments), the European Investment Bank (EIB), for example, recommends that banking systems offer banking services specifically targeted at migrants — including mortgage products, remittance-tailored bank accounts and investments funds — in order to channel remittances into productive investments (de Haas, 2006). Such innovative initiatives promise to promote both household and community investment of remittances in human development.

Portrait 12.1

Entrepreneurship for Development

Thomas was born in Ghana almost 41 years ago. Arriving in Naples in 1988, he soon moved to Modena in northern Italy where, friends had told him, it was easier to find a job. "At first, Italy was a big disappointment. In Ghana we thought that Italy was like paradise: a sunny, friendly place where you could become rich easily. This was not the case, of course. And for us, coming from Africa, the big shock was the fact that winter is cold, that people live indoors and are actually not as friendly as we had been told. But you know, life is not only relationships, nice people and fun, it is also work and commitment. We all need to survive and to carry on. In fact, even if it was not really what I expected, Italy was able to give me the chance to carry on with my own work."

For Thomas, commitment, seriousness and willpower are key to realizing almost everything. Within a few weeks of his arrival in Modena, he started to work for a company specialized in waterproofing. After that, he worked for six years in a metal workshop. In the meantime, he attended language courses and obtained his driving licence. He married in Ghana, and his wife joined him in Modena in 1991. In the years that followed, he changed jobs, and his attitudes to Italy gradually evolved.

"There comes a moment in life when you start to feel different: one day you wake up, you look out of your window and you feel at home. Now I can say that 80 per cent of me wants to stay in Italy and 20 per cent to return to Ghana for good. I have two daughters, they were born here but I have already taken them several times to Ghana. They feel like Italians, but they have not forgotten their African roots".

In 2005 came the big change: he decided to leave his job and become president of Ghanacoop – a challenging and also risky decision. Ghanacoop is a cooperative run by the Ghanaian migrant community in the Province of Modena, set up with the help of the IOM Rome Office's MIDA-Italia (Migration for Development in Africa) Pilot Project.

This initiative started by importing pineapples from small Ghanaian producers to Italy with the aim of enhancing sustainable trading flows of typical Ghanaian produce and consumer goods between Ghanaian migrant associations in Italy and the small producers in Ghana.

The Ghanaian community in Modena counts about 4,000 people, and the initiative of starting an entrepreneurial activity stemmed from the will to make a concrete contribution to the development of the home country and to build the basis for the creation of social enterprises in Ghana. So far, Ghanacoop has proven to be successful; the pineapples imported to Italy, called

Missghananas, are sold in many regions by three leading retailers and will very soon be distributed nationwide. "I work 12 hours a day, but I really believe that it is worthwhile: we are doing something huge for our community and for our homeland as well. The success of Ghanacoop will be of historic importance and significance for the coming generations."

In February 2004, Thomas obtained Italian citizenship. After 20 years, Thomas is now in the midst of a new challenge, but the first, that of integration, has already been won.

Source: *IOM Rome.*

Co-development projects, pioneered by France, while still relatively modest in numbers and scale, include projects in the home countries involving migrants living in developed countries (i.e. business people, academics, health personnel, engineers). Migrants are encouraged to promote commercial activities or implement social development projects (by building schools or health centres), or lend their expertise to their home country. Moreover, the concept of co-development also includes helping migrants to better direct their savings towards productive investments in their countries of origin. This concerns especially the transfer of monies as well as strengthening the capacities of microcredit institutions. As such, an increasing concern to co-development is how to catalyze and amplify the effects of social investments made with remittances (OECD, 2007).

7. Conclusion

Better management of labour migration promises greater gains for migrants, countries of origin and countries of destination. This chapter has explored the potential costs and benefits developing countries should take into account as they seek to gain more from the labour migration and development equation. The chapter has argued that the economic gains from migration depend upon three effects of emigration: changes in labour supply, induced changes in productivity and receipt of remittances. At different points in a country's migration cycle, the relative contribution – positive or negative – of each of these effects differs; so too, the appropriate policies differ at different points in the migration cycle.

The chapter advocates genuine partnerships between destination and origin countries for the latter to gain more from migration. Destination countries bring to such a partnership the commitment to look at their migration policies through a development lens: what is the impact of these policies on migrants' countries of origin? This does not mean subordinating migration policies to the objectives of development cooperation, but rather taking advantage of complementarities between both policy domains. Origin countries, conversely, commit themselves to take a fresh look at their development policies through a migration lens: how does the fact of large-scale emigration change optimal policy decisions in the macroeconomic, human resources, education, infrastructure and regional cooperation spheres? This does not invite origin countries to pursue emigration as a development strategy, but rather to adapt decision-making to the realities of labour mobility.

Destination and origin countries alike must commit themselves to more coherent policymaking, as the labour migration and development equation is affected by a broad range of policies, including trade, agriculture, investment, labour, social security and national security policies – as well as development and immigration/emigration policies. Policy coherence will require new institutional set-ups to facilitate greater information-sharing, negotiation and consensus building across ministries and agencies within governments and, indeed, between governments.

Finally, more effective partnerships for migration management are not just a job for governments. Diaspora networks, with anchors at each end of the migration corridor, can be uniquely effective partners for governments of countries of destination and of origin. They can serve as intermediaries in integration and labour market policies in destination countries, and as partners in development cooperation policies with both destination and origin countries. The private sector, too, has a role to play. Banks and other financial institutions can, if given appropriate incentives, reduce the costs of transferring money back home and increase access to financial services for migrants' families and communities in remote and rural parts of origin countries.

REFERENCES

Adams, R. and J. Page
2005   "Do International Migration and Remittances Reduce Poverty in Developing Countries?" *World Development*, 33: 1645-1669.

Borodak, D.
2006   "Migration et Développement Economique en Moldavie", Unpublished manuscript, Organisation for Economic Co-operation and Development (OECD) Development Centre, Paris.

Burnside, C. and D. Dollar
2004   "Aid, Policies, and Growth: Reply", *The American Economic Review*, 94(3): 781-784.

Clemens, M.
2007   "Do visas kill? Health effects of African health professional emigration", Working Paper No. 114, March, Center for Global Development, Washington, D.C., http://www.cgdev.org/content/publications/detail/13123.

Cogneau, D. and F. Gubert
2005   "Migrations du Sud, pauvreté et développement" in E.M. Mouhoud (Ed.), *Les nouvelles migrations, un enjeu Nord-Sud de la mondialisation*, Editions Universalis, Paris.

Dayton-Johnson, J. and L.T. Katseli
2006a   "Migration, Aid and Trade: Policy Coherence for Development", Policy Brief No. 28, OECD Development Centre, Paris, http://www.oecd.org/dataoecd/55/26/37860544.pdf.

2006b   "Plus d'aide, moins d'immigration? Une solution en trompe-l'oeil", *Le Monde*, 12 December.

Dayton-Johnson, J. and T. Xenogiani
2006   "Immigration, Development and Policy Trade-offs", paper presented at the Fourth Agence française de développement (AFD)/European Development Network (EUDN) Conference on Migrations and Development: Who benefits?, 8 November, Paris, http://www.eudnet.net/download/Dayton%20Johnson.pdf.

Dayton-Johnson, J., L.T. Katseli, G. Maniatis, R. Münz and D. Papademetriou
2007   *Gaining from Migration: Towards a New Mobility System*, September, OECD Development Centre, Paris.

de Haas, H.
2006   "Engaging Diasporas: How governments and development agencies can support diaspora involvement in the development of origin countries", June, study prepared for Oxfam Novib, The Hague, International Migration Institute (IMI), University of Oxford, http://www.imi.ox.ac.uk/pdfs/engaging-diasporas-hein-de-haas.pdf.

European Commission
2005   *Policy Coherence for Development - Accelerating progress towards attaining the Millennium Development Goals*, COM (2005) 134, 12 April, Brussels.

2006   Joint statement by the Council and the representatives of the governments of the Member States meeting within the Council, the European Parliament and the Commission on European Union Development Policy: "The European Consensus", OJ 2006 C46/1, Brussels.

Faini, R. and A. Venturini
1993   "Trade, Aid and Migrations: Some Basic Policy Issues", *European Economic Review*, 37: 435-442.

Fajnzylber, P. and J.H. López
2007   *Close to Home: The Development Impact of Remittances in Latin America*, The World Bank, Washington, D.C., http://siteresources.worldbank.org/INTLACOFFICEOFCE/Resources/ClosetoHome.pdf.

Hatton, T. and J. Williamson
1998   *The Age of Mass Migration: Causes and Impact*, Oxford University Press, New York.

2002   "What Fundamentals Drive World Migration?", paper presented at the Conference on Poverty, International Migration and Asylum, 27-28 September, Helsinki.

Ionescu, D.
2006   *Engaging Diasporas as Development Partners for Home and Destination Countries: Challenges for Policymakers*, IOM Migration Research Series No. 26, International Organization for Migration (IOM), Geneva, http://www.iom.int/jahia/webdav/site/myjahiasite/shared/shared/mainsite/published_docs/serial_publications/MRS26.pdf.

Iskander, N.

2005   "Social Learning as a Productive Project: The Tres por uno [Three for one] experience at Zacatecas, Mexico", in OECD, *Migration, Remittances and Development*, OECD, Paris, 249-264.

Katseli, L.

2006   "EU Policy Coherence on Security and Development: A New Agenda for Research and Policy Making" in H.G. Brauch (Ed.), *Institutional Security Concepts Revisited for the 21st Century*, ch. 60, Springer Verlag, Berlin.

Katseli, L.T., R.E.B. Lucas and T. Xenogiani

2006a   "Effects of Migration on Sending Countries: What Do We Know?", OECD Development Centre Working Paper No. 250, Paris, http://www.oecd.org/dataoecd/24/54/37053726.pdf.

2006b   "Policies for Migration and Development: A European Perspective", Policy Brief No. 30, OECD Development Centre, Paris, http://www.oecd.org/dataoecd/55/37/37862315.pdf.

Levy, S.

2006   *Progress against Poverty. Sustaining Mexico's Progresa-Oportunidades Program*, Brookings Institution Press, Washington, D.C.

Lucas, R.E.B.

2006   "Migration and Economic Development in Africa: A Review of Evidence", *Journal of African Economies*, 15(2): 337-395.

Organisation for Economic Co-operation and Development (OECD)

2005   *Migration, Remittances and Development*, OECD, Paris.

2007   *Policy Coherence for Development 2007: Migration and Developing Countries*, OECD Development Centre, Paris.

Ratha, D. and W. Shaw

2007   "South-South Migration and Remittances", Working Paper No. 102, The International Bank for Reconstruction and Development/The World Bank, Washington, D.C., http://siteresources.worldbank.org/INTPROSPECTS/Resources/334934-1110315015165/SouthSouthMigrationandRemittances.pdf.

Ratha, D., S. Mohapatra, K.M. Vijayalakshmi and Z. Xu

2007   "Remittance Trends 2007", Migration and Development Brief 3, Migration and Remittances Team, Development Prospects Group, The World Bank, Washington, D.C., http://siteresources.worldbank.org/EXTDECPROSPECTS/Resources/476882-1157133580628/BriefingNote3.pdf.

Rindoks, A., R. Penninx and J. Rath

2006   "What works in networks? Examining economically related benefits accrued from greater economic linkages, migration processes and diasporas", Unpublished manuscript, Institute for Migration and Ethnic Studies (IMES), University of Amsterdam, OECD Development Centre, Paris.

Spencer, S. and B. Cooper

2006   "Social Integration of Migrants in Europe: A Review of the European Literature 2000 – 2006", 28 September, COMPAS, University of Oxford/OECD Development Centre, Paris, http://www.compas.ox.ac.uk/publications/papers/Spencer%20Literature%20Review.pdf.

Stark, O. and J.E. Taylor

1991   "Migration Incentives, Migration Types: The Role of Relative Deprivation", *The Economic Journal*, 101: 1163-1178.

Suwa-Eisenmann, A. and T. Verdier

2006   "The Coherence of Trade Flows and Trade Policies with Aid and Investment Flows: A Background Paper", OECD Development Centre Working Paper No. 254, August, Paris, http://www.oecd.org/dataoecd/9/63/37450734.pdf.

Sweden

2003   *Shared Responsibility: Sweden's Policy for Global Development*, Government Bill 2002/03:122, 15 May, http://www.regeringen.se/content/1/c6/02/45/20/c4527821.pdf.

United Nations Development Programme (UNDP)

2007   *Informe sobre desarrollo humano México 2006-2007, Programa de las Naciones Unidas para el Desarrollo*, UNDP, Mexico City.

Vogler, M. and R. Rotte

2000   "The Effects of Development on Migration: Theoretical Issues and New Empirical Evidence", *Journal of Population Economics*, 13: 485-508.

World Bank

1998   *Assessing Aid: What Works, What Doesn't, and Why*, November, Policy Research Report, Development Research Group, The World Bank, Washington, D.C., http://www-wds.worldbank.org/external/default/WDSContentServer/IW3P/IB/2000/02/23/000094946_99030406212262/Rendered/PDF/multi_page.pdf.

2006   *Global Economic Prospects 2006: Economic Implications of Remittances and Migration*, The World Bank, Washington, D.C., http://econ.worldbank.org/WBSITE/EXTERNAL/EXTDEC/EXTDECPROSPECTS/GEPEXT/EXTGEP2006/0,,menuPK:1026834~pagePK:64167702~piPK:64167676~theSitePK:1026804,00.html.

Xenogiani, T.

2006   "Migration Policy and its Interactions with Aid, Trade and Foreign Direct Investment Policies: A Background Paper", OECD Development Centre Working Paper No. 249, June, Paris, http://www.oecd.org/dataoecd/60/28/37036220.pdf.

Textbox 12.3 - Challenges in Assessing the Economic Impacts of Migration and Remittances

McKenzie, D. and M. Sasin

2007   "Migration, Remittances, Poverty and Human Capital: Conceptual and empirical challenges", MOVe Operational Notes 1, The World Bank, Washington, D.C.

McKenzie, D., J. Gibson and S. Stillman

2006   "How Important is Selection? Experimental versus Non-Experimental Measures of the Income Gains from Migration", World Bank Policy Research Working Paper 3906, May, Washington, D.C., http://www-wds.worldbank.org/external/default/WDSContentServer/IW3P/IB/2006/05/01/000016406_20060501143118/Rendered/PDF/wps3906.pdf.

Textbox 12.4 - Diaspora Linkage in Development: A Bangladesh Case

Amin, K.S.

2004   "Water World in Nandan Park Opens", Aviatour: Internet Edition, http://www.weeklyholiday.net/300504/aviatour.html#top.

British-Bangladeshi Youth.net

2007   "4th Dialogue on Transnationalism and Development Opportunities and Challenges of NRB Investment: Experiences of the Nandan Group", British-Bangladeshi Youth.net, http://www.bbyouth.net/dialogues4.php.

de Bruyn, T. and U. Kuddus

2005   *Dynamics of Remittance Utilization in Bangladesh*, IOM Migration Research Series No. 18, IOM, Geneva, http://www.iom.org.bd/images/publications/Dynamics_of_Remittance_Utilization_in_Bangladesh.pdf.

Ionescu, D.

2006   *Engaging Diasporas as Development Partners for Home and Destination Countries: Challenges for Policymakers*, IOM Migration Research Series No. 26, IOM, Geneva, http://www.iom.int/jahia/webdav/site/myjahiasite/shared/shared/mainsite/published_docs/serial_publications/MRS26.pdf.

Knights, M.

1996   "Bangladeshi immigrants in Italy: from geopolitics to micropolitics", *Transactions of the Institute of British Geographers*, 21(1) (March): 105-123.

Siddiqui, T.

2004   *Institutionalising Diaspora Linkage: The Emigrant Bangladeshis in UK and USA*, Ministry of Expatriates' Welfare and Overseas Employment/Government of Bangladesh and IOM, February, IOM, Dhaka, http://www.iom.org.bd/images/publications/Institutionalising_Diaspora_Linkage_The_Emigrant_Bangladesh.pdf.

2005a   "Introduction" in T. Siddiqui (Ed.), *Migration and Development: Pro Poor Policy Choices*, The University Press Limited, Dhaka.

2005b   "International Migration as a Livelihood Strategy of the Poor: The Bangladesh Case" in T. Siddiqui (Ed.), *Migration and Development: Pro Poor Policy Choices*, The University Press Limited, Dhaka.

Zeitlyn, B.

2006   "Migration from Bangladesh to Italy and Spain", Occasional Paper for the South Asia Migration Resource Network (SAMReN) and the Refugee and Migratory Movements Research Unit (RMMRU), June, Dhaka, http://www.samren.org/Fellowships/papers/Beji.pdf.

ACHIEVING BEST OUTCOMES FROM GLOBAL, REGIONAL AND BILATERAL COOPERATION*

CHAPTER 13

1. Introduction

Migration is by its very nature a transnational process. No country can claim to be in a position to respond to and manage these movements on its own, all the more so since the policies of other countries influence migration flows and the effectiveness of domestic policies. The awareness of the ineffectiveness of unilateral actions, increased diversity of migratory routes and patterns of flows (cutting across regions and continents; reacting to changes in external factors such as immigration policies, economic situations and employment opportunities), and interlinkages with other global issues such as trade, development and human rights have increasingly led states to acknowledge the need for international cooperation in migration management.

However, states have generally been reluctant to translate this growing awareness into concrete action by accepting trade-offs between sovereignty and international regulatory mechanisms. Progress has mainly occurred at the regional and bilateral levels, where common interests between countries of origin and destination are more easily identified

and mutual benefits worked out. But even at these levels, the general tendency has been to engage in informal, as opposed to legal or more formal means of cooperation.

Among the main obstacles to entering into binding legal frameworks on migration are the divergences of opinion on the respective merits of liberalizing or restricting migration flows; administrative and financial burdens of adapting national frameworks; concerns about limiting the state's capacity to intervene because of the nature and extent of the rights to be granted to migrant workers and, especially, to irregular migrants; the diverging views between countries of origin and destination regarding the categories of workers to be given access to domestic labour markets, e.g. skilled, low-skilled or both; and, perhaps most importantly, the general preference for a high degree of flexibility in determining national migration policy.

This chapter provides an overview of the formal and less formal mechanisms in place for managing labour mobility at the multilateral, regional and bilateral levels, with a particular focus on temporary migration for employment, and considers their respective advantages and disadvantages in practice.

---

* This chapter has been written by Sophie Nonnenmacher, Migration Policy Specialist, Migration Policy, Research and Communications, IOM, Geneva.

2. Multilateral Approaches

Although a limited number of instruments cover specific aspects of cross-border mobility for economic purposes, there are no comprehensive global agreements or international conventions in place to manage temporary labour migration.

2.1 ILO and UN Conventions

The International Labour Organization (ILO) has adopted two conventions (Nos. 97 and 143) and two accompanying non-binding recommendations (Nos. 86 and 151) applying to persons moving from one country to another for the purpose of employment.[1] The first convention and its accompanying recommendation, adopted in 1949, focus on setting standards for the recruitment of migrant workers and their conditions of work, while the two other instruments, adopted in 1975 in the wake of the oil crisis, reflect a growing concern about the resulting increase in unemployment, and emphasize the need to prevent irregular migration and the unauthorized employment of migrants (ILO, 2004). Both conventions cover issues related to the entire migration process and provide for equal treatment between lawfully resident migrant workers and nationals. Convention No. 143 obliges states parties to respect the basic human rights of **all** migrant workers and also provides for equal treatment between irregular and regular workers in respect of rights arising out of past employment, such as remuneration, social security and other benefits.[2] Both conventions exclude certain categories of workers from their scope, such as the self-employed, seafarers, frontier workers, and artistes and members

of liberal professions who have entered the country on a short-term basis. In addition, Convention No. 143 excludes students and trainees and temporary workers sent by their employer to perform specific duties or assignments in the destination country from its Part II on equality of opportunity and treatment.

In its 2004 report *Towards a fair deal for migrant workers in the global economy*, the ILO recognizes that international labour standards "were not drafted with the protection of temporary migrant workers in mind and the provisions applicable to other lawfully admitted migrant workers may not always be well suited to their situation" (ILO, 2004: 89). For example, while movements of temporary workers who are sent by their employers to perform a specific duty or assignment for a limited period of time are increasing and are the subject of discussion under Mode 4 of the World Trade Organization's General Agreement on Trade in Services (GATS),[3] as noted above, such workers are excluded from the provisions on equality of opportunity and treatment in Part II of Convention No. 143,[4] together with artistes and members of the liberal professions who have entered the country on a short-term basis.[5] In addition, these instruments do not adequately reflect the increasing role of private actors in the world of work and international mobility for employment, in particular of private employment agencies. This trend led to

---

[1] See respectively: Convention No. 97 concerning Migration for Employment (Revised 1949); Convention No. 143 concerning Migrations in Abusive Conditions and the Promotion of Equality of Opportunity and Treatment of Migrant Workers (1975); Recommendation No. 86 concerning Migration for Employment (Revised 1949); and Recommendation No. 151 concerning Migrant Workers (1975). These instruments can be accessed from the ILO website at http://www.ilo.org/global/What_we_do/InternationalLabourStandards/lang--en/index.htm.

[2] Articles 1 and 9(1) respectively.

[3] See Textbox Int. 1.

[4] Part II is also concerned with, inter alia, the obligation of a state to facilitate family reunion (Art 13), the right to free choice of employment and geographical mobility (Art 14(a)), as well as to recognition of qualifications (Art 14(b)).

[5] But "project-tied" (Article 2(2)(f)) and "specified-employment" workers (Article 2(2)(g)) are covered in the 1990 UN Migrant Workers Convention, discussed below, subject to some limitations (see Part V). The identification of gaps in international standards related to the protection of seasonal workers, project-tied workers, special purpose workers, cross-border service providers, students and trainees resulted in the adoption by the ILO of "Guidelines on special protective measures for migrant workers in time-bound activities" covering such issues as housing, tied employment, wages and other terms of employment, family migration and reunification, freedom of association, social security and return issues for regular migrants during its Tripartite Meeting of Experts on Future ILO Activities in the Field of Migration, 21-25 April 1997 (Doc. MEIM/1997/d.4, Annex I).

the adoption by the ILO in 1997 of Convention No. 181 concerning Private Employment Agencies.[6]

In 1990, the UN adopted the International Convention on the Protection of the Rights of All Migrant Workers and Members of Their Families, which represents an important step towards the more effective protection of the rights of migrant workers and their families by providing in a single instrument a comprehensive set of standards for the protection of all migrant workers, including migrants in an irregular situation (Part III), and more extensive safeguards for regular migrant workers (Parts IV

and V) (see Textbox 13.1),[7] including categories of workers not covered by ILO Conventions Nos. 97 and 143 (i.e. seafarers, frontier workers and the self-employed). The UN Convention is more detailed and specific regarding the rights of **temporary** migrant workers than are the ILO Conventions.[8] Nonetheless, the UN Convention underlines in explicit terms that it does not interfere with the sovereign competence of states to design their own rules on the admission of foreigners. Article 79 stipulates that "nothing in the present convention shall affect the right of each state to establish the criteria governing admission of migrant workers and members of their families".

---

[6] Convention No. 181 contains provisions for preventing abuses of migrant workers in the placement and recruitment processes; e.g. Article 7 states: "Private employment agencies shall not charge directly or indirectly, in whole or in part, any fees or costs to workers." To date, the Convention has received 20 ratifications.

[7] Part IV provides for additional rights to all lawfully resident migrant workers, except as otherwise provided for in Part V (limitations can be applied to seasonal workers (Art. 59), itinerant migrant workers (Art. 60), project-tied migrant workers (Art. 61) and specified-employment workers (Art. 62)).

[8] However, ILO offers potentially better protection to seasonal migrant workers, itinerant migrant workers, technically unqualified project-tied migrant workers, whose rights can be limited according to Part V of the UN Convention, and to students and trainees not covered by the latter (Böhning, 2003).

Textbox 13.1

The International Convention on the Protection of the Rights of All Migrant Workers and Members of Their Families*

The Convention, which came into force on 1 July 2003, establishes minimum standards for migrant workers and members of their families. As of September 2008, 39 countries had ratified the Convention.

Article 2(1) of the Convention defines a migrant worker as "a person who is to be engaged, is engaged or has been engaged in a remunerated activity in a state of which he or she is not a national". It should be noted that the protection provided under the Convention can be invoked not only in the country of employment, but already before departure in the country of origin, during the travel in the country of transit and again upon return in the country of origin.

The Convention distinguishes between migrants who are either in a regular or in an irregular situation. All migrant workers enjoy basic human rights, including irregular migrants, while additional rights are foreseen for regular or documented migrant workers. Parties to the Convention are under an obligation not to discriminate against migrant workers on the grounds of sex, race, colour, language, religion or conviction, political or other opinion, national, ethnic or social origin, nationality, age, economic position, property, marital status, birth or other status (Part II, Article 7).

One of the more interesting features of the Convention is contained in Part VI, which calls for the promotion of humane conditions of migration.[1] States parties undertake to cooperate with each other and maintain appropriate services, such as the exchange of information and assistance, recruitment of migrant workers, orderly return of migrant workers and members of their families, prevention and elimination of illegal and clandestine movements, and employment of migrant workers in an irregular situation.

Concerning labour mobility, of most relevance are the rights of documented migrant workers set out in Part IV of the Convention.[2] Part IV includes not only the right of migrant workers and members of their families to be fully informed by the state of origin or of employment, as appropriate, of all conditions applicable to their admission (particularly concerning their stay and the remunerated activities in which they may engage), but they also have the right to be fully informed of the terms on which temporary absences from the state of employment are authorized and which the state is required to make every effort to provide to them without this adversely affecting their right to remain or work.[3] In addition, Part IV includes the obligation for the state to take measures to avoid double taxation of migrants' earnings and savings, as well as the right of migrant workers to equal (national) treatment in the host country in such fields as access to vocational training and placement services, exemption from import and export duties for household effects and professional equipment, and the transfer and repatriation of their earnings and savings.

Part III of the Convention concerns the rights of all migrant workers and members of their families, including those in an irregular situation, and establishes the right to equality with nationals of the country of employment regarding wages and working conditions (Article 25). The aim of this provision, as set out in the Preamble, is not only to ensure humane and decent working conditions for migrant workers, but also to discourage the employment of undocumented workers by removing any inducement for employers to hire such labour.

The Convention's monitoring body, the Committee on the Protection of the Rights of All Migrant Workers and Members of Their Families (Committee on Migrant Workers), commenced its work in 2004 and started to examine the reports submitted by states parties to the Convention at its 4th Session in April 2006. In its first observations on the reports, the Committee emphasized the need for cooperation to effectively combat illegal or clandestine movements of migrants, and paid special attention to the particular vulnerability of women and children, as well as domestic and agricultural migrant workers.

On the occasion of the High-Level Dialogue on International Migration and Development, held at the General Assembly of the United Nations in September 2006, the Committee organized a "Day of General Discussion on Protecting the Rights of all Migrant Workers as a Tool to Enhance Development".[4] It then adopted a written statement highlighting the human-rights based approach to migration and emphasized the shared responsibility of all states to guarantee the human rights of migrants, as well as the importance of international consultations and cooperation in order to promote and ensure humane conditions of migration.

Notes:
[*] Adopted by UN General Assembly Resolution 45/158 of 18 December 1990. The Convention entered into force on 1 July 2003.
[1] Part VI: Promotion of sound, equitable, humane and lawful conditions in connection with international migration of workers and members of their families.
[2] Part IV: Other rights of migrant workers and members of their families who are documented or in a regular situation.
[3] Articles 37 and 38, respectively.
[4] See http://www2.ohchr.org/english/bodies/cmw/mwdiscussion.htm.

Source: *Carla Edelenbos, Secretary, Migrant Workers Committee, Office of the United Nations High Commissioner for Human Rights, Geneva.*

All these instruments recognize the importance of interstate cooperation in addressing labour migration. ILO Conventions Nos. 97 and 143 contain provisions on the exchange of information on national policies, laws and regulations. The UN Convention (in Part VI) requests states parties to consult and cooperate with the competent authorities of other states parties on measures regarding the orderly return of migrants. Both the UN Convention and ILO Convention No. 143 also envisage interstate cooperation to suppress clandestine movements of migrants for employment and to act against organizers of irregular migration and the unauthorized employment of migrant workers.

The exact form of cooperation is not prescribed and it is for the states parties to determine. However the drafters were of the view that, while general principles or standards can be spelled out at the multilateral level, the differences in situations and legal frameworks between countries call for more specific, complementary modes of cooperation at other levels of operation. The ILO Conventions refer to bilateral agreements as an appropriate means of putting general principles into practice, and Recommendation No. 86 of 1949, provides, in an Annex, for a model bilateral agreement covering the different stages of the migration process which includes a model contract for employment (Article 22). The model agreement also recommends the conclusion of separate bilateral agreements with respect to social security.[9] The UN Convention acknowledges, in its Preamble, the progress made in bilateral and multilateral regional agreements towards the protection of the rights of migrant workers, and their importance and usefulness, and also specifies in Article 81(1)(b) that nothing in the Convention shall affect more favourable rights granted to migrant workers and members of their families by virtue of any bilateral or multilateral treaty in force for the state party concerned.

However, these instruments have been ratified by a limited number of states only[10] and, in so far as the UN Convention is concerned, by no major developed destination country.[11]

2.2 General Agreement on Trade in Services (GATS)

The GATS provides for the liberalization of trade in services. Under Mode 4, the GATS offers a multilateral framework for negotiations,[12] with a set of principles (covering domestic regulations, transparency requirements and other issues) designed to facilitate the movement of service providers. However, the GATS does not create universal criteria for the admission of defined categories of service providers and their access to labour markets. Indeed, it does not provide a definition of service providers nor does it prescribe the range, depth or sectoral coverage of country commitments. Inclusion of individual sectors within the GATS schedules is at the discretion of WTO Member States, which must define the commitment they are prepared to make on market access and national treatment on a sector-by-sector basis. States can also make "horizontal commitments", i.e. cross-sectoral commitments given by Member States for market access (e.g. categories of stay, duration of stay, and conditions of entry and compliance by natural persons). Moreover, the GATS does not require its members to offer market access or conditions that are more liberal than those in national policy settings. Departures from market access and national treatment are not prohibited per se under the GATS, but must be identified in schedules as limitations.[13] Therefore, each party defines in its commitments the category of service providers to be granted freer access and, to date, these commitments reflect merely what is already permitted under existing immigration policies.[14]

---

[9] Migrant workers can face difficulties in benefiting from social security provision as such systems are generally based on contributions and the period of employment or residence (see also Chapter 11). Social security provides another illustration of complementarity between multilateral and bilateral approaches. While ILO Convention No. 157 of 1982 on the Maintenance of Social Security Rights and its accompanying Recommendation No. 167 provide an international framework for the maintenance of acquired rights or rights in the course of acquisition by workers who change their country of residence, they recommend the conclusion of bilateral and multilateral agreements and the Recommendation contains model provisions for such agreements.

[10] ILO Convention Nos. 97 and 143 have been ratified by 48 and 23 states, including both countries of origin and destination, respectively, and the UN Convention has been ratified by 39 states (as of September 2008).

[11] Two destination countries, which have ratified the UN Convention, are Argentina and Libya. Important transit countries that have ratified include Libya, Mexico and Morocco. For obstacles cited by governments to ratification of the ILO Conventions on migrant workers, see ILO (1999). For obstacles relevant to the UN Convention, see the country and regional reports commissioned by UNESCO on the webpage of the UNESCO Project on the International Migrants' Rights Convention at http://portal.unesco.org/shs/en/ev.php-URL_ID=6554&URL_DO=DO_TOPIC&URL_SECTION=201.html.

[12] See the WTO's website at http://www.wto.org/english/tratop_e/serv_e/gatsqa_e.htm#14 (GATS: objectives, coverage and disciplines).

[13] Limitations to market access can take the form of quota restrictions and economic needs or labour market tests, including wage parity requirements (for a fuller description of these mechanisms, see Chapter 11).

[14] Current commitments focus mainly on the highly skilled, such as executive managers and professionals. These categories usually already enjoy quite liberal access in national immigration admission policies (see Chapter 2), while lower-skilled migrants have fewer or no possibilities to enter the country (see Chapter 3).

Each party also determines its own admission criteria. The only limitation to a member's competence to regulate the entry and temporary stay of natural persons within its borders is the obligation to ensure that such measures are not applied in such a way as to nullify or impair the benefits accruing to another.[15] However, some members would like to see the scope of the GATS expanded with the adoption of multilateral rules in the area of admission (such as a standard GATS visa) (Winters, 2005). Other commentators take this idea one step further and would like WTO to monitor and/or participate in the allocation of visas concerning the movement of natural persons.[16] The proposed inclusion of migration management issues within WTO competences is highly controversial and probably unlikely to secure the support of all WTO Member States as required for an amendment of its mandate.[17]

A further contentious aspect is that GATS Mode 4, as a trade agreement, focuses only on one aspect of the migration process, namely the entry and access of service providers, and does not refer to social and labour standards, such as the quality of working conditions for service providers. The argument usually advanced in this context is that the WTO is a trade body and therefore not the appropriate forum to set social or labour standards for the protection of workers worldwide. However, this question is present in the negotiations in an oblique fashion through the notification of limitations to market access in countries' schedules. Indeed, over 50 WTO members stipulate in their commitments that they require wage parity. In addition, 22 members have reserved the right to suspend Mode 4 commitments in the event of labour-management disputes with a view to precluding employers from hiring foreigners

as "strike-breakers" (to replace national workers) (Dommen, 2005). A number of recent regional and bilateral trade agreements also contain explicit references to social issues or core labour standards, either in the text of the agreement or, indirectly, through side agreements on labour cooperation.[18] These provisions do not generally secure any particular labour protection for migrant workers and/or service providers, but they can benefit from broader requirements, such as the obligation to enforce domestic labour standards in a non-discriminatory manner.[19] From a legal point of view, however, these provisions and/or their enforcement mechanisms appear to remain generally weak.

Would it be possible to include a social clause in the GATS to ensure respect for core labour standards (such as non-discrimination in the payment of wages) at the multilateral level? Those in favour of such a clause argue that it will protect local workers from "social dumping", whereas those against express the view that it will reduce the advantage for a country in being involved in recruiting/sending workers abroad. However, to date, it seems that there are no strong voices to advance this issue apart from those of trade unions and some NGOs (GURN, 2007).

While multilateral trade negotiations stalled at Cancun in September 2003, and no significant progress was made in Hong Kong SAR in December 2006, the number of bilateral and regional trade agreements and negotiations has been growing, reigniting a debate about whether such regional

---

[15] GATS, Annex on movement of natural persons supplying services under the Agreement. See http://www.wto.org/english/tratop_e/serv_e/8-anmvnt_e.htm.

[16] See e.g. Ng and Whalley (2007), who envisage this possibility for the WTO or a new international body.

[17] However, some commentators argue that visas already fall within the GATS Mode 4 mandate as they can be part of "measures" referred to in the Annex on the movement of natural persons.

[18] The U.S.-CAFTA-D.R. (U.S.-Central America-Dominican Republic Free Trade Agreement) and the U.S.-Chile Free Trade Agreement (FTA) include commitments to core labour standards (except for the ILO core conventions on discrimination and equal remuneration). In parallel to the Canada–Costa Rica FTA, there is also an agreement on labour cooperation (Canada-Costa Rica Agreement on Labour Cooperation (CCRALC) signed in April 2001). In this agreement, the parties are obliged to embody in their labour legislation the principles enshrined in the 1998 ILO Declaration on Fundamental Principles and Rights at Work and to enforce this legislation effectively (ICFTU, 2004).

[19] E.g. the 11th Principle of the North American Agreement on Labour Cooperation under the North American Free Trade Agreement (NAFTA) provides migrant workers on a state party's territory with the same legal protection as that provided to the state party's nationals in respect of working conditions.

and/or bilateral agreements complement multilateral trade agreements, or undermine them (Brown et al., 2005; ICFTU, 2004; see also Textbox 13.7 at the end of this chapter).

2.3 Other International Instruments

There are a number of other binding international legal instruments of relevance to labour migration. They can be divided into two broad categories: instruments indirectly and directly related to migration. Under the first category are human rights treaties protecting the fundamental rights of all migrant workers as human beings (the two International Covenants on Civil and Political Rights, and Economic, Social and Cultural Rights, 1966), as women (International Convention on the Elimination of All Forms of Discrimination against Women, 1979), as children (Convention on the Rights of the Child, 1989) and as foreigners (Migrant Workers Convention, 1990).[20] Like any other workers, migrants are also covered by ILO international labour standards.[21] Under the second category, it is necessary to mention the 2000 UN Convention against Transnational Organized Crime and its two protocols addressing trafficking in human beings and smuggling of migrants.[22]

2.4 Non-binding Initiatives

In addition, a number of non-binding initiatives have been taken or are taking place at the multilateral level with a view to fostering dialogue and effective practices in managing labour migration, either by focusing exclusively on this objective or as part of a broader migration agenda. Focusing on the protection of the human and labour rights of migrants, in 1999 the UN Commission on Human Rights (now the Human Rights Council) established the mandate of the UN Special Rapporteur on the human rights of migrants,[23] who has since issued a number of reports focusing specifically on migrant workers and conducted several country visits. In 2006, the ILO Governing Body endorsed the non-binding Multilateral Framework on Labour Migration (ILO, 2006), which comprises principles and guidelines promoting a rights-based approach to labour migration, and provides guidance to governments, and employers' and workers' organizations on the formulation and implementation of national and international policies (see Textbox 10.6).[24] IOM's International Dialogue on Migration (IDM) offers a platform for its Membership to exchange information and effective practices in the formulation and implementation of migration policy.[25] An International Agenda for Migration Management (IAMM), published in December 2005, was the outcome of the Berne Initiative, a states-owned process sponsored by the Swiss Government and for which IOM provided the Secretariat (IOM/ Swiss Federal Office for Migration, 2005a). More recently, and as discussed in the Introduction and Chapter 12, the international community has been preoccupied with the theme of international migration and development, which includes an important labour mobility component.[26]

---

[20] See also here the Vienna Convention on Consular Relations, 1963.

[21] The 1998 ILO Declaration on Fundamental Principles and Rights at Work requires ILO Member States to respect four categories of principles and rights at work, even if they are not signatories to the relevant conventions: freedom of association and rights of collective bargaining, equality of opportunity and treatment, abolition of forced labour, and the elimination of child labour.

[22] Protocol to Prevent, Suppress and Punish Trafficking in Persons, Especially Women and Children, and Protocol Against the Smuggling of Migrants by Land, Sea and Air. These Protocols were adopted at Palermo on 15 November 2000 and, as of September 2008, have been ratified by 123 and 114 states, respectively. See also Chapter 8.

[23] For more information on the Special Rapporteur's work, see the website of the Office of the UN High Commissioner for Human Rights at http://www2.ohchr.org/english/issues/migration/rapporteur/index.htm.

[24] The Framework focuses on areas such as inter alia decent work, international cooperation, the effective management of migration and the protection of migrant workers.

[25] See the IDM webpages at http://www.iom.int/jahia/Jahia/lang/en/pid/385 for the recent themes addressed. For example, in 2007 the overarching theme of the IDM, "Migration Management in the Evolving Global Economy", was closely tied to the subject matter of this Report and a workshop was convened on 8-9 October on Global Making Labour Mobility a Catalyst for Development. See http://www.iom.int/jahia/Jahia/pid/1826.

[26] See the UN General Assembly's High-Level Dialogue on International Migration and Development (New York, September 2006) and the Global Forum on Migration and Development (GFMD) (Brussels, July 2007). For an overview of labour mobility in the context of the GFMD, see Textbox Int. 2.

ECOWAS Member States are searching for policies that would enhance the prospects for greater labour mobility in the sub-region, and priorities for action include:

- The establishment of a Permanent Observatory to provide up-to-date information on labour migration patterns and facilitate internal labour mobility within ECOWAS with limited travel documentation.
- The setting up and/or revamping of an Advisory Board on Migration as a forum for formulating and monitoring the status of implementation of national laws and ECOWAS decisions relating to labour migration.
- Raising migration discourse to the top of the political agenda, showcasing the potential contribution of migrant workers to development and underlining the positive outcomes of migration for migrants and countries of origin and destination.
- Harmonizing national laws and employment codes that regulate the types of economic activity that nationals of Community Member States can practice according to the terms of the ECOWAS Protocol on Free Movement of Persons, Establishment and Settlement.
- Concretely addressing the right of residence and establishment of migrants and obligations of the host countries, and ensuring that the rights of migrant workers in the host countries are protected.
- Enhancing capacity of immigration, customs, police and security officials to help transform their role into that of migration managers, assisting to facilitate rather than restrict regular migration within the sub-region. Officials have to be sensitized to the revised national laws and treaties and ECOWAS protocols.
- Mounting an intensive and sustained public education campaign to raise awareness of the ECOWAS passport and travel certificate and its benefits to Community citizens for travel within the sub-region and also to help halt hostility against migrant workers.
- Promoting student exchange and study programmes to help break language and colonial barriers among countries and peoples, and promoting labour migration and more effective utilization of human resources.
- Promoting access of Community nationals to employment and settlement, and easing remitting of earned income through formal banking channels.
- Harmonizing and implementing the policies of trade, investment, transport and movement of persons in a coherent and integrated manner.

Source: *Aderanti Adepoju, Coordinator, Network of Migration Research on Africa (NOMRA) and Chief Executive, Human Resources Development Centre (HRDC), Lagos, Nigeria.*

The European Union represents the most far-reaching form of regional economic integration, and its principal characteristics are discussed below. The right of free movement of workers within the region was introduced by the 1957 Treaty of Rome and expanded to include the free movement of all EU citizens in 1993.[28] The EU has succeeded in creating an area where **all** workers who are nationals of EU Member States are entitled to equal treatment regardless of their nationality with respect to employment, remuneration and other working conditions, access to accommodation and the right to be joined by family members.[29] This means, inter alia, that any national of a Member State is entitled to take up and engage in gainful employment on the territory of another Member State in conformity with the relevant regulations applicable to national workers. In order not to jeopardize this right through improper requirements concerning entry into and residence in Member States, workers must be admitted to their territory simply on the production of a valid identity card or passport and be granted the right of residence.[30] Spouses and, where applicable, registered partners, as well as their children up to the age of 21, are authorized to reside with them.

---

[28] Consolidated Version of the Treaty Establishing the European Community (EC Treaty), OJ 2006 C 321/E/37, Arts. 39 and 18, respectively.

[29] Arts. 12 and 39(2) of the EC Treaty and Council Regulation 1612/68/EEC of 15 October 1968 on freedom of movement for workers within the Community (OJ Sp. Ed. 1968-69, 475, JO 1968 L 257/2, as amended).

[30] For a stay of more than three months the requirement for a residence permit has been abolished, but Member States may require EU citizens to register with the relevant authorities (see Directive 2004/38/EC of the European Parliament and of the Council of 29 April 2004 on the right of citizens of the Union and their family members to move and reside freely within the territory of the Member States, OJ 2004 L 229/35, Article 8).

Under the system of mutual recognition of qualifications, EU citizens fully qualified in one Member State are entitled to exercise a regulated profession[31] in another Member State. Depending on the activity in question and the training completed, recognition will be either automatic or subject to a period of probation or an aptitude test. Self-employed persons and service providers can also exercise free movement rights by virtue of Articles 43-48 (Chapter 2 on the Right of Establishment) and 49-55 (Chapter 3 on Services) of Part Three, Title III of the EC Treaty. Moreover, national social security systems are coordinated at the EU level to prevent discrimination against persons who are exercising their right to free movement.[32]

With regard to service providers, the EC Treaty enables an economic operator providing services in one Member State to also offer services on a temporary basis in another Member State, without having to

be established there. In particular, "services" covers activities of an industrial and commercial character; craftspersons' activities; and professional activities. In those instances where restrictions on the provision of specific services have not yet been abolished, the application of such restrictions must be applied without discrimination based on nationality.

The possibility of derogating from the general rules governing the mobility of EU workers has nonetheless been envisaged for workers from countries joining the EU after the 2004 and 2007 enlargements.[33] "Transitional arrangements", as this label suggests, permit the former EU-15 to derogate temporarily from the principle of free movement of workers in respect of workers coming from the new EU Member States for a maximum period of seven years. These arrangements only apply to workers and not service providers, with some limited exceptions for Austria and Germany (see Textbox 13.3).[34]

---

[31] Regulated professions imply de jure professional recognition, because either the education leading to a professional activity or the pursuit of the particular professional activity are regulated by legal acts (i.e. laws, regulations, administrative provisions), and the final decision on mandatory recognition is in the hands of professional or governmental bodies, or both. The professions regulated vary among countries, generally motivated by consumer protection and public interest concerns. Many countries regulate professions which can have an impact on health or life or result in material or moral loss, such as professions relating to medicine and pharmacy, veterinary medicine, architecture, law or transport.

[32] Article 42 of the EC Treaty and Council Regulation 1408/74/EEC of 14 June 1971 on the application of social security schemes to employed persons, to self-employed persons and to members of their families moving within the Community (JO Sp. Ed. 1971, 416, JO 1971 L 149/2, as amended).

[33] Over a three-year period (2004-2007) the EU has been transformed from a 15-country Union to one of 27 countries. In May 2004, 10 countries joined the 15 EU Member States: Cyprus, Czech Republic, Estonia, Hungary, Latvia, Lithuania, Malta, Poland, Slovakia and Slovenia. In January 2007, Bulgaria and Romania also became members.

[34] The transitional arrangements in the Accession Treaties of 16 April 2003 provide that for workers from the 8+2 new EU Member States in Central and Eastern Europe (the transitional arrangements do not apply to Cyprus and Malta), access to the labour markets of the former EU-15 will depend on the national laws and policies of those Member States. These arrangements only apply to the taking up of employment, with the exception of Austria and Germany, where the movement of service providers in a limited number of sectors, for example construction and industrial cleaning, may also be restricted in the event of serious disturbances in the service sectors in question.

Textbox 13.3

EU Enlargement – Free Movement of Workers

General Provisions

On 1 January 2007, Bulgaria and Romania joined the European Union, taking the total to 27 Member States. While nationals of all 27 Member States are also EU nationals, not all enjoy from the outset equal rights of free movement. All EU nationals are entitled to move freely among the Member States without visas or other pre-entry conditions. They are entitled to remain on the territory of any other Member State for a period of not more than three months without further formalities and longer if they are self-employed, service providers or recipients, or as students, retirees or economically inactive persons, provided they produce evidence of sufficient independent means and will not have to rely on the social security/welfare system of the respective EU host country.

For the nationals of eight of the ten 2004 accession states (i.e. the Czech Republic, Estonia, Hungary, Latvia, Lithuania, Poland, Slovakia and Slovenia, collectively referred to as "A8 states"), the right to employment and to remain in the country to work has been limited, though not for Cyprus and Malta. Thus, "A8" nationals are subject to a gradual labour market liberalization scheme under which pre-2004 Member States (the former EU-15) are entitled to restrict labour market access in their regard for an initial two-year period and, subject to notification, for a further three years. In the presence of serious disturbances in a Member State's labour market, these restrictions may be extended for a further two years. However, A8 workers who have completed twelve months or more of lawful employment in a Member State acquire full Treaty rights and are no longer subject to the transitional provisions.

Among the substantial issues that arise in restricting access to the labour market for workers only, and not for the self-employed and service providers, is the suspicion that the self-employed and service providers might be "abusing" the rules against labour market access by falsely presenting their economic activity as self-employment. Similarly, the fact that companies have the right to bring in workers to carry out service provision, though these workers have no right of access to the labour market, has lead to tensions regarding the working conditions applicable to such posted workers (who tend to be from the EU Member State of origin) and the effect on competition.

Free Movement of Workers: Current Situation of A8 Workers

At present, of the pre-2004 Member States, ten have opened their labour markets completely: Ireland, Sweden and the United Kingdom did so as of 1 May 2004; Finland, Greece Portugal and Spain (1 May 2006); Italy (27 July 2006); the Netherlands (1 May 2007); and France (1 July 2008). The U.K. is continuing its Worker Registration Scheme[1] and Finland is developing one.

While the remaining pre-2004 Member States (Austria, Belgium, Denmark, Germany and Luxembourg) extended the transitional arrangements for a further three years as of 1 May 2006, they have relaxed their labour market access rules for A8 workers, either generally or on a sectoral basis.

Concerning the new EU Member States, Hungary proceeds on a reciprocal basis, while Poland and Slovenia first applied and subsequently removed such reciprocity measures.

Free Movement of Workers: Bulgaria and Romania

Ten Member States (the Czech Republic, Cyprus, Estonia, Finland, Latvia, Lithuania, Poland, Slovakia, Slovenia and Sweden) have introduced no restrictions in regard to workers from Bulgaria and Romania, while Denmark, Hungary and Italy have relaxed their labour market access rules in their regard. However, concerns have been raised in some Member States over the application of general national regulations rather than EU rules to foreigners, particularly in the case of expulsions.

Note:

[1] In the U.K., an A8 worker is obliged to register under the Worker Registration Scheme (WRS) within one month of starting employment. A8 nationals who have been lawfully employed in the U.K. for a continuous 12-month period or who are self-employed or service providers are not required to register. The registration fee is GBP 90, to be paid by the worker who is then issued a registration card and certificate. Employers may face sanctions if they violate this obligation and a fine of up to GBP 5,000. For more information on the WRS, see the UK Border Agency website at http://www.ukba.homeoffice.gov.uk/workingintheuk/wrs/.

Source: Elspeth Guild, Centre for European Policy Studies (CEPS), Brussels, Belgium.

One of the unique EU features is a specific approach to the management of migration flows from regions outside the EU through the development of a common policy on asylum and immigration.[35] However, progress on the adoption of a common EU law and policy on regular or legal migration has been relatively slow. Member States have found it easier to adopt measures in the fields of visa policy; external border controls, including the establishment of the European External Border Agency (FRONTEX); prevention of irregular migration (e.g. through information exchange and measures to combat smuggling and trafficking in human beings);[36] and the establishment of an EU return policy involving the negotiation of EU-wide readmission agreements with third countries (agreements with Albania, Hong Kong SAR, Macao SAR and Sri Lanka have already come into force), and common measures on the return of third-country nationals who are resident without authorization within their territories.[37]

While Directives on the right to family reunification (see also Chapter 6), on the status of third-country nationals who are long-term residents and on the admission of students and researchers have been

adopted,[38] Member States have demonstrated a reluctance to engage at the EU level with the issue of economic-related migration from third countries. In order to break this impasse, in January 2005 the European Commission (2005a) presented a Green Paper on an EU approach to managing economic migration, a consultative document which paved the way for the adoption in December 2005 of a Policy Plan on Legal Migration (European Commission, 2005c).[39] This plan led to two legislative initiatives presented in October 2007. The first is a proposed Directive on the conditions of entry and residence of highly skilled migrants from third countries (European Commission, 2007d), the so-called "Blue Card" proposal, and the second a proposed Directive on a single application procedure for a single permit for third-country nationals to reside and work in the territory of a Member State, as well as a common set of rights for lawfully resident third-country workers (European Commission, 2007e).[40]

A further characteristic of EU migration policy is close cooperation with countries of origin on managing migration flows, which is supported by a special budget line (originally AENEAS, recently replaced by a new programme, the Thematic Cooperation Programme with Third Countries on the Development

[35] EC Treaty, Part Three, Title IV. Key elements of this policy were identified by the European Council in Tampere in 1999: the adoption of a comprehensive approach to the management of migratory flows so as to find a balance between admissions for humanitarian and those for economic purposes; fair treatment for third-country nationals; and forging partnerships with countries of origin, including policies of co-development. The Hague Programme (2004-2009) reinforced these elements and identified new ones. See also n. 39 below. It should be noted that one of the ultimate objectives of the Southern African Development Community (SADC) 2005 Protocol on the Facilitation of the Movement of Persons (which has not yet come into force) is also to eliminate obstacles to the **movement of persons into** the Community (Williams, 2008).
[36] One the most recent initiatives to address irregular migration is the proposed Directive on employer sanctions (European Commission, 2007c).
[37] In June 2008, the Council of Ministers and the European Parliament reached agreement on a Directive on Common standards and procedures in Member States for returning illegally staying third-country nationals. The Directive includes common measures on the voluntary return, detention and expulsion of irregular migrants, and Member States will be required to transpose these measures into their domestic legal and administrative systems within a period of two years from the Directive's formal adoption.

[38] See, respectively, Council Directive 2003/86/EC of 22 September 2003 on the right to family reunification, OJ 2003 L 251/12; Council Directive 2003/109/EC of 25 November 2003 concerning the status of third-country nationals who are long-term residents, OJ 2004 L 16/44; Council Directive 2004/114/EC of 13 December 2004 on the conditions of admission of third-country nationals for the purposes of studies, pupil exchange, non-remunerated training or voluntary service, OJ 2004 L 375/12; and Council Directive 2005/71/EC of 12 October 2005 on a specific procedure for admitting third-country nationals for the purpose of scientific research, OJ 2005 L 289/15.
[39] The Policy Plan defines a roadmap for the remaining period (2006-2009) of the European Council's Hague Programme, a five-year programme for the development of the Area of Freedom, Security and Justice adopted in November 2004. The Policy Plan was one of the priorities identified in the Hague Programme and lists the actions and legislative initiatives that the Commission intends to take to pursue the consistent development of an EU legal migration policy.
[40] Proposed directives on seasonal workers, intra-corporate transferees and remunerated trainees are in the process of formulation (European Commission, 2005c).

Aspects of Migration and Asylum).[41] This cooperation now encompasses the global approach to migration management adopted at the end of 2005.[42] It also builds on earlier initiatives, such as the support of a linkage between migration and non-related issues as a means to secure greater cooperation on migration issues,[43] and the inclusion of migration concerns in EU external and development policies and agreements (European Commission, 2005b).[44] The recent introduction of mobility partnerships to better manage migration flows between the EU and specific third countries is the latest development in the construction of a comprehensive cooperation framework.[45]

All these elements make the EU the most advanced regional entity in managing external and internal movements of persons, even though it took several decades to reach that level. However, the framework applicable to the movement and treatment of non-EU nationals is still incomplete and does not cover admission for employment, which remains within the competence of individual Member States.

Other regional economic integration processes (e.g. Andean Community, Caribbean Community and Common Market (CARICOM), COMESA, ECOWAS SADC and MERCOSUR), which support free movement to various extents,[46] are some distance from the progress made at the level of the European Union, although the EU experience also demonstrates that such an advanced degree of integration is the result of a lengthy and painstaking process and requires the support of an institutional infrastructure and a strong resource base. It should also be underscored that each region is unique on account of its history and level of economic and social development with the result that migration management objectives, whether they are to be applied in an internal or external context, or both, are often also quite different. Nevertheless, this does not mean that progress cannot be achieved through other less formal regional mechanisms, as discussed in the section below.

3.2 Regional Consultative Processes

The purpose of Regional Consultative Processes (RCPs) is to discuss migration-related issues in a cooperative manner with a view to reaching a common understanding of, and where possible, effective solutions for regional migration management (IOM/Swiss Federal Office for Migration, 2005b). A number of factors explain their emergence and breadth:

- RCPs offer a structure for dialogue, exchange of information and expertise without requiring a government to enter into formal commitments. This facilitates confidence building, the identification of like-minded partners and the search for common understandings and approaches. It also allows the discussion of sensitive issues in a non-confrontational manner.

---

[41] See the European Commission website at http://ec.europa.eu/europeaid/where/worldwide/migration-asylum/index_en.htm (External cooperation programmes - Migration and Asylum).

[42] In December 2005, the European Council adopted the "Global Approach to Migration", which brings together migration, external relations and development policy to address migration in an integrated, comprehensive and balanced way in partnership with third countries.

[43] Every cooperation and association agreement concluded by the EU must contain a clause on joint management of migration flows and on compulsory readmission in the event of irregular migration (see the Conclusions of the European Council in Seville in June 2002).

[44] See e.g. the Partnership Agreement between the Members of the African, Caribbean and Pacific (ACP) Group of States and the European Community and its Members States, Cotonou, 23 June 2000, and the European Neighbourhood Policy with countries to the South and East of the EU (European Commission, 2007a).

[45] In May 2007, the European Commission (2007b) presented a Communication on *Circular migration and mobility partnerships between the European Union and third countries*. The Communication proposes partnerships between the EU and third countries interested in working with the EU to address irregular migration, while facilitating regular migration and circular migration. In June 2008, two joint declarations on mobility partnerships were signed between the EU and Cape Verde (in cooperation with four EU Member States) and Moldova (in cooperation with 14 EU Member States).

[46] While free movement of persons has not been advanced in the context of the Association of Southeast Asian Nations (ASEAN), the protection of migrant workers is a particular concern, as reflected in the ASEAN Declaration on the Protection and Promotion of the Rights of Migrant Workers, adopted by the Heads of State/Government in Cebu, the Philippines on 13 January 2007. See the ASEAN website at http://www.aseansec.org/19264.htm.

- States are more willing to join RCPs since they can withdraw from them just as easily if they so desire.
- States interact on equal terms, which favours a broad sense of ownership of the process.
- Membership can be open to states sharing migratory routes (countries of origin, transit and destination). Unlike more formal entities based on economically or politically motivated membership, RCPs may select participants according to their potential contribution to the advancement of the migration agenda (e.g. the 5+5 Dialogue on Migration in the Western Mediterranean[47]).

- They can extend participation to non-state actors, such as intergovernmental organizations or NGOs, and bring together officials from different ministries (IOM/Swiss Federal Office for Migration FOM, 2005b).

RCPs' agendas are flexible and responsive to members' main concerns, hence the evolving nature of their work priorities. RCPs typically revolve around a key theme. In the past, many of them focused on issues linked to irregular migration, such as the return of irregular migrants and readmission agreements, visa policy, border management, and human smuggling and trafficking. They are now inclined to have a broader work programme and increasingly cover development issues, labour mobility (see Textbox 13.4), remittances, protection of the human rights of migrants, integration or visa facilitation.

---

[47] The 5+5 Dialogue involves Algeria, France, Italy, Libya, Malta, Mauritania, Morocco, Portugal, Spain and Tunisia. It is an informal process in which governments cooperate and exchange information and analyses on topics such as migration trends, irregular migration and trafficking in human beings, migration and co-development (e.g. the role of diasporas), human rights and duties of migrants, integration, movement of people and management of regular migration, labour migration and vocational training, migration and health, local cooperation and gender equality in the context of migration. For more information, see IOM's website at http://www.iom.int/jahia/Jahia/pid/860.

Textbox 13.4

Regional Consultative Processes and Labour Mobility

Regional Consultative Processes (RCPs) are informal, non-binding and regularly scheduled meetings attended by government representatives – generally at senior official, but sometimes at ministerial level – to discuss issues of mutual concern related to migration. In keeping with the non-institutional character of RCPs, their administrative structures are kept simple, often in the form of small secretariats hosted by an international organization.

RCP membership is wide and varied. The meetings may be attended by either both home and host countries or, alternatively, only countries of origin or destination. Some of the better known RCPs are:

- Intergovernmental Conference on Migration, Asylum and Refugees (IGC). Established in 1985, it involves destination countries in Europe, North America and Australia and New Zealand, and examines border control, asylum, immigration (regular and irregular) and security issues.
- Regional Conference on Migration (RCM) (Puebla Process). Established in 1996, it includes Canada, the United States, Mexico and Central American countries, and focuses on migration policy, rights of migrants and development.
- 5 + 5 Dialogue on Migration in the Western Mediterranean. Established in 2002, it includes five southern European and five North African countries and examines migration, trafficking in human beings, rights of migrants, health, gender equality and public awareness.
- Migration Dialogue for Southern Africa (MIDSA). Established in 2000, it includes Botswana, the Democratic Republic of the Congo (DRC), South Africa and 12 other Southern African countries. It focuses on migration/border management, health, development, rights of migrants, return and readmission, and trafficking in human beings.
- Intergovernmental Asia-Pacific Consultations on Refugees, Displaced Persons and Migrants (APC). Established in 1996, the APC brings together 29 countries from the Asia-Pacific region. It focuses on return, refugees, trafficking in human beings, remittances, public awareness, burden sharing and capacity building.

- Bali Process. Established in 2002, it includes a wide range of countries of origin, transit and destination from many different regions of the world. It focuses on trafficking and smuggling in human beings and related transnational criminal activities.
- Ministerial Consultations on Overseas Employment and Contractual Labour for Countries of Origin in Asia (Colombo Process). Established in 2003, its membership consists of Afghanistan, Bangladesh, China, India, Indonesia, Nepal, Pakistan, the Philippines, Sri Lanka, Thailand and Viet Nam. In addition, certain countries of destination, viz. Bahrain, Italy, Kuwait, Malaysia, Qatar, Republic of Korea (South Korea), Saudi Arabia and the United Arab Emirates (UAE) participated as observers in the Ministerial Consultations in September 2005. The Colombo Process focuses on three thematic clusters: protection of vulnerable migrants and provision of support services; optimization of the benefits of organized labour migration; and capacity building, data collection and interstate cooperation (see also Textbox 10.5).
- Abu Dhabi Dialogue. The Abu Dhabi Dialogue was launched in January 2008. It brings together Colombo Process countries and countries of destination in Asia for consultations focusing on the facilitation of labour mobility and the protection of temporary contractual workers (see also Textbox 10.5).

RCP agendas have evolved considerably over the years. The initial focus on individual topics of interest (such as asylum policies and procedures, trafficking in human beings or border control) has gradually given way to broader, comprehensive perspectives on migration management in which labour mobility now occupies an increasingly important place. Even issues that appear less directly related to labour mobility – trafficking and irregular migration, for instance – have implications for labour mobility, in the sense that the effective control of borders can contribute to the development of a climate of public confidence supportive of the facilitation of the movement of migrant workers. Two RCPs, the Colombo Process and the related Abu Dhabi Dialogue, have chosen labour mobility as their prime focus of interest and have developed a range of capacity-building activities to equip participating countries with the legislative and administrative tools needed to manage their labour flows effectively.

Source: Randall Hansen, Canada Research Chair in Immigration and Governance, Department of Political Science, University of Toronto, Canada.

Regional consultations often lead to the adoption of recommendations, action plans or regional strategies setting shared principles and goals. Financial mechanisms are sometimes devised to sustain a component of technical cooperation assistance (e.g. joint training). Past experiences have proven that the success of RCPs may result from the choice of a limited number of participants combined with the support of an ad hoc (e.g. IGC) or internationally-based (IOM, UNHCR, UN Institute for Training and Research - UNITAR) secretariat. A participating state or a regional intergovernmental organization (e.g. Association of Southeast Asian Nations – ASEAN) may also host the process.

RCPs dedicated to labour migration issues do not create openings within the regional labour market. Rather, they facilitate movements through the adoption of recommendations or guidelines on issues such as visa facilitation (e.g. Asia-Pacific Economic Cooperation - APEC), or the protection and training of the labour force (e.g. Colombo Process[48]), which in turn can create the impetus for the realization of projects in these fields (e.g. training of labour attachés or the establishment of migrant resource centres). Although APEC is not a typical RCP, its pro-mobility activities are a good illustration of the levels of progress that can be achieved in a regional forum on the basis of consensus and voluntary commitments (see Textbox 13.5).

---

[48] This is the short title for the RCP on overseas employment and contractual labour for countries of origin in Asia. See also Textbox 13.4.

Textbox 13.5

Asia-Pacific Economic Cooperation (APEC)

APEC,[1] which gathers members bordering the Pacific Ocean and often separated by large geographical distances (e.g. Australia, China, Peru), does not increase access to the labour markets of its members. Rather it is committed to facilitating labour mobility for certain categories of highly skilled persons through (1) exchanging information on regulatory regimes; (2) streamlining the processing of short-term business visitor visas and procedures for temporary residence of business people; and (3) maintaining a dialogue on these issues with the business community. This work is coordinated by the Informal Experts' Group on Business Mobility.

The APEC Business Travel Card (ABTC) is one of the key initiatives being pursued. This card provides pre-cleared short-term entry to the 17 APEC economies participating in the scheme. The card holders do not need to individually apply for visas or entry permits each time they travel, as the card provides for multiple entries into participating economies during its three-year period of validity. In addition, immigration processing on arrival is accelerated via fast-track entry and exit through special APEC lanes at major airports. APEC has also developed an electronic APEC Business Travel Handbook providing a quick reference guide to the visa and entry requirements of APEC participating economies.[2]

The introduction of the ABTC followed a pathfinder approach, allowing countries to join when ready (conditions include: sufficient resources, necessary legislative frameworks in place and capacity to be an equal partner) and providing technical assistance to developing economies. The principles and procedures of the programme are compiled in an ABTC Operating Framework (including card manufacturing standards, eligibility criteria and service standards), which should be followed on a "best endeavour basis", and are not legally binding.

> Applications for the ABTC card are made to the designated home country agency (each state determines which particular agency accepts applications). The home country then carries out necessary vetting procedures in order to select bona fide applicants: it was agreed that the country of origin is in the best position to implement the specific procedures to determine who is eligible for the ABTC, and thereby maintain the integrity of the scheme. Although the basic eligibility requirements are set out in the Operating Framework, economies may use additional criteria to ensure bona fide applicants. Applications approved by the country of origin are sent to the participating economies and, if accepted, are given a pre-clearance permission. Member states are not required to give reasons for refusing pre-clearance to any applicants. Finally, the home country can issue the ABTC card, which allows entry into all economies that have given a pre-clearance permission. The ABTC pre-clearance system ensures that states retain the control over the movement of people across their borders and over the eligibility of domestic applicants. The ABTC members also benefit from the increased integrity of the scheme, which results from the double-screening procedure by home and destination countries. The programme inspires a high degree of confidence in both government officials and the business community: in the history of the ABTC, no instances of fraud have been discovered (David Watt, Department of Immigration, Multicultural and Indigenous Affairs, Australia, speaking at the OECD/World Bank/IOM Seminar on Trade and Migration, Geneva, 12-14 November 2003).

One of the keys to the success of the scheme is that it is designed and supported by a major destination country, Australia, which has considerable experience in migration management and pre-entry clearance, thereby reassuring other destination countries of the efficiency of the entire system. Nonetheless, despite this and the good record of the scheme, it is important to note that Canada has not yet joined, while the U.S. only became a transitional member in September 2007 (with the aim of full participation within three years).

Other pro-mobility initiatives include a 30-day processing standard for applications for, and extensions of, temporary residence permits for APEC intra-company transferees, the development of standards in all major immigration areas,[3] assistance to regional economies to develop Advance Passenger Information (API) Systems (information about incoming airline passengers supplied to the destination government) and Advance Passenger Processing (using API provided by airlines to run checks against electronic immigration records for pre-arrival screening); as well as the creation of a Regional Movement Alert System (RMAS – provision of real-time access to a database of lost and stolen passports).[4] Since 2002, APEC has also paid more attention to remittances with a working group established by finance ministers to examine the economic, structural and regulatory factors that encourage the use of remittances in the APEC economies. The APEC initiative on remittances systems has helped launch research projects (undertaken by the World Bank and the Asian Development Bank, in particular) and led to the organization of two symposia.[5]

Notes:

[1] APEC's 21 member economies are: Australia, Brunei Darussalam, Canada, Chile, China, Hong Kong SAR, Indonesia, Japan, Republic of Korea (South Korea), Malaysia, Mexico, New Zealand, Papua New Guinea, Peru, Philippines, Russian Federation, Singapore, Taiwan Province of China, Thailand, United States and Viet Nam.

[2] The Business Travel Handbook is available at http://www.businessmobility.org/travel/index.asp. It lists the basic eligibility criteria and procedures for applying for visas and the terms and conditions that apply to business travellers. This information is provided for both short-term business visits and temporary residence for business purposes in APEC economies. The Handbook also provides contact details for the embassies, consulates and other visa-issuing agencies of each member economy.

[3] Including pre-arrival, entry, stay and departure. Standards and/or best practice guidelines have been agreed by the Business Mobility Group covering short-term and temporary residence arrangements, transparency, API implementation, e-commerce, immigration legislation, travel document examination, travel document security, professional immigration services and the APEC Business Travel Card scheme.

[4] See http://www.businessmobility.org/key/index.html.

[5] APEC Symposia on Alternative Remittances Systems, Tokyo, 3-4 June 2004 and The Role of the Private Sector in Shifting from Informal to Formal Remittance Systems, Bangkok, 26-27 May 2005.

RCPs' perceived success is based partly on the common interest of participants in the topical issues considered by the group of states concerned. RCPs are well positioned to add coherence to the broader regional agenda and complement formal regional processes by involving neighbouring or like-minded states in special or ad hoc discussions. They are particularly useful when progress in formal arrangements is lagging, as they allow continuation of dialogue. They are similarly well placed to enhance bilateral cooperation (see Section 4 below) by creating trust relationships between countries and generating opportunities for interactions in a broader setting. The number of RCPs specializing in international labour mobility is still rather limited and their impact on the development of national labour migration policies is difficult to assess owing to the non-normative approach adopted. The informality of these processes may therefore be regarded both as a strength (as this fosters broader participation) and as a weakness (as the concretization of identified goals is left to the discretion of each country).

4. Facilitating and Managing Temporary Labour Migration through Bilateral Cooperation

Bilateral labour migration agreements were first used extensively at the end of the Second World War, when large emerging economies in "New World" countries

decided to meet their considerable labour market needs through large-scale immigration programmes.[49] They have regained currency more recently as a flexible policy instrument used by two countries in the management of migratory flows (OECD, 2004). Such agreements can target specific groups of migrants, contain provisions enabling policies to adapt to labour market fluctuations in countries of destination and equitably attribute responsibilities between countries of origin and destination for the monitoring and overall management of the labour migration process.

The scope of these agreements varies. Their provisions generally specify the purpose of the agreement; define the categories of labour concerned; and provide for admission criteria, the terms of migration, fair and equitable treatment and annual quotas, where applicable. However, some specific issues, such as social security and double taxation, recognition of qualifications and irregular migration, are often dealt with in separate agreements (e.g. the bilateral social security agreements signed by the U.S. with 20 countries, including Chile, France and South Korea, or

---

[49] For more information on the historical context of bilateral labour migration agreements, see the textbox written by the author for IOM (2005: Textbox 12.2: "Bilateral Labour Agreements: Effective Tools for Managing Labour Flows?"), from where the material in this section is mainly drawn.

the readmission agreements in force, signed or under negotiation between Switzerland and 33 countries[50]). The diversity of agreements and their provisions reflect the differences in the economic environment and the nature of labour market shortages, as well as a variety of broader economic, social and political objectives for entering into bilateral cooperative approaches for the management of these flows.

4.1 Objectives of Countries of Destination

When engaging in bilateral labour agreements, countries of destination follow mainly four broad types of objectives that are not mutually exclusive. The first of these is to satisfy their labour market needs and to better manage the labour migration process. Through such agreements, a country of destination can respond to its labour market needs by recruiting workers from other countries. Alternatively, where regular channels for migration are already in place, bilateral agreements may help to better match supply and demand, for instance by streamlining recruitment procedures or by stipulating the activities and responsibilities of public authorities and private partners. The most comprehensive agreements cover all phases of the migratory process and various issues related to movement (e.g. access to health care, pre-departure information on labour laws and the cultural and social environment of the destination country, and vocational and language training).

A second objective is to prevent or reduce irregular migration by affording regular migration opportunities. The motivations to offer such opportunities are twofold. First, the idea is to relieve the pressure to migrate from countries of origin and curb the number of irregular migrants by channelling such movements into regular avenues.[51] Second, the opening up of a regular channel is sometimes used as a negotiation tool to secure the willingness of countries of origin to cooperate on managing irregular migration, and especially on the readmission of their nationals who are in an irregular situation (e.g. rejected asylum seekers).

A third objective is the use of bilateral labour agreements to promote and support broader economic relations with countries of origin. The movement of workers in this case is aimed at facilitating regional economic integration and the development of countries of origin. The bilateral agreements signed by Germany with some central and eastern European countries (CEECs) are good examples (OECD, 2004). They establish several forms of temporary migration for work purposes (e.g. seasonal work, contract work and "guest worker" programmes). In that sense, their purpose goes beyond the satisfaction of German labour market needs to the strengthening of economic relations between Germany and CEECs.

A final specific objective is to preserve or strengthen ties between countries sharing historical (sometimes post-colonial) and cultural links. For example, the United Kingdom operates a "working holidaymaker" scheme with participating Commonwealth countries, allowing persons aged between 17 and 30 to come

---

[50] Information taken from the IGC Matrix on Countries of Origin/Transit Countries parties to IGC States' and the EC's Readmission Instruments (in force, signed or under negotiation).

[51] Some bilateral labour agreements are signed at the time of a regularization programme and target the principal countries of origin of irregular migrants. The idea behind this approach is to encourage irregular migrants to leave the destination country, return home and benefit from regular work opportunities set out in the agreements. Special clauses on the implementation of the regularization programme can figure in the agreement (with a limited period of validity), e.g. migration agreements between Argentina and Bolivia, and Argentina and Peru, signed in February 1998 and May 1999, respectively, and their additional Protocols. The agreement between Spain and Ecuador concerning the regulation and control of migratory flows (*Acuerdo entre España y Ecuador relative a la regulación y ordenación de los flujos migratorios*) (Madrid, 29 May 2001), stipulates in Article 14(3) that migrants returning home to regularize their situation will have their visa and work permit applications treated as a priority: "[T]he authorities of the requesting contracting party undertake to facilitate the departure and gradual and voluntary repatriation of undocumented persons in their territory, so that those who so request are guaranteed that the respective embassy will provide fast-track treatment for their residence and work visas, with the guarantee of a job in the requesting contracting party."

Until this issue is fully addressed, the growth of those sectors of the economy that rely on intensive, less-skilled labour – tourism, for instance – will be constrained and least developed countries (LDCs) with a surplus of less-skilled labour will struggle to overcome intra-regional disparities (Caldentey and Schmid, 2006). In the meantime, as unmet labour demands persist and important countries of origin (e.g. Haiti) and destination (e.g. the Bahamas) remain outside the CSME, one may expect an increase in irregular intra-regional migration.

The regulation and facilitation of less skilled labour flows is also of critical significance for the management of extra-CARICOM migration, whether to the nearby Dominican Republic or farther afield to the U.S., Canada, the United Kingdom, France and the Netherlands, all the more so because of the role played by remittances in the regional economy (IADB, 2007; World Bank, 2005) and because of the current and/or projected demographic and economic profiles and associated demands for migrant workers among various countries of destination.

In the light of such unresolved concerns over how best and to what extent to integrate labour markets at the lower end of the skills spectrum, bilateral labour agreements (BLAs) may constitute promising instruments for the flexible matching of labour supply and demand, both seasonal and structural and according to national requirements and capacities, while mitigating irregular migration pressures. Several BLAs already exist, including those under the Commonwealth Caribbean Seasonal Agriculture Workers Program (SAWP) with Canada[1], and others concluded by CARICOM Member States with the U.S. for the temporary employment of farmers and hospitality workers.

If the coverage of destination countries and worker categories of such agreements is to be expanded successfully (World Bank, 2005), public education and awareness of their benefits, and significant improvements in their design to ensure feasibility, will be critical.

The benefits of well-designed BLAs for countries of origin include, among others, expanded access to the international labour market and "brain circulation". Destination countries meanwhile can gain from cooperation in ensuring that access to their territory generally remains temporary and responds more efficiently to verifiable labour shortages and sectoral shifts in demand. Effectively meeting these objectives requires that these agreements and/or accompanying unilateral initiatives incorporate incentives for temporary and circular migration; adequate quotas; and relatively low transaction costs for employers and migrants alike (Mansoor and Quillin, 2007; Ruhs, 2005).

BLAs could also potentially serve as development policy instruments by offering less-skilled nationals of LDCs preferential access to employment quotas, the impact of which may support the attainment of the Millennium Development Goals (MDGs) (Pritchett, 2006). By targeting the less-skilled, these agreements could partly address the reservation that skill-biased admission policies may exacerbate income disparities within countries of origin by raising the local skill premium (Pritchett, 2006; Caldentey and Schmid, 2006) and skewing remittance flows towards the presumably better-off. However, at the moment, Haiti, for instance, has a fairly even distribution of remittance recipients among the lowest and highest income quintiles, according to the Haiti Remittance Survey 2006 of the Inter-American Development Bank (IADB, 2007), although this could change. Nevertheless, further research is required to determine whether any such effects are offset by the human capital and/or employment generated through higher returns to education and the local investment of remittances from highly skilled workers (World Bank, 2005).[2] Such development objectives may be most realistic where the agreements address labour shortages that are of a temporary nature.

BLAs may furthermore reduce the vulnerability of migrant workers to exploitation during recruitment and employment. Beyond obliging countries of origin to better regulate recruitment agencies, the agreements could assist them in negotiating limited freedom of movement for their nationals within assigned occupational sectors, thereby also potentially raising labour market efficiency in the destination country (Ruhs, 2005).

More rigorous research on the effectiveness of such agreements in terms of their implementation and impact and, possibly, the formation of a regional consultative process (RCP) on migration to complement the CSME, where good practices and experiences can be shared, would likely assist the Member States of the Caribbean Community to develop expanded and more effective BLAs.

To conclude, well-designed BLAs can assist countries of origin and destination to cultivate the multi-stakeholder cooperation and public support necessary to address politically sensitive issues in migration management and help to bring migration policies more into line with those on trade and foreign investment (Ruhs, 2005). In so doing, BLAs may assist in securing the interests of all parties and facilitate a more equitable integration of less-developed countries of origin into the regional and global economies.

Notes:
1 Implementation of the SAWP commenced in 1966 based on negotiations between Canada and Jamaica, and the programme was subsequently extended to Trinidad and Tobago and Barbados in 1967, Mexico in 1974, and the Organization of East Caribbean States in 1976.
2 Other remittance issues under discussion include the direction of causality in the association between remittance inflows and relatively high unemployment among migrant-sending households in some countries such as the Dominican Republic, and the potential for remittances to result in exchange rate appreciation and reduced competitiveness of exports among small economies.

Source: *Jennifer Zimmermann, Darfur Coordinator, IOM Sudan (formerly Project Development Officer, IOM Haiti).*

4.3 Different Forms of Bilateral Arrangements and their Scope

As discussed above, bilateral cooperation on temporary labour migration may aim to fulfil various economic, social and political purposes and take a number of different approaches. But how does this cooperation take shape? Bilateral cooperation arrangements can be distinguished according to their legal status, the comprehensiveness or specificity of the migratory issues addressed and the categories of workers covered.

(a) Legal status

Bilateral arrangements can cover a wide variety of devices, from legally binding agreements (i.e. formal treaties) to less formal Memoranda of Understanding (MoUs) and very informal practical arrangements, such as those involving primarily the national employment agencies of the two countries concerned.

Bilateral arrangements can take the form of a treaty, i.e. a legally binding instrument between the two governments concerned governed by international law. Such agreements may or may not include a formal mechanism (e.g. arbitration) for the settlement of disputes, but where they do, the parties to the agreement are required to follow the decisions of any such body. Furthermore, bilateral agreements are often published in the official journal of laws of the countries concerned, although their method of adoption and publication will normally depend on the administrative and constitutional rules of those countries.

A country may, however, prefer to conclude MoUs or Cooperation Arrangements (CA),[57] which have a status similar to that of administrative or private "arrangements", and which are not legally binding on the state. While MoUs/CAs may also contain mechanisms for resolving disputes, these are usually in the form of further political dialogue or consultations between representatives of the parties concerned.

Memoranda of Understanding can be of the "government to government" type (e.g. MoU between Canada and Mexico or the Caribbean states on the Seasonal Agriculture Worker Program (SAWP) – see Textbox 13.6), of the "government to private sector" type (e.g. Guatemalan Ministry of Labour with FERME, an employer association in the Canadian Province of Québec on the recruitment of seasonal agriculture workers - see Textbox 10.2) or between national administrations (e.g. between Germany's and Slovenia's employment services for "guest workers"). While under a MoU, the actions or decisions taken

---
57 MoUs and CAs are two out of a large variety of informal arrangements used. For example, the U.K. operates a youth exchange scheme with Japan, "Japan yes", on the basis of a *Note verbale* agreed with Japan, and the Philippines has signed a "Memorandum of Agreement" with Iraq, Jordan and Qatar.

- Bilateral agreements **facilitating (or addressing the consequences of) mobility**, while paying no attention to international border-crossing issues:

    a. Mutual recognition arrangements on the criteria and procedures for the recognition of diplomas, or the right to practice a profession or trade in another country.
    b. Social security and double taxation agreements (e.g. portability of pensions, prevention of double taxation).

The diversity of instruments available often implies that a wide range of actors are involved in bilateral cooperation on labour migration. The leading roles in the negotiations and discussions are typically taken by one or several ministries (for instance, the ministry of labour and social affairs, or interior or foreign affairs, or the ministry of immigration or emigration where such specific entities exist). Administrations and institutions under their umbrella (e.g. public employment agencies, universities) may also initiate bilateral agreements with a local or national scope. Some agreements are concluded between private entities and foreign public and/or private authorities. Added to this is the fact that the authorities in charge of negotiating an agreement are often not the same as those responsible for their implementation.

Given these complexities, one of the main challenges consists in achieving coherence in the framing of bilateral labour migration policies, especially as they relate to both the identification of economic and social objectives and their realization through policymaking and implementation. This requires a relatively high degree of national coordination on the part of countries of origin and destination, which is typically lacking owing to the real or perceived inability to reconcile conflicting objectives pursued by diverse public and private stakeholders at various levels (e.g. between different ministries; by businesses; and representatives of employers, workers and civil society), and/or the lack of institutional

capacity and financial resources (especially when developing countries are involved).

The high degree of informality, the diversity of objectives and the variety of actors involved make it all the more difficult to track the dynamics of bilateral negotiations on facilitating and regulating labour migration; to identify the trade-offs resulting in the opening up of new channels for migrant workers from particular countries; and to weigh the importance of particular migration management issues (e.g. addressing irregular migration) and their success in securing regular openings for migrant workers.

4.4 Impediments to Bilateral Agreements

It would be mistaken to assume that the relatively limited number of bilateral labour arrangements that have been concluded and are being implemented to date are a reflection of the asymmetry of relations between countries of origin and destination, where the former would be willing to enter into bilateral arrangements but lack the capacity to convince the latter to do so. It is true that many destination countries have declined offers from countries of origin to negotiate such arrangements. Spain has declined 40 such requests (Schulman, 2003), whereas the Philippines and Moldova have not been successful in securing bilateral agreements with some major destination countries (e.g. Saudi Arabia, in the case of the Philippines; and 24 countries relying to some extent on Moldovan migrant workers in the case of Moldova[66]). However, the reasons for this lack of success are complex.

Some of the difficulties may stem from the fact that a number countries adopt a position of principle not to resort to bilateral agreements, but to pursue a

---

[66] These include Bosnia and Herzegovina, Bulgaria, Canada, the Czech Republic, Estonia, France, Germany, Greece, Hungary, Israel, Italy, Kuwait, Lithuania, Former Yugoslav Republic of Macedonia (FYROM), Poland, Slovakia, the then Serbia and Montenegro, and Slovenia (Sleptova, 2003).

more universal approach regarding labour migration, i.e. one that does not distinguish on the basis of nationality.[67] Other destination countries have engaged in bilateral agreements, but may be unwilling to expand the number of current beneficiaries for various reasons, such as reservations regarding countries that do not figure prominently on their list of priorities, or they may entertain other concerns (e.g. domestic labour market conditions or a source country's standards regarding governance and human rights). Obstacles may also arise from a divergence of opinions between countries of origin and destination about the terms of a bilateral agreement, or from a lack of institutional capacity to pursue the negotiation and implementation of such agreements.

(a) Preference for a unilateral/universal approach

Certain destination countries do not feel the need for bilateral agreements as foreign workers have access to their labour markets through their general immigration policy, and the rights of migrant workers are protected under national legislation. They may also have concerns that concluding bilateral agreements would result in conferring additional rights on migrants not enjoyed by local workers.

For countries that favour a universal immigration policy and offer the same access and conditions to workers of all nationalities, bilateral arrangements may be regarded as discriminatory which, by privileging nationals from one country over others, are susceptible to create political tensions. Indeed, entering into a bilateral labour agreement with one

country is likely to create expectations for other countries that their nationals should similarly benefit from the favourable treatment and may, in consequence, affect the quality of diplomatic relations by generating resentment in case of refusal.

With regard to skilled and highly skilled workers, in a context where such competences are scarce and the challenge of global competition to attract such workers is acutely felt, restricting labour market access to professionals from selected nationalities may not appear advisable.

As far as **opening up access** to their labour market is concerned, most destination countries, when declining an offer to negotiate, point to the situation of their employment market and their unemployment rates. Parallel reasons include the general opposition expressed by public opinion to regular migration and fears relating to overstay and the fuelling of irregular migration. As far as **working conditions** are concerned, there may be a reluctance on the part of the government to take decisions which could translate into more obligations beyond those set down in national and international labour standards, and higher costs for the employers of foreign workers (e.g. by regulating issues such as accommodation, overtime pay, rest periods and similar concerns). Certain governments are of the view that the determination of wages and the conditions surrounding the hiring of workers more generally is essentially a private matter between employers and employees, or should be left to labour market forces to determine.

While an argument in favour of BLAs is the prevention of abuse by the private sector (e.g. overcharging of fees, contract substitution) through the involvement of the state in the recruitment process, it has also to be considered that governments or public administrations are not necessarily immune to malpractices themselves and that their involvement can be misdirected to satisfy "political patronage". Furthermore, unnecessarily bureaucratic

---

[67] This policy is sometimes also qualified as a unilateral approach. However, universal and unilateral approaches are not necessarily the same. Indeed, a unilateral approach suggests that one country has established a policy on its own and on the basis of objectives identified by its government. A universal policy (applying no differences in terms of migrants' origins) may result from such a unilateral process. However, there is nothing to preclude a country from entering into consultations with source countries with a view to improving its universal policy, and therefore departing from a purely unilateral approach (see also Chapter 11 and the discussion regarding the adoption of "development-friendly" policies).

administrative requirements can be an obstacle to effective implementation of the agreement.

The general tendency among major destination countries today is still concerned with the management of ports of entry on the basis of a universal system and closer cooperation with countries of origin on issues related to irregular migration at the bilateral level. Moreover, some countries believe that their commitments under GATS Mode 4 (see Textbox Int. 1), which could be invoked by non-parties on the basis of the Most Favoured Nation Clause of the GATS, preclude such a bilateral approach to admission.

(b) Negotiation and implementation problems

Destination countries usually limit their readiness to enter into bilateral agreements to countries that are potential sources of migratory flows. The number of BLAs they accept to enter into is limited for several reasons, in addition to those connected with the existence of less favourable labour market conditions. Any additional BLA a country concludes will have the effect of limiting or diluting the relative advantage of other beneficiary countries, and may create discontent. Another source of tension emerges when a BLA does not generate movements; countries of origin often regard the availability of jobs in a country of destination as an entitlement rather than a mere prospect, and quotas (where they exist) more as targets than ceilings. Some countries of destination experience this problem with their trainee programmes for foreign nationals, which are typically underused to the dissatisfaction of countries of origin, especially when the programme was negotiated together with a readmission agreement (OECD, 2004). Lack of implementation or utilization can be due to inadequacies in recruitment mechanisms; employer preferences; mismatches between admission criteria and labour force profiles in countries of origin; the balance between earning possibilities (wages, duration of stay) and the costs of migration (i.e. travel, medical examination,

lodgings and such like); administrative inefficiency; and the presence of community networks from other countries acting as intermediaries for job matching for their nationals.

It may also be difficult to terminate a bilateral agreement, or to resist pressure for its expansion, even if conditions in the labour market have changed or if countries prefer to change their future immigration policy and restrict their intervention (and related costs) to visa delivery, so as not to be involved in the administration and monitoring of the entire process. Indeed, bilateral agreements are time and resource (financial and human) intensive, as they might imply extensive public administration involvement in their implementation and monitoring; the more countries involved, the higher the administrative complexity, especially if, as is often the case, the terms of the agreements vary.

Countries of destination enter into bilateral labour agreements for two main reasons: (a) normalizing a pre-existing situation with a source country by regularizing irregular flows and reorganizing them in a satisfactory manner; or (b) encouraging/ facilitating new recruitment channels for persons whose qualifications are in high demand on the basis of the resources available in **specific** countries (e.g. agreements on nurses by the U.K. with the Philippines and Spain[68]). Consequently, countries of origin that are outside the scope of these interests experience difficulties in building the bargaining capacity necessary to enter into bilateral cooperation.

Obstacles to negotiations and prospective implementation on the part of countries of origin may arise from a lack of institutional capacity to analyse the existing labour demand in destination countries, determine their priorities and pursue

---

[68] However, changes in the demand for certain categories of foreign labour can affect the functioning of these agreements. For instance, "general nursing" occupations were removed from the U.K. shortage occupation list in August 2006, which impacted on the recruitment of nurses from the Philippines.

a lengthy process of negotiation.[69] Countries of origin may also suffer from the absence of adequate public or private recruitment agencies to "market" their national workforce and facilitate the implementation of labour migration programmes. Further impediments include the educational level, skills and language proficiency of their nationals, whose attributes do not always correspond to those in demand in destination countries.

Countries of origin may also be reluctant to accept a bilateral arrangement requiring, in exchange for some limited market access, the return of nationals in an irregular situation in the destination country. Indeed some countries of origin may feel that it is beyond their capacity to prevent the departure of irregular migrants whose job expectations cannot be accommodated at home, and whose families rely on remittances from abroad to make ends meet. Furthermore, when wages are agreed under BLAs while other sources of foreign recruitment exist, such types of agreement may undermine their competitiveness. For some countries, bilateral agreements are of limited interest as they typically offer few mechanisms for enforcement and redress, and unequal power relationships between countries of origin and destination make it difficult to negotiate equitable agreements that truly protect migrant workers.

Even when parties are willing to enter into BLAs, the terms under discussion might put too much pressure on one party to reach an accord. It is sometimes difficult for the parties to identify common goals when each is advocating its own agenda and is unwilling to make compromises regarding its own perceived interests. Among some of the common subjects of contention are: social and medical insurance, family reunification, conditions of readmission of irregular migrants, recognition of qualifications, and mechanisms supporting circular

migration between host and home country to limit disruption to families.

In the context of GATS Mode 4 negotiations and development considerations, the likelihood of bilateral agreements being a complementary tool to the multilateral framework by providing for further openings for the low and semi-skilled workforce should not be overestimated.[70]

It would nonetheless be worthwhile to explore in more depth the other ways in which bilateral agreements may assist in liberalizing the movement of workers, either through further research on examples of good practices of migration management extracted from bilateral agreements, which could lead developed destination countries to adopt a more open attitude towards them, and/or through using these examples for the elaboration of a pre-commitment mechanism which would guarantee access to the labour markets of WTO Members to any countries of origin meeting the stated criteria. Both options offer the advantage of providing solutions for all developing countries because they are not discriminatory and support efforts in the direction of the establishment of a workable global framework.

5. Conclusion

In recent years, the international community has come to recognize migration as a key global issue. There are few who would dispute that migration affects virtually every country in the world in one way or another, and frequently to a very significant degree. This has created previously unforeseen challenges for policymakers, but it has also led to the acknowledgement that no country can realistically hope to manage migration on its own; and, in turn, provided impetus for cooperation

---

[69] And once the agreement is signed, to discuss the modalities for its implementation and monitoring.

[70] Another issue when exploring bilateral possibilities is the fact that an agreement covering movements of persons only in the context of service provision would normally be incompatible with the Most Favoured Nation principle of the WTO which requires all Member States to be treated equally.

towards the development of common approaches to the management of international migration.

At the global level, there are elements of a normative framework "dispersed across a number of treaties, customary law provisions, non-binding agreements and policy understandings" (GCIM, 2005: 55). There are challenges for the international community in both articulating clearly these provisions and ensuring that they are implemented. The GATS Mode 4 negotiations are an ambitious worksite where advances on the access and entry of service providers is, to a large extent conditioned to progress on much larger portfolios of interest such as agriculture. For the foreseeable future however, most of the effort at the global level is likely to be applied to the Global Forum on Migration and Development, where the migration and development agenda offers a commonly acceptable discussion platform for countries of origin and destination.

At the regional level, the most significant outcomes have been achieved when migration management objectives are linked to broader economic integration endeavours supported by well-developed institutional frameworks and considerable financial resources, as best exemplified within the European Union. By providing a normative framework, such regional undertakings create predictability and a legal basis for safeguarding the rights of migrants. However, in many regions, movements of workers are still restricted, with the exception of the highly skilled in carefully defined situations, and the prospects of fuller integration of labour markets and freer movements of workers are clouded by economic disparities and fear of massive inflows by the strong economies of regional groupings. For this reason, most of the considerable activity at this level is of an informal and non-binding nature. Regional frameworks are sometimes seen as relay stations for the non-coercive implementation of standards and principles adopted at the global level. Regional cross-border movements create shared concerns and elicit

interest in their management. The limited number of countries involved offers a more manageable environment for consensus building, allocation of financial resources and technical assistance, and reduction in transaction costs through joint activities. In response to the emergence or evolution of issues of interest to more than one region, inter-regional processes, such as the Bali Process or the Abu Dhabi Dialogue (see Textbox 13.4), can be established as broader consultative or cooperative platforms.

Finally, the bilateral level offers a wide range of possibilities for cooperation, including very concrete partnerships to enable the movement of targeted contingents of migrant workers. Bilateral arrangements are very diverse in form and content. In considering why and how they work, it should be noted that the principal motivations for engaging in such cooperation for the facilitation of movement may frequently be unrelated to the improved matching of labour demand and supply. Other social, economic or political considerations come into play, and the specific objectives pursued by countries influence the way these agreements/arrangements are designed and in turn their capacity to function effectively as instruments fostering labour movements. Other internal and external factors are also relevant. Internal conditions relate, for instance, to the efficiency of the mechanisms in the agreement or arrangements for matching demand and supply, the criteria outlined for migrants to participate in the scheme, the complexity of administrative procedures, and the cost of the process to workers and employers. Among external conditions are the existence of other migration routes;[71] the language and vocational skills available in the country of origin; the availability of a pool of irregular migrants;[72] the deterrent effect

---

[71] E.g. possibilities to enter under other migration/visa programmes for foreign workers, under family migration/reunion or even humanitarian schemes.

[72] Irregular migrants are attractive to employers because they are cheaper (employers do not respect minimum wage requirements, or pay contributions to the social security system, etc.) and allow considerable flexibility in hiring and firing according to the needs of enterprises.

of policies against unauthorized employment; and the preference of employers for workers of certain nationalities (e.g. for reasons of cultural affinity, geographical proximity).

The bilateral, regional and global levels of cooperation afford differing advantages and disadvantages to countries in terms of bargaining strategies and outcomes. The bilateral approach generally allows the more powerful party a stronger say, while offering the ability to both parties to arrive at tailor-made arrangements reflecting an agreed balance of interests. Regional cooperation, even when dominated by the stronger economies in the group, provides possibilities for countries with a weaker voice to be heard, and the commitments made in such circles tend to be measured and practicable. The global arena is a more level playing field, in theory at least, with each country having an equal voice and weaker countries being in a position to develop effective alliances with like-minded partners, bearing in mind that in global institutions developing countries are superior in number to developed countries. Countries interested in becoming more involved in international cooperation on labour mobility may explore all these available opportunities according to their respective merits.

Textbox 13.7

Skilled Migration and Regional, Bilateral and Multilateral Agreements

The flow of global talent across borders is growing continuously, spurred by such diverse factors as demographic profiles, developments in information and communication technologies, and the growing internationalization of goods and services production and delivery. Earlier, skilled labour flows were primarily directed from developed to developing countries. Increasingly, skilled migration also occurs within and among developing countries, reflecting the integration of developing economies in global markets and the growth in South-South trade and investment relations.

Today, there is a distinct shift in migration patterns towards the highly skilled, and countries of destination are pursuing various approaches to attract talent globally (see Chapter 2). In countries of origin, there has also been a shift in thinking on skilled outflows, from viewing such flows as brain drain to seeing them as sources for brain exchange and circulation, especially in view of the temporary and repeat nature of much of these flows in key source sectors like information technology and within global firms. Thus, although economic and social push and pull factors in countries of origin and countries of destination, respectively, have been and remain the primary drivers in migratory flows, changes in host country policies and shifts in source country attitudes have also played a role in driving the growth in cross-border skilled flows.

As more and more host countries compete for global talent and as more and more source countries seek to reap benefits from their skilled labour base and capitalize on their demographic dividend, labour mobility is becoming an important issue in bilateral, regional, and multilateral discussions. Several trade and investment agreements today include labour mobility provisions and commitments on movement and entry of workers among countries. Such agreements are intended to ensure an appropriate framework for managed migration among the parties, in a manner that benefits both sides and at times also go beyond to address issues of capacity building, education and training policies, as well as coordinating screening, monitoring and deployment issues. In the context of skilled migration, these agreements entail shaping the sectoral and regional dynamics of skilled labour movements so as to lower transactions costs for trade and business flows and to leverage complementarities in labour supply and demand between partner countries.

At the multilateral level, the General Agreement on Trade in Services (GATS), negotiated under WTO auspices, provides a framework for the discussion of international movements of service providers at all skill levels. However, despite a few improved offers in the Doha Round discussions that touch on certain categories of interest to developing countries and remove certain conditions on entry and stay, there has been little progress made in the Mode 4 discussions under the GATS and no commercially meaningful improvement in market access conditions so far (see Textbox Int. 1). Thus, the prospects for liberalizing skilled labour flows do not seem promising under the GATS at this time.

On the other hand, regional and bilateral approaches have been more successful in handling migration issues.[1] Regional and bilateral agreements, such as free trade agreements (FTAs), economic partnership agreements (EPAs) and comprehensive economic cooperation agreements (CECAs), generally cover labour mobility under the separate headings of labour and investment. These agreements tend to focus on skilled labour categories similar to those under GATS, as these raise fewer concerns over labour displacement and cultural and social impacts. Regional and bilateral arrangements need not be viewed separately as the approach towards liberalizing migration is not affected by the number of the participating countries or the size of the region covered by such arrangements. Several of these agreements use the GATS model with specific schedules of commitments for various categories of persons. Some, such as the U.S.-Jordan FTA, also go beyond GATS to include specific visa commitments for such categories as independent traders, treaty investors and investment-related entry.

The approach adopted by regional and bilateral agreements towards skilled labour mobility can be broadly classified into three groups.

The **first** concerns agreements such as those concluded under European Union (EU), European Economic Area (EEA) and European Free Trade Association (EFTA) auspices, as well as the Australia-New Zealand Closer Economic Relations Agreement that cover skilled movements under the broader heading of labour movements, which is a general right among member countries. Such agreements tend to be concluded among developed countries.

The **second** group consists of agreements which specifically focus on movements associated with investment and business flows, such as business visitors and investment treaty-related movements. The Asia-Pacific Economic Cooperation (APEC) Forum, for example, excludes self-employed and low or semi-skilled labour and includes arrangements to facilitate labour mobility through information exchange, business dialogue, harmonization of immigration procedures and standards, and the streamlining of procedures for entry, processing and stay for business purposes. There is an in-principle agreement to reduce the processing time for temporary entry applications for intra-corporate transferees, specialists and business visitors. An APEC Business Travel Card valid for three years provides for multiple short-term business entries and accelerated airport processing and entry for business travellers from within APEC (see Textbox 13.5). Likewise, the U.S.-Jordan FTA specifies visa commitments for independent traders and persons entering in connection with investment activities. Jordanian nationals can obtain E-1 and E-2, i.e. U.S. treaty-trader and treaty-investor visas, respectively. The Japan-Singapore Economic Partnership Agreement regulates movement for business purposes, covering business visitors, intra-corporate transferees and certain categories of professionals and investors. However, parties to such agreements continue to retain the right to refuse entry, and national laws on employment, entry and stay take precedence over the agreement provisions on mobility. The Trade in Services Agreement (TIS), concluded under the Framework Agreement on Comprehensive Economic Cooperation between China and the Association of Southeast Asian Nations (ASEAN), similarly provides for improved market access and national treatment for select service suppliers with the objective of facilitating greater investment in the region.

The **third** group of regional or bilateral agreements focuses on liberalizing market access for select business and professional categories to address skills shortages in particular areas. These agreements also discuss associated regulatory issues such as harmonization of standards and mutual recognition of professional and academic qualifications among the parties. For instance, the India-Singapore CECA relaxes visa restrictions for Indian professionals in 127 categories, including information technology (IT), medicine, engineering, nursing, accountancy and university lecturers, by introducing one-year multiple entry visas and removing economic needs tests and labour market tests together with the social security contribution requirement for these categories. By adopting this targeted approach, the agreement clearly builds on the complementarity in the supply of and demand for skilled service providers between India and Singapore, respectively. It also provides for mutual recognition of degrees issued by specified universities and technical education boards of both countries, and a framework for negotiations in other areas where there are requests for recognition. The agreement further addresses the issue of wage parity by adding special allowances paid in India and Singapore to the basic pay of Indian professionals to achieve salary equivalence requirements for market entry into Singapore. Thus, under this bilateral agreement, India has been able to address and make some headway on critical regulatory and market access issues, which the government has also raised in the context of the GATS negotiations. In turn, India hopes to use the CECA as a benchmark in negotiations on other regional trade agreements.

Two points should be noted concerning discussions on labour mobility in the context of bilateral and regional frameworks.

The first point is that, although more progress on skilled movements may be achieved in the regional and bilateral context than under the GATS, discussions have not always been easy even as regards the former. Agreement on skilled movement and labour mobility is often particularly difficult. Thus, the Japan-Philippines Economic Partnership Agreement (JPEPA) was initially unable to progress concerning the admission of Filipino nurses onto the Japanese market. This was the first free trade agreement to be negotiated by Japan to include provisions on the movement of labour. Japan's new economic strategy aims to boost the number of foreign workers in Japan and this agreement is a step in that direction. The Japanese Government has decided to introduce a new facilitated licence for nursing caretakers, which will certify those who have completed relevant courses at vocational schools, colleges and universities, but have not passed a national exam, as "practical" nursing caretakers. This will enable nurses who have not passed the state exam to work at nursing care facilities. Japan will accept 400 nurses and 600 nursing caretakers under this FTA. As a result, hundreds of Filipino nurses, caregivers and nursing care trainees are expected to enter Japan. Some organizations have already been training Filipino nurses in anticipation of this development. Other countries, such as Thailand and Indonesia, that are interested in free trade agreements with Japan are also likely to seek greater market access for skilled and semi-skilled service providers to the Japanese market. However, the Japan-Philippines FTA shows that the passage of labour mobility provisions is not a smooth one, although it could also be argued that more has been achieved by the Philippines in the bilateral than might have been possible in a multilateral context, from a traditionally closed host country like Japan.

Likewise, China's request for admission of its skilled workers to New Zealand has been a matter of debate, as New Zealand negotiators wish to protect working conditions and their local labour force in any agreement. Trade unions in New Zealand are concerned that to admit such labour would reduce incentives to train and upgrade the skills of local workers and affect their working conditions. However, some associations in New Zealand, such as the Engineering, Printing and Manufacturing Union, view such provisions as a means to fill critical skills gaps in manufacturing and other areas, and thus potentially as beneficial. New Zealand may grant access to select groups of skilled Chinese workers, such as teachers of Mandarin, specialists in Chinese medicine and working holidaymakers from China. Therefore, labour mobility issues clearly evoke a wide range of responses and raise host country sensitivities on such issues as wages, the displacement of local workers and the effect on working conditions, similar to those in the multilateral context and, therefore, progress is not easily made.

A second point worth noting is that bilateral and regional agreements may involve substantial concessions by developing countries to their partners to the agreement, particularly in sectors that are in high demand, in exchange for market access for their skilled workers. In the discussions between China and New Zealand, New Zealand has demanded major concessions from China in return for increased access for Chinese skilled workers. In the discussions taking place between India and the EU, the free movement of professionals, especially in such activities as IT, medicine and engineering, and the recognition of professional qualifications are among India's main demands. However, such access is likely to require India's commitments on investment in, for example, the financial, telecom and retail distribution services sectors, and in other areas such as tariffs for industrial products as well as competition policy and regulatory transparency. Thus, the quid pro quo, especially for countries such as India and China, which have large pools of skilled labour but are also very attractive markets for investment, is likely to be much more pronounced in bilateral and regional discussions and also a necessary condition for realizing any gains on skilled movement.

The real value of bilateral and regional agreements, however, lies beyond the market access gained through any particular agreement. Such agreements also provide developing countries with experience and the institutional and regulatory capacity to negotiate with large trading partners on issues such as visas and standards. India is expected to use the CECA concluded with Singapore as a benchmark for its mutual recognition and visa discussions with the EU. Likewise, China, which is seeking market access for its skilled workers on temporary permits as part of a planned free trade deal with New Zealand, is looking to use this agreement as a precedent in its future discussions with larger OECD economies.

Thus, bilateral and regional agreements can potentially serve as building blocks for multilateral frameworks such as the GATS by providing countries with negotiating experience, enabling regulatory capacity building and instilling confidence among policymakers to undertake commitments initially on a bilateral or regional scale before moving on to the multilateral level.

This is particularly so for complex issues such as standards, mutual recognition and labour market policies where there can be no single agreed technical formula for liberalization and where multilateral discussions are more likely to falter. Ideally, these regional and bilateral pacts should pave the way for more liberal multilateral commitments. Whether or not this will be so depends on the overall state of play and the confidence of member countries in the multilateral trading system and the intersectoral trade-offs involved. There is, of course, the frequently referred to concern that some smaller countries may be marginalized in these regional and bilateral processes. But, given the growing number of small countries that are entering into EPAs and FTAs with developed countries, and the accelerating rate of South-South pacts, such marginalization need not occur. Additional issues, such as the classification of occupations and occupational categories, could be addressed multilaterally building on the experience and successful cases of regional and bilateral pacts.

Note:

[1] Much of the discussion on bilateral and regional agreements and their typologies is based on Nielson (2003) and miscellaneous articles from the bilaterals.org website.

Source: Rupa Chanda, Professor of Economics, Indian Institute of Management, Bangalore.

REFERENCES

Al-Shammary, H.
2003   "Recruitment of workers from Bangladesh resumes", *The Arab News* (Saudi Arabia), 19 August.

Böhning, W.R.
2003   "The Protection of Temporary Migrants by Conventions of the ILO and the UN", paper presented to the Workshop on Temporary Migration – Assessment and Practical Proposals for Overcoming Protection Gaps, 18-19 September, International Institute for Labour Studies, International Labour Organization (ILO), Geneva, http://www.ilo.org/public/english/bureau/inst/download/bohning.pdf.

Brown, O., F.H. Shaheen, S.R. Khan and M. Yusuf
2005   "Regional Trade Agreements: Promoting conflict or building peace?", October, International Institute for Sustainable Development (IISD), Winnipeg, http://www.iisd.org/pdf/2005/security_rta_conflict.pdf.

Dommen, C.
2005   "Migrants' Human Rights: Could GATS Help?", *Migration Information Source*, March, Migration Policy Institute (MPI), Washington, D.C., http://www.migrationinformation.org/Feature/display.cfm?id=290.

European Commission
2005a   *Green Paper on an EU approach to managing economic migration*, COM (2004) 811, 11 January.

2005b   *Migration and Development: Some concrete orientations*, COM (2005) 390, 1 September.

2005c   *Policy Plan on Legal Migration*, COM (2005) 669, 21 December.

2007a   *Communication applying the Global Approach to Migration to the Eastern and South-Eastern Regions neighbouring the European Union*, COM (2007) 247, 16 May.

2007b   *Communication on circular migration and mobility partnerships between the European Union and third countries*, COM (2007) 248, 16 May.

2007c   *Proposal for a Directive of the European Parliament and of the Council providing for sanctions against employers for illegally staying third-country nationals*, COM (2007) 249, 16 May.

2007d   *Proposal for a Council Directive on the conditions of entry and residence of third-country nationals for the purposes of highly qualified employment*, COM (2007) 637, 23 October.

2007e   *Proposal for a Council Directive on a single application procedure for a single permit for third-country nationals to reside and work in the territory of a Member State and on a common set of rights for third-country workers legally residing in a Member State*, COM (2007) 638, 23 October.

Fonseca, L., J. Macaísta Malheiros and S. Silva
2005   "Portugal" in J. Niessen, Y. Schibel and C. Thompson (Eds.), *Current Immigration Debates in Europe: A Publication of the European Migration Dialogue*, September, Migration Policy Group (MPG), Brussels/Lisbon, http://www.migpolgroup.com/multiattachments/3011/DocumentName/EMD_Portugal_2005.pdf.

Geronimi, E.
2004   *Acuerdos bilaterales de migración de mano de obra: Modo de empleo*, International Migration Paper No. 65, International Migration Programme, International Labour Office, Geneva, http://www.ilo.org/public/english/protection/migrant/download/imp/imp65s.pdf.

Global Commission on International Migration (GCIM)
2005   *Migration in an Interconnected World: New directions for action*, Report of the GCIM, October, SRO-Kundig, Geneva, http://www.gcim.org/attachements/gcim-complete-report-2005.pdf.

Global Union Research Network (GURN)
2007   Bilateral and Regional Trade Agreements, GURN online discussion, http://www.gurn.info/topic/trade/.

International Confederation of Free Trade Unions (ICFTU)
2004   "The Spread of Bilateral and Regional Trade Agreements", Draft Paper, June, ICFTU, http://www.gurn.info/topic/trade/icftu_0604.pdf.

International Labour Organization (ILO)

1999   *General Survey on Migrant Workers*, Committee on the Application of Conventions and Recommendations, Report III (1B), International Labour Conference, 87th Session, June, International Labour Office, Geneva, http://www.ilo.org/public/english/standards/relm/ilc/ilc87/r3-1b.htm.

2004   *Towards a fair deal for migrant workers in the global economy*, Report VI, International Labour Conference, 92nd Session, June, International Labour Office, Geneva, http://www.ilo.org/wcmsp5/groups/public/---dgreports/---dcomm/documents/meetingdocument/kd00096.pdf.

2006   *ILO Multilateral Framework on Labour Migration: Non-binding principles and guidelines for a rights-based approach to labour migration*, International Labour Office, Geneva, http://www.ilo.org/public/english/protection/migrant/download/multilat_fwk_en.pdf.

International Organization for Migration (IOM)

2005   *World Migration 2005: Costs and Benefits of International Migration*, IOM, Geneva, http://www.iom.int/jahia/Jahia/cache/offonce/pid/1674?entryId=932.

IOM and Swiss Federal Office for Migration

2005a   *International Agenda for Migration Management*, IOM/Swiss Federal Office for Migration, Geneva/Berne, http://www.iom.int/jahia/Jahia/cache/offonce/pid/1674?entryId=8005.

2005b   *Interstate Cooperation and Migration*, Berne Initiative Studies, IOM/Swiss Federal Office for Migration, Geneva/Berne, http://www.iom.int/jahia/Jahia/cache/offonce/pid/1674?entryId=8008.

Ng, E. and J. Whalley

2007   "Visas and Work Permits: Possible Global Negotiating Initiatives", paper prepared for a Centre for International Governance and Innovation (CIGI) project and resubmitted to the *Review of International Organizations*, September, http://economics.uwo.ca/grad/Ng/AdditionalPaper1~Oct2007.pdf.

Organisation for Economic Co-operation and Development (OECD)

2004   *Migration for Employment – Bilateral Agreements at a Crossroads*, OECD, Paris.

Piper, N. and R. Iredale

2003   *Identification of the Obstacles to the Signing and Ratification of the UN Convention on the Protection of the Rights of all Migrant Workers: The Asia-Pacific Perspective*, United Nations Educational, Scientific and Cultural Organization (UNESCO) Series of Country Reports on the Ratification of the UN Convention on Migrants, Doc. SHS/2003/MC/1 REV, UNESCO, Paris, http://unesdoc.unesco.org/images/0013/001395/139528E.pdf.

Santestevan, A.M.

2007   "Free Movement Regimes in South America: The Experience of MERCOSUR and the Andean Community" in R. Cholewinski, R. Perruchoud and E. Macdonald (Eds.), *International Migration Law: Developing Paradigms and Key Challenges*, T.M.C. Asser Press, The Hague, 363-386.

Shulman, R.

2003   "Underage, Illegal and taking their Chances in Spain: Moroccan Girls defy Social Convention to Escape Poverty, Violence and Despair", *Washington Post*, 2 November.

Sleptova, E.

2003   "Labour Migration in Europe: Special focus on the Republic of Moldova", Institute for Public Policy (IPP), Moldova Republic, http://www.ipp.md/public/biblioteca/50/en/St~Sleptova~fin.doc.

Williams, V.

2008   "Interstate Cooperation in Migration Management in the Southern African Development Community (SADC)", revised draft paper presented at the IOM-University of Toronto Workshop on Migration and International Cooperation: South-South Perspectives, 7-8 August, Geneva.

Winters, L.A.

2005   "Developing Country Proposals for the Liberalization of Movements of Natural Service Suppliers", Working Paper T8, January, Development Research Centre on Migration, Globalisation and Poverty, University of Sussex, Brighton, http://www.migrationdrc.org/publications/working_papers/WP-T8.pdf.

Textbox 13.1 - The International Convention on the Protection of the Rights of All Migrant Workers and Members of Their Families

Office of the United Nations High Commissioner for Human Rights (OHCHR)

2008   International Convention on the Protection of the Rights of All Migrant Workers and Members of Their Families, General Assembly resolution 45/158 of 18 December 1990, OHCHR, http://www2.ohchr.org/english/law/cmw.htm.

2005   Committee on Migrant Workers, 15 December 2005: Day of General Discussion: Protecting the rights of all migrant workers as a tool to enhance development, OHCHR, http://www2.ohchr.org/english/bodies/cmw/mwdiscussion.htm.

Textbox 13.6 - Exploring the Role of Reformed Bilateral Labour Agreements: The Caribbean Community and the Temporary Movement of Less-skilled Labour

Caldentey, E.P. and K. Schmid

2006   "The Performance of CARICOM Economies in the 1990s: The Current Effect on Migration and Conflict Potential" in T. Lesser, B. Fernández-Alfaro, L. Cowie and N. Bruni (Eds.), *Intra-Caribbean Migration and the Conflict Nexus,* Human Rights Internet (in collaboration with the IOM, Association of Caribbean States and The University of West Indies), Ottawa.

Caribbean Community (CARICOM)

2007   CARICOM Secretariat Law website, http://www.caricomlaw.org/doc.php?id=557.

Cholewinski, R., J. Redpath, S. Nonnenmacher and J. Packer

2006   "The International Normative Framework with Reference to Migration in the Greater Caribbean" in T. Lesser, B. Fernández-Alfaro, L. Cowie and N. Bruni (Eds.), *Intra-Caribbean Migration and the Conflict Nexus.* Human Rights Internet (in collaboration with the IOM, Association of Caribbean States and The University of West Indies), Ottawa.

Council on Hemispheric Affairs (COHA)

2005   *Neighborly Quarrels: The Dominican Republic and the Perennial Haitian Immigrant Issue,* Memorandum to the Press, 30 June, COHA, Washington, D.C., http://www.coha.org/2005/06/30/neighborly-quarrels-the-dominican-republic-and-the-perennial-haitian-immigrant-issue/.

Ferguson, J.

2003   *Migration in the Caribbean: Haiti, the Dominican Republic and Beyond,* July, Minority Rights Group International, London, http://www.minorityrights.org/1038/reports/migration-in-the-caribbean-haiti-the-dominican-republic-and-beyond.html.

Fuchs, D. and T. Straubhaar

2003   *Economic Integration in the Caribbean: The development towards a common labour market,* International Migration Papers 61, May, Social Protection Sector, International Migration Programme, International Labour Office, Geneva, http://www.ilo.org/public/english/protection/migrant/download/imp/imp61e.pdf.

Hendrikx, M.

2006   *Appropriate social security for migrant workers: Implementation of agreements on social security,* paper prepared for the International Social Security Association (ISSA) Regional Conference for the Americas, 28-31 May, Belize City, http://www.issa.int/pdf/belize06/2hendrikx.pdf.

Inter-American Development Bank (IADB)

2007   *Haiti Remittance Survey 2006,* presented at the IADB and the Multilateral Investment Fund (MIF) Conference on Sending Money Home: Remittances to Haiti, 6 March, Port-au-Prince, http://www.iadb.org/news/docs/HaitiSurvey.pps.

International Organization for Migration (IOM)

2005   "Bilateral Labour Agreements: Effective Tools for Managing Labour Flows?", Textbox 12.2 in *World Migration 2005: Costs and Benefits of International Migration,* IOM, Geneva, 238-251.

2008   Website on Migration and Trade, http://www.iom.int/jahia/page1172.html.

in relation to both domestic and international labour market needs taking account of, inter alia, demographic projections. Policies required for the specific management of labour mobility then follow. Foremost among these are measures to uphold the integrity of recruitment processes and, more generally, protect migrant workers from exploitation and abuse. Access to authoritative, accurate and up-to-date information is of great importance, but so are welfare and support services for the workers while abroad and, when needed, appropriate arrangements to facilitate their return and reintegration in the home country.

From the perspective of countries of destination, the starting point is also the definition of explicit mobility-related objectives and desired outcomes, followed by the formulation of appropriate policies. These policies are not narrowly limited to the admission of foreign workers to fill existing labour shortages, but relate more broadly to economic and demographic planning, and cover the entire migration cycle from departure in countries of origin, the treatment and adequate protection of migrant workers (and their families) in the host society and the workplace, including appropriate integration strategies, to their return and reintegration, where appropriate, as well as possible continued movement between the country of origin and of destination. Such policies should be sufficiently flexible to be able to respond to changing labour market needs. They may need to accommodate both temporary labour migration and (permanent) employment-based immigration and, in certain instances, to provide a bridge between the two types of movement.

Both countries of origin and destination stand to benefit from securing the involvement and cooperation of the widest range of stakeholders, including employers, private recruitment agencies, trade unions, migrant and diaspora associations, and international organizations.

Bilateral cooperation offers many possibilities. Bilateral agreements are flexible instruments that can be used to match labour supply and demand in a planned, predictable and rights-based manner, while also contributing to the mitigation of irregular migration. They enable employers in countries of destination to recruit trained and competent individuals with the needed skills, while countries of origin obtain assurances that employment contracts will be adhered to and workers enjoy decent and safe working conditions. Cooperation does not stop there. Human mobility is increasingly the subject of international cooperation at the sub-regional, regional, inter-regional and global level, although it is true that progress in the management of labour migration is yet to match what has been achieved at the international level in other domains of economic and social affairs.

The discretion to determine who may or may not enter its territory remains a prerogative of the nation state, and this may limit the state's willingness to engage in cooperative endeavours. A second issue is the difficulty in achieving nationally coordinated policy positions addressing labour mobility among interested domestic agencies, such as those concerned with employment, foreign affairs, development, trade or welfare, prior to multilateral engagement. Yet another obstacle is differences in priorities among countries: while they are all affected by migratory flows, they are not all affected at the same time or in the same way, nor do they share the same circumstances or objectives. Despite these hurdles, however, numerous consultative mechanisms on migration policy have emerged over the last decade or so. The Abu Dhabi Dialogue, held in early 2008, is a good example of how consultations among countries of origin and destination can lead to the development of concrete projects to facilitate the movement of workers and improve their welfare (see Textbox 10.5). Such consultative processes, characterized by their informality and open-endedness, deserve to be further developed as forums for confidence building and information exchange and as "workplaces" where governments can meet to discuss the challenges of managing mobility, improve their grasp of issues and identify viable policy options.

Considerable amounts of time, resources and effort have been invested in non-binding consultative exercises in recent years. The Berne Initiative, IOM's International Dialogue on Migration, the UN General Assembly's High-Level Dialogue on International Migration and Development, and the Global Forum on Migration and Development have been or are, in many ways, large-scale community learning exercises. The Global Commission on International Migration (GCIM) was another parallel and intensive effort at developing a "framework for the formulation of a coherent, comprehensive and global response to the issue of international migration" (GCIM, 2005: vii). The outcomes of all these exercises are strikingly convergent. All of them take as their starting point the increasing political visibility and importance of international migration; all of them acknowledge that mobility is an unavoidable economic and social reality; all of them point to benefits that flow from properly managed flows; all of them draw attention to the risks of not managing those flows; all of them assert that it is possible to arrive at common understandings and principles, and propose remarkably consistent lines of action. They also confirm the need for clearer linkages to be established between the domain of human mobility proper and closely adjoining policy fields, especially those of development and trade.

Accordingly, the migration and development equation has become a foremost subject of research and policy debate. It has now been established beyond any doubt that migration can and does contribute to poverty reduction at both the individual and community level. Migrants can benefit directly by obtaining access to higher wages and improved living conditions, and there are follow-on benefits for the family members and communities, who are

the recipients of flows of remittances that had an estimated global value of USD 337 billion in 2007 (Ratha et al., 2008). Other longer-term gains accrue from the establishment of expatriate communities. Under the right circumstances, these diasporas have demonstrated that they can develop and sustain extensive social and cultural networks, promote and conduct trade, become providers of investment funding and business know-how, offer humanitarian assistance in times of crisis and even make a meaningful contribution to democratic processes in countries of origin. There are, however, downsides to the picture. Countries of origin – especially the smaller ones – are concerned about the impact on their economies of the departure of large proportions of their highly skilled workers. Developing countries are therefore keenly interested in the development of legislative and policy frameworks that will provide a balanced set of solutions affording opportunities and rights for migrants while meeting their concerns regarding brain drain.

For all countries, progress in this continuously evolving and complex area is first and foremost subject to a better understanding of the impact of international labour mobility on domestic labour supply; the impact of migration on productivity in the domestic economy; and the impact of remittance flows on development. It will also depend on the establishment of genuine partnerships between countries of origin and destination to attain mutually satisfactory outcomes.

The migration and trade nexus is at least as complex as the migration and development equation. At the global level, tariffs and other barriers to cross-border investment and trade in goods have been very substantially reduced in recent decades with the consequent growth in the global exchanges of capital, goods and services. Facilitation of the movement of people has been identified as a potential avenue to further economic gains through trade liberalization, but the policy intersections between migration and trade need to be more clearly mapped out and more fully explored. One specific issue to be addressed is the fundamental tension between trade-oriented policy objectives driven by market dynamics and premised on planning and predictability, and approaches to migration management that favour discretion and the adaptation of policy strategies to changing circumstances. At the doctrinal level, trade theories have yet to agree whether trade and migration are substitutes (viz. supporting local economic growth and boosting exports would have the effect of easing migration pressure) or complements (viz. both trade and migration can increase, and can be mutually supportive). Trade theories need to be reviewed from the trade-migration vantage point and relevant supporting evidence gathered to better inform policies aimed at managing international labour mobility, all the more so as current globalization trends are predominantly characterized by the growth in trade in services and knowledge-based trading patterns, both of which rely heavily on the mobility of human resources. In the context of international trade negotiations, GATS Mode 4 is seen as a promising means to facilitate the temporary movement of service personnel; however, so far its scope of application has been largely limited to the international movement of highly skilled personnel, and considerable creativity and persistence are still needed to allow these

negotiations to move forward. Regional and bilateral initiatives will similarly have to be nurtured and encouraged to yield the intended results. In fact, regional and bilateral trade agreements that already incorporate labour mobility may turn out to be learning stations where states acquire the confidence to work on broader approaches (see Textbox 13.7). Finally, policy coherence requires improvement in two ways: first, through the integration of worker mobility in national, regional and international employment and migration policies and strategies and, second, the definition of the particular roles and responsibilities of all key stakeholders, including the private sector.

The elucidation of the connections between migration, development and trade needs to take full account of the rights of migrant workers, in particular those who, for various reasons, such as age, gender, low-skill profile or work in unregulated sectors, are not covered by national labour laws and find themselves in vulnerable situations. Similarly, issues such as the management of change while maintaining social cohesion and adherence to core values, environmental impacts on mobility and vice versa (see Textbox Conc. 1) and migrant health should be taken into account in the development of effective migration management strategies.

Textbox Conc. 1

Climate Change and Labour Mobility

The importance of the reciprocal impact of climate change and migration is expected to grow incrementally over the coming decades. Altered rainfall patterns, rising sea levels and increasingly frequent natural disasters are all likely to exceed the absorption capacity of large areas of the world, and to critically affect problems of food and water security in marginal areas.

A number of analysts, of whom Norman Myers of Oxford University is perhaps the best known, have undertaken to estimate the number of people who will be forced to move over the long term as a direct result of climate change. Myers predicts that, by 2050, "there could be as many as 200 million people overtaken by disruptions of monsoon systems and other rainfall regimes, by droughts of unprecedented severity and duration, and by sea-level rise and coastal flooding" (Myers, 2005: 1).

This is a staggering number and, should it come to pass, some two per cent or one in forty-five people alive in 2050 would have been displaced by climate change at some point in their lives, and their total number would exceed the estimated current global migrant population of 200 million.

Such predictions are, of course, inherently speculative. There are so many and diverse factors at play – population growth, urbanization and local politics, to name just three – that establishing a causal relation between climate change and migration is difficult and fraught with uncertainties. However, it is clear that climate change will lead to large areas becoming increasingly less able to sustain peoples' livelihoods and lead to large-scale moves to areas still able to offer better opportunities.

Migration is, and always has been, an important response mechanism to climate stress. While pastoralists have since time immemorial migrated to and from water sources and grazing lands as part of their normal way of life as well as in response to climate changes, it is becoming apparent that migration as a response to environmental change is no longer limited to nomadic societies.

In Western Sudan, for example, studies have shown that one adaptive response to drought is to send an older male family member to the capital, Khartoum, to find paid work so as to tide the family over until the end of the drought (McLeman and Smit, 2004). Temporary labour migration in times of climate stress can supplement a family's income through remittances from paid work elsewhere, and reduce the demand on local resources as there will be fewer mouths to feed.

But the picture is nuanced. Recent studies in the West African Sahel have revealed the recourse to temporary labour migration as an adaptive mechanism to climate change. The region has suffered a prolonged drought for much of the past three decades. One way that households have adapted has been to send their young men and women in search of wage labour after each harvest. But **how far** they go depends on the success of the harvest.

A good harvest might give the family sufficient resources to send a member to Europe in search of work. While the potential rewards in terms of remittances are high, the journey is dangerous and the migrant is unlikely to be back in time for the next planting season. But, in a drought year, when harvests are poor, the young men and women tend to stay much closer to home and travel instead to nearby cities for paid work with which to supplement the household income. In such years the risk of losing the "migration gamble" is simply too great (McLeman, 2006).

In the past, the rich developed countries focused mainly on mitigating climate change by setting emissions targets for the OECD countries and deliberating on how to gain new adherents to an emissions control agreement after the Kyoto Protocol expires in 2012. More recently, greater attention has been paid to helping developing countries to adapt to the impacts of climate change, for instance by altering irrigation techniques, building better storm shelters and developing drought-resistant crops.

This approach to adaptation is fundamentally based on the idea of adapting "in situ". Migration is somehow viewed as a failure to adapt. The United Nations Framework Convention on Climate Change, for example, has supported the development of National Adaptation Programmes of Action (NAPA) to help the Least Developed Countries to identify and rank their priorities for adaptation to climate change. However, none of the fourteen NAPAs submitted so far mention migration or population relocation as a possible policy response. Likewise, the developed countries are very resistant to the idea of relaxing their immigration or asylum policies and to consider environmental strain as a legitimate reason for migration.

It may be said that the international community is, in fact, ignoring labour mobility as a coping strategy for climate stress. Instead, there is a collective, and rather successful, attempt to ignore the scale of future climate-induced migration. However, how the international community reacts to climate-driven labour migration will have a real effect on the larger development impacts of climate change.

Some analysts are beginning to argue that migration is both a necessary element of global redistributive justice and an important response to climate change; and that greenhouse gas emitters should accept an allocation of "climate migrants"[2] in proportion to their historical greenhouse gas emissions. Andrew Simms of the New Economics Foundation argues: "Is it right

---

[2] IOM applies the term "environmental migrants" to describe persons moving primarily as a result of climate change and environmental degradation. In its 2007 Discussion Note on "Migration and the Environment", IOM defined environmental migrants as "persons or groups of persons who, for reasons of sudden or progressive changes in the environment that adversely affect their lives or living conditions, are obliged to leave their habitual homes, or choose to do so, either temporarily or permanently, and who move either within their country or abroad" (IOM, 2007: 1-2, para. 6). This term is broader than "climate migrants" and encompasses population movements that are resulting both from climate and non-climate related environmental processes and events.

that while some states are more responsible for creating problems like global climate change, all states should bear equal responsibility to deal with their displaced people?"

There is a dilemma here. Relaxing immigration rules as part of a concerted policy to "release the population pressure" in areas affected by climate change could accelerate the brain drain of talented individuals from the developing world to the developed – and thereby worsen the "hollowing out" of affected economies, which is itself a driver of migration. On the other hand, closing borders in both source and destination countries undermines remittance economies and denies developing countries the benefits of access to the international labour market.

Clearly, there has to be a balance of policies that promotes the incentives for workers to stay in their home countries, whilst not closing the door to international labour mobility. The first steps are to acknowledge, assess and plan for the role of climate change and environmental degradation in future population movements.

Source: Oli Brown, International Institute for Sustainable Development (IISD), Geneva.

Accurate and reliable data on migrant stocks, flows and trends are indispensable to develop, monitor and evaluate migration policies and programmes. However, the collection, sharing and management of migration data is a highly time-consuming and resource-intensive process. Data are frequently gleaned from a multitude of sources not actually designed for migration-related analysis. In addition, since migration data are frequently considered to be sensitive, the sharing of data among institutions at the national level, let alone with other governments or non-government specialists, is often avoided. Special efforts are needed to improve the reliability and comparability of existing data sources; to identify and gather new data on emerging issues; and to ensure the dissemination and utilization of data and research on labour migration.

For many countries, migration is a new administrative area, and comprehensive systems to track, process and facilitate inward and outward movements of people are weak or non-existent. What is needed is a renewed focus on building the capacity of all governments, in particular those of developing countries or of countries newly affected by migratory flows; to formulate policy and legislation; to improve labour migration and related human resource development programmes through experimentation and innovation; to properly administer them; and to monitor progress and evaluate outcomes.

A new spirit of partnership in outlook and action is both possible and essential to realizing beneficial outcomes for the international community as a whole, including countries of origin, countries of destination and the migrants and their families. Such a partnership will be the key to the success or failure of the efforts to manage the international labour mobility challenges of the twenty-first century.

REFERENCES

European Commission

2007   *Proposal for a Council Directive on the conditions of entry and residence of third-country nationals for the purposes of highly qualified employment*, COM (2007) 637, 23 October.

Global Commission on International Migration (GCIM)

2005   *Migration in an Interconnected World: New directions for action*, October, GCIM, SRO-Kundig, Geneva, http://www.gcim.org/attachements/gcim-complete-report-2005.pdf.

International Organization for Migration (IOM)

2007   "Discussion Note: Migration and the Environment", 1 November, IOM Council, 94th Session, Doc. MC/INF/288, IOM, Geneva, http://www.old.iom.int//DOCUMENTS/GOVERNING/EN/913208461788198.pdf.

Ratha, D., S. Mohapatra, K.M. Vijayalakshmi and Z. Xu

2008   *Revisions to Remittance Trends 2007*, Migration and Development Brief 5, 10 July, Migration and Remittances Team, Development Prospects Group, The World Bank, Washington, D.C., http://siteresources.worldbank.org/INTPROSPECTS/Resources/334934-1110315015165/MD_Brief5.pdf.

Textbox Conc. 1 - Climate Change and Labour Mobility

Dupont, A. and G. Pearman

2006   "Heating up the Planet: Climate Change and Security", Lowry Institute for International Policy, Paper 12, Sydney, http://lowyinstitute.richmedia-server.com/docs/AD_GP_ClimateChange.pdf.

McLeman, R.

2006   "Global warming's huddled masses", *The Ottawa Citizen*, 23 November, http://www.canada.com/ottawacitizen/news/opinion/story.html?id=f4f4a221-e39e-42ac-9d19-5f0bd4b0ee3e.

McLeman, R. and B. Smit

2004   "Climate change, migration and security", Canadian Security Intelligence Service, March, Commentary No. 86, Ottawa, http://www.csis-scrs.gc.ca/pblctns/cmmntr/cm86-eng.asp.

Myers, N.

2005   "Environmental Refugees: An emergent security issue", 13th Economic Forum, 23-27 May, Session III – Environment and Migration, Organization for Security and Co-operation in Europe (OSCE), Prague, Doc. EF.NGO/4/05, http://www.osce.org/documents/eea/2005/05/14488_en.pdf.

Pielke, R. Jr, G. Prins, S. Rayner and D. Sarewitz

2007   "Lifting the taboo on adaptation: renewed attention to policies for adapting to climate change cannot come too soon", *Nature*, 445 (8 February): 597-598.

REGIONAL OVERVIEWS

INTRODUCTION

While *World Migration 2008* lays emphasis on the global nature of contemporary migratory activity, it is nonetheless true that each major geographic region displays characteristics that distinguish it from the others. The following brief Regional Overviews are intended to complement the information provided in the rest of this Report by drawing attention to the key features typifying each region. Given the known difficulty of obtaining up-to-date, comprehensive and comparable data on migratory phenomena, the overviews are not intended to be read as statistically accurate accounts, but rather as impressionistic depictions of the migratory dynamics in operation within the regions.

Based on a review of many different and not infrequently conflicting sources, each overview offers information on the stocks and distribution of migrants; the major types of flows encountered and their magnitude and determinants; and some of the topical migration management issues to which they give rise. Wherever possible, preference has been given to graphs and illustrations over lengthy word descriptions.

AFRICA

- With an increase of just over half a million migrants from 16.3 to 16.9 million between 2000 and 2005, Africa[1] experienced the lowest growth rate in international migrants of any region in the world, and, at two per cent, the continent also registers the lowest proportion of migrants as a share of the population. Its share of the global migrant stock has remained stable at nine per cent (UN DESA, 2005).

- Migrants are widely distributed across the continent, with a disproportionate number in sub-Saharan countries. In absolute terms, it is the large West and Southern African countries that are most affected by migration, but relative to the size of their population the smallest countries or territories receive more migrants (see Figure 1).

---

[1] **East Africa**: Burundi, Comoros, Djibouti, Eritrea, Ethiopia, Kenya, Madagascar, Malawi, Mauritius, Mozambique, Reunion, Rwanda, Seychelles, Somalia, Uganda, Tanzania, Zambia, Zimbabwe. **Central Africa**: Angola, Cameroon, Central African Republic, Chad, Congo, Democratic Republic of the Congo (DRC), Equatorial Guinea, Gabon, Sao Tome and Principe. **North Africa**: Algeria, Libya, Morocco, Sudan, Tunisia. **Southern Africa**: Botswana, Lesotho, Namibia, Republic of South Africa and Swaziland. **West Africa**: Benin, Burkina Faso, Cape Verde, Côte d'Ivoire, Gambia, Ghana, Guinea, Guinea-Bissau, Liberia, Mali, Mauritania, Niger, Nigeria, Saint Helena, Senegal, Sierra Leone, Togo (division of countries according to UN DESA, 2005). Egypt is considered in the Migration Overview on the Middle East.

Figure 1:

Stock of migrants in Africa, top ten destinations, 2000 and 2005

Part A: Total number of migrants

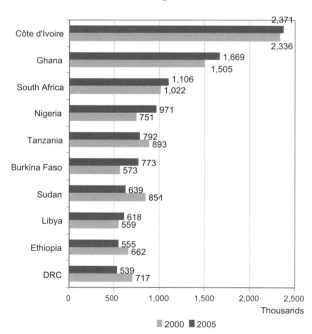

Part B: As a share of total population

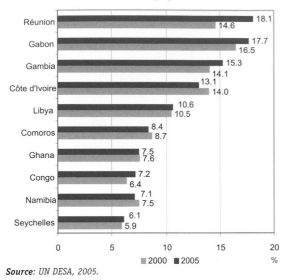

Source: UN DESA, 2005.

- Most of the recorded migration in Africa occurs within the region; out of a total of 14.5 million migrants originating in sub-Saharan Africa, 10 million migrants (or 69%) move within the region (Ratha and Shaw, 2007).
- On the other hand, data from North Africa[2] show that South-South migration represents only 19 per cent of total migration from this sub-region while South-North migration accounts for 80 per cent of total migration (Ratha and Shaw, 2007).
- Africa has the world's highest concentration of internally displaced persons (IDPs), with 12.7 million in 20 countries at the end of 2007 (IDMC, 2008), largely outnumbering the refugee population which declined from approximately six million to about three million in the 1995-2005 decade (UNHCR, 1995 and 2007).
- Refugees as a percentage of total international migrants decreased by four percentage points to 18 per cent of the current migrant population (UN DESA, 2005).

----

[2] North Africa here includes the Middle East. While the Middle East region is analyzed in a separate overview, a reference to this region is made here because the findings cited from the South-South remittances analysis aggregate data for North Africa and the Middle East (Ratha and Shaw, 2007).

- Africa received USD 23.1 billion in remittances[3] in 2007, the smallest share of global transfers (World Bank, 2008).
- Coastal migration and environmental migration are among the emerging features of migration in Africa.

EAST AND CENTRAL AFRICA

- The four leading East African countries of destination for migrants from the sub-region registered a decline in their migrant populations between 2000 and 2005. With nearly a million migrants, Tanzania is host to the largest contingent of migrants; while migrants make up a larger share of the populations of the smaller islands. Thus, the share of migrants in the total population of La Réunion increased from 14.6 per cent to 18 per cent between 2000 and 2005, and the Comoros and Seychelles host, respectively, 8.4 and 6.1 migrants per 100 habitants (UN DESA, 2005) (see Figure 2).

Figure 2:

Stock of migrants in East Africa, top ten destinations, 2000 and 2005

Part A: Total number of migrants

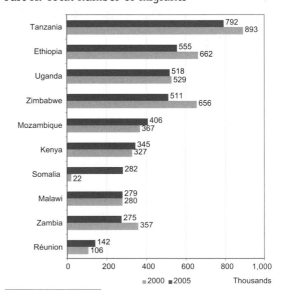

----

[3] Unless otherwise stated, remittance figures in these overviews refer to officially recorded flows and do not capture amounts transmitted through informal channels.

Part B: As a share of total population

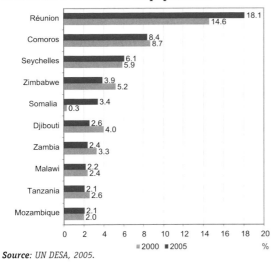

Source: UN DESA, 2005.

- Even though between 2000 and 2005 the migrant population in the Democratic Republic of the Congo (DRC) dropped from 717,000 to 539,000, at the end of that period their numbers continued to be the highest in Central Africa. As a share of the population, they represented only 1.4 per cent in 2000 and 0.9 per cent in 2005. In 2005, migrants in Gabon represented 17.7 per cent of the local population, the largest share in any Central African country (see Figure 3).

Figure 3:

Stock of migrants in Central Africa, by destination, 2000 and 2005

Part A: Total number of migrants

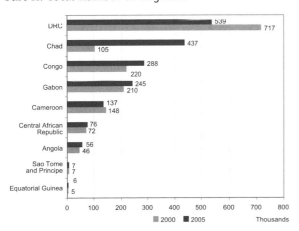

Part B: As a share of total population

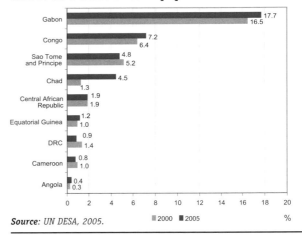

Source: UN DESA, 2005.

The number of IDPs exceeds that of refugees in East African countries

- At the end of 1995, the number of IDPs concentrated in the countries of the Greater Horn of Africa[4] (GHA) amounted to less than half of the total regional refugee population of 3.2 million (Oucho, 2006); however, by 2007, owing to the conflicts in the ten GHA countries, their numbers relative to refugees increased dramatically (see Figure 4).

Figure 4:

Greater Horn of Africa: Refugees and IDPs in 2007

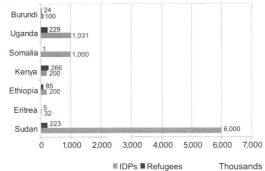

Note: Djibouti, Rwanda and Tanzania are not included in Figure 4 for lack of data on IDPs.

Sources: UNHCR, 2008a, IDMC, 2008.

---

4   The "Greater Horn of Africa" (GHA) comprises ten countries: the two Great Lakes region states of Burundi and Rwanda; the three countries of East Africa – Kenya, Tanzania and Uganda; and the "Horn of Africa" (HOA) states of Djibouti, Eritrea, Ethiopia, Somalia and Sudan.

- African visits to South Africa increased from 550,000 to four million; and
- SADC visits to South Africa increased from 500,000 to 3.7 million (Crush and Williams, 2005).

Health worker migration is a growing phenomenon ...

- Medical doctors from South Africa are emigrating at an annual rate of about 1,000, and it is estimated that 30-50 per cent of all medical school graduates emigrate to the U.K. or U.S. every year. More than 75 per cent of skilled South African emigrants relocate in only five countries: the U.K., the U.S., Australia, Canada and New Zealand (IOM, 2007a). Doctors from South Africa make up 9.7 per cent of total foreign-trained doctors in Australia and seven per cent in the U.K. (IOM, 2007b).
- While Zambia had an estimated 1,600 doctors in the 1980s, only 400 remained by 2002. Similarly, of the 1,200 doctors trained in Zimbabwe in the 1990s, only 360 were practicing in the country in 2003 (IOM, 2007a).
- Between 2000 and 2004, nearly 40,000 foreign nurses registered to work in the U.K. according to the government's official statistics. Over a period of four years, 6,028 nurses left South Africa for the U.K., 1,561 left Zimbabwe, 1,496 left Nigeria, 660 left Ghana, 444 left Zambia, 386 left Kenya, 226 left Botswana and 192 left Malawi (IOM, 2007a).
- Lesotho and Namibia present a physician emigration rate[6] of over 30 per cent, while this rate rises to over 50 per cent in Malawi, Tanzania and Zambia and to 75 per cent in Mozambique. South Africa, Swaziland and Botswana (11%) are the only countries in Southern Africa with a physician emigration rate below the average for sub-Saharan Africa (IOM, 2007a).

... but South Africa is also a destination country for health professionals of all categories

- By 2003, South Africa reported 32,000 vacancies for nurses and 4,000 for doctors in the public health sector alone (IOM, 2007b).
- Even as South Africa is losing skilled health workers, the country is also the major destination for skilled health workers from other parts of Africa, most recently from Botswana, DRC, Ghana, Nigeria and Zimbabwe. In Africa, South Africa has the highest physician and nurse ratio to the population: 56.3 physicians and 471.8 nurses per 100,000 inhabitants, compared to a ratio of only 6.2 and 44.2, respectively, in the DRC, another SADC country (IOM, 2007b).
- South Africa has sought to address staff shortages in the public health sector through the hiring of Iranian and Cuban health personnel to work in rural areas (IOM, 2007b).

WEST AFRICA

- While Côte d'Ivoire is the leading destination country for migrants in West Africa (2.4 million international migrants in 2005), at 15.3 per cent, Gambia has the highest proportion of migrants in its population. Guinea is the only country in the sub-region to register a drop in the number of international migrants in both absolute and relative terms (from 8.7% in 2000 to 4.3% in 2005) (UN DESA, 2005) (see Figure 8).

---

[6] The **physician emigration rate** is the physician emigration stock compared to the total number of doctors originating from the source country (residents plus emigrants).

Figure 8:

Stock of migrants in West Africa, top ten destinations, 2000 and 2005

Part A: Total number of migrants

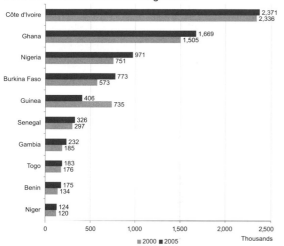

Part B: As a share of total population

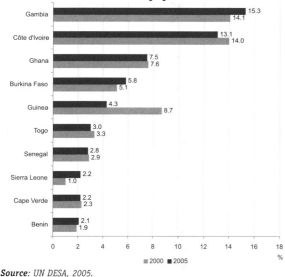

Source: UN DESA, 2005.

- Regular migration from ECOWAS[7] Member States to the EU-15[8] increased from 23,557 to 71,653 from 2000 to 2004 (European Commission, 2007).

---

[7] The Economic Community of West African States (ECOWAS) is a regional grouping of 16 countries: Benin, Burkina Faso, Cape Verde, Côte d'Ivoire, Gambia, Ghana, Guinea, Guinea Bissau, Liberia, Mali, Mauritania, Niger, Nigeria, Senegal, Sierra Leone and Togo.

[8] The EU-15 refers to the 15 European Union Member States before the enlargements of the EU to 25 and 27 Member States in May 2004 and January 2007, respectively.

- Recently, West African migration to North America has become more diversified. While in 1994, the inflows of citizens of ECOWAS Member States to the U.S. stood at 9,498, they had reached 24,820 in 2004. Inflows to Canada increased from 2,093 to 4,337 during that same period (see Figure 9).

Figure 9:

Diversification of West African diaspora

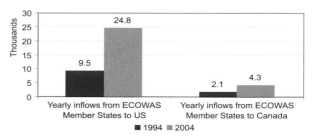

Source: European Commission, 2007.

- Currently, 56 per cent of the West African population is under 20 years of age and 66 per cent are under 25 years of age compared to 12 per cent and 15 per cent, respectively, in Europe. By the year 2020, West Africa could have about 200 million people under the age of 20 (OECD, 2006).

The outmigration of health professionals is a major concern

- According to World Health Organization (WHO) figures, over 900 physicians trained in Ghana are working in an OECD country, compared with 3,240 practicing in Ghana itself (UNECA, 2006).

Environmental migration is an emerging major issue in West Africa

- Yields from rain-fed agriculture, the most important part of sub-Saharan agriculture, are projected to fall by up to 50 per cent by 2020 (IPCC, 2007), seriously compromising agricultural production and access to food. Labour migration has already become an important part of the annual coping strategy against the prolonged drought that has been affecting the West African Sahel for the past three decades (Brown, 2007).

- Under the worst climate change migration scenario, it has been estimated by the Intergovernmental Panel on Climate Change (IPCC) that more than 200 million people might be displaced globally by climate change, and the Sahelian region could become uninhabitable on a permanent basis (Brown, 2008).

SOME TOPICAL POLICY ISSUES IN MIGRATION MANAGEMENT IN AFRICA

Remittances

Remittance flows are significant but Africa receives the smallest share of global transfers

- According to World Bank estimates for 2007, the African continent received USD 23.1 billion in remittances, with USD 11.7 billion to sub-Saharan Africa and USD 11.4 billion to North Africa (World Bank, 2008) (see Figure 10).

Figure 10:

Remittances received in Africa, 2007 (billions of USD)

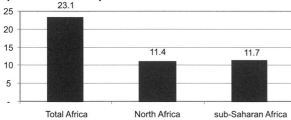

Note: Egypt is not included in these calculations.

Source: World Bank, 2008.

- In 2007, Africa received 6.8 per cent of global remittance flows of USD 337 billion (World Bank, 2008).

- Remittances to sub-Saharan Africa accounted for around 2.5 per cent of GDP on average between 2000 and 2005, which is considerably lower than in some other developing countries. However, there are striking exceptions such as Lesotho, where remittances represent almost 28 per cent of GDP, and Cape Verde, Guinea-Bissau and Senegal, with more than five per cent (see Figure 11). For many countries, remittances are an important source of foreign exchange: for Lesotho, Cape Verde, Uganda and Comoros, for instance, remittances have since 2000 amounted on average to more than 25 per cent of export earnings (Gupta et al., 2007).

Figure 11:

Leading ten recipients of remittances in sub-Saharan Africa, 2005-2006

Part A: Total flows (millions of USD)

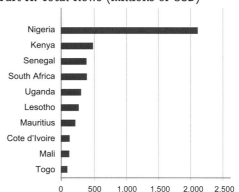

Part B: Ratio to GDP (%)

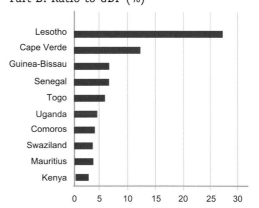

Part C: Ratio to export earnings (%)

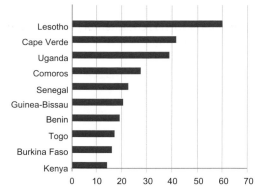

Note: Rankings are based on average remittance inflows for 2005-2006.
Source: Gupta et al., 2007.

- South–South remittances in Africa can be significant, a good example being the flows within the Southern Africa sub-region, where South Africa is the major remittance-sending country to other SADC countries (Genesis Analytics, 2005).

Major remittance flows in the SADC

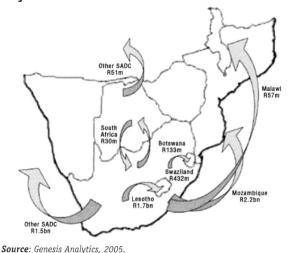

Source: Genesis Analytics, 2005.

Contrary to other regions, in Africa foreign direct investment flows are higher than remittance flows

- While remittances to African countries more than doubled from USD 7 billion to 17 billion between

1995 and 2005, foreign direct investment (FDI) increased fivefold from about USD 5 billion to USD 25 billion over the same period (World Bank, 2007) (see Figure 12).

Figure 12:

Total remittances and FDI received by Africa, 1995-2005 (billions of USD)

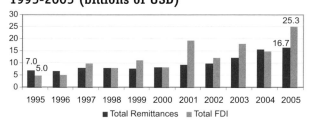

Note: Egypt is not included in these calculations.
Source: UNCTAD, 2006 and World Bank, 2007.

Irregular Migration

Irregular migration, both within and from Africa, is growing but still represents only a small proportion of all irregular migrants in Europe

Various locations on the West African coastline are used as staging posts for smuggling and trafficking operations into Europe

- Although the European Union has introduced extensive control operations in recent years, there are still substantial numbers of irregular migrants who attempt to cross in an irregular manner from West Africa to Italy or Spain. Some 34,000 irregular migrants were apprehended on or off the Canary Islands in 2006 (*Migration News Sheet*, February 2007), and, in 2007, increasing numbers of Asians joined Africans crossing from the West African coast to the Canary Islands (de Haas, 2007b). In 2007, however, these numbers dropped due to greater vigilance by countries of departure and surveillance missions conducted by Spain alone or within the framework of the EU border agency, FRONTEX (*Migration News Sheet*, September 2007).

Saharan routes are commonly used by Asian migrants seeking to reach southern European countries

- In recent years, migrants from Bangladesh, China, India and Pakistan have begun to migrate to the Maghreb overland via Saharan routes. Most of them fly from Asia to West African capitals, sometimes via the Gulf states. From there, they follow the common Saharan trail via Niger and Algeria to Morocco. Others enter North Africa through Egypt to Libya and Tunisia, from where they cross to Italy and Malta (de Haas, 2007b).

Some of the irregular migratory flows in Africa are intra-continental, for instance those involving migrants moving in search of life and work opportunities, whether to South Africa ...

- More than 300,000 migrants were deported from South Africa in 2007, up from approximately 250,000 in 2006 (CoRMSA, 2008).

- According to the Government of South Africa, 50,000 Zimbabweans were returned to their country between January and March 2007 (ReliefWeb, 2007).

... or to islands in the Indian Ocean

Mayotte has become the pole of attraction for between 45,000 to 60,000 irregular migrants principally from other islands of the Comoro Archipelago with smaller numbers from Madagascar (*Le Monde*, 15 August 2007).

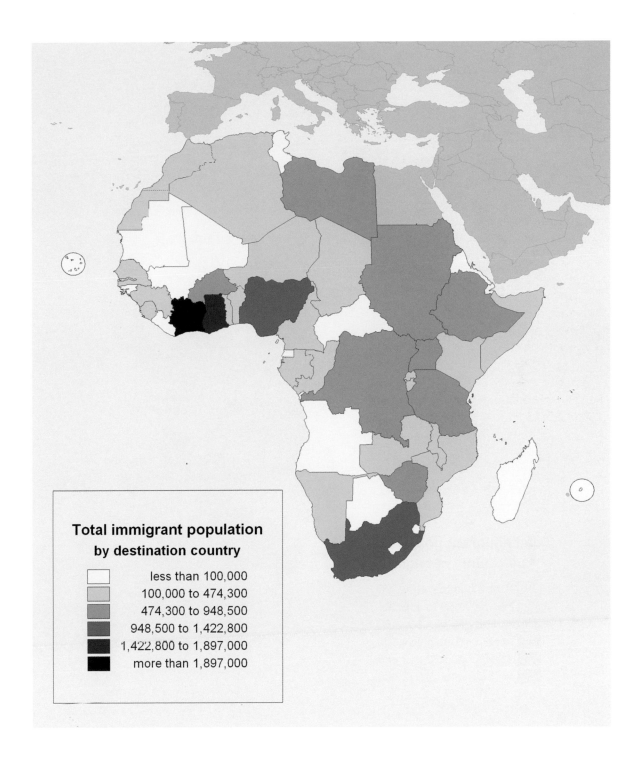

Total immigrant population
by destination country

less than 100,000
100,000 to 474,300
474,300 to 948,500
948,500 to 1,422,800
1,422,800 to 1,897,000
more than 1,897,000

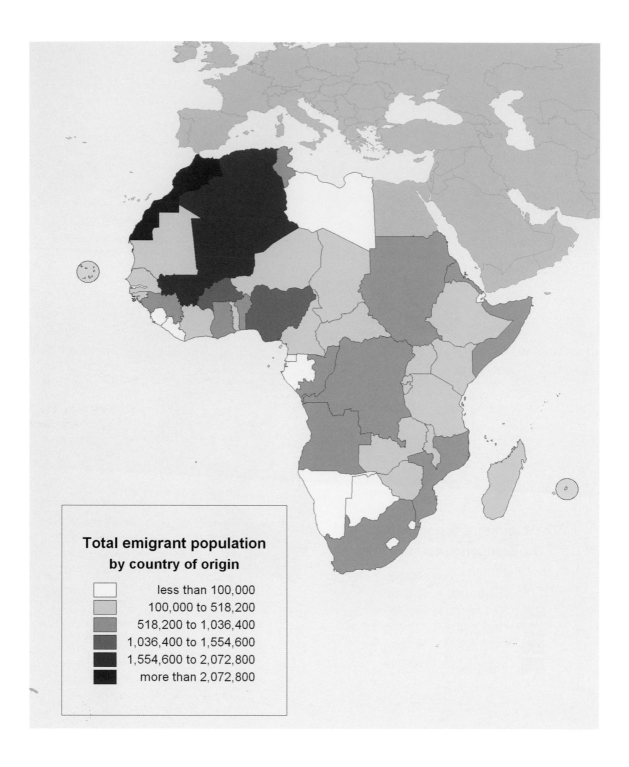

**Total emigrant population
by country of origin**

less than 100,000
100,000 to 518,200
518,200 to 1,036,400
1,036,400 to 1,554,600
1,554,600 to 2,072,800
more than 2,072,800

REFERENCES

Adepoju, A.
2006   "Policy-driven Research on International Migration in sub-Saharan Africa" in K. Tamas and J. Palme (Eds.), *How Migration can Benefit Development*, Institute for Future Studies, Stockholm, 69-84.

Brown, O.
2007   "Climate change and forced migration: Observations, projections and implications", background paper for the 2007 Human Development Report, http://hdr.undp.org/en/reports/global/hdr2007-2008/papers/brown_oli.pdf.

2008   *Migration and Climate Change*, Migration Research Series, No. 31, International Organization for Migration (IOM), Geneva.

Cross, C., D. Gerdelblom, N. Roux and J. Mafukukidze (Eds.)
2006   *Views on Migration in Sub-Saharan Africa: Proceedings of an African Migration Alliance Workshop*, HSRC Press, Cape Town.

Crush, J. and V. Williams
2005   "International Migration and Development: Dynamics and Challenges in South and Southern Africa", paper prepared for the United Nations Expert Group Meeting on International Migration and Development, United Nations Department for Economic and Social Affairs (UN DESA), 6-8 July, New York, Doc. UN/POP/MIG/2005/05, http://www.un.org/esa/population/meetings/ittmigdev2005/P05_Crush&Williams.pdf.

de Haas, H.
2007a   "North-African Migration Systems: evolution, transformations and development linkages", International Migration Institute (IMI) Working Paper 6, University of Oxford, http://www.imi.ox.ac.uk/pdfs/WP6%20North%20African%20Migration%20Systems.pdf.

2007b   "The myth of invasion – Irregular migration from West Africa to the Maghreb and the European Union", IMI Research Report, October, University of Oxford, http://www.imi.ox.ac.uk/pdfs/Irregular%20migration%20from%20West%20Africa%20-%20Hein%20de%20Haas.pdf.

European Commission
2007   "Migration from Africa: A Case Study on Root Causes and Factors Contributing to Migration from Senegal to the EU", Technical Note IPSC/TN/2007/xxx.

Genesis Analytics
2005   "Supporting Remittances in Southern Africa", Genesis Analytics, Johannesburg, http://www.microfinancegateway.com/files/27700_file_27700.pdf.

Gupta, S., C. Pattillo and S. Wagh
2007   "Making Remittances Work for Africa", *Finance and Development*, 44:2 (June).

Hugo, G.
2005   "Migration in the Asia-Pacific Region", paper prepared for the Policy Analysis and Research Programme of the Global Commission on International Migration (GCIM), September, Geneva, http://www.gcim.org/mm/File/Regional%20Study%202.pdf.

Internal Displacement Monitoring Centre (IDMC) of the Norwegian Refugee Council
2008   *Internal Displacement: Global Overview of Trends and Developments in 2007*, April, IDMC, Geneva, http://www.internal-displacement.org/8025708F004BE3B1/(httpInfoFiles)/BD8316FAB5984142C125742E0033180B/$file/IDMC_Internal_Displacement_Global_Overview_2007.pdf.

International Organization for Migration (IOM)
2005   *World Migration 2005: Costs and Benefits of International Migration*, IOM, Geneva, http://www.iom.int/jahia/Jahia/cache/offonce/pid/1674?entryId=932.

2007a   "Health Workers Migration in South and Southern Africa: Literature Review", October, IOM Regional Office for Southern Africa, Pretoria.

2007b   "Facilitation of the Recruitment and Placement of Foreign Health Care Professionals to Work in the Public Sector Health Care in South Africa", Assessment conducted in the Netherlands, the United Kingdom and the United States, November, IOM Pretoria in consultation with the National Department of Health, Republic of South Africa, Pretoria, http://www.iom.int/Template/health_worker_assessment_report.pdf.

highest number of migrants (29.4%), followed by Saint-Pierre-et-Miquelon (22.4%) and Greenland (21.4%). Compared to 2001, all countries and territories in North America have seen an increase in immigration in both absolute and relative terms.

Figure 1:

Stock of migrants in North America, by destination, 2000 and 2005

Part A: Total number of migrants

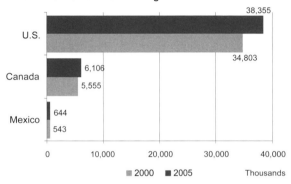

Part B: As a share of total population

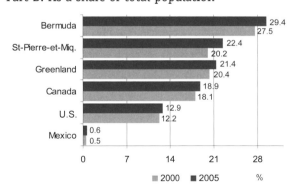

Source: UN DESA, 2005.

UNITED STATES

Intra-regional migration accounts for more than half of total immigration in the United States

- In absolute numbers, the United States remains the dominant country of destination in the Americas and in the world. In 2005, of the 38.3 million migrants living in the U.S., 55 per cent were from the Americas: 10.8 million from Mexico, 4.6 million from Latin America, 3.2 million from the Caribbean and 692,000 from Canada and other parts of North America (see Figure 2).

Figure 2:

Stock of foreign-born population in the U.S., by region of origin, 1995 to 2005

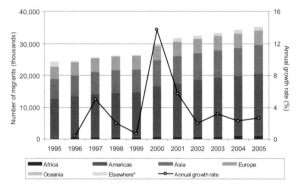

Note: *Includes region not known.

Source: Urban Institute tabulations from public-use files from the U.S. Census Bureau, Current Population Survey, March Supplement, 1995 to 2005.

- Persons of Hispanic origin are the fastest growing ethnic group in the U.S., becoming the largest minority group in 2004.

Changes in settlement patterns have profoundly affected migration in the U.S.

- The impact of immigration on the United States has also been influenced by changes in the settlement patterns of immigrants in recent years (MPI, 2004). California and New York continue to be the top receiving states of migrants, hosting 27 and 11 per cent of the total foreign-born population, respectively. From 1990 to 2005, however, their combined percentage of total migration fell by 9.3 per cent (California losing 6% and New York 3.3%). The loss of the big "gateway" states was partially compensated by non-traditional immigration states like Arizona, Georgia, Virginia, North Carolina, Colorado and Nevada. In these new immigration states, the foreign-born population grew on average by over 200 per cent with some states experiencing even higher growth rates (North Carolina and Georgia led with a growth rate of 412% and 382%, respectively – MPI, 2004).

- Finally, it is important to mention that while in the past agriculture was the main sector employing migrant labour, new arrivals are now distributed more widely, notably in the food and service industries.

CANADA

Canada is not only a country of destination but also has a long history of emigration to the U.S.

- Immigration trends in Canada from 2000 to 2005 show a rise in the foreign-born population of 0.55 million. Immigration to Canada has grown at a 9.2 per cent average quintennial rate since 1960. In 2005, Canada's foreign-born population of 6.1 million represented 18.9 per cent of the total population, a figure higher than in the U.S. (see Figure 3).
- Nearly one-quarter of the 235,808 new permanent residents admitted in Canada in 2004 were selected through Canada's "points system" that tests them inter alia for skills and education (see Chapter 11). Family members accompanying these migrants account for a little over another quarter of admissions, with subsequent family reunification and humanitarian migrants making up the remainder (O'Neil et al., 2005).

- Canada is not only a destination country but has a long history of emigration to the United States. In 2005, the foreign-born from Canada, 674,000 people, made up the ninth-largest immigrant group in the U.S. (U.S. Census Bureau, 2005).

Figure 3:

Estimated number of migrants in Canada by gender at mid-year and quintennial growth rate

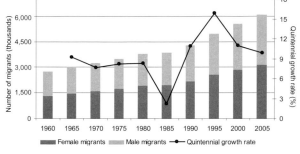

Source: UN DESA, 2005.

MEXICO

Mexico is not only a significant country of origin but has also become an important country of transit

- Mexico is characterized primarily by the mass emigration of Mexicans to the United States. With 10.8 million migrants, or 90 per cent of the country's total emigration, Mexico is the top country of origin of the foreign-born population in the U.S. (U.S. Census Bureau, 2005). In addition, one in every five immigrants who obtained U.S. permanent residence status in 2002 was from Mexico (Grieco, 2003).
- Immigrants do not represent a large proportion of Mexico's population. In 2005, the percentage of the foreign-born population in Mexico was around 0.6 per cent, or 644,361 (UN DESA, 2005). Of these, the majority (69% in 2000) were from the United States (Castillo, 2006). Most are thought to be

the U.S.-born children of Mexican migrants or of Mexican border residents; however, an increasing number of U.S.-born senior citizens are settling in Mexico after their retirement. In 2000, the Mexican census showed 28,247 U.S.-born senior citizens in Mexico, representing an increase of 17.3 per cent over 1990 (MPI, 2006). There are also temporary workers from Central America, for example, from Guatemala, who tend to work in border areas in sectors such as agriculture, construction and domestic service.

- Over the last two decades or so, Mexico has become a significant country of transit, especially for Central American migrants. In 2006, over 270,000 Central Americans entered Mexico through its southern border trying to reach the U.S. Around 216,000 were detained and returned to their countries of origin. A smaller number of transit migrants originate from South America (mainly Ecuador and Brazil), China, Cuba, other Caribbean countries and Africa (around 3,000 for all nationalities) (CONAPO, 2006).

LATIN AMERICA AND THE CARIBBEAN[3]

- Argentina, hosting 1.5 million migrants in 2005, is the top country of destination in Latin America and the Caribbean, followed by Venezuela (one million) and Brazil (641,000) (see Figure 4). These countries remain as the top three destination countries of the sub-region despite a decrease in the stock of migrants relative to 2000. Costa Rica, ranking fourth as country of destination in 2005, experienced the greatest increase in the stock of

migrants (130,000) compared to 2000. Dependent territories or overseas departments of larger countries, have the highest number of immigrants relative to the size of their population. French Guiana is at the top of the list with 44.9 per cent, followed by Anguilla (42.5%) and the British Virgin Islands (38.3%) (UN DESA, 2005).

Figure 4:

Stock of migrants in Latin America and the Caribbean, top ten destinations, 2000 and 2005

Part A: Total number of migrants

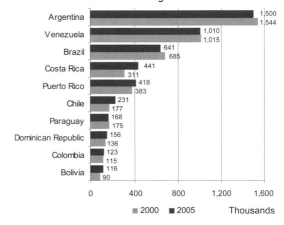

Part B: As a share of total population

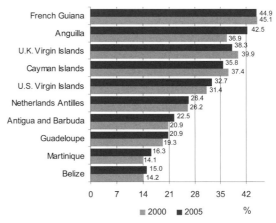

Source: UN DESA, 2005.

---

[3] This section covers 14 **Caribbean countries** (Antigua and Barbuda, Bahamas, Barbados, Cuba, Dominica, Dominican Republic, Grenada, Grenadines, Haiti, Jamaica, Saint Kitts and Nevis, Saint Lucia, Saint Vincent, and Trinidad and Tobago); seven **Central American countries** (Belize, Costa Rica, El Salvador, Guatemala, Honduras, Nicaragua and Panama); 12 **South American countries** (Argentina, Brazil, Bolivia, Colombia, Chile, Ecuador, Guyana, Paraguay, Peru, Suriname, Uruguay and Venezuela), and ten **dependent territories or overseas departments** (Anguilla, British Virgin Islands, Cayman Islands, French Guiana, Guadeloupe, Martinique, Netherlands Antilles, Puerto Rico, United States Virgin Islands and Turks and Caicos Islands).

The U.S. continues to host the highest number of Latin American and Caribbean migrants ...

- According to the Population Division of the Economic Commission for Latin America and the Caribbean (ECLAC), the number of Latin American and Caribbean migrants increased considerably from an estimated total of 21 million in 2000 to 25 million in 2005,[4] accounting in 2005 for four per cent of the population of their home countries (ECLAC, 2006a). Relative to the approximately 191 million international migrants in the world in 2005 (UN DESA, 2005), this sub-region accounts for over 13 per cent of all international migrants worldwide. In 2001, half of those migrants resided in the Americas (70% in the U.S. and 30% within Latin America and the Caribbean) and half in other parts of the world.

... and yet the flow of Latin American and Caribbean migrants towards Europe has increased during the last 15 years

- In geographical terms, the destinations of Latin American and Caribbean migrants have been expanding and diversifying. Owing to push factors, the demand for specialized workers and the emergence of social networks, the flows of migrants from Latin America and the Caribbean towards Europe (particularly Spain, Portugal and Italy), as well as Japan and Canada, increased over the period 1990-2005 (ECLAC, 2006a). According to ECLAC estimates, approximately three million people from Latin America and the Caribbean are living outside the sub-region in countries

other that the U.S. Figure 5 shows the evolution of Latin American and Caribbean migration as a percentage of total immigration in some of the main countries of destination.

Figure 5:

Volume of Latin American and Caribbean migrants as a percentage of total migration, by main destination, 1995-2005

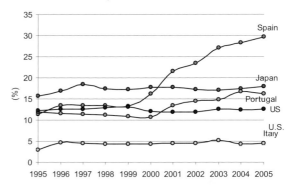

Source: *OECD, Stocks of foreign population by nationality and stocks of foreign-born population by country of origin, online database.*

- The changing migration patterns affecting Latin America and the Caribbean are complex. However, some of the larger trends in the sub-region have been shaped by natural and economic crises, gradual economic and political change, the feminization of migration flows and the diversification of countries of destination for Latin American migrants (O'Neil et al., 2005).

The importance of crises and economic change in migration trends

- Emigration trends from Latin America and the Caribbean can sometimes be traced clearly to specific crises, but flows triggered by general economic and cultural changes are more difficult to identify. Natural disasters and conflicts are the most obvious causes of migration, especially in Central America where natural disasters have

---

[4] The 2000 and 2005 figures of the total number of Latin American and Caribbean migrants include the number of migrants from Mexico, which accounts for around half of Latin American and Caribbean citizens living outside their country of origin. The importance of including Mexico as part of Latin American migration is that, in terms of migrant characteristics (reasons for migrating, migration conditions, living conditions in the host countries, etc.), Mexican migrants are more similar to the rest of Latin American and Caribbean citizens living outside their country of origin than to U.S. and Canadian citizens living outside their country of origin.

contributed to maintaining emigration flows, originally provoked by political violence two or three decades earlier. This migration is often between fairly close neighbouring countries, as in the case of Costa Rica, which hosted 296,461 migrants in 2000; 75 per cent of those migrants came from Nicaragua. But it can also occur at the sub-regional level as in the case of Panama, where most migrants come from South America (especially Colombia which contributed 26 per cent of the total migrant stock for 2000) and the Caribbean (O'Neil et al., 2005).

- Economic crises have played a powerful role in migration in Latin America, shaping new migration trends in some countries and even reversing migration patterns in some others. In Argentina, the economic crisis of 2001 caused a dramatic reversal in migration flows. Originally a magnet for migrants during the 1990s, Argentina experienced an exodus of 255,000 people from 2001 to 2003, nearly six times as many as during the period 1993-2000. Argentine emigration slowed down as the country recovered from the crisis (O'Neil et al., 2005).

- Two other countries, Venezuela and Brazil, show evolving migration trends due to changing economic circumstances. Venezuela, a net destination for migrant labour from other countries in the sub-region and southern Europe since the oil boom 50 years ago, has started to experience some migration outflows, especially to the U.S. and Spain. As to Brazil, the number of Brazilians in the U.S. and in Portugal has been rising to reach 356,000 in 2005 (U.S. Census Bureau, 2005) and 70,400 in 2005 (OECD, online datasets, 2007), respectively. In addition, Brazilians numbering 302,100 in 2005 accounted for the third-largest foreign group in Japan (OECD, online datasets, 2007).

- Ecuador provides another example of the importance of economic crises in shaping migration trends in Latin America, and also of the emergence of new migration patterns in the sub-region. After the crisis that began in 1998, 550,000 Ecuadorians left the country (O'Neil et al, 2005). The Ecuadorian case shows two interesting transformations in emigration that can be observed in other Latin American countries as well. First, the major country of destination of Ecuadorian migrants has changed, with Spain receiving a yearly average inflow of 69,453 Ecuadorians from 2000 to 2004, compared to fewer than 1,000 migrants per year before the crisis in 1998, replacing the U.S. as the top destination (OECD, online datasets, 2007). Other countries where emigration patterns have shifted away from the U.S. as the top destination are Argentina, Bolivia, Peru and Venezuela.

- The second significant new trend observed in Ecuador, and that can be extended throughout Latin America, is the increased importance of women in intra-regional migration. According to ECLAC estimates, on the American continent as a whole, there has been a shift replacing predominantly female migration in the 1970s and 1980s by mainly male migration thereafter (González and Sánchez, 2002). However, if the analysis is restricted to cross-border migration between Latin American countries, there is a strong increase in the number of women relative to total emigration. Figure 6 shows the trend in gender balance among international migrants in Latin America between 1970 and 2000. Latin America records the highest proportion of women among international migrants in the developing parts of the world (ECLAC, 2006a). Female migration in Latin America and the Caribbean has also been characterized by the increased participation of women in the labour market, which confirms the increase in the feminization of migration in this sub-region. In addition, according to the United Nations International Research and Training Institute for the Advancement of Women (UN INSTRAW), 54 per cent of Latin American migrants are women, and the majority of their remittances (30% of their income, compared to 10% for men) is used for education, health care and small businesses that benefit their families. The amount of money female migrants send home accounts for more than half of total remittances transferred (LP, 2007).

Figure 6:

Gender ratio of the stock of intra-regional migration from Latin America and the Caribbean, 1970-2000

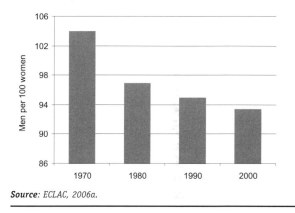

Source: ECLAC, 2006a.

SOME TOPICAL ISSUES IN MIGRATION MANAGEMENT IN THE AMERICAS

Irregular migration in the region is substantial and rising

- In the Americas, as in many other parts of the world, irregular migration is substantial and rising (see also Chapter 8). In the U.S., for example, although the irregular migration problem has been felt for some considerable time, rising numbers during the last decade have pushed the topic towards the top of the national agenda. According to the OECD (2006), net irregular immigration to the United States is estimated to be in the vicinity of 500,000 persons per year, which amounts to around 0.15-0.20 per cent of the total population per year. The Pew Hispanic Center (Passel, 2006) estimated the stock of irregular migrants at between 11.5 and 12 million persons in March 2006, and suggests that

most irregular migrants arrived since 1990. These numbers concur broadly with the estimates of the U.S. Department of Homeland Security, according to which the volume of the irregular migration flow increased from 120,000 per year in the 1980s to 440,000 per year during the period 1990-1994, and to 650,000 per year during the period 1995-1999, to reach 850,000 migrants per year during the period 2000-2005 (Passel, 2006). Mexico is the major country of origin and transit for irregular migration to the U.S. (over 450,000 a year). This flow has become more pronounced since the 1990s, even though Mexico has strengthened its migration control measures. According to Mexico's National Migration Institute (Instituto Nacional de Migración, 2005), the number of apprehensions and deportations of irregular migrants increased from 215,695 in 2004 to 240,269 in 2005 but decreased to 167,437 during the first ten months of 2006.

- During the last ten years, South America has become characterized by intensive outmigration towards North America and Europe, while traditional intra-regional movements have declined. The most important source countries for irregular migration to Europe are Ecuador and Peru, but also traditional destination countries like Argentina and Brazil. In Spain, for example, in 2003 a majority of irregular migrants came from Latin America (the top three source countries being Ecuador – 20%, Colombia – 8% and Bolivia – 7%). The same is true of Portugal, where six per cent of irregular migrants came from Brazil in 2004 (Kostova Karaboytcheva, 2006).

Remittances are increasing in the region and play a central role in economic development

- An important emerging migration issue in the Americas is the increasing role of remittances in economic development. According to the World Bank (2008), in 2007 the countries of Latin America and the Caribbean received USD 60.7

billion in remittances, over 16 per cent more than in 2006, with this sub-region receiving 24.14 per cent of total remittances sent to developing countries in 2007 (World Bank, 2008) (see Figure 7). Moreover, the Inter-American Development Bank (2003) estimates that the actual impact of remittances on local economies can be enhanced by a factor of three through their multiplier effects. At the national level, the country with the highest remittance inflows in the region is Mexico (41% of total flows) (World Bank, 2008), which is estimated to have received USD 25.1 billion in 2007, making it the third largest recipient of remittances in the world, after India and China and followed by the Philippines. In addition, in 2006, in seven countries in the region remittances accounted for more than ten per cent of GDP (World Bank, 2008): Honduras (25.6%), Guyana (24.3%), Haiti (21.6%), Jamaica (18.5%), El Salvador (18.2%), Nicaragua (12.2%) and Guatemala (10.3%) (World Bank, 2008).

Figure 7:

Workers' remittances sent to developing countries, 2001-2007

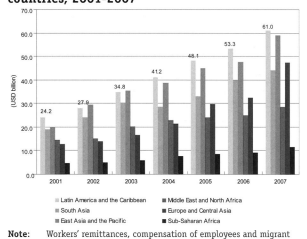

Note: Workers' remittances, compensation of employees and migrant transfers.

Source: *World Bank (2008), based on the International Monetary Fund's Balance of Payments Statistics Yearbook 2007.*

Brain drain is a growing concern in the region

- Brain drain in the Caribbean has become an issue of particular relevance, given the rate of emigration against the size of the pool of highly qualified persons. While in South America and Mexico brain drain accounts for ten and five per cent of the college and high-school educated population respectively, in the case of Caribbean countries nearly one-third of college and high-school educated citizens live in the U.S. (Lowell and Suro, 2002). Jamaica and Haiti have some of the highest rates of emigration of the highly skilled in the world, with two-thirds of their college graduates abroad (O'Neil et al., 2005). Even if the emigration of highly skilled persons is considered to yield some direct beneficial effects to countries of origin, Beine et al. (2002) argue that in the case of Jamaica and Haiti they are made unambiguously poorer.

The movement of refugees and displaced persons is no longer a concern on the scale of the previous two decades

- Finally, the movement of refugees and displaced persons in Latin America and the Caribbean, while still of significance, is no longer experienced on the scale of the previous two decades. The number of refugees leaving the sub-region has fallen considerably compared to the 1980s and 1990s. According to the Office of the United Nations High Commissioner for Refugees (UNHCR), as of the end of 2005, there were 2.51 million "persons of concern" from Latin America and the Caribbean, compared to 8.86 million in Asia, 5.17 in Africa, 3.68 million in Europe, 716,806 in North America and 82,492 in Oceania (UNHCR, 2006). However, the estimated number of displaced people in some Latin American countries is substantial. For instance, according to one reliable source, there were in 2007 between 2.39 and four million internally displaced persons in Colombia, the second highest IDP figure in the world after Sudan (IDMC, 2008). In addition, more than 400,000 Colombians have refugee status within the region and in the U.S. (O'Neil et al., 2005), and the number of asylum applications by Colombians in Ecuador has increased from 36 in 1999 to 11,388 in 2003 totalling 37,143 applications during the period 2000-2005 (UNHCR, 2006). This trend represents a significant challenge not only for Colombia, but also for all host countries in the region.

The access of migrants and mobile populations to health care is an important issue

In the Americas, as indeed in other regions, speedy and adequate access of migrants and mobile populations to HIV prevention, care and treatment is considered essential to combating the virus, and a number of interventions have been undertaken in the region to this effect (see Textbox Reg. 1).

Textbox Reg. 1

Universal Access to HIV Prevention, Care and Treatment: Targeting Migrants and Mobile Populations in the Americas

Many socio-economic and psychosocial factors that drive migration, such as poverty, unemployment, political instability and conflicts, are also closely associated with the proliferation of HIV infections, as their spread traces rural-urban migration paths within countries and subsequent return migration to areas and communities of origin. At the global level, the spread of HIV is often associated with the flow of people fleeing armed conflicts and civil unrest, but also accompanies the growth of international tourism, business travel and commercial activities, while the rise in international criminal activities, such as the smuggling and the trafficking in human beings, has also become an important factor in the spread of the disease. In the destination country, migrants can be perceived as potential sources of HIV infections, while they themselves face important obstacles in accessing health services and advice on either prevention or care and support in living with HIV, and are frequently barred from permanent residence status if mandatory tests show them to be HIV positive.

Young, lonely and isolated adult migrant men living and working far away from home, from disadvantaged socio-economic backgrounds, with little or no knowledge of the local language, frequently undocumented, are particularly vulnerable to becoming infected with HIV, a situation further compounded by exploitative working conditions, lack of access to health and social services and a high number of sexual partners, including same-sex partners and prostitutes, as well as excessive drinking, substance abuse and risky conduct under stress (Hirsch et al., 2002; Organista and Kibo, 2005). Studies have shown that on the Mexico-Guatemalan border, 70 per cent of truck drivers (*traileros*), who are either married or in a stable relationship, neglect the use of condoms to protect themselves and their partner, even though 40 per cent would have engaged in extramarital sex, including prostitution (Bronfman-Pertzovsky and Leyva, 2000). Female migrant workers are especially vulnerable to abuse, including trafficking, forced labour and prostitution. An estimated 60 per cent of undocumented migrant women would have been exposed to some kind of sexual activity during their migration experience, ranging from sexual abuse, coerced sex or new sexual partners (Aguilar, 1996). Different cultural factors and attitudes to sexuality in the destination country contribute to a migrant's vulnerability, as do the different approaches to healthcare and medical practice, together with unfamiliar legal and administrative rules.

In the Americas, a major risk factor for HIV transmission is unprotected sex between men, though the heterosexual transmission of HIV has also become a major risk factor for the wives and female partners of returnees. In the Caribbean, the high HIV prevalence reflects the significant level of population mobility and poses a major challenge for the control of the epidemic (Borland et al., 2004).

Unmet health needs are common among migrant workers and their access to healthcare is often affected by a migrant's legal status. Some of the most frequently reported obstacles to healthcare cited by Latino migrants in the U.S. is their irregular status and fear of deportation (Brown et al., 2002; Cunningham, et al., 2000), insufficient economic means, lack of health insurance and competing essential needs (e.g. housing, food, transportation) as well as language, cultural factors and stigma (Solorio, et al., 2004). According to a 2006 New York City Department of Health report, foreign-born adults with low incomes are less likely to have Medicaid than others born in the U.S. (29% and 42%, respectively) and foreign-born adults under the age of 65 who speak only Spanish are nearly twice as likely to be unable to obtain medical care when needed as those who speak English (15% and 8%, respectively). They are also less likely to use preventive measures, and low-income migrants in New York are less likely to have tested for HIV during the past year (Kim et al., 2006).

Because of the higher vulnerability to HIV infection among migrants and other mobile populations, a number of countervailing initiatives have been launched throughout the region. Thus, since 2001, the HIV/AIDS Mobile Population Project for Central America, Mexico and the U.S., developed under the auspices of the National Institute of Public Health, Mexico, and the IMPSIDA project[1] of the United Nations, have been active at eleven border-crossing points throughout Mesoamerica with educational initiatives, access to free condoms and to HIV counselling and testing services (Bronfman-Pertzovsky and Leyva, 2000). Similar HIV-testing initiatives were launched in El Salvador at the San Cristobal border-crossing point, providing guidelines for the care of mobile populations as well as pamphlets, posters and other tools to raise general awareness and knowledge about HIV and AIDS among mobile populations (Bortman et al., 2006).

Another example of effective practice in the region is the 1990 AIDS Law in Argentina, which guarantees full access to healthcare and treatment regardless of the migrant's status (Art. 8),[2] and various programmes, services and guidelines are being offered and implemented in response to this political mandate (Vásquez et al., 2005).

Among the positive examples of prevention exercises for highly mobile populations is an innovative programme in Brazil aimed at truck drivers. As they wait for customs clearance at the Brazil-Argentina-Paraguay border, two outreach educators hand them educational material and invite them to a mobile trailer for health services, including testing and counselling for HIV and syphilis, as well as the management of sexually transmitted infection (STI) syndromes. In addition, they have their blood pressure taken, are screened for diabetes and asked to return for a follow-up visit two weeks later. Interviews were conducted with a random sample of 1,775 male truck drivers before the screening exercise and with another 2,408 eighteen months later. Of the truck drivers interviewed during the post-intervention period, half had participated in the programme; one-third had participated in HIV testing and counselling; and only around 13 per cent were unaware of the project. Nearly 2,000 truck drivers participated in pre-test counselling for HIV and syphilis. Of the 1,795 who gave blood samples, 83 per cent returned for post-test counselling and results. Only 0.3 per cent tested positive for HIV and 4.7 per cent for Syphilis.

However, examples of successful initiatives are few and far between, and regular and large-scale services for HIV/AIDS testing, prevention, care and treatment, and systematic and reliable information for mobile populations, in particular irregular migrants, on how to access them are lacking or, at best, uneven throughout the Caribbean, Latin America and North America. In order to combat and control the spread of HIV/AIDS, governments and policymakers need to devote more attention and means to the issues at stake and strive towards universal access to prevention, care and treatment for mobile and hard-to-reach populations, such as migrants. To be effective, such service outreach must also aim to breach the social isolation and stigma frequently experienced by migrants, and to gain an insight and understanding of their social networks, relationships and dynamics, and not limit itself to the mere handout of condoms and HIV/AIDS testing and education.

By the end of 2008, IOM Washington and the HIV/STI Unit of the Pan American Health Organization (PAHO) will publish research on migrants' access to health in the Caribbean, with a particular focus on HIV, as a follow-up to a Baseline Assessment on mobile populations, conducted in 2004 (Borland et al., 2004).[3]

Notes:

[1] Iniciativa Mesoamericana para Prevenir la expansión del VIH-SIDA [Mesoamerican Initiative for Prevention of the Spread of HIV/AIDS].

[2] Argentina, Ley Nacional de SIDA [Aids Law] No. 23.798, Republic of Argentina, Buenos Aires, 16 August 1990.

[3] *HIV/AIDS in the Caribbean* (forthcoming). On the basis of a comparison between five countries (Bahamas, Dominican Republic, Guyana, Haiti and Trinidad and Tobago), the study covers the different facets of the relationship between HIV/AIDS and migration in the region. It includes an analysis of vulnerability factors in the migration process, dynamics and impact of health workers' migration, and legal and political responses to the phenomenon.

Source: HIV/STI Unit, PAHO, Washington, D.C.

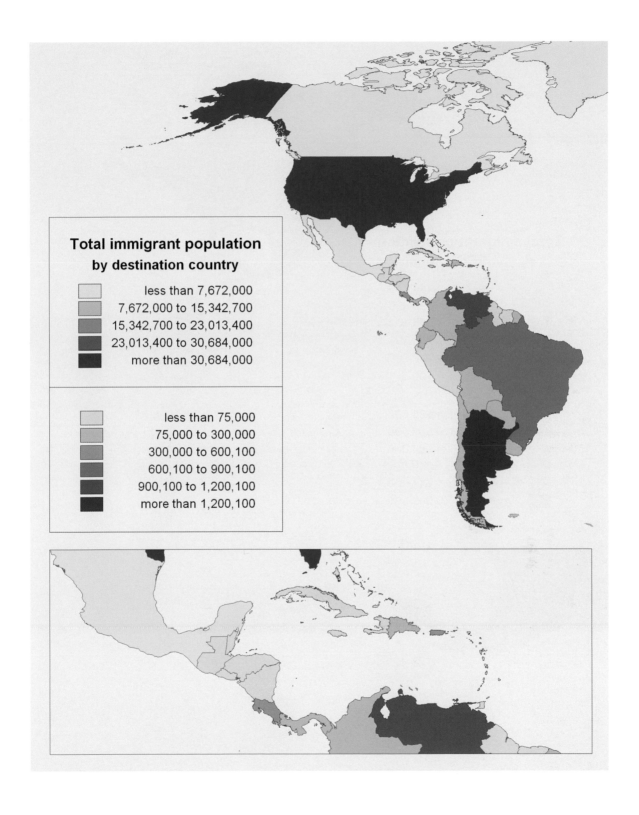

Total immigrant population
by destination country

less than 7,672,000
7,672,000 to 15,342,700
15,342,700 to 23,013,400
23,013,400 to 30,684,000
more than 30,684,000

less than 75,000
75,000 to 300,000
300,000 to 600,100
600,100 to 900,100
900,100 to 1,200,100
more than 1,200,100

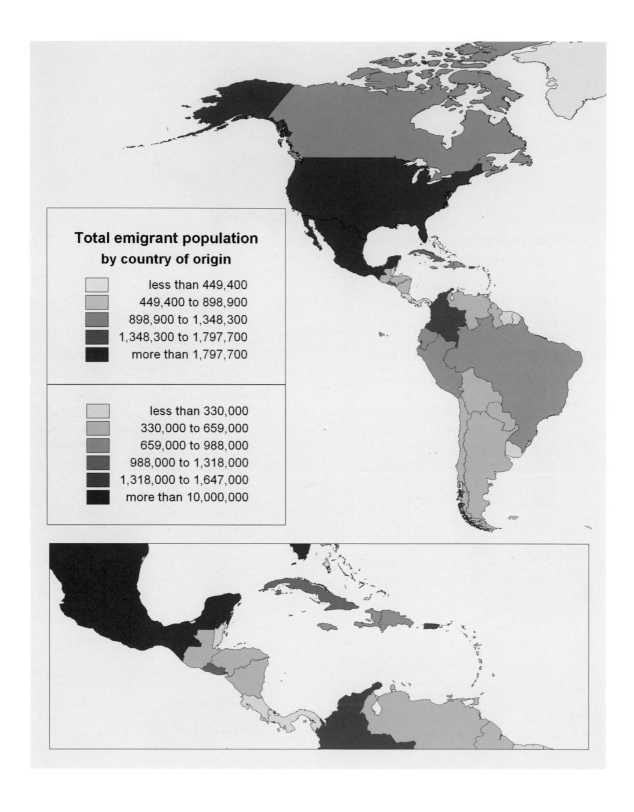

Total emigrant population
by country of origin

less than 449,400
449,400 to 898,900
898,900 to 1,348,300
1,348,300 to 1,797,700
more than 1,797,700

less than 330,000
330,000 to 659,000
659,000 to 988,000
988,000 to 1,318,000
1,318,000 to 1,647,000
more than 10,000,000

REFERENCES

Castillo, M.A.

2006   "Mexico: Caught Between the United States and Central America", *Migration Information Source*, April, Migration Policy Institute (MPI), Washington, D.C., http://www.migrationinformation.org/feature/display.cfm?ID=389.

Consejo Nacional de Población (CONAPO)

2002   *Dinámica reciente de las migraciones en América* [Recent migration trends in America], Año 6, núm. 18/2002/.

2006   *Ajustes al Censo Nacional de Población de 2005* [Modifications to the 2005 National Population Census]. Taken from: Informe presidencial del 1 de septiembre 2006 [Presidential report of 1 September 2006].

Cooper, B. and E. Grieco

2004   "The Foreign Born from Canada in the United States", *Migration Information Source*, August, MPI, Washington, D.C., http://www.migrationinformation.org/USFocus/display.cfm?ID=244.

Economic Commission for Latin America and the Caribbean (ECLAC)

2006a   *International Migration in Latin America and the Caribbean*, Latin America and the Caribbean Demographic Observatory, April, United Nations, ECLAC, Santiago de Chile.

2006b   *International Migration, Human Rights and Development in Latin America and the Caribbean*, 31st Session of ECLAC, Montevideo, 20-24 March, Doc. LC/G.2303 (SES.31/11), http://www.eclac.org/publicaciones/xml/4/24024/DGI-2303(SES.31-11)-Migration-web.pdf.

Fajnzylber, P. and H. López

2006   *Close to Home: The Development Impact of Remittances in Latin America*, The World Bank, Washington, D.C., http://siteresources.worldbank.org/INTLACOFFICEOFCE/Resources/ClosetoHome.pdf.

García, M.C.

2006   "Canada: A Northern Refuge for Central Americans", *Migration Information Source*, April, MPI, Washington, D.C., http://www.migrationinformation.org/feature/display.cfm?ID=390.

González Alvarado, I. and H. Sánchez

2002   "Migration in Latin America and the Caribbean: A view from the ICFTU/ORIT", *Labour Education Online*, 4:129 (Migrant Workers), 101-108, http://www.ilo.org/public/english/dialogue/actrav/publ/129/19.pdf.

Grieco, E.

2003   "The Foreign Born from Mexico in the United States", *Migration Information Source*, April, MPI, Washington, D.C., http://www.migrationinformation.org/USFocus/display.cfm?ID=163.

Instituto Nacional de Migración

2006   Estadísticas del Instituto Nacional de Migración: "Extranjeros asegurados en la EMDF según continente de procedencia, año y sexo, 2005" [National Migration Institute's Statistics: "Foreigners insured in the EMDF according to region of origin, year and sex, 2005"], Centro de Estudios Migratorios del INM [Centre for Migration Studies], Mexico.

Internal Displacement Monitoring Centre (IDMC) of the Norwegian Refugee Council

2008   *Internal Displacement: Global Overview of Trends and Developments in 2007*, April, IDMC, Geneva, http://www.internal-displacement.org/8025708F004BE3B1/(httpInfoFiles)/BD8316FAB5984142C125742E0033180B/$file/IDMC_Internal_Displacement_Global_Overview_2007.pdf.

Kostova Karaboytcheva, M.

2006   "Una Evaluación del Último Proceso de Regularización de Trabajadores Extranjeros en España (Febrero-Mayo de 2005)" ["Evaluation of the Latest Regularization Process for Foreign Workers in Spain (February-May 2005)"], Un Año Despues DT No. 15, Real Instituto Elcano de Estudios Internacionales y Estratégicos [Royal Elcano Institute for International Studies], http://www.realinstitutoelcano.org/documentos/252.asp.

Latinamerica Press (LP)

2007   http://www.latinamericapress.org/index.asp# (accessed 13 August).

Lowell, B.L. and R. Suro

2002   *The Improving Educational Profile of Latino Immigrants,* A Pew Hispanic Center Report, 4 December, Washington, D.C., http:// pewhispanic.org/files/reports/14.pdf.

Migration Policy Institute (MPI)

2004   *Building the New American Community: Newcomer Integration and Inclusion Experiences in Non-Traditional Gateway Cities*, Washington, D.C.

        Fact Sheet on the Foreign Born: The United States, MPI Data Hub, Online information, February, Washington, D.C., http://www. migrationinformation.org/DataHub/state. cfm?ID=US.

2006   *America's Emigrants: US Retirement Migration to Mexico and Panama*, MPI, Washington, D.C., http://www.migrationpolicy.org/pubs/ americas_emigrants.pdf.

O'Neil, K., K. Hamilton and D. Papademetriou

2005   "Migration in the Americas", paper prepared for the Policy Analysis and Research Programme of the Global Commission on International Migration (GCIM), September, Geneva, http:// www.gcim.org/attachements/RS1.pdf.

Organisation for Economic Co-operation and Development (OECD)

2006   *International Migration Outlook*, SOPEMI 2006 Edition, OECD, Paris.

Passel, J.S.

2006   *Changing Dynamics and Characteristics of Immigration to the United States*, June, Pew Hispanic Center, Washington, D.C..

Ratha, D. and W. Shaw

2007   "South-South Migration and Remittances", 19 January, Development Prospects Group, The World Bank, Washington, D.C., http:// siteresources.worldbank.org/INTPROSPECTS/ Resources/South-SouthmigrationJan192006. pdf.

United Nations, Department of Economic and Social Affairs (UN DESA), Population Division

2002   *International Migration Report 2002*, UN DESA, Population Division, New York, http:// www.un.org/esa/population/publications/ ittmig2002/ittmigrep2002.htm.

2005   *Trends in Total Migrant Stock: The 2005 Revision*, UN DESA, Population Division, New York, http://esa.un.org/migration/index. asp?panel=1.

United Nations High Commissioner for Refugees (UNHCR)

2006   *Statistical Yearbook 2005*, UNHCR, Geneva, http://www.unhcr.org/statistics/STATISTICS/ 464478a72.html.

United States Census Bureau

2006   Urban Institute tabulations from public-use files from the Current Population Survey, March Supplement, 1995 to 2005.

Van Hook, J., F.D. Bean and J. Passel

2005   "Unauthorized Migrants Living in the United States: A Mid-Decade Portrait", *Migration Information Source*, September, MPI, Washington, D.C., http://www. migrationinformation.org/feature/display. cfm?ID=329.

World Bank

2006   *Global Economic Prospects 2006: Economic Implications of Remittances and Migration*, The World Bank, Washington, D.C., http://econ. worldbank.org/WBSITE/EXTERNAL/EXTDEC/ EXTDECPROSPECTS/GEPEXT/EXTGEP2006/ 0,,contentMDK:20709766~menuPK:1026823~pa gePK:64167689~piPK:64167673~theSitePK:1026 804,00.html.

2008   *Revisions to Remittance Trends 2007*, July, The World Bank, Washington, D.C., http://econ. worldbank.org/WBSITE/EXTERNAL/EXTDEC/ EXTDECPROSPECTS/0,,contentMDK:21121930~me nuPK:3145470~pagePK:64165401~piPK:6416502 6~theSitePK:476883,00.html.

Textbox Reg. 1 - Universal Access to HIV Prevention, Care and Treatment: Targeting Migrants and Mobile Populations in the Americas

Aguilar, H.S.
1996   *VIH/SIDA en Guatemala. Una Bibliografía anotada*, Mimeo, Julio, Guatemala, Guatemala.

Borland, B., L. Faas, D. Marshall, R. McLean, M. Schroen, M. Smit and T. Valerio
2004   *HIV/AIDS and Mobile Populations in the Caribbean: A Baseline Assessment. Final Report*, June, International Organization for Migration (IOM), Santo Domingo, Dominican Republic, http://www.iom.int/jahia/webdav/site/myjahiasite/shared/shared/mainsite/published_docs/books/hiv_mobile_carribbean.pdf.

Bortman, M., L.B. Saenz, I. Pimenta, C. Isern, A.E. Rodríguez, M. Miranda, L. Moreira and D. Rayo
2006   *Reducing HIV/AIDS Vulnerability in Central America: El Salvador: HIV/AIDS Situation and Response to the Epidemic*, December, Latin America and the Caribbean Region and The Global HIV/AIDS Program, The World Bank, Washington, D.C.

Bronfman-Pertzovsky, M. and R. Leyva
2000   *Traileros en la frontera México-Guatemala. Impacto de una intervención informativa sobre ETS/VIH/SIDA y promoción del uso del condón*, SSA Instituto Nacional De Salud Pública.

Brown, E.R., N. Ponce, T. Rice and S.A. Lavarreda
2002   *The State of Health Insurance in California: Findings from the 2001 California Health Interview Survey*, June, University of California, Los Angeles (UCLA) Center for Health Policy Research, Los Angeles, http://www.healthpolicy.ucla.edu/pubs/files/shic062002.pdf.

Cunningham, W.E., D.M. Mosen, L.S. Morales, R.M. Andersen, M.F. Shapiro and R.D. Hays
2000   "Ethnic and racial differences in long-term survival from hospitalization for HIV Infection", *Journal of Health Care for the Poor and Underserved*, 11(2): 163-178.

Hirsch, J.S., J. Higgins, M.E. Bentely and C.A. Nathanson
2002   "The Social Construction of Sexuality: Marital Infidelity and Sexually Transmitted Diseases – HIV Risk in a Mexican Migrant Community", *American Journal of Public Health*, 92: 1227-1237.

Kim, M., G. Van Wye, B. Kerker, L. Thorpe and T.R. Frieden
2006   *The Health of Immigrants in New York City*, A Report from the New York City Department of Health and Mental Hygiene, June, New York, http://www.nyc.gov/html/doh/downloads/pdf/episrv/episrv-immigrant-report.pdf.

Organista, K. and A. Kubo
2005   "Pilot Survey of HIV Risk and Contextual Problems and Issues in Mexican/Latino Migrant Day Laborers", *Journal of Immigrant Health*, 7(4): 269-281.

Solorio, M.R., J. Currier and W. Cunningham
2004   "HIV health care services for Mexican migrants", *Journal of Acquired Immune Deficiency Syndromes*, 37(Supp. 4): S240-S251.

Vásquez, M., G. Wald and K. Frieder
2005   *Guía para promotores comunitarios Prevención del VIH/SIDA en Población Migrante*, 2nd Ed., Fundación Huésped, Buenos Aires.

ASIA

- Over the past three decades, international labour mobility has become an increasingly important feature of the Asian economic landscape. The estimated current stock of Asian migrant workers abroad may be around 25 million (Hugo, 2005), including both within and beyond the Asian region.[1] Much of these movements are undocumented and are not included in the available official statistics.

- Asian migration has become an increasingly intra-regional phenomenon. In mid-2000, a quarter of the 25 million international migrants worked in East and Southeast Asia – and their number increases to 7.5 million if unauthorized workers are included (Hugo, 2005).

- From 2000 to 2005, the estimated number of international migrants in South-Central Asia dropped from 15 to 13 million, while it increased in both East Asia (from 5.7 to 6.5 million) and Southeast Asia (from 4.7 to 5.6 million) (UN DESA, 2005).

- Some of the countries/areas that are most affected by international migration are in Asia. For instance, approximately 56 percent of the total population of Macao SAR is foreign-born, while the proportion of foreign-born in Hong Kong SAR and Singapore is nearly 43 per cent. In Brunei, about one-third of the population is foreign-born (Hugo, 2005).

- Countries/areas in Asia can be roughly classified according to their international labour migration situation as "mainly emigration" (Bangladesh, Cambodia, China, India, Indonesia, Laos, Myanmar, Nepal, Pakistan, the Philippines, Sri Lanka, Viet Nam); "mainly immigration" (Brunei, Hong Kong SAR, Japan, Macao SAR, Malaysia, Singapore, Republic of Korea (South Korea), Taiwan Province of China) and "both significant immigration and emigration" (Thailand) (Hugo, 2005). Some countries, such as Cambodia, China, Indonesia, the Philippines and Thailand, are also transit countries.

EAST ASIA

- The two Special Administrative Regions of China, Hong Kong and Macao, have the highest

[1] For the purpose of this Migration Overview, Asia includes: **East Asia** (China (China mainland, Hong Kong Special Administrative Region of China, Macao Special Administrative Region of China – hereafter Hong Kong SAR and Macao SAR, respectively - and Taiwan Province of China), the Democratic People's Republic of Korea (North Korea), Japan, Mongolia and the Republic of Korea (South Korea)); **Southeast Asia** (Brunei, Cambodia, Indonesia, Laos, Malaysia, Myanmar, the Philippines, Singapore, Thailand, Timor-Leste, Viet Nam); and **South-Central Asia** (Afghanistan, Bangladesh, Bhutan, India, Iran, Maldives, Nepal, Pakistan and Sri Lanka). Countries in Western Asia and Central Asia are addressed in the Migration Overviews on the Middle East and Europe, respectively.

concentration of international migrants in East Asia (43% and 56% of their total population, respectively). With about three million international migrants, Hong Kong SAR is also the major destination in the sub-region, followed by Japan with two million international migrants (UN DESA, 2005) (see Figure 1).

Figure 1:

Stock of migrants in East Asia, by destination, 2000 and 2005

Part A: Total number of migrants

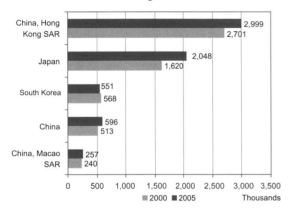

Part B: As a share of total population

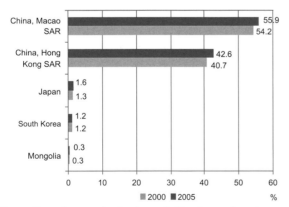

Note: East Asian countries showing negligible values on the scale are not included in this table.

Source: UN DESA, 2005.

Many East Asian countries/areas, together with Thailand and Singapore, show a high dependence on foreign labour

- The Migrant Labour Dependency Ratio (MLDR)[2] has significantly increased in recent years in all East Asian countries/areas with the exception of Hong Kong SAR, which experienced a decrease from 95 in 1993 to 72 in 2000 but still shows the highest MLDR in the region (Athukorala, 2006).

Japan receives migrant workers from less-developed Asian countries ...

- Japan hosts the third largest number of overseas Filipino workers (258,977), after the U.S. (2.7 million) and Saudi Arabia (one million), representing nearly a third of all foreign workers in Japan, totalling 910,000 in 2005 (POEA, 2006).
- In Japan, migrants from China make up almost one-quarter of new arrivals (*Financial Times*, 9 July 2007).

... and also from Russia

- The growing presence of Russians in Japan's northern provinces had hardly been researched until recently. Japanese Government statistics put the number of Russians entering Japan at around 37,000 per year, and the number of Russians residing in the country for 90 days or longer at a little over 6,000. Also, several tens of thousands of Russian seafarers and tourists visit Japanese port cities each year on a temporary landing permit while their ships are at anchor (Akaha, 2004).

China depends on its internal migrant workers ... and domestic remittances

- Labour migration in China has been characterized by the large outflow of agricultural labourers from

---

[2] The Migrant Labour Dependency Ratio is defined as the number of migrant workers per 1,000 workers in the labour force.

inland villages to work in the manufacturing and service sectors in the coastal provinces, mostly on a temporary basis. This pattern of domestic and temporary migration has helped to generate a very large inflow of money from migrant workers to their families at home that has contributed to raise the income and welfare of farmers, and to reduce poverty. On average, a migrant worker remits between ¥500-1,000 (EUR 50-100[3]) three to six times a year. In 2006, domestic remittances averaged ¥331 billion[4] (EUR 33 billion). Approximately 75 per cent of the total domestic remittance volume of ¥223 billion in 2004 was captured by formal financial institutions. The remaining 25 per cent were either hand-carried home or sent through other channels (Cheng and Zhong, 2005).

Highly skilled emigration from East Asia is still an issue ...

- South Korean professionals continue to emigrate, with 4,600 leaving for Canada and 4,200 for the U.S. in 2003. Some 188,000 South Koreans were studying abroad in April 2004 (*Migration News*, 2005), a step that often leads to permanent settlement abroad.
- It is estimated that more than half of the graduating class of Beijing University's engineering students will seek opportunities overseas. Between 1979 and 1998, only about a third of all Chinese students benefiting from government assistance to study abroad returned home. The return rate, at around 10 per cent, is lowest for students going to the United States (from Canada the rate is around 50%) (Asia Pacific Foundation of Canada, 2000).

... but there are also signs that talent can be encouraged to return home

- Incentives schemes have been launched to encourage the return of highly skilled diaspora both to Taiwan Province of China and to South Korea.
- In China, the number of returned students jumped from less than 10,000 in 2000 to about 25,000 in 2004. However, returnees, as a percentage of persons going overseas, have not increased, as liberalization of the policy on travelling abroad on the basis of own funds has resulted in a very significant increase in the number of persons going abroad (Zweig, 2006).

SOUTH–CENTRAL ASIA

- Though India is the main destination country in South-Central Asia, the 5.7 million international migrants living there account for only 0.5 per cent of the total population. At the other extreme, the 818,582 international migrants living in Nepal represent three per cent of the local population, the highest share in this part of the world (UN DESA, 2005) (see Figure 2).

Figure 2:

Stock of migrants in South-Central Asia, by destination, 2000 and 2005

Part A: Total number of migrants

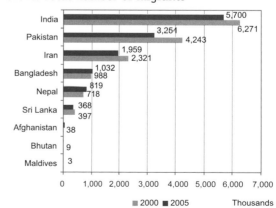

---

[3] One China Yuan Renminbi = EUR 0.099 (exchange rate, August 2008).

[4] The above estimate is based on the assumption that 75 per cent of the 126 million migrant workers in China in 2006 sent on average ¥3,500 home per year (Cheng and Zhong, 2005).

Part B: As a share of total population

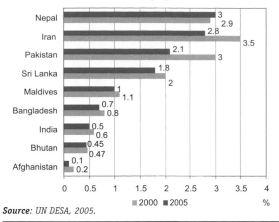

Source: UN DESA, 2005.

Many South-Central Asian countries are major sources of migrant workers

- Bangladesh, India, Nepal and Sri Lanka are major countries of origin of migrant workers (see Figure 3).
- While India is also a country of destination and transit, its levels of emigration increased in 2005 and accounted for almost eight per cent of total inflows in Australia (compared to 5% for the period 1990-2004), 11 per cent in Canada (8%) and eight per cent in the United States (5%) (OECD, 2007).

Figure 3:

Labour migration outflows for South-Central Asia, 2001-2005

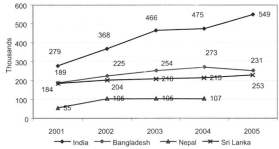

Note: Figures based on official statistics for the South-Central Asian region and the Nepal Institute of Development Studies (NIPS).

Source: IOM, 2005.

- According to research conducted in 2002 by the Nepal Institute for Development Studies (NIDS) for the United Nations Women's Fund (UNIFEM), approximately 170,000 Nepalese were in East and Southeast Asia,[5] nearly 36,000 in Europe and over 10,000 in North America. However, most Nepali workers abroad were to be found in the Gulf states; over 465,000 Nepalese were working in countries such as Saudi Arabia (42% of all Nepali expatriate workers) and Qatar (11%) (Seddon, 2005).

These movements continue to comprise mainly low-skilled workers ... and involve women

- The majority of Nepali women migrant workers present outside of India, mainly in the Middle East, East Asia, and Southeast Asia, were concentrated in two destinations – Hong Kong SAR (44%) and Japan (9%) – with 56.5 per cent in East and Southeast Asia. The remainder were employed in the U.K. (12%), the U.S. (9%), Australia (6%), Bahrain (4%) and other countries. Most of them were working in domestic service or in other areas of the services sector (Seddon, 2005).

South-Central Asia is also characterized by large outflows of students

- Indian students in the U.S. accounted for 13.9 per cent of all foreign students in the period 2003-2004, the largest percentage for the third year in a row, followed by students from China, South Korea, Japan, Canada, and Taiwan Province of China. In 2004-2005, India continued to be the main country of origin for students leaving to study in the U.S., with 80,466 students (Khadria, 2006).

---

[5] In February 2001, the Malaysian Government officially "opened" its labour market to workers from Nepal. Within six months, over 12,000 migrant workers had left for Malaysia and, a year later, Malaysia was hosting some 85,000 Nepali migrant workers.

During the last decade, labour migration flows from South-Central Asia have become more diverse: while Asian destinations now receive many more migrants, the Middle East continues to be the most popular destination

- An estimated 8.7 million temporary contractual workers from different Asian countries live and work in the Middle East (Hugo, 2005) (see Figure 4).

Figure 4:

Estimated stock of Asian origin temporary contractual workers in the Middle East

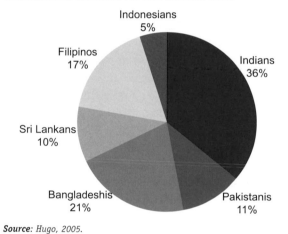

Source: Hugo, 2005.

- Bangladesh, India and Pakistan supply workers to realize infrastructure projects in the Gulf states, while Indonesia and Sri Lanka have secured the greatest part of the labour market for domestic workers, which has also spurred the feminization of migration in the Gulf region (Asis, 2005).
- Outflows of Pakistani workers to the Gulf countries fluctuate from year to year. The number of Pakistani workers who moved to Kuwait was 400 in 2001, but reached 12,087 in 2003 and then declined to 6,895 in 2005. Likewise, 18,421 Pakistani workers went to the United Arab Emirates (UAE) in 2001, whereas in 2003 the number was 61,329, then 47,441 in 2005. Around 90 per cent of Pakistani temporary contractual workers to the Gulf

countries are in semi to low-skilled employment categories (IDB, 2006).

SOUTHEAST ASIA

- Southeast Asian countries are grouped in the ASEAN[6] regional block and most of their migrant populations originate within this system (Battistella, 2002). In Southeast Asia, Singapore has the highest number of international migrants on its territory (1.8 million), followed by Malaysia with 1.6 million. In terms of concentration, Singapore still leads with nearly 43 migrants per 100 inhabitants, while Malaysia has a much lower migrant share of 6.5 per cent. The country of Brunei Darussalam ranks second in concentration with about 33 migrants per 100 habitants (UN DESA, 2005) (see Figure 3).

Figure 5:

Stock of migrants in Southeast Asia, by destination, 2000 and 2005

Part A: Total number of migrants

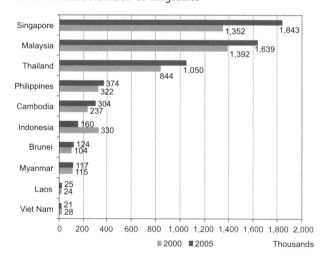

---

[6] ASEAN is the Association of Southeast Asian Nations and comprises 10 countries: Brunei, Cambodia, Indonesia, Laos, Malaysia, Myanmar, Philippines, Singapore, Thailand and Viet Nam.

Part B: As a share of total population

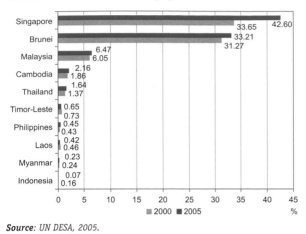

Source: UN DESA, 2005.

Although Malaysia, Thailand and Singapore show a dependence on foreign labour, ...

- Singapore's non-resident workforce increased 170 per cent, from 248,000 in 1990 to 670,000 in 2006. About 580,000 foreign workers are lower-skilled workers (Yeoh, 2007).
- The number of regular foreign workers in Malaysia, as per official sources, was reported to be as high as 2.2 million[7] in 2008 or up to 2.5-3 million if irregular migrant workers are included.[8] In 2006, Indonesians made up 65 per cent of all regular migrants, followed by Nepalese (11%) and Indian nationals (7%). About 32 per cent of migrants were employed in manufacturing and the remainder in the services, construction and plantation sectors (EIU, 2006).
- The Economist Intelligence Unit (EIU, 2006) forecast suggests that between 2005 and 2015 Singapore and Thailand (along with Hong Kong SAR and Taiwan Province of China) will face a situation where the growth in labour demand will

exceed growth in the working age population. Thailand's MLDR increased from 5 in 1990 to 15 in 2003 (Athukorala, 2006). These countries/areas are thus expected to face incremental pressure on the demand for labour in connection with continued economic growth. The problem is most acute in Singapore (EIU, 2006).

... many Southeast Asian countries are major sources of migrant labour

- A newcomer to labour migration, Viet Nam, has expanded its overseas employment programme, with the result that over 70,000 workers go abroad per annum (Asis, 2005). Some 75,000 migrants went abroad in 2003, when there was a stock of 350,000 Vietnamese migrants abroad, including 75,000 in Malaysia and 40,000 in Taiwan Province of China; other destinations are Japan, South Korea and the Middle East (*Migration News*, 2004).
- The Philippines have the largest stock of migrant workers in foreign countries. Official figures from the Philippine Overseas Employment Administration (POEA, 2006) reveal that, as at the end of 2006, the total stock of overseas Filipinos was 8.2 million distributed as follows: 3.6 million permanent residents, 3.8 million temporary residents and 875,000 irregular migrants.
- Indonesia is a quintessential labour-surplus country. At the end of 2006, an estimated 11 per cent of Indonesian workers (11.6 million) were unemployed, and underemployment stood at over 20 per cent (i.e. 45 million workers) (Hugo, 2007). Official governmental sources in July 2006 reported that two million Indonesians worked abroad, 70 per cent of whom were low-skilled (*Migration News*, 2006).
- On the other hand, the number of Thai nationals officially in employment overseas fell steadily from 202,000 in 1999 to about 150,000 in 2003, owing to increased competition from more populous countries and their large supply of low-wage

---

[7] Malaysia showed the highest dependency on migrant workers in the region with about 220 migrants per 1,000 workers in 2003, having experienced an increase of 65 per cent since 1994 (Athukorala, 2006).

[8] The discrepancy with the UN DESA estimates provided in Figure 3 and those reported by the Malaysian government is likely to be due to the different reference year of the two sources.

labour, and to stricter labour migration regulations in Thailand and in destination countries (Huguet and Punpuing, 2005).

These outflows are also directed to non-ASEAN destinations

- The vast majority of Filipino workers abroad is to be found either in the Middle East or in other Asian countries (see Figure 6).

Figure 6:

Deployment of overseas Filipino workers, by destination, (new employees and returnees, excluding seafarers), 1998-2006

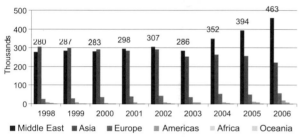

Source: POEA, 2006.

- Out of some 200,000 migrant workers in the Lebanon, about 34,000 were from the Philippines in mid-2006, mostly in domestic service (*Migration News*, 2006).
- Since 2001, the Middle East has again become the leading destination for Indonesian overseas workers, with their number peaking at over 226,000 in 2006 (Hugo, 2007).
- Taiwan Province of China is the major destination for Thais migrating for employment, followed by Singapore. While Israel has been steadily attracting Thai workers during the last decade, South Korea has emerged as a new top destination only during the last five years and is now the third largest destination for Thai temporary migrant workers. Brunei is also becoming another significant destination for Thais and migration of Thais to

non-Asian destinations, such as Europe, is steadily increasing (TOEA, 2007) (see Figure 7).

Figure 7:

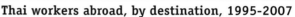

Thai workers abroad, by destination, 1995-2007

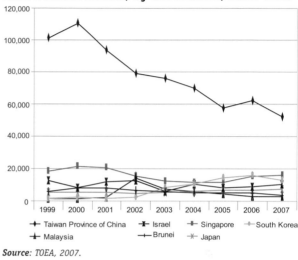

Source: TOEA, 2007.

... but there are signs that talent can be encouraged to return home

- Malaysia has introduced a programme under which the estimated 10,000 Malaysian professionals abroad can apply to return with the government guaranteeing their previous foreign salary. In 2004, 250 out of 650 applications to return had been accepted (*Migration News*, 2004).

SOME TOPICAL ISSUES IN MIGRATION MANAGEMENT IN ASIA

Increasing numbers of Asian migrants are leaving to work in African countries

- The number of Filipino nationals working in Africa has steadily increased over the last years (see Figure 8).

Figure 8:

Overseas Filipino workers in Africa, (new employees and returnees), 1998-2006

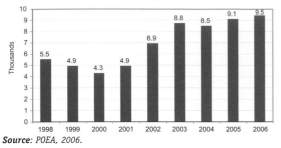

Source: POEA, 2006.

- China is also rapidly becoming an important country of origin for migrants going to Africa, especially to South Africa where an estimated 100,000 to 200,000 Chinese migrants are working either as regular or irregular entrants (*SAMP Migration News*, January 2006).

- Lesotho is home to about 5,000 Chinese nationals (mainly investors in the textile industry) both from Taiwan Province of China and the mainland, making it the largest foreign community ever to reside there (MPI, 2004).

South-Central and Southeast Asian migration is increasingly feminized

- With employment opportunities and the number of destinations increasing worldwide, many more women are joining the migrant flows from Asian countries to Europe, the Middle East and North America, and also within the Asian region itself.

Figure 9:

Selected Asian countries of origin: proportion of women in international labour migration flows

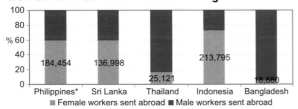

*Sources: POEA, 2006 (*only new employees); Sri Lanka Bureau of Foreign Employment 2005; Chalamwong, 2005 for Thailand; Soeprobo, 2004 for Indonesia; Bangladesh Bureau of Manpower, Employment and Training (BMET), 2006.*

- Women represent about 60 per cent of all migrants from the Philippines, Sri Lanka and Indonesia (POEA, 2006; Sri Lanka Bureau of Foreign Employment 2005; Soeprobo, 2005) (see Figure 9).

- Women make up just over 15 per cent of Thai migrant workers, but the actual number may be considerably higher given that much female migration is undocumented (Hugo, 2005) and that most women migrant workers from Thailand work in the domestic sector which is not a recognized category of employment.

- Countries with a traditionally higher proportion of female migrants, such as Sri Lanka and the Philippines, have experienced a slower rate of increase in the number of female migrants than countries where women have only relatively recently joined the migration flows and where their numbers are still relatively low, for instance, Bangladesh (POEA, 2006; Sri Lanka Bureau of Foreign Employment, 2005) (see Figures 10 and 11).

Figure 10:

Trends in female labour migration from the Philippines and Sri Lanka

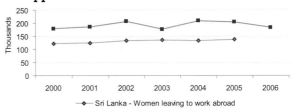

Sources: POEA, 2006 (only new employees) and Sri Lanka Bureau of Foreign Employment, 2005.

Figure 11:

Trends in female labour migrant flows from Bangladesh

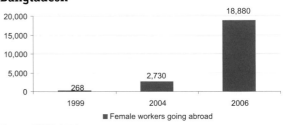

Source: BMET, 2006.

- Although Bangladesh did introduce a selective ban on female migration owing to cases of abuse and sexual exploitation of women migrants abroad, according to the recently adopted overseas employment policies by the Government of Bangladesh, both men and women are free to migrate abroad to work and the earlier ban on female migration is being reviewed on a case-by-case basis.[9]
- The evidence provided by Blanchet (2008) suggests that the official statistics on both male and female Bangladeshi migrant workers have been significantly underestimated. In sharp contrast to the official figure of 18,880 for 2006, this study provides an estimate of 430,000 Bangladeshi women migrant workers abroad. On the other hand, while the official statistics indicate that there are 3.8 million male migrant workers, the paper gives an estimate of 2.9 million. Given these new estimates, the proportion of female migrants as compared to their male counterparts stands at approximately 15 per cent.
- The majority of the ten main destinations for Bangladeshi women between mid-2004 and mid-2007 are in the Middle East (BMET, 2007) (see Figure 12).

Figure 12:

Top destinations for Bangladeshi women, mid-2004-mid-2007

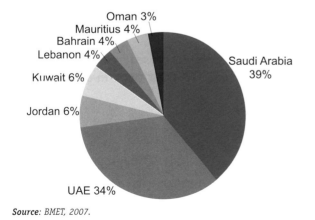

Source: BMET, 2007.

Asia is increasingly attracting highly trained individuals from more developed countries/areas within and outside Asia

- ASEAN-6[10] countries have been net destinations for skilled individuals in recent years: Malaysia, Singapore and Thailand have attracted some 60,000-70,000 foreign workers, with some 10,000 to 20,000 migrants also working in Indonesia and the Philippines in 2002-2003 (Bathnagar and Manning, 2005). Professional posts requiring greater skills and experience are largely filled by workers from Singapore, the G-8 countries and Australia and New Zealand (EIU, 2007).
- Indonesia is also experiencing an influx of skilled expatriates owing to the inability of Indonesian training institutions to supply a sufficient number of professionals (in particular engineers, scientists, managers and accountants) commensurate with the country's structural changes and economic growth. Experts have come from Australia and other developed countries, as well as the Philippines and India (Hugo, 2007).
- While India can generally meet its need for skilled workers from its large pool of university graduates, there has been a recent trend to hire foreign nationals already working with Indian companies around the world. Foreigners are being employed in India's information technology (IT) sector, and this trend is likely to continue (EIU, 2007).
- Many Hong Kong SAR residents work outside their territory, particularly in mainland China. According to a survey conducted in Hong Kong SAR in early 2004, close to 80 per cent out of a total of 240,000 held administrative and professional positions in mainland China. Chinese authorities offer three-year multiple-entry visas to visiting third-country nationals who are permanent residents in Hong Kong SAR. Most of those working in China do so on a temporary basis; annual departures from the territory as a whole are relatively low at just 9,800 in 2004 (EIU, 2007).

---

[9] Information obtained via personal email contact with Shahidul Haque (IOM).

[10] ASEAN-6 refers to those countries that are long-standing members of the World Trade Organization (WTO): Brunei-Darussalam, Indonesia, Malaysia, the Philippines, Singapore and Thailand.

remains within Asia is around 80 per cent and, for Singapore, this share is over 70 per cent (IOM calculations based on the World Bank bilateral remittances dataset, 2006).

Figure 16:

Selected Asian sending and receiving countries of remittances (%, estimates in USD millions)

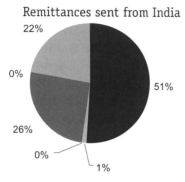

Remittances sent from India

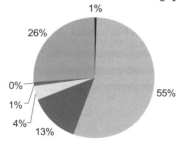

Remittances sent from Singapore

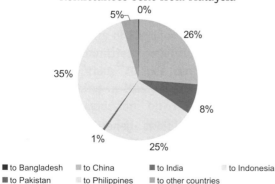

Remittances sent from Malaysia

■ to Bangladesh　■ to China　■ to India　■ to Indonesia
■ to Pakistan　■ to Philippines　■ to other countries

Note: IOM calculations using figures from the "Bilateral Remittance Flows using Migrant Stocks" dataset by Ratha and Shaw (World Bank, 2006).

Source: *IOM, 2007b.*

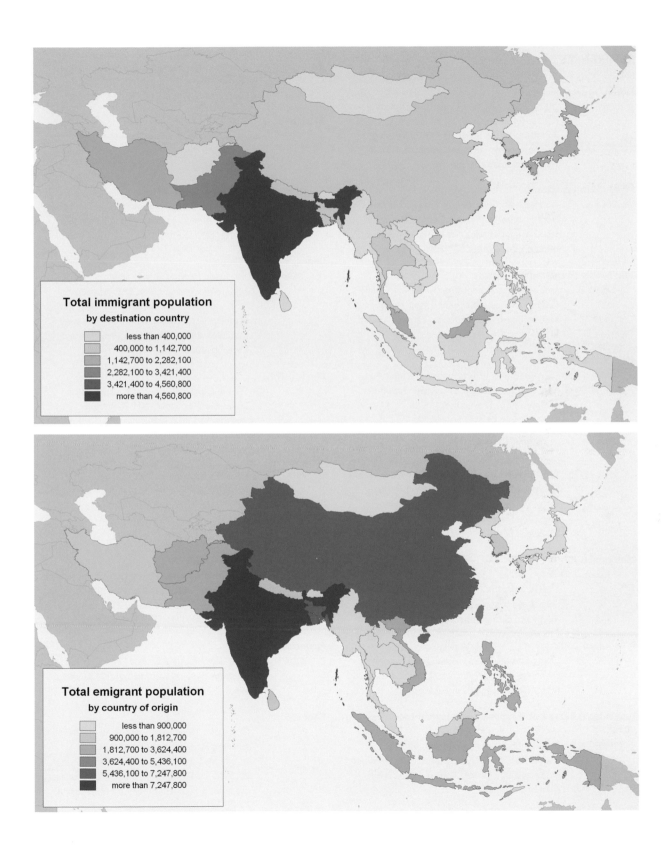

Total immigrant population
by destination country

less than 400,000
400,000 to 1,142,700
1,142,700 to 2,282,100
2,282,100 to 3,421,400
3,421,400 to 4,560,800
more than 4,560,800

Total emigrant population
by country of origin

less than 900,000
900,000 to 1,812,700
1,812,700 to 3,624,400
3,624,400 to 5,436,100
5,436,100 to 7,247,800
more than 7,247,800

REFERENCES

Akaha, T.
2004   "Cross-Border Human Flows in Northeast Asia", *Migration Information Source*, October, Migration Policy Institute (MPI), Washington, D.C., http://www.migrationinformation.org/Feature/display.cfm?id=257.

Amnesty International
2006   "Republic of Korea (South Korea): Migrant Workers are Also Human Beings", Amnesty International, http://www.amnesty.org/en/library/info/ASA25/007/2006.

Asia Pacific Foundation of Canada
2000   China-Canada Immigration Workshop, Final Report, 28 June, Shanghai, http://www.asiapacific.ca/analysis/pubs/28jun00-shanghai.html.

Asis, M.M.B.
2005   "Recent Trends in International Migration in Asia and the Pacific", *Asia-Pacific Population Journal*, 20(3) (December): 15-38.

2006   "Gender Dimensions of Labor Migration in Asia", paper submitted to the High-Level Panel on The Gender Dimensions of International Migration, UN Commission on the Status of Women, 50th Session, 27 February - 10 March, New York, http://www.un.org/womenwatch/daw/csw/csw50/statements/CSW%20HLP%20Maruja%20MB%20Asis.pdf.

Athukorala, P.
2006   "International Labour Migration in East Asia: Trends, Patterns and Policy Issues", Asia-Pacific School of Economics and Government, The Australian National University, Canberra.

Bangladesh Bank
2007   "Wage Earners Remittance Flows", Foreign Exchange Policy Department, Bangladesh Bank, http://www.bangladesh-bank.org/.

Bangladesh, Bureau of Manpower, Employment and Training (BMET)
2007   Government of the People Republic's of Bangladesh, Ministry of Expatriates Welfare and Overseas Employment, BMET website, http://www.bmet.org.bd/.

Bathnagar, P. and C. Manning
2005   "Regional Arrangements for Mode 4 in the Services Trade: Lessons from the ASEAN Experience", *World Trade Review*, 4(2): 171-199.

Battistella, G.
2002   "Unauthorized Migrants as Global Workers in the ASEAN Region", *Southeast Asian Studies*, 40(3): 350-371.

Blanchet, T., A. Razzaque and H. Biswas
2008   *Documenting the Undocumented: Female Migrant Workers from Bangladesh*, Drishti Research Centre, Pathak Shambesh, Dhaka.

Cheng, E. and X. Zhong
2004   "Domestic Money Transfer Services for Migrant Workers in China", report prepared for the Consultative Group to Assist the Poor, October, http://www.microfinancegateway.com/files/28874_file_China_Remittance_Study_Workshop20Oct_.doc.

Chishti, M.A.
2007   "The Phenomenal Rise in Remittances to India: A Closer Look", MPI Policy Brief, May, Washington, D.C., http://www.migrationpolicy.org/pubs/MigDevPB_052907.pdf.

Cobbe, J.
2004   "Lesotho: Will the Enclave Empty?", *Migration Information Source*, September, MPI, Washington, D.C., http://www.migrationinformation.org/Profiles/display.cfm?ID=248.

Economist Intelligence Unit (EIU)
2007   "Labour Mobility and Migration - Trends in the Asia Region", EIU Research Paper prepared for the Asia-New Zealand Foundation, http://www.asianz.org.nz/files/labour_mobility.pdf.

Financial Times
2007   "The New Melting Pot: Asia Learns to Cope with a Rise in the Flow of Immigrants", *Financial Times*, 19 July.

Haque, S.
2005   "Migration Trends and Patterns in South Asia and Management Approaches and Initiatives", *Asia-Pacific Population Journal*, 20(3) (December): 39-60, http://www.unescap.org/esid/psis/population/journal/Articles/V20N3A2_Ab.asp.

Hugo, G.
2005 "Migration in the Asia-Pacific region", paper prepared for the Policy Analysis and Research Programme of the Global Commission on International Migration (GCIM), September, Geneva, http://www.gcim.org/mm/File/Regional%20Study%202.pdf.

2007 "Indonesia's Labor Looks Abroad", *Migration Information Source*, April, MPI, Washington, D.C., http://www.migrationinformation.org/Profiles/display.cfm?ID=594.

Huguet, J.W and S. Punpuing
2005 *International Migration in Thailand*, International Organization for Migration (IOM), International Labour Organization (ILO), United Nations Children's Fund (UNICEF), United Nations Development Programme (UNDP), UN Economic and Social Commission for Asia and the Pacific (UNESCAP), World Bank, World Health Organization (WHO), Bangkok, http://www.iom.int/jahia/webdav/site/myjahiasite/shared/shared/mainsite/published_docs/books/iom_thailand.pdf.

International Organization for Migration (IOM)
2005 "In-house Workshop on Labour Migration and Project Development", 29-31 May, IOM Dhaka.

2007a "Migration, Development and Natural Disasters: Insights from the Indian Ocean Tsunami", IOM *Migration Research Series*, No. 30, Geneva, http://www.iom.int/jahia/Jahia/cache/offonce/pid/1674?entryId=14556.

2007b "Migration Dynamics in South Asia: Overview of Labour Migration in Bangladesh, India, Nepal and Sri Lanka", presentation, 29 May, IOM Dhaka.

Islamic Development Bank (IDB)
2006 *Brain Drain in IDB Member Countries: Trends and Development Impact*, IDB Occasional Paper No. 12, May.

Khadria, B.
2006 "Uncharted Contours of a Changing Paradigm - Skilled Migration and Brain Drain in India", *Harvard International Review*, July 17, http://hir.harvard.edu/articles/1445/.

Li, K.
2007 "Millions affected by floods in Bangladesh face a 'desperate situation'", 7 August, UNICEF, http://www.unicef.org/infobycountry/bangladesh_40538.html.

Migration News
2004 "South-East Asia", *Migration News*, 11(4) (October), University of California at Davis.

2005 "Japan-Korea", *Migration News*, 12(1) (January), University of California at Davis.

2006 "Philippines, Indonesia", *Migration News*, 13(4) (October), University of California at Davis.

Migration Policy Institute (MPI) and Globalization, Urbanization and Migration (GUM) Project
2007 "Global City Migration Map, 2007", MPI/GUM, http://www.migrationinformation.org/datahub/gcmm.cfm#map1.

Philippine Overseas Employment Administration (POEA)
2006 "OFW Global Presence – A Compendium of Overseas Employment Statistics", POEA, http://www.poea.gov.ph/stats/2006Stats.pdf.

Rofi, A. and C. Robinson
2006 "Tsunami Mortality and Displacement in Aceh Province, Indonesia", *Disasters* 30(3): 340 350.

Seddon, D.
2005 "Nepal's Dependence on Exporting Labour", *Migration Information Source*, January, MPI, Washington, D.C., http://www.migrationinformation.org/Feature/display.cfm?id=277.

Siddiqui, T.
2005 "International Labour Migration from Bangladesh: A Decent Work Perspective", Working Paper No. 66, November, Policy Integration Department, National Policy Group, ILO, Geneva.

Skeldon, R.
2004 "China: From Exceptional Case to Global Participant", *Migration Information Source*, April, MPI, Washington, D.C., http://www.migrationinformation.org/Profiles/display.cfm?id=219.

various reasons: the number of migrants dropped in Latvia and Estonia during this five-year period, while in Liechtenstein immigration actually increased, but at a lower rate than population growth.

Figure 1:

Stock of migrants in western and central Europe, top ten destination countries, 2000 and 2005

Part A: Total number of migrants

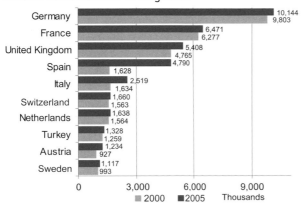

Part B: As a share of total population

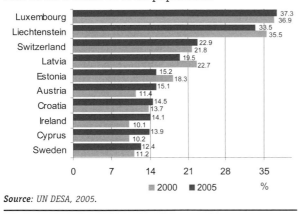

Source: UN DESA, 2005.

Western and central Europe is one of the most important regions of destination for migratory flows ...

• While most regions of the world experienced fluctuations in migratory flows over the last 50 years, nowhere have the changes been as pronounced as in Europe. Having been primarily countries of emigration for more than two centuries, most countries in the region became countries of immigration in the late 20th century. Many reasons have been advanced to account for this reversal, covering factors as diverse as economic disparities between Europe and its neighbours to the south and east, the large humanitarian inflows of the 1980s and 1990s, and the emergence of organized trafficking and smuggling networks. The role of growing demand for migrant workers to fill gaps in local labour markets is also widely acknowledged.

... leading to a steady growth of its migrant population

• As the membership of the EU grew from 12 to 25 between 1990 and 2004, the number of migrants across the combined territories of EU Member States and other countries in western and central Europe likewise increased from 14.5 to 44.1 million. Migration to this sub-region has grown on average at a 14.5 per cent quintennial rate since 1990. In 2005, the foreign-born living in western and central Europe represented 7.6 per cent of its total population, and 23.2 per cent of all international migrants worldwide (see Figure 2).

Figure 2:

Estimated number of migrants in western and central Europe, by gender and as a percentage of total population

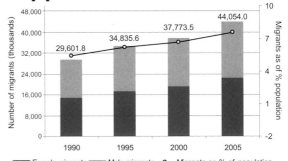

Source: UN DESA, 2005.

- The former EU-15 (except the Netherlands), Norway and Switzerland have a positive migration balance, as do six of the 10 new EU Member States (Cyprus, the Czech Republic, Hungary, Malta, Slovenia and Slovakia). Several countries, in particular the Czech Republic, Italy, Greece, Slovenia and Slovakia, registered population growth only in 2005, and that because of migration. In Germany and Hungary, the population decline would have been much larger without a positive migration balance (see Figure 3). In absolute numbers, the EU-25 registered a net gain of 1.8 million people in 2005 owing to international migration, accounting for almost 85 per cent of Europe's total population growth.

Figure 3:

Net migration in Europe per 1,000 population, 2005

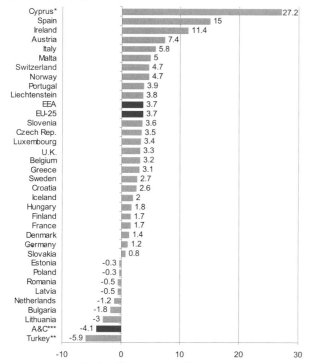

Notes: *Area under the effective control of the Government of the Republic of Cyprus.
        **Data for Turkey on net migration are from 2003.
        ***Accession and Candidate countries excluding the Former Yugoslav Republic of Macedonia.

Source: *Eurostat. Data taken from Münz, 2006.*

The majority of migrants come from within the region or adjacent countries

- One interesting but often overlooked feature of the migratory patterns in Europe is the prevalence of intra-regional movements. The OECD online datasets on migration show that intra-regional movements in Europe represented around 30 per cent of total migration in the period 1998-2004. Figure 4 shows the stock of intra-regional migrants as a percentage of total migration in EU-25 countries, Switzerland and Norway. In most of the countries analyzed, the bulk of migrants from the EU-25 accounts for at least 25 per cent of total migration. In some countries (e.g. Belgium, Ireland, Luxembourg, the Slovak Republic and Switzerland), migrants from within the region equal or exceed 50 per cent of total migration. However, in all countries reviewed besides Italy, the contribution of intra-regional migration to total migration has decreased over time. Yet, in absolute terms, with the exception of Germany and the Czech Republic, the European foreign population in these countries increased, but by less than the number of migrants from outside Europe.

Figure 8:

Labour force participation rate of foreign-born and native-born population in selected European countries, 2005

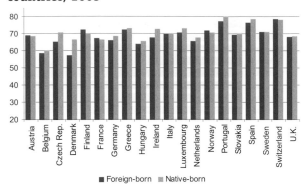

Source: *European Community Labour Force Survey (data provided by Eurostat) except for Denmark (Population Register), taken from OECD, 2007.*

EASTERN EUROPE AND CENTRAL ASIA[3]

- As host to 12 million migrants in 2005, the Russian Federation is the leading country of destination in this region, followed by Ukraine (6.8 million) and Kazakhstan (2.5 million) (see Figure 9). While Russia registered a 1.6 per cent increase in the stock of migrants from 2001 to 2005, the other nine countries reviewed saw their stock of migrants fall over the same period. With the exception of Ukraine and Russia, the number of migrants as a share of their total populations fell in all countries.

Figure 9:

Stock of migrants in eastern Europe and Central Asia, top ten destinations, 2000 and 2005

Part A: Total number of migrants

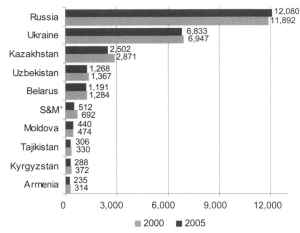

Note: * The then Serbia and Montenegro.

Part B: As share of total population

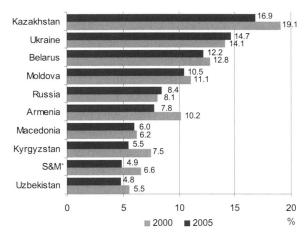

Note: * The then Serbia and Montenegro.

Source: UN DESA, 2005.

---

[3] Albania, Armenia, Azerbaijan, Belarus, Bosnia and Herzegovina, Georgia, Kazakhstan, Kyrgyzstan, Former Yugoslav Republic of Macedonia (FYROM) (granted EU candidate country status in December 2005), Moldova, the Russian Federation, the then Serbia and Montenegro, Tajikistan, Turkmenistan, Ukraine and Uzbekistan.

Two broad migration systems operate in this sub-region

- The nature and patterns of migratory movements in this sub-region since 1990 have been shaped by the combined effects of economic transition, political and social liberalization, and the break-up of two federal countries (the former Soviet Union, and former Federal Republic of Yugoslavia). They also account for the difficulty of accessing and compiling reliable migration data concerning this sub-region. The direction and magnitude of migration flows have changed significantly following the lifting of political constraints on movement, as has the emergence of 22 new countries and the resulting diversification of migratory flows throughout the region. Finally, with the break-up of the former Soviet Union a new category of migrants, the "statistical" migrants, emerged, who may not have moved physically, but were defined as migrants under UN practice (World Bank, 2006).

- According to Mansoor and Quillin (2006), two broad migration systems have developed in the region: the first concerns migrants from eastern European countries who move to western Europe; and the second involves the majority of migrants from Central Asia who travel to the wealthier countries of the Commonwealth of Independent States (CIS), particularly the Russian Federation and Kazakhstan. Figures 10a and 10b clearly show this bipolar migration system, with Russia registering by far the largest population gain from migration. Most of the migration to Russia is shaped by migrants leaving the other countries of the former Soviet Union.

Figure 10:

Net migration in eastern Europe and Central Asia as a percentage of total population, 1989-1999 and 2000-2003

10a: In the CIS

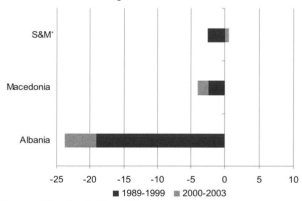

10b: In Eastern Europe

Note: * The then Serbia and Montenegro.
Turkmenistan and Bosnia and Herzegovina are not included owing to migration data difficulties.

Source: *National statistical offices and UNICEF, TransMONEE Database, Mansoor and Quillin (2006).*

- Yet, the two migration systems in the sub-region are not exclusively bipolar. Indeed, there are significant subsidiary flows from the poorer CIS economies, particularly from Moldova, to western European countries; and from Central Asia towards the EU and Turkey.

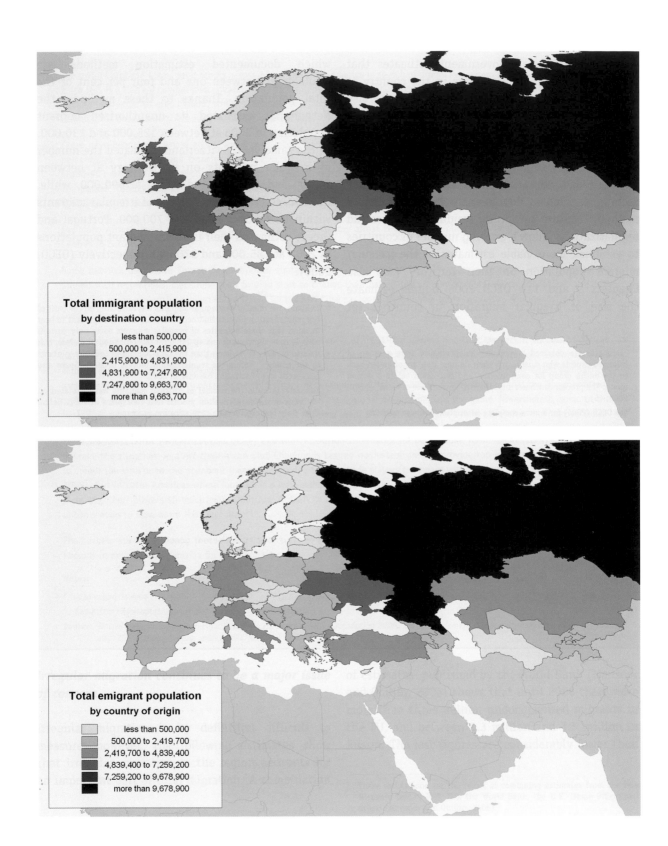

REFERENCES

Drew, C. and D. Sriskandarajah

2007   "EU Enlargement in 2007: No Warm Welcome
         for Labor Migrants", *Migration Information
         Source*, January, Migration Policy Institute
         (MPI), Washington, D.C., http://www.
         migrationinformation.org/feature/display.
         cfm?ID=568.

Jandl, M.

2003   "Estimates on the Numbers of Illegal and
         Smuggled Immigrants in Europe", presentation
         of the International Centre for Migration
         Policy Development (ICMPD) at the Eighth
         International Metropolis Conference, 17
         September, Vienna, http://www.mighealth.
         net/eu/images/5/5b/Icmpd.pdf.

2004   "The Estimation of Illegal Migration in Europe",
         Studi Emigrazione/ Migration Studies, 61(153)
         (March): 141–155.

Mansoor, A. and B. Quillin (Eds.)

2006   *Migration and Remittances: Eastern Europe and
         Former Soviet Union*, Chapter 1: "Overview of
         Migration Trends in Europe and Central Asia,
         1990-2004", The World Bank, Washington, D.C.

Münz, R.

2004   "Towards a Common European Migration
         Regime?", *Migration Information Source*,
         February, MPI, Washington, D.C., http://www.
         migrationinformation.org/events/021804_sum.
         php.

2006   "Europe: Population and Migration in
         2005", *Migration Information Source*,
         June, MPI, Washington, D.C., http://www.
         migrationinformation.org/feature/display.
         cfm?ID=402.

**Organisation for Economic Co-operation and Development
(OECD)**

2006   *International Migration Outlook*, SOPEMI 2006
         Edition, OECD, Paris.

2007   *International Migration Outlook*, SOPEMI 2007
         Edition, OECD, Paris.

Ratha, D. and W. Shaw

2007   "South-South Migration and Remittances",
         19 January, Development Prospects Group,
         The World Bank, Washington, D.C., http://
         siteresources.worldbank.org/INTPROSPECTS/
         Resources/South-SouthmigrationJan192006.
         pdf.

Russian News and Information Agency (Novosti)

2006   "Russia loses over $9 bln/yr from illegal
         immigration – govt.", Novosti, 3 November,
         http://en.rian.ru/russia/20061103/55351198.
         html.

**United Nations, Department of Economic and Social Affairs
(UN DESA), Population Division**

2002   *International Migration Report 2002*, Doc. ST/
         ESA/SER.A/220, UN DESA, Population Division,
         New York, http://www.un.org/esa/population/
         publications/ittmig2002/2002ITTMIGTEXT22-
         11.pdf.

2005   *Trends in Total Migrant Stock: The 2005 Revision*,
         Population Database, UN DESA, Population
         Division, New York, http://esa.un.org/
         migration/index.asp?panel=1.

United Nations Economic and Social Council (UN ECOSOC)

2006   *World population monitoring, focusing on
         international migration and development*, Report
         of the Secretary-General, Doc. E/CN.9/2006/3,
         UN ECOSOC, Commission on Population and
         Development, 39th Session, 3-7 April, New York.

**United Nations Educational, Scientific and Cultural
Organization (UNESCO)**

2007   *Global Education Digest 2006: Comparing
         Education Statistics Across the World*, UNESCO
         Institute for Statistics, Montréal, http://www.
         uis.unesco.org/TEMPLATE/pdf/ged/2006/
         GED2006.pdf.

World Bank

2006   *Global Economic Prospects 2006: Economic
         Implications of Remittances and Migration*, The
         World Bank, Washington, D.C., http://econ.
         worldbank.org/WBSITE/EXTERNAL/EXTDEC/
         EXTDECPROSPECTS/GEPEXT/EXTGEP2006/0,,cont
         entMDK:20709766~menuPK:1026823~pagePK:64
         167689~piPK:64167673~theSitePK:1026804,00.
         html.

Part B: As a share of total population

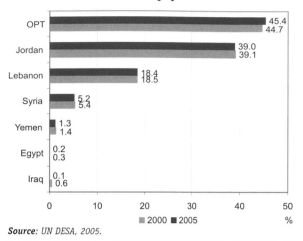

Source: UN DESA, 2005.

- The number of migrants as a proportion of the total population has remained stable in all countries except Iraq: the Occupied Palestinian Territories (OPT) are in first place with international migrants making up 45 per cent of their population, followed by Jordan (39%) and Lebanon (18%) (UN DESA, 2005) (see Figure 1).
- The figures for the OPT consist of Palestinian refugees coming under the mandate of the United Nations Relief and Works Agency for Palestine Refugees in the Near East (UNRWA). As at 30 June 2008, the total registered refugee population in the Gaza Strip and the West Bank stood at 1.06 million and 754,263, respectively (UNRWA, 2008).

People flows from the Arab Mashrek to GCC States are considerable, but mobility between Arab Mashrek countries is also significant

- In 2005, 461,211 Syrian citizens left their country to go to Saudi Arabia, the second most popular destination for Syrians after Lebanon (in 2005, 2.45 million Syrian citizens entered Lebanon) (CARIM, 2005).
- In 2003, an estimated 400,000 Syrians were cross-border commuters, who lived in Syria and worked in Lebanon (Sadeldine, 2005).

- In 2005, 1.68 million Lebanese citizens, or 29 per cent of all annual arrivals, came to Syria, followed by Jordanians, whose numbers increased from 609,000 to 940,000 over the 2001-2005 period (CARIM, 2005).

Lately, the Arab Mashrek has also been characterized by significant migration to destinations further afield, especially from Lebanon and Egypt ...

- Recent data indicate that Europe is increasingly becoming a destination for migrants from Egypt and Lebanon, with stocks of 127,060 and 111,691 migrants, respectively, followed by Syria with 70,879 migrants (Fargues, 2006) (see Figure 2).
- Italy has become a popular destination for Egyptians. In 2006, there were 46,834 Egyptians regularly residing[2] in Italy, compared to 32,381 in 2001 (ISTAT, 2006).
- The U.S. is another popular destination for Arab Mashrek migrants, with Egypt and Lebanon ranking first and second among countries of origin (113,995 and 105,920 migrants, respectively) (Fargues, 2006) (see Figure 2).

Figure 2:

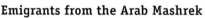

Emigrants from the Arab Mashrek

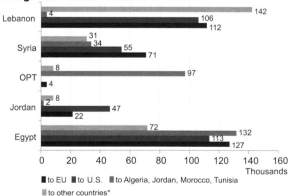

Note: * Data for countries of destination were collected from countries providing the latest available census data on foreign residents by country of nationality/birth. Some of the world's major destination countries for overseas temporary workers, such as Saudi Arabia, the UAE and other Gulf states could not be included for lack of accurate data.

Source: Fargues, 2006.

---

[2] i.e. all migrants who hold a residence permit.

... leaving more room for low-skilled workers from Asian countries

- Lebanon, together with Jordan and Egypt, are destinations for increasing numbers of workers mainly from Sri Lanka and the Philippines. More than 55,000 work permits are issued in Lebanon each year to East Asians, mostly to women (Fargues, 2006).

Arab Mashrek countries are a source of both highly skilled and low-skilled migrants

- The active migrant workforce originating from the Middle East Arab countries is predominantly low or semi-skilled, but some countries, such as Lebanon, Jordan and Egypt, also experience a high degree of highly skilled emigration. While migrants from Jordan, for instance, are predominantly hired as service workers (35%), lawyers and managers account for 33 per cent of migrants leaving the country (Fargues, 2006) (see Figure 3).

Figure 3:

Migrants from Jordan, according to occupation

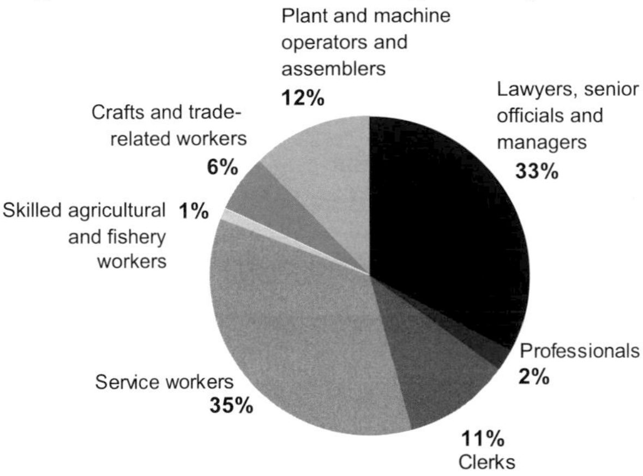

Note: *Only the following countries of residence providing the distribution by occupation of Jordanian migrants are included in the Figure: Austria, Canada, France, Spain and the U.S.*

Source: *Fargues, 2006.*

The region is strongly affected by the presence of refugees and IDPs

- At mid-2005, Jordan was host to 1.8 million refugees (UN DESA, 2005). Most of them were Palestinians (on 30 June 2008, 1.93 million Palestinians refugees were registered in Jordan with UNRWA[3]) constituting 31 per cent of the total population of the country (5.7 million), the highest ratio in any of UNRWA's operational regions.
- Syria also has a sizable Palestinian refugee population, estimated at 424,650 or 2.2 per cent of its total population in 2005 (UNRWA, 2006; UN DESA, 2005).
- Nearly one million people were displaced at the height of the Middle East conflict in the summer of 2006 – the vast majority of them in Lebanon. Some 200,000 are estimated to remain in a situation of displacement (IDMC, 2006).

Arab Mashrek countries are important sources of remittances ...

- The remittances sent from the Arab Mashrek countries were estimated at USD 3.7 billion in 2007, with USD 2.8 billion from Lebanon alone (World Bank, 2008).

... but they are mostly significant recipients of remittances

- The total amount of remittances sent to Arab Mashrek countries reached USD 17.2 billion in 2007 (World Bank, 2008). Egypt and Lebanon received almost USD 6 billion each and alone

---

[3]   See UNRWA (2008). Under UNRWA's operational definition, Palestinian refugees are persons whose normal place of residence was Palestine between June 1946 and May 1948, and who lost both their homes and means of livelihoods as a result of the 1948 Arab-Israeli conflict (http://www.un.org/unrwa/refugees/whois.html). UNRWA's definition of a refugee also covers the descendants of persons who became refugees in 1948 and, as a consequence, the number of registered Palestinian refugees continues to rise due to natural population growth.

ISRAEL

- From 2000 to 2005, the number of international migrants in Israel increased by about 20 per cent from 2.3 million in 2000, or 37 per cent of the population, to 2.7 million in 2005, or 40 per cent of the population (UN DESA, 2005) (see Figure 7).

Figure 7:

Stock of migrants in Israel, 2000 and 2005

Part A: Total number of migrants

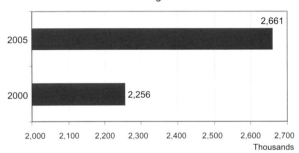

Part B: As a share of total population

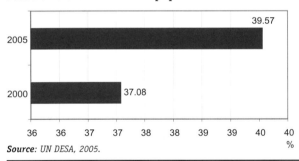

Source: UN DESA, 2005.

- Persons of Jewish ancestry account for a large share of total immigration to Israel, facilitated by the "Law of Return" of 1950 and its subsequent amendments. Ethiopian Jews, or *Falasha*, constitute another important migrant group, estimated in 2005 by the Israel Association for Ethiopian Jews to number around 85,000, of whom some 20,000 were already born in Israel.

The largest immigration flow of the last 20 years occurred in the wake of the dissolution of the former Soviet Union, when approximately 900,000 Soviet Jews settled in Israel (Kruger, 2005).

- In addition, non-Jewish and non-Palestinian temporary migrant workers have lately been accepted by Israel to support its prosperous economy. 2003 estimates put the number of migrant workers at about 189,000. They come mainly from Southeast Asia and eastern Europe and are hired as low-skilled workers. The largest groups are from the Philippines (around 50,000) working mainly as home health carers, followed by Thai migrant workers (some 30,000) who work in agriculture, and Chinese (15,000) active in construction. Another approximately 65,000 foreign workers are from eastern Europe (over half of whom are from Romania) who work mainly in construction. Women constitute around one-third of all migrants and are mainly employed in the 24-hour home healthcare sector (Kruger, 2005).

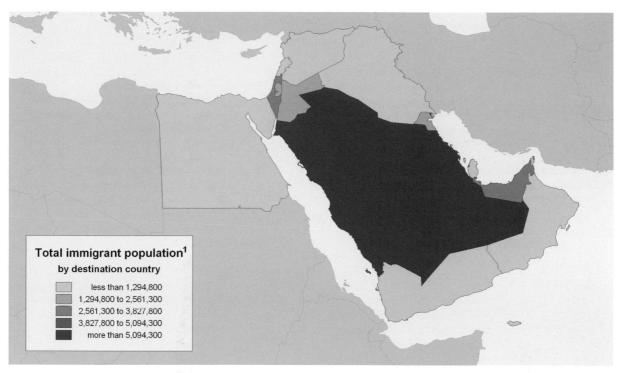

Total immigrant population[1]
by destination country

- less than 1,294,800
- 1,294,800 to 2,561,300
- 2,561,300 to 3,827,800
- 3,827,800 to 5,094,300
- more than 5,094,300

Note 1: It should be noted that the Gulf Cooperation Council (GCC) States do not refer to non-nationals as "immigrants" or "migrants" because they view these terms as being associated with permanent immigration or settlement. Most non-nationals resident in the GCC States are temporary contractual workers.

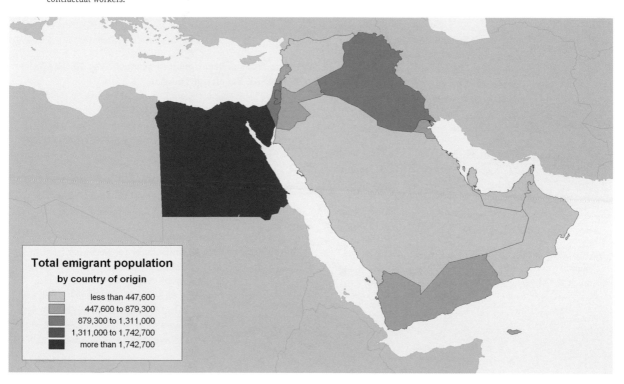

Total emigrant population
by country of origin

- less than 447,600
- 447,600 to 879,300
- 879,300 to 1,311,000
- 1,311,000 to 1,742,700
- more than 1,742,700

REFERENCES

Baldwin-Edwards, M.

2005   "Migration in the Middle East and Mediterranean", paper prepared for the Policy Analysis and Research Programme of the Global Commission on International Migration (GCIM), September, Geneva, http://www.gcim.org/attachements/RS5.pdf.

Euro-Mediterranean Consortium for Applied Research on International Migration (CARIM)

2005   Database on Demographic and Economic Dimensions of Migration, CARIM, European University Institute, The Robert Schuman Centre for Advanced Studies, Florence, http://www.carim.org/index.php?areaid=4&contentid=5.

Fargues, P. (Ed.)

2005   *Mediterranean Migration: 2005 Report*, Cooperation project on the social integration of immigrants, migration, and the movement of persons – financed by the European Commission-MEDA Programme, CARIM, European University Institute, The Robert Schuman Centre for Advanced Studies, Florence, http://www.carim.org/publications/AR2005CARIM.pdf.

Fargues, P.

2006   "International Migration in the Arab Region: Trends and Policies", paper prepared for the United Nations Expert Group Meeting on International Migration and Development in the Arab Region, United Nations, Department of Economic and Social Affairs (UN DESA), Population Division, 15-17 May, Beirut.

International Labour Organization (ILO)

2006   "Facts on Labour Migration in Asia", August, 14th Asian Regional Meeting, Bangkok, http://www.ilo.org/public/english/bureau/inf/download/factsheets/pdf/14asrm/migration_asia.pdf.

International Organization for Migration (IOM)

2005   *World Migration 2005: Costs and Benefits of International Migration*, IOM, Geneva.

Internal Displacement Monitoring Centre (IDMC) of the Norwegian Refugee Council

2006   "Lebanon: Displaced Return Amidst Growing Political Tension", 15 December, IDMC.

Islamic Development Bank (IDB)

2006   *Brain Drain in IDB Member Countries: Trends and Development Impact,* IDB Occasional Paper No. 12, May.

Kruger, M.

2005   "Israel: Balancing Demographics in the Jewish State", *Migration Information Source*, July, Migration Policy Institute (MPI), Georgetown University, Washington, D.C., http://www.migrationinformation.org/Profiles/display.cfm?id=321.

Nassar, H.

2006   "A perspective from the Arab Region on Migration and Development" in K. Tamas and J. Palme (Eds.), *How Migration can Benefit Development,* Institute for Future Studies, Stockholm, 97-112.

Sadeldine, S.

2005   "Syria: the Demographic and Economic Dimension of Migration" in P. Fargues (Ed.), *Mediterranean Migration: 2005 Report*, CARIM, European University Institute, Robert Schuman Centre for Advanced Studies, Florence, 265-271.

United Nations Department of Economic and Social Affairs (UN DESA), Population Division

2002   *International Migration Report 2002*, Doc. ST/ESA/SER.A/220, UN DESA, Population Division, New York, http://www.un.org/esa/population/publications/ittmig2002/2002ITTMIGTEXT22-11.pdf.

2005   *Trends in Total Migrant Stock: The 2005 Revision, Population Database*, UN DESA, Population Division, New York, http://esa.un.org/migration.

United Nations High Commissioner for Refugees (UNHCR)

2006   *2005 Global Refugee Trends - Statistical Overview of Populations of Refugees, Asylum-Seekers, Internally Displaced Persons, Stateless Persons, and Other Persons of Concern to UNHCR*, 9 June, UNHCR, Geneva, http://www.unhcr.org/cgi-bin/texis/vtx/events/opendoc.pdf?tbl=STATISTICS&id=4486ceb12.

United Nations Relief and Works Agency for Palestine Refugees in the Near East (UNRWA)

2008   "Total Registered Refugees per Country and Area (as at 30 June, 2008)", UNRWA, http://www.un.org/unrwa/publications/pdf/rr_countryandarea.pdf.

World Bank

2004   *Unlocking the Employment Potential in the Middle East and North Africa: Toward a New Social Contract*, The World Bank, Washington, D.C., http://web.worldbank.org/WBSITE/EXTERNAL/COUNTRIES/MENAEXT/0,,contentMDK:20260961~pagePK:146736~piPK:146830~theSitePK:256299,00.html.

2006   *Global Economic Prospects 2006: Economic Implications of Remittances and Migration*, The World Bank, Washington, D.C., http://econ.worldbank.org/WBSITE/EXTERNAL/EXTDEC/EXTDECPROSPECTS/GEPEXT/EXTGEP2006/0,,contentMDK:20709766~menuPK:1026823~pagePK:64167689~piPK:64167673~theSitePK:1026804,00.html.

2008   *Revisions to Remittance Trends 2007*, July, The World Bank, Washington, D.C., http://econ.worldbank.org/WBSITE/EXTERNAL/EXTDEC/EXTDECPROSPECTS/0,,contentMDK:21121930~menuPK:3145470~pagePK:64165401~piPK:64165026~theSitePK:476883,00.html.

OCEANIA

- Oceania[1] is host to five million international migrants (UN DESA, 2005), representing 15.2 per cent of its population, the largest share in any region in the world, and accounting for 2.6 per cent of the global migrant stock.
- Migration accounts for one-quarter of population growth in Australia, New Zealand and Pacific Ocean island countries, with the number of migrants in the Oceania region increasing from 4.8 million to five million over the period 1990-2005 (UN, 2005).
- Women migrants in Oceania have outnumbered men since 2000, when they constituted 50.6 per cent of international migrants. Their share has since risen to 51.3 per cent of total international migrants (UN, 2005).

AUSTRALIA AND NEW ZEALAND

- Migrants make up a fifth of the population of Australia, the highest proportion for any country in the world with a population of 20 million or more.[2] While in Australia the migrant population has increased since 1995, in New Zealand the number of migrants decreased from 708,000 to 642,000 (UN DESA, 2005).

Figure 1:

Stock of migrants in Australia and New Zealand, 2000 and 2005

Part A: Total number of migrants

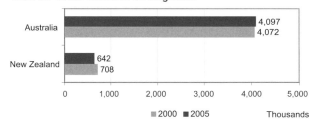

Part B: As a share of total population

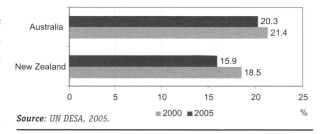

Source: UN DESA, 2005.

---

[1] Oceania includes the following countries and territories: Australia, New Zealand, **Melanesia** (Fiji, New Caledonia, Papua New Guinea, Solomon Islands, Vanuatu**), Micronesia** (Guam, Kiribati, Marshall Islands, Micronesia (Federated States of), Nauru, Northern Mariana Islands, Palau) and **Polynesia** (American Samoa, Cook Islands, French Polynesia, Niue, Pitcairn, Samoa, Tokelau, Tonga, Tuvalu, Walis and Futuna Islands).

[2] Only single countries and not sub-regions are referred to in this statistic. Therefore, GCC countries are not included, although their total share of migrants is higher than in Australia.

- In both Australia and New Zealand the number of migrants as a share of the total population declined between 2000 and 2005 (UN DESA, 2005) (see Figure 1). Three main factors may explain this development.[3] First, from 2000 to 2005, the rules concerning migration for family reunion, which in the past had accounted for a substantial share of immigration to both countries, have been tightened. Second, while skilled immigration continued to grow significantly, much of it was, in fact, of a temporary nature of between six months and two years, and therefore does not show up in some statistics. Third, though of less immediate impact, particularly in Australia, the numbers of the older post-World War II immigrants are declining as old age takes its toll (Connell, 2007).

Australia and New Zealand are among the few countries in the world to have active immigration programmes and are the major destinations in the region for both migrants and refugees

- The U.K. has traditionally been the leading country of origin for immigrants in Australia. In 1996, however, arrivals from New Zealand, outnumbered British immigrants, reaching 25,000 in 2001. In 2003, the U.K. regained its first position until 2005, when the differential between these two top groups of migrants decreased with 18,220 and 17,345 arrivals from the U.K. and New Zealand, respectively (MPI, 2005).
- In 1996, China became the third country of origin for migrants arriving in Australia, and has maintained this position since (MPI, 2005) (see Figure 2).

Figure 2:

Australia – leading countries of origin, by country of birth, 1991-2005

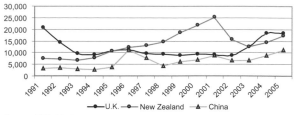

Source: MPI, 2005.

- The stock of foreign-born workers in Australia increased steadily from 1995 to 2005, while, as a proportion of the total labour force, it declined slightly during the period 2003-2004 (OECD, 2007) (see Figure 3).

Figure 3:

Stock of foreign workers in Australia

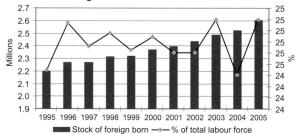

Source: OECD, 2007.

Family reunification has been the traditional cornerstone of migration policies ...

- During the period 1990-2002, family reunification accounted for 37 per cent of immigrant entries to Australia. For New Zealand, the share of admissions for family reasons was lower and continued to decline over the same period (UN, 2005).

... but many more highly skilled migrants are now admitted under the "points system" ...

- Between 2006-2007, 97,920 permanent residents were granted permanent residence in Australia under the skills programme, compared to 50,079

---

[3] Email communication with Professor John Connell, University of Sydney, Australia.

under the family reunification programme (DIAC, 2007).

... and the student population remains large

- In 2006-2007, a total of 228,592 student visas were granted, which represents a significant increase of almost 20 per cent over the 2005-2006 figure of 190,674 visas. The two leading source countries were China and India with 28,949 and 24,915 visa grants, respectively (DIAC, 2007).
- In 2004-2005, foreign graduates of Australian Universities accounted for 20 per cent of Australian immigrants under the skills programme, led by Chinese and Indians (*Migration News*, January 2006).

Temporary migration for work is gaining in importance

- The number of temporary workers in Australia has increased noticeably since 1996, when the government introduced a new temporary business entry visa that allows employers to sponsor skilled workers from overseas for a stay of up to four years (OECD, 2007) (see Figure 4).

Figure 4:

Inflows of foreign workers to Australia, 1995-2005 (thousands)

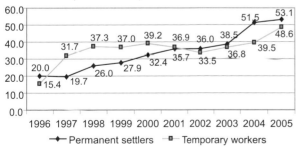

Source: OECD, 2007.[4]

---

[4] **Permanent settlers:** Skilled workers including the following categories of visas: employer nominations, business skills, occupational shares system, special talents and independent, including accompanying dependants. Period of reference: Fiscal year (July to June).
Temporary workers: Skilled temporary resident programme, including accompanying dependants. Includes Long-stay Temporary Business Programme as from 1996-97. Period of reference: Fiscal year (July to June).

- Temporary migration also increased in New Zealand over the last ten years (see Figure 5). In line with this general trend, a pilot programme for seasonal workers from Vanuatu was launched in April 2007 (IMF, 2007).

Figure 5:

Inflows of foreign workers into New Zealand, 1998-2005 (thousands)

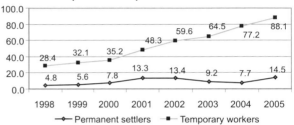

Source: OECD, 2007.

Female migration is also gaining greater prominence

- Recent data show that women are migrating to Australia to take up managerial, professional and other positions that cannot be filled locally. For example, Australia is projecting nursing deficits of 40,000 during the next four to five years (UNFPA, 2006). According to the New Zealand nurse registry figures for 2002, 23 per cent of nurses were foreign-born.

The relatively high emigration levels from Australia and New Zealand primarily reflect the desire of educated young citizens to seek work experience abroad

- Australia has an overall emigration rate[5] of 1.75 and New Zealand 10.7. The highly skilled emigration rate[6] is 3.68 and 17, respectively (OECD, 2005).

---

[5] The emigration rate is calculated by dividing the expatriate population from that country by the total native-born population of the country (native-born = expatriates + resident native-born) (OECD, Database on Immigrants and Expatriates, 2005).

[6] The emigration rate of highly educated persons is calculated by dividing the highly educated expatriate population from that country by the total highly educated native-born population.

moderate) is driven by the strong growth rate of the working-age population combined with a low increase in jobs. Papua New Guinea, Solomon Islands and Vanuatu are likely to be the most affected (World Bank, 2007) (see Figure 9).

Figure 9:

Working-age population of Papua New Guinea, Solomon Islands and Vanuatu not employed in the formal sector, 2004 and 2015

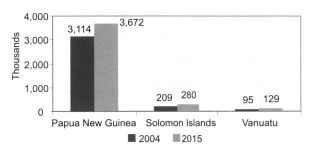

Source: World Bank, 2007.

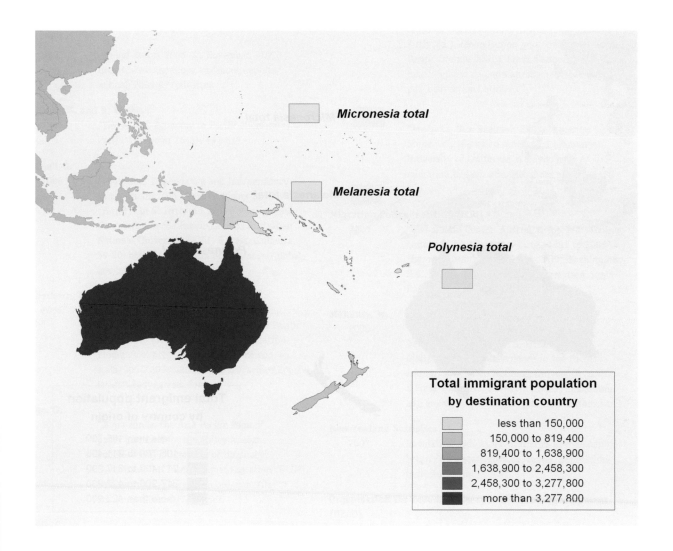

Micronesia total

Melanesia total

Polynesia total

Total immigrant population
by destination country

less than 150,000
150,000 to 819,400
819,400 to 1,638,900
1,638,900 to 2,458,300
2,458,300 to 3,277,800
more than 3,277,800

Rokoduru, A.

2005   "Contemporary Migration within the Pacific
        Islands: the Case of Fijian Skilled Workers in
        Kiribati and Marshall Islands" in S. Firth (Ed.),
        *Globalisation and Governance in the Pacific
        Islands*, ANU E Press, Canberra, 173-186,
        http://epress.anu.edu.au/ssgm/global_gov/
        pdf_instructions.html.

Small, C.A. and D.L. Dixon

2004   "Tonga: Migration and the Homeland",
        Migration Information Source, February,
        MPI, Washington, D.C., http://www.
        migrationinformation.org/Profiles/print.
        cfm?ID=198.

United Nations (UN)

2005   "International Migration and Development",
        Regional Fact Sheet on Oceania, UN,
        Department of Public Information, in
        cooperation with the Population Division of the
        UN Department of Economic and Social Affairs
        (UN DESA), http://www.un.org/migration/
        presskit/factsheet_oceania.pdf.

**United Nations Department of Economic and Social Affairs
(DESA), Population Division**

2005   *Trends in Total Migrant Stock: The 2005 Revision*,
        Population Database, UN DESA, Population
        Division, New York, http://esa.un.org/
        migration/index.asp?panel=1.

United Nations Population Fund (UNFPA)

2006   "Migration by Region: Oceania", UNFPA, http://
        www.unfpa.org/swp/2006/presskit/docs/
        factsheet_oceania.doc.

World Bank

2006   *Global Economic Prospects 2006: Economic
        Implications of Remittances and Migration*,
        The World Bank, Washington, D.C.,
        http://www-wds.worldbank.org/external/
        default/WDSContentServer/IW3P/
        IB/2005/11/14/000112742_20051114174928/
        Rendered/PDF/343200GEP02006.pdf.

2007   *At Home and Away: Expanding Job Opportunities
        for Pacific Islanders through Labor Mobility*, The
        World Bank, Washington, D.C., http://web.
        worldbank.org/WBSITE/EXTERNAL/COUNTRIES/
        EASTASIAPACIFICEXT/PACIFICISLANDSEXTN/
        0,,contentMDK:21020027~pagePK:141137~piPK:
        141127~theSitePK:441883,00.html.

2008   *Revisions to Remittance Trends 2007*, July, The
        World Bank, Washington, D.C., http://econ.
        worldbank.org/WBSITE/EXTERNAL/EXTDEC/
        EXTDECPROSPECTS/0,,contentMDK:21121930~me
        nuPK:3145470~pagePK:64165401~piPK:6416502
        6~theSitePK:476883,00.html.

MIGRATION TERMINOLOGY*

admission: The granting of entry into a state.

alien: *See non-national.*

amnesty: A general pardon, "regularization" or "legalization" that is extended to people who can show residence in a country for which the amnesty is granted, despite the fact that such residence was unauthorized.

assimilation: Adaptation of one ethnic or social group – usually a minority – to another, involving the subsuming of language, traditions, values and behaviour or even fundamental vital interests.

assisted voluntary return: Logistical, financial and reintegration support to rejected asylum seekers, victims of trafficking in human beings, stranded migrants, qualified nationals and other migrants unable or unwilling to remain in the host country, who volunteer to return to their countries of origin. *See also voluntary return.*

asylum seeker: A person who seeks safety from persecution or serious harm in a country other than her/his own and awaits a decision on the application for refugee status under relevant international and national instruments. *See also refugee.*

best (effective) practices: Means to further the application of the existing norms and principles, both at the international and the national levels. Best practices may be translated into operational directives, codes of conduct or other manifestations of soft law, but should not lead to a weakening or erosion of positive law. They are characterized by: being innovative, developing creative solutions; showing a positive impact on the level of

implementation of the rights of migrants; having a sustainable effect, especially by involving migrants themselves; and having potential for replication.

bilateral labour migration agreements: Formal mechanisms concluded between states, which are essentially legally binding treaty commitments concerned with inter-state cooperation on labour migration. The term is also used to describe less formal arrangements regulating the movement of workers between countries entered into by states as well as a range of other actors, including individual ministries, employer organizations, etc.

biometrics: The study of measurable biological characteristics. "Biometric identifiers" (BIs) are pieces of information that encode a representation of a person's unique biological make up (e.g. fingerprints, facial recognition photographs, retinal scans or voice scans).

bonded labour: Service rendered by a worker under condition of bondage arising from economic considerations, notably indebtedness through a loan or an advance. Where debt is the root cause of bondage, the implication is that the worker (or dependents or heirs) is tied to a particular creditor for a specified or unspecified period until the loan is repaid.

border control: A state's regulation of the entry of persons to its territory, in the exercise of its sovereignty.

---

* Many of the terms in this section are drawn or adapted from the terms found in a similar section in *World Migration 2005* and IOM's *Glossary on Migration,* November 2004.

forced return: The compulsory return of a person to the country of origin, transit or third country, on the basis of an administrative or judicial act. Also referred to as mandatory return.

foreigner: A person belonging to, or owing an allegiance to, another state. *See also alien and non-national.*

freedom of movement: A human right which comprises three basic elements: the freedom of movement within the territory of a country (*Article 13(1), Universal Declaration of Human Rights, 1948*: "Everyone has the right to freedom of movement and residence within the borders of each state"); the right to leave any country; and, the right to return to his or her own country (*Article 13(2), Universal Declaration of Human Rights, 1948*: "Everyone has the right to leave any country, including his own, and to return to his country."). Freedom of movement is also referred to in the context of freedom of movement arrangements between states at the regional level (e.g. European Union).

frontier worker: A migrant worker who retains his or her habitual residence in a neighbouring state to which he or she normally returns every day or at least once a week (*International Convention on the Protection of the Rights of All Migrant Workers and Members of Their Families, 1990, Article 2(2)(a)). See also migrant worker.*

globalization: A process of interaction and integration among the people, corporations, and governments of different states; a process driven by international trade and investment and aided by information technology. This process has effects on the environment, culture, political systems, economic development and prosperity, and human well-being in societies.

green card: An identity card issued by the U.S. Government to non-nationals who have been granted permanent resident status in the United States. Also called a Permanent Resident Card, it is evidence of a non-national being a lawful permanent resident with a right to live and work permanently in the United States.

highly skilled/qualified migrant: While there is no internationally agreed definition, two overlapping meanings are often intended. In very general terms a highly skilled migrant is considered to be a person with tertiary education, typically an adult who has completed a formal two-year college education or more. In a more specific sense, a highly skilled migrant is a person who has earned, either by tertiary level education or occupational experience, the level of qualifications typically needed to practice a profession.

host country: *See country of destination, receiving country, state of employment.*

human rights: Those liberties, benefits and entitlements, which, by accepted contemporary values, all human beings should be able to claim "as of right" in the society in which they live; e.g. as contained in the *Universal Declaration of Human Rights, 1948* and the *International Covenants on Economic, Social and Cultural Rights*, and *on Civil and Political Rights*, 1966 (together frequently referred to as the "International Bill of Rights"), and developed by other treaties from this core.

illegal/irregular/unauthorized entry: Act of crossing borders without complying with the necessary requirements for legal entry into the receiving state (*Art. 3(b), Protocol Against the Smuggling of Migrants by Land, Sea and Air, supplementing the United Nations Convention against Transnational Organized Crime, 2000*).

illegal migrant/migration: *See irregular migrant/migration.*

immigration: A process by which non-nationals move into a country for the purpose of settlement.

immigration status: Status which a migrant is accorded under the immigration law of the host country.

integration: While the term is used and understood differently in different countries and contexts, "integration" can be defined as the process by which migrants become accepted into society, both as individuals and as groups. It generally refers to a two-way process of adaptation by migrants and host societies, while the particular requirements for acceptance by a host society vary from country to country. Integration does not necessarily imply permanent settlement. It does, however, imply consideration of the rights and obligations of migrants and host societies, of access to different kinds of services and the labour market, and of identification and respect for a core set of values that bind migrants and host communities in a common purpose.

internal migration: A movement of people from one area of a country to another for the purpose or with the effect of establishing a new residence. This migration may be temporary or permanent. Internal migrants move but remain within their country of origin (e.g. rural to urban migration). *See also internally displaced persons.*

internally displaced persons (IDPs): Persons or groups of persons who have been forced or obliged to flee or to leave their homes or places of habitual residence, in particular as a result of or in order to avoid the effects of armed conflict, situations of generalized violence, violations of human rights or natural or human-made disasters, and who have not crossed an internationally recognized state border (*Para. 2, Guiding Principles on Internal Displacement, UN Doc. E/CN.4/1998/53/Add.2*).

international law: The legal principles governing relationships between states. The contemporary law of international relations embraces not only states, but also such participants as international organizations and even individuals (such as those who invoke their human rights or commit war crimes). Also termed law of nations, public international law, *jus gentium*.

international migration: Movement of persons who leave their country of origin, or the country of habitual residence, to establish themselves either permanently or temporarily in another country.

international migration law: Instruments of international law applicable to migration.

international minimum standard: A state is required to observe minimum standards set by international law with respect to treatment of non-nationals present on its territory (or the property of such persons) (e.g. denial of justice, unwarranted delay or obstruction of access to courts are in breach of international minimum standards required by international law).

intra-corporate transferee: An employee of a firm who is temporarily transferred to a foreign affiliate of that firm (branch, subsidiary, office, joint venture, etc.).

irregular migrant: A person who, owing to unauthorized entry, breach of a condition of entry, or the expiry of his or her visa, lacks legal status in a transit or host country. The definition covers inter alia those persons who have entered a transit or host country lawfully but have stayed for a longer period than authorized or subsequently taken up unauthorized employment. *See also undocumented migrant, illegal migrant, clandestine migration.*

irregular migration: Movement that takes place outside the regulatory norms of the origin, transit and destination countries.

***jus sanguinis* (Latin):** The rule that a child's nationality is determined by its parents' nationality, irrespective of the place of its birth.

***jus soli* (Latin):** The rule that a child's nationality is determined by its place of birth (although it can also be conveyed by the parents).

labour migration: Movement of persons from their home state to another state or within their own country of residence for the purpose of employment.

lawful admission: Legal entry of a non-national into the country, including under a valid immigrant visa.

legalization: The act of making lawful; authorization or justification by legal sanction. *See also amnesty, regularization.*

less/low-skilled and semi-skilled migrant worker: There is no internationally agreed definition of a less or low-skilled and semi-skilled migrant worker. In broad terms, a semi-skilled worker is considered to be a person who requires a degree of training or familiarization with the job before being able to operate at maximum/optimal efficiency, although this training is not of the length or intensity required for designation as a skilled (or craft) worker, being measured in weeks or days rather than years, nor is it normally at the tertiary level. Many so-called "manual workers" (e.g. production, construction workers) should therefore be classified as semi-skilled. A less or low-skilled worker, on the other hand, is considered to be a person who has received less training than a semi-skilled worker or, having not received any training, has still acquired his or her competence on the job.

long-term migrant: A person who moves to a country other than that of his or her usual residence for a period of at least a year, so that the country of destination effectively becomes his or her new country of usual residence. From the perspective of the country of departure, the person will be a long-term emigrant and from that of the country of arrival, the person will be a long-term immigrant. *See also short-term migrant.*

migrant flow: The number of migrants counted as moving, or being authorized to move, to or from a given location in a defined period of time.

migrant/worker in an irregular situation: *See irregular migrant, undocumented migrant/worker.*

migrant stock: The number of migrants residing in a given location at a particular point in time.

remittances: Monies earned or acquired by non-nationals that are transferred back to their country of origin.

removal: *See deportation, expulsion.*

repatriation: The return of a refugee or a prisoner of war to his/her country of nationality under specific conditions laid down in various international instruments (*Geneva Conventions, 1949 and Protocols, 1977, Regulations Respecting the Laws and Customs of War on Land, Annexed to the Fourth Hague Convention, 1907,* the human rights instruments as well as in customary international law).

replacement migration: Internal migration that occurs where the vacuum created by workers departing for another country is filled by workers from other parts of the country, or international migration that a country would need to offset population decline and population ageing resulting from low fertility and mortality rates (see Chapter 7).

resettlement: The relocation and integration of people (refugees, internally displaced persons, etc.) into another geographical area and environment, usually in a third country.

residence: The act or fact of living in a given place for some time; the place where one actually lives as distinguished from a domicile. Residence usually just means bodily presence as an inhabitant in a given place, while domicile usually requires bodily presence and an intention to make the place one's home. A person thus may have more than one residence at a time but only one domicile.

residence permit: A document issued by a state to a non-national, confirming that s/he has the right to live in the state concerned. *See also residence.*

return migration: The movement of a person returning to his/her country of origin or habitual residence usually after at least one year in another country. The return may or may not be voluntary. *See also circular migration, forced return, voluntary return.*

reverse brain drain: *See brain gain.*

right to leave: "Everyone has the right to leave any country, including his own…" (*Art. 13(2), Universal Declaration of Human Rights, 1948*). This right was set down in other international law instruments, for example in *Art. 12(2), International Covenant on Civil and Political Rights, 1966,* which states: "Everyone shall be free to leave any country, including his own." Some restrictions on this right can be legitimately imposed however (Art. 12(3), *International Covenant on Civil and Political Rights, 1966*: "The above-mentioned [right] shall not be subject to any restrictions except those which are provided by law, are necessary to protect national security, public order (*ordre public*), public health or morals or the rights and freedoms of others, and are consistent with the other rights recognized in the present Covenant"). The right to leave is an aspect of the right to freedom of movement, and it applies to all persons without distinction. There is however, no corollary right to enter the territory of a foreign country under international law. *See also freedom of movement, international minimum standard, repatriation, return.*

seafarer: Migrant worker employed on board a vessel registered in a state of which he or she is not a national (includes fishermen) (*Art. 2(2)(c), International Convention on the Protection of the Rights of All Migrant Workers and Members of Their Families, 1990*). *See also migrant worker.*

seasonal migrant worker/migration: A migrant worker whose work, or migration for work that, by its character is dependent on seasonal conditions and is performed only during part of the year (*Art. 2(2)(b), International Convention on the Protection of the Rights of All Migrant Workers and Members of Their Families, 1990*). *See also migrant worker.*

self-employed migrant worker: A migrant worker who is engaged in a remunerated activity otherwise than under a contract of employment and who earns his or her living through this activity normally working alone or together with members of his or her family, and any other migrant worker recognized as self-employed by applicable legislation of the state of employment or bilateral or multilateral agreements. (*Art. 2(2)(h), International Convention on the Protection of the Rights of All Migrant Workers and Members of Their Families, 1990*). *See also migrant worker.*

sending country: A country from which people leave to settle abroad permanently or temporarily. *See also country of origin.*

short-term migrant: A person who moves to a country other than that of his or her usual residence for a period of at least three months, but less than a year, except in cases where the movement to that country is for purposes of recreation, holiday, visits to friends or relatives, business or medical treatment. For the purpose of international migration statistics, the country of usual residence of short-term migrants is considered to be the country of destination during the period they spend in it. *See also long-term migrant, temporary migrant workers.*

skilled migrant: A migrant worker who, because of his/her skills or acquired professional experience, is usually granted preferential treatment regarding admission to a host country. *See also highly skilled migrant, qualified national.*

slavery: The status or condition of a person over whom any or all the powers attaching to the right of ownership are exercised (*Art. 1, Slavery Convention, 1926, as amended by the 1953 Protocol*).

smuggler (of migrants): An intermediary who is moving people by agreement with them, in order to transport them in an unauthorized manner across an internationally recognized state border. *See also smuggling, trafficking.*

smuggling: The procurement, in order to obtain, directly or indirectly, a financial or other material benefit, of the illegal [or unauthorized] entry of a person into a state party of which the person is not a national or a permanent resident (*Art. 3(a), Protocol Against the Smuggling of Migrants by Land, Sea and Air, supplementing the United Nations Convention against Transnational Organized Crime, 2000*).

sovereignty: As a concept of international law, sovereignty has three principal aspects: external, internal and territorial. The external aspect of sovereignty is the right of the state freely to determine its relations with other states or other entities without the restraint or control of another state. This aspect of sovereignty is also known as independence. The internal aspect of sovereignty is the state's exclusive right or competence to determine the character of its own institutions, to enact laws of its own choice and ensure their respect. The territorial aspect of sovereignty is the exclusive authority which a state exercises over all persons and things found on, under or above its territory. In the context of migration, this means the sovereign prerogative of a state to determine which non-citizens should be admitted to its territory subject to the limitations of the *non-refoulement* principle, human rights and provisions in bilateral or regional agreements (e.g. free movement or integration agreements). *See also non-refoulement, human rights.*

specified-employment worker: A migrant worker: (i) Who has been sent by his or her employer for a restricted and defined period of time to a state of employment to undertake a specific assignment or duty; or (ii) Who engages for a restricted and defined period of time in work that requires professional, commercial, technical or other highly-specialized skill; or (iii) Who, upon the request of his or her employer in the state of employment, engages for a restricted and defined period of time in work whose nature is transitory or brief; and who is required

to depart from the state of employment either at the expiration of his or her authorized period of stay, or earlier if he or she no longer undertakes that specific assignment or duty or engages in that work (*Art. 2(2)(g), International Convention on the Protection of the Rights of All Migrant Workers and Members of Their Families, 1990*). *See also migrant worker.*

sponsorship: The act of promising support, in particular financial support, for a non-national seeking entry to the state, generally for a defined period of time. Some states require either sponsorship or proof of adequate income as a condition of entry for certain categories of migrants as well as visitors.

source country: *See also country of origin, sending country.*

state: A political entity with legal jurisdiction and effective control over a defined territory, and the authority to make collective decisions for a permanent population, a monopoly on the legitimate use of force, and an internationally recognized government that interacts, or has the capacity to interact, in formal relations with other entities.

state of employment/state of origin/state of transit: *See country of destination, country of origin, country of transit.*

stateless person: A person who is not considered a national by any state under the operation of its law (*Art. 1, United Nations Convention Relating to the Status of Stateless Persons, 1954*). As such, a stateless person lacks those rights attributable to nationality: the diplomatic protection of a state, the inherent right of sojourn in the state of residence and the right of return in case s/he travels.

step migration: Where a person moves to one or more locations within the country before emigration to another country, or from one country to another before moving to his/her ultimate or final country of destination.

technical cooperation: The sharing of information and expertise on a given subject usually focused on public sector functions.

temporary (labour) migration: Migration of workers who enter a foreign country for a specified limited period of time before returning to the country of origin.

temporary migrant workers: Skilled, semi-skilled or low-skilled workers in the destination country for definite periods, for example under a work contract with an individual employer or a service contract with an enterprise.

Research - 12-15, 23, 35, 38, 41, 52-53, 60, 62, 67-70, 97, 111, 115-116, 127, 145-146, 152-154, 163, 167, 173-174, 178-179, 183, 185-186, 192-193, 202, 207, 219, 223, 237, 248, 250-251, 252, 258, 261, 263, 265, 267, 277, 293, 308, 315, 342, 372, 376, 383, 397, 400, 432, 442
    Policy-relevant research - 251
Research and development (R&D) - 53, 67, 69
Research Networks - 250-251
        Asia Pacific Migration Research Network (APMRN) - 192
        European Migration Network (EMN) - 251
Residence - 9, 11, 54-55, 58, 61-62, 107, 160-161, 179, 189, 202, 214, 240, 242, 247, 299, 303, 311, 332, 363-364, 367, 393, 463-464, 532
    Definition - 498
    → Permanent residence
    → Residence permit
    Temporary - 58, 141, 371,
Residence permit - 59, 61, 115, 118-120, 142, 160-161, 189, 210, 243-244, 314, 363, 371, 462, 532
    Definition - 498
Resident worker test → Labour market test
Return migration - 64-65, 94, 174, 179-180, 182, 247, 302, 431
    Definition - 498
    → Forced return
    → Circular migration
    Incentive to - 66, 69, 93, 100, 374
    Orderly return - 357-358
    Sustainable return - 303
    "Virtual return" - 348
Romania - 85, 107, 145, 219, 223, 365-366, 458, 476, 525, 529, 532, 537
Russian Federation (Russia) - 88, 106-107, 112, 144, 146, 206, 219, 245, 272, 285-286, 291, 316, 317, 339, 440, 455, 458, 460-464, 466-467, 528
    Federal Migration Service (FMS) - 316
    Pilot regularization project -
Rwanda - 4, 329

S
SADC - Southern African Development Community - 79, 88, 189, 251, 367, 411, 412, 415
    Protocol on the Facilitation of the Movement of Persons (2005) - 367, 368
Saint Lucia - 109, 265, 312, 426
SAMP - Southern African Migration Project - 79, 248, 251
Sao Tome and Principe - 407
Saudi Arabia - 84, 98, 107, 220, 221, 280, 339, 370, 380, 440, 442, 471, 472, 474, 475, 507
Savings - 63, 93, 183, 186, 226, 274, 302, 304, 305, 336, 339, 343, 349, 358, 374
    High-interest bearing savings accounts - 301
Scandinavia - 100, 241
Schengen - 136, 208
Science and technology (S&T) - 53, 67, 110, 261, 263, 290
Seafarers - 262, 271, 277, 356, 357, 440, 445
    Definition - 498
Seasonal (migrant) worker - 34, 80, 82, 83, 87, 90, 91, 97, 127, 173, 174, 176, 177, 185, 213, 219, 269-270, 295, 302, 304, 310, 332, 335, 356, 357, 367, 379, 483
Seasonal migration - 80, 85, 86, 86, 88, 176, 177, 178, 181, 186, 269-270, 272, 311, 373, 374, 376, 377
    Definition - 498
Security and migration - 5, 9, 43, 46, 58, 222, 288, 306, 312, 313, 317, 332, 340, 362, 369, 379
    Biometrics, definition of - 491
    National security policies - 288, 328, 349
    → Organized crime
    September 11, 2001 - 118, 222, 312, 340
    → Terrorism
    → Travel documents

Self-employed migrant (worker) - 6, 7, 139, 159, 202, 356, 365, 366, 386
    Definition - 498
Senegal - 107, 109, 121, 129, 145, 179, 180, 182, 189, 215, 216, 223, 339, 363, 407, 413, 414
Serbia - 59, 317, 380, 460, 461, 562, 519
Service providers - 3, 40, 80, 99, 114, 127, 139, 281, 289, 319, 345, 356, 359, 360, 365, 366, 384, 385, 386, 387,
    → GATS
Short-term migrant - 51, 173
    Definition - 498
Sierra Leone - 89, 121, 189, 407, 413
Singapore - 26, 84, 113, 117, 131, 132, 140, 151, 182, 218, 251, 264, 280, 289, 296, 302, 310, 372, 386, 387, 439, 440, 443, 444, 445, 447, 449, 450
    Foreign worker levy - 296
    Japan-Singapore Economic Partnership Agreement - 262, 386
    Ministry of Manpower - 296, 310
Skill(s)
    Formation - 260, 332
    Profile(s) - 34, 398
    Shortages - 265, 292, 386
    Transfer of - 2, 295, 302, 304
Slavery - 44, 83, 204, 466, 493
    Definition - 499
Slavery-like practices - 313, 493
Slovakia - 35, 87, 309, 365, 366, 380, 455, 457, 462
Slovenia - 35, 365, 366, 377, 380, 455, 457, 462, 511
Small and medium enterprises (SMEs) - 30, 139
Smuggling (of migrants) - 9, 15, 203, 221, 222, 272, 281, 289, 314, 319, 367, 369, 370, 374, 431
    Definition - 499
    Networks - 44, 209, 267, 415, 456
    Protocol against the Smuggling of Migrants by Land, Sea and Air (2000) - 361
    Smuggler (of migrants), definition of - 499
    → Trafficking
Social cohesion - 16, 43, 250, 286, 288, 292, 305, 308, 309, 332, 345, 398
Social costs - 43, 46
    of migration - 46, 69, 70, 153
Social exclusion - 226, 266
    Marginalization - 174, 308, 316, 329, 346
    Risk of - 301
Social justice - 17
Social security (benefits) - 10, 45, 97, 190, 214, 241, 278, 305, 311-312, 316, 349, 356, 359, 365, 372, 386
    Aggregation of - 312
    Bilateral arrangements (agreements) - 375, 379, 380
    CARICOM Agreement on Social Security (1996) - 312
    Convention No. 157 on the Maintenance of Social Security Rights (1982) - 359
    Council Regulation 1408/71/EEC on the application of social security schemes (1971) - 312, 365
    Cumulative rights - 311
    Maintenance of acquired rights - 311, 359
    → Pensions
    Portability of - 311
    Qualifying period(s) - 312
    Recommendation No. 167 on the Maintenance of Social Security Rights (1983) - 359
    → Social (welfare) benefits
    Systems - 27, 312, 365, 384
    Transfer/export of - 301, 342
Social services - 43, 44, 272, 308, 310, 344, 345, 431
    Access to - 44, 344, 431
    Delivery systems - 341
Social (welfare) benefits - 9, 10, 112, 161, 297, 311

MAP 2: Foreign Students in Higher Education in Selected Countries, 2004*

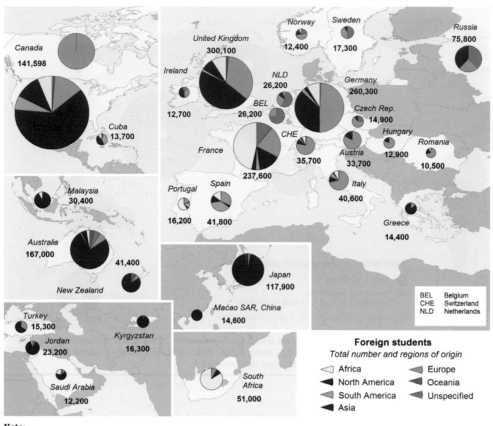

Foreign students
Total number and regions of origin

◁ Africa   ◀ Europe
◀ North America   ◀ Oceania
◀ South America   ◀ Unspecified
◀ Asia

BEL	Belgium
CHE	Switzerland
NLD	Netherlands

Note:

The size of each pie chart shown on this map is proportional to the total number of foreign students hosted by the relevant country, while the size and colours of each pie slice highlight the importance of the different regions of origin in numerical terms. The data for Canada, drawn from Citizenship and Immigration Canada statistics, did not allow a breakdown by region although it did list the ten top places of origin, namely (in order of magnitude): China, South Korea, U.S., Japan, France, India, Taiwan Province of China, Hong Kong SAR, Mexico, Germany, U.K.

Sources: UNESCO, Global Education Digest 2006: Comparing Education Statistics Across the World, Paris. For Canada: Citizenship and Immigration Canada, Stocks of Foreign Students 2004, http://www.cic.gc.ca/english/resources/ statistics/facts2006/temporary/10.asp.

Map 2 shows the global distribution of international students in tertiary education by region of origin. The data in this map primarily refer to the 2004 school year and only countries hosting more than 10,000 students have been selected in each region.

The U.S. and the U.K. had the largest number of foreign students in 2004, hosting 572,500 and 300,100 individuals, respectively. Germany, France, Australia, Canada and Japan follow with totals ranging from about 260,300 students (Germany) to 100,000 (Japan). While the U.S. figure is more than twice that of France and Germany, and nearly twice that of the U.K, Europe considered as a whole is the largest recipient of foreign students globally. Most of them come from within Europe as students from the European Union (EU) finding it convenient and cheaper to study in another EU Member State. Half, or more than half, of the foreign students in Austria, Germany, Hungary, Italy, Norway, Romania, Sweden and Switzerland are from the EU. On the other hand, nearly half of the foreign students in France and more than half in Portugal are from Africa, and these two countries are globally the largest recipients of African students after South Africa, while in the U.K. and Greece most international students come from Asia. Spain is the country hosting the highest proportion of foreign students from South America (37%).

Globally, Asia produces the highest number of students going abroad to pursue higher education. Within Asia, more than 90 per cent of foreign students in Japan and Macao SAR are from within the region, while in Malaysia they account for 89 per cent. In Australia and New Zealand, Asians account for about 77 per cent of all the overseas students. Students from Asia also make up the majority in Saudi Arabia and Jordan. With a total of 12,200 and 23,200 foreign students, respectively, these two countries are the largest poles of attraction in the Middle East.

Finally, with a total of 51,000 international students, South Africa is the most significant country of destination for foreign students in Africa with the majority (43,176) coming from countries within the continent.

MAP 5: Proportion of Women Migrants by Region, 1975, 1990, 2005

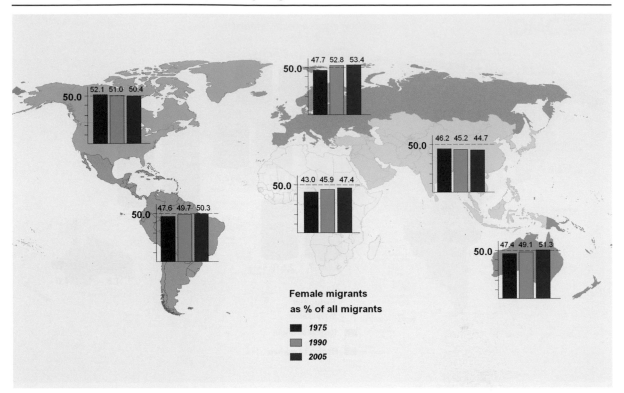

Source: *Population Division of the Department of Economic and Social Affairs of the United Nations Secretariat, Trends in Total Migrant Stock: The 2005 Revision, New York, http://esa.un.org/migration.*

Map 5 shows the proportion of women migrants residing in different world regions in the period 1975 to 2005. This proportion rose globally by more than two per cent from 47.4 to 49.6 per cent, the steepest increases being recorded in Europe and the Russian Federation, with a rise of about six per cent. Asia and North America were the only two regions where the share of female migrants declined during this period from 46.2 to 44.7 and 52.1 to 50.4 per cent, respectively.

In all regions the share of female migrants is higher than 50 per cent, except for Africa and Asia (including the Middle East).

MAP 6: Population Change in the EU-27, EEA and Switzerland, 2005

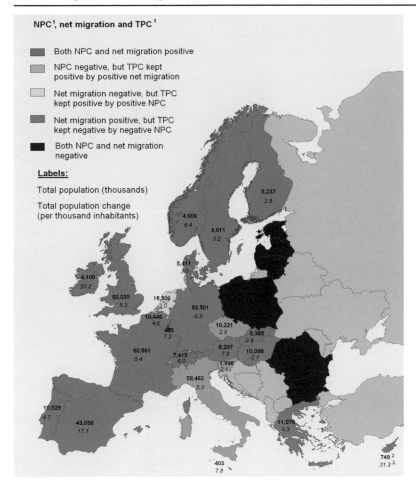

NPC¹, net migration and TPC¹

- Both NPC and net migration positive
- NPC negative, but TPC kept positive by positive net migration
- Net migration negative, but TPC kept positive by positive NPC
- Net migration positive, but TPC kept negative by negative NPC
- Both NPC and net migration negative

Labels:

Total population (thousands)

Total population change (per thousand inhabitants)

Notes:
¹ NPC refers to "natural population change"; TPC refers to "total population change"
² Figures refer to the area under the effective control of the Government of the Republic of Cyprus.

Source: Münz, R. 2006, "Europe: Population and Migration in 2005", Migration Information Source, June, Migration Policy Institute (MPI), Washington, D.C., http://www.migrationinformation. org/feature/display.cfm?ID=402.

Map 6 presents the demographic indicators for the EU-27 Member States, the European Economic Area (EEA) countries and Switzerland in the year 2005. The map shows that both the natural population change (births minus deaths) and the net migration were positive in 15 of the countries analyzed in 2005. In three of the countries examined (Czech Republic, Italy and Slovenia), the natural population change was either zero or negative, but the total change was positive through net migration. In The Netherlands, the total population change was kept positive on the strength of a positive natural population change, despite negative net migration. For Germany and Hungary, the strongly negative natural change kept the total population change negative, in spite of the clearly positive net migration. Finally, for Bulgaria, Estonia, Latvia, Lithuania, Poland and Romania, both natural population change and net migration were negative for that year.

MAP 7a: Main Regularizations and Amnesty Programmes in the Americas and Europe

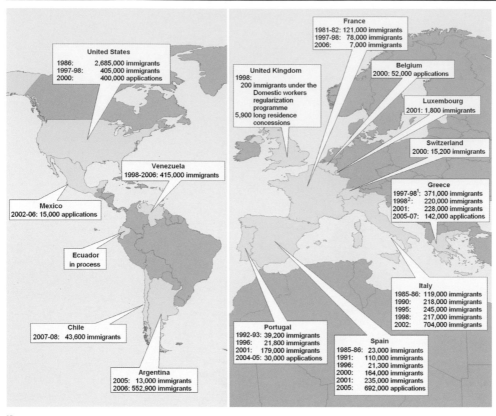

Notes:

1 and 2 In 1997-98 371,000 immigrants in Greece obtained a "white card". Of these, 220,000 obtained the "green card" in 1998. The "white card" provided a six-month residence permit and was a prerequisite for obtaining the "green card", which provided a one-to-five year residence permit.

Sources for both Maps 7a and 7b: *OECD 2004, Trends in International Migration, SOPEMI 2003, Paris; OECD 2007, International Migration Outlook, SOPEMI 2007, Paris; Government of New Zealand; Government of Portugal; Thailand, Ministries of Labour and Interior; the Philippines, Ministry of Labour; Republic of Korea, Ministry of Justice; Government of Malaysia; Levinson, A. 2005, The Regularization of Unauthorized Migrants: Literature Survey and Country Case Studies, Centre on Migration, Policy and Society (COMPAS), University of Oxford, http://www.compas.ox.ac.uk/publications/papers/Regularisation%20Report.pdf.*

Obtaining accurate estimates of the number of irregular or undocumented migrants in a country is problematic and prone to a considerable margin of error. The estimates quoted in Maps 7a and 7b are compiled from a variety of sources. While it is difficult to state estimates with confidence, it is possible to at least identify the different indicators used to calculate these estimates (Levinson, 2005).

One useful indicator is the number of persons participating in regularization or amnesty programmes, which enable irregular migrants to acquire lawful status. Not all irregular migrants can benefit from these measures, as regularization often depends on the number of years a person has lived in a country or whether he or she is in employment. Therefore, the figures in Maps 7a and

MAP 7b: Main Regularizations and Amnesty Programmes in Asia and Oceania

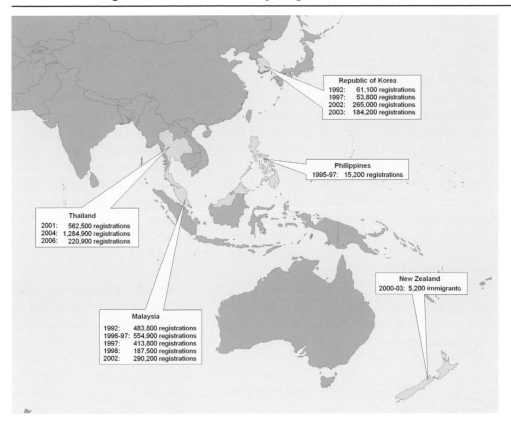

7b can only be indicative of the number of irregular migrants residing in a country at a particular point in time. Other factors limiting participation in such programmes are that employers may not wish to reveal their recourse to unauthorized labour, or may prefer to keep workers in an irregular situation so that they can pay lower wages. Furthermore, regularization frequently does not offer permanent residence status. Many of these migrants fall back into an irregular situation, owing to the insecurity or short duration of the status offered under certain programmes and the burdensome administrative procedures involved in renewing their regular status (OECD, 2004). Whatever the merits of regularization in the different regions of the world, the process itself does allow the movements due to unauthorized entry or overstay to enter the immigration statistics and thus to provide some idea of the scale of such movements (OECD, 2007).

Comparability of Data

It is important to note that the regularization figures published by governments can refer either to the number of applications for, or the number of persons granted, regular status. Each country has its own individual system for collecting data. For instance, the figures for Belgium and Switzerland for 2000 count the number of applications received and the dependants named therein, and include asylum seekers. Countries on the northern shores of the Mediterranean (France, Greece, Italy, Portugal,

Spain) have carried out successive regularization programmes, which principally target undocumented migrant workers.

The majority of regularization applicants in Spain are from Latin America; in Portugal they are from Brazil; in Belgium from the Democratic Republic of the Congo; and in France the majority of such applicants are from the Maghreb region. Many irregular migrants in Europe also originate from central and eastern Europe and China. In many countries, China ranks among the top five countries of origin. In the last regularization programme conducted in Italy in 2002, most applicants were from Romania and Ukraine (OECD, 2004).

Regarding the Americas, the 1997-98 figure for the U.S. counts the number of persons granted residence permits, which excludes dependants, while the figure for 2000 only shows the number of applications received. The U.S. regularization programmes have principally targeted agricultural workers (1986), Nicaraguans and Cubans (1997-98) and irregular migrants generally (2000). Latin American countries also implement regularization programmes (see Textbox 8.3). In Argentina, the National Programme for the Regularization of Migrants *"Patria Grande"*

in its first phase (2005) granted residence status to migrants who were not citizens of countries belonging to the Common Market of the South (MERCOSUR) and, in 2006, facilitated the regularization of migrants from MERCOSUR and associated countries. Mexico has been implementing a large regularization programme, which benefited 15,000 migrants in the period 2002-2006, most of whom came from countries in Central America. The *"Mision Identidad"* (Identity Mission), implemented by Venezuela, has provided documentation to migrants who had been living in the country for many years and who did not possess identity cards. Finally, Ecuador is in the process of carrying out a regularization programme benefitting undocumented migrants from the neighbouring countries of Colombia and Peru.

In many countries in Asia and Oceania, periods of rapid economic growth have resulted in significant intakes of migrant workers, not all of whom have immediately been furnished with the requisite documentation for residence and work. Therefore, certain destination countries in this region have repeatedly offered the possibility for undocumented migrant workers to register and obtain valid documentation. In the case of New Zealand's regularization programme, carried out in 2000-2003, 5,200 overstayers were identified.

MAP 8: Remittances and Foreign Aid by Region, 2006

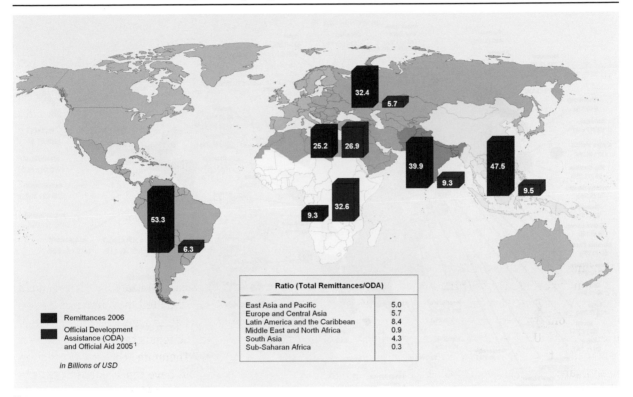

Ratio (Total Remittances/ODA)	
East Asia and Pacific	5.0
Europe and Central Asia	5.7
Latin America and the Caribbean	8.4
Middle East and North Africa	0.9
South Asia	4.3
Sub-Saharan Africa	0.3

Remittances 2006

Official Development Assistance (ODA) and Official Aid 2005 [1]

In Billions of USD

Note:
[1] Foreign aid includes Official Development Assistance (ODA) and official aid.

Sources: *World Bank Staff Estimates based on the International Monetary Fund's Balance of Payments Statistics Yearbook 2007; World Development Indicators 2007, The World Bank, Washington, D.C.*

In 2006, officially recorded remittances amounted to USD 281 billion. Of that amount, USD 207 billion was sent back to developing countries. In 2005, foreign aid (Official Development Assistance (ODA) and official aid) was less than half that amount (USD 90.4 billion), which underscores the importance of remittances as a source of income for developing countries.

The economic importance of migrant remittances varies across the globe. Some developing countries and regions receive considerably higher amounts of remittances than foreign aid, while in other regions foreign aid plays a larger role in development. In the Latin American and Caribbean region, remittances were 8.4 times higher than foreign aid received in 2005. The Middle East and Africa were the only two regions where foreign aid exceeded remittances in 2005-2006. As in previous years (see *World Migration 2005*), sub-Saharan Africa received the smallest nominal amount of remittances, but the region received the highest percentage of foreign aid (32.6%). Total remittances accounted for only 0.4 times the amount of all the foreign aid.

Note: Maps 8 to 12 have been produced on the basis of the World Bank 2006 remittance figures. The World Bank released new figures on remittance trends in July 2008, and the Regional Migration Overviews include such data, but the trends indicated in these maps remain essentially the same.

MAP 11: Remittances to Select Countries in Asia and Oceania, 2006

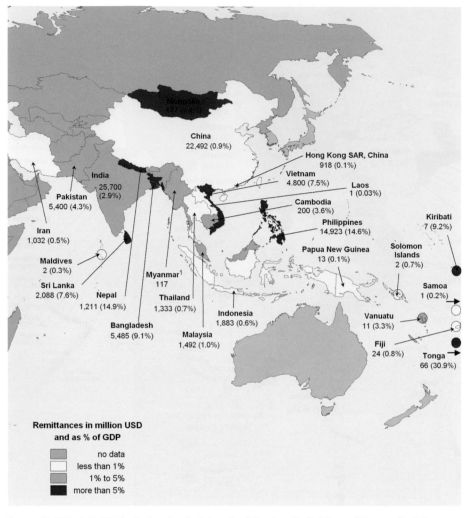

Source: *World Bank Staff Estimates based on the International Monetary Fund's Balance of Payments Statistics Yearbook 2007.*

In 2006, the Asia-Pacific region received a total of USD 91 billion in migrant remittances, with South-Central Asia in the lead with a total of USD 41 billion and East Asia and Southeast Asia each receiving a total of USD 25 billion. India has consistently been one of the foremost receivers of remittances and, in 2006, ranked first in Asia and the world as a whole with USD 25.7 billion (nearly 3% of its GDP). At USD 22.5 billion, China was the second largest recipient of remittances in Asia in absolute terms, but as a percentage of GDP they account for less than one per cent. The Philippines, on the other hand, was not only one of the foremost receivers of remittances (USD 14.9 billion) in absolute terms, but also as a percentage of GDP (14.6%), which in the region was only surpassed by Nepal (with USD 1.2 billion, the equivalent of 14.9% of its GDP). Remittances account for more than five per cent of GDP in Bangladesh, Sri Lanka and Viet Nam.

MAP 12: Remittances to Countries in Transition in Europe and Central Asia, 2006

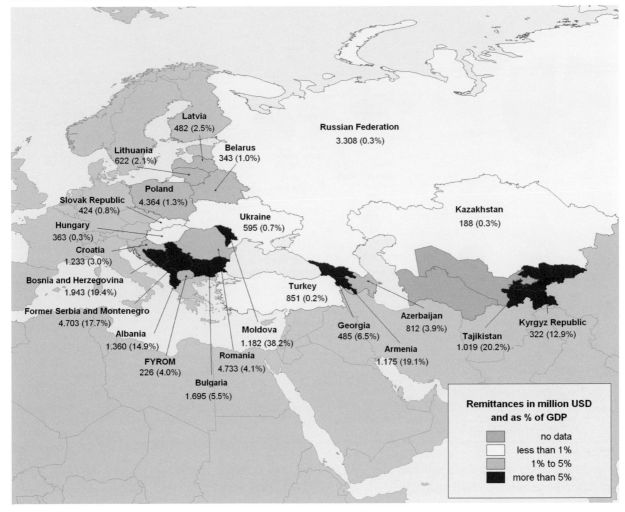

Source: World Bank Staff Estimates based on the International Monetary Fund's Balance of Payments Statistics Yearbook 2007.

Total migrant remittances to countries in transition in Europe and Central Asia in 2006 amounted to USD 32.4 billion, an increase of 11.1 per cent from 2005. The largest receivers in the region were Romania, the then Serbia and Montenegro and Poland, with all three recording absolute remittance figures of over USD 4 billion. In terms of remittances as a share of GDP, the highest proportions were to be found in Armenia, Bosnia and Herzegovina, Tajikistan and Moldova, with shares of GDP ranging between 19 and 39 per cent.

Only the countries considered by the United Nations as "countries in transition from centrally planned to market economies", and for which information is available, have been taken into account for the purpose of this map.

MAP 13: Highly Skilled Migrants by Destination Country, 2000

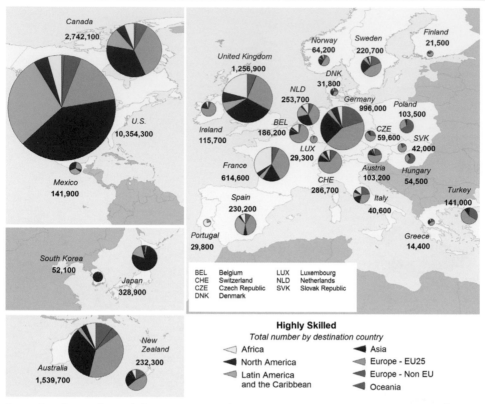

Canada
2,742,100

U.S.
10,354,300

Mexico
141,900

Norway
64,200

Sweden
220,700

Finland
21,500

United Kingdom
1,256,900

DNK
31,800

NLD
253,700

Germany
996,000

Poland
103,500

Ireland
115,700

BEL
186,200

CZE
59,600

SVK
42,000

France
614,600

LUX
29,300

CHE
286,700

Austria
103,200

Hungary
54,500

Turkey
141,000

Spain
230,200

Italy
40,600

Portugal
29,800

Greece
14,400

South Korea
52,100

Japan
328,900

New Zealand
232,300

Australia
1,539,700

BEL	Belgium	LUX	Luxembourg
CHE	Switzerland	NLD	Netherlands
CZE	Czech Republic	SVK	Slovak Republic
DNK	Denmark		

Highly Skilled
Total number by destination country

◁ Africa   ◀ Asia

◀ North America   ◀ Europe - EU25

◀ Latin America   ◀ Europe - Non EU
and the Caribbean
    ◀ Oceania

Source: Docquier, F. and A. Marfouk. 2006, "International Migration by Education Attainment, 1990-2000" in C. Özden and M. Schiff (Eds.), International Migration, Remittances, and the Brain Drain, The World Bank and Palgrave Macmillan, Washington D.C./New York, 151-199.

Map 13 shows the global distribution of highly skilled migrants by country of destination.

The map clearly shows that, with more than ten million, the U.S. is the most important recipient of highly skilled migrants, followed by Canada and Australia, with 2.7 and 1.5 million, respectively. Even though each individual OECD country in Europe, with the exception of the U.K., shows figures below one million, when considered as an entity, Europe is the second largest destination, hosting five million highly skilled migrants.

Highly skilled Asian migrants are well represented across the regions of the world, accounting for 41 per cent of all the highly skilled migrants in the U.S., 35 per cent in both Australia and Canada, and 33 per cent in the U.K. Latin America and the Caribbean rank second, accounting for 29 per cent of the highly skilled migrants to the U.S., and 35 per cent to Spain, while Mexico has the highest share of highly skilled migrants from Latin America and the Caribbean (34%). Highly skilled migrants from Africa are mostly found in Europe, where they account for 79 per cent of all highly skilled immigrants in Portugal and 34 per cent in France. European highly skilled migrants are most likely to move among European countries, accounting for 43 per cent of all highly skilled migrants in Germany and 39 per cent in Spain.

MAP 14: Highly Skilled Migrants by Region of Origin, 2000

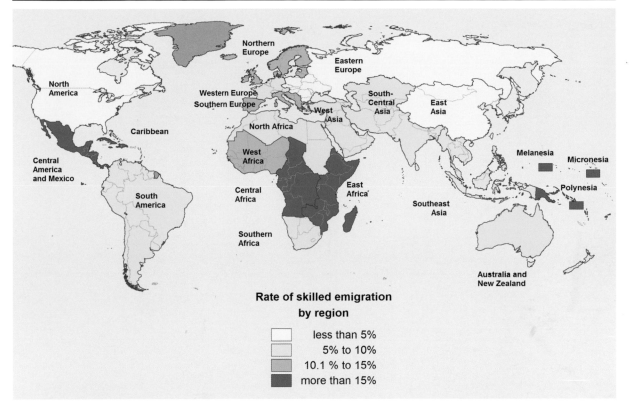

Rate of skilled emigration by region

☐ less than 5%
☐ 5% to 10%
☐ 10.1 % to 15%
■ more than 15%

Source: Docquier, F. and A. Marfouk. 2006, "International Migration by Education Attainment, 1990-2000" in C. Özden and M. Schiff (Eds.), International Migration, Remittances, and the Brain Drain, The World Bank and Palgrave Macmillan, Washington, D.C./New York, 151-199.

To complement Map 13, Map 14 shows the global distribution of highly skilled migrants by region of origin.

The map shows that, in relative terms, East Africa, Central America and Mexico, and the Caribbean, together with the Pacific Islands, are the most affected sub-regions with more than 15 per cent of their highly skilled nationals migrating abroad. On the other hand, the sub-regions least affected by the emigration of their highly skilled nationals in 2000 are North America, eastern Europe and East Asia.